HANDBOOK OF TECHNOLOGY-BASED TRAINING

HANDBOOK OF TECHNOLOGY-BASED TRAINING

Brian Tucker

Forum for Technology in Training

Gower

© Gower Publishing Limited 1997

All rights reserved. No part of this publication may be reproduced, stored in a retrieval system, or transmitted in any form or by any means, electronic, mechanical, photocopying, recording or otherwise without the permission of the publisher.

Published by
Gower Publishing Limited
Gower House
Croft Road
Aldershot
Hampshire GU11 3HR
England

Gower
Old Post Road
Brookfield
Vermont 05036
USA

Brian Tucker has asserted his right under the Copyright, Designs and Patents Act 1988 to be identified as the author of this work.

British Library Cataloguing in Publication Data
Tucker, Brian
　Handbook of technology-based training
　1. Employees – Training of – Data processing
　I. Title
　658.3'124'0285

　ISBN 0 566 07809 0

Library of Congress Cataloging-in-Publication Data
Tucker, Brian, 1934–
　Handbook of technology-based training/Brian Tucker.
　　p.　cm.
　Includes index.
　ISBN 0–566–07809–0 (cloth)
　　1. Computer-assisted instruction—Handbooks, manuals, etc.
　2. Internet (Computer network) in education—Handbooks, manuals, etc.　3. Educational technology—Handbooks, manuals, etc.
　I. Title.
　LB1028.5.T76　1997
　371.33'4—dc21　　　　　　　　　　　　　　　　　　　　　　　96–52107
　　　　　　　　　　　　　　　　　　　　　　　　　　　　　　　　　CIP

Typeset in Century Old Style by Intype London Ltd
Printed in Great Britain by Biddles Ltd, Guildford.

Contents

Preface   vii
The Forum for Technology in Training   ix

Part I   Technology-based Training

1 **What is Technology-Based Training?**   3
Computer-based training – Interactive audio – Interactive video – Digital video interactive – Expert systems/artificial intelligence – Multimedia – CD-ROM – CD-ROM (XA) – Compact disc interactive – Digital video disc – Simulation – Virtual reality – Video conferencing – Desk-to-desk conferencing – Satellite broadcasting – Networks/Internet/ intranets – Electronic peformance support systems

2 **The Benefits of Using Technology-Based Training**   23
The organisational benefits of TBT – The learner benefits of TBT

3 **Implementation**   33
Availability of TBT – Selling TBT to line management – Selling TBT to the individual – Publicising TBT – Administration of TBT – Supporting TBT – Case study

4 **How to use TBT**   39
TBT as a distance-learning tool – TBT as pre-course work – TBT as part of the course – TBT as post-course work

5 **Generic Training**   43
Why buy generic training? – Customising – Subject matter available on the market –

Choosing generic courseware – Evaluating generic courseware

6 **Bespoke Training** 47
In-house or external? – Choosing a supplier – Defining the project – Subject-matter experts – Project management

7 **Evaluation** 51
Have the training objectives been met? – Has the learning been put into practice? – Has there been a business benefit?

8 **The Future** 55
9 **Case Studies** 59
Use of computer-based testing to assist with training needs analysis at NPI – Induction training at Sun Life – The drive for better training at Vauxhall – Multimedia training in Specsavers – Multimedia training at Lloyds Bank – A catalogue of training at Argos – TBT open-learning material in the newly restructured British Gas – The effectiveness of integration of technology-based training with traditional methods at British Steel – IT training in the virtual classroom

Index to Part I 81

Part II The Directory

Introduction to Part II 87
Alphabetical list of categories and subcategories 91
Directory of Courses 97
Index 1 Alphabetical List of all Courses 373
Index 2 List of Courses by Delivery Method 393
Index 3 List of Courses by Supplier 415

Preface

When I started to write this book I thought back to the days when I was first looking at *computer-based training*. At that stage, it was all relatively new. Equally, when I was writing the feasibility study to introduce computer-based training into Royal Insurance and started to look at *interactive video*, that too was new. So new were these aspects of training, in fact, that many of the examples which I was shown or saw demonstrated at conferences were still only pilot projects and were not being used in real life. It was exciting to be in at that early stage and be involved in an emerging industry.

The industry has moved on a long way since those days, yet it is all just as exciting now as it was then – I would go so far as to say that it's even more exciting now. The convergence of computers with video has been followed quickly by *multimedia*, and undoubtedly the combination of communications, computers and video is offering great potential and will continue to do so as the true superhighway emerges.

The other major change that is taking place is the transfer of the responsibility for learning to the individual and the concept of lifelong learning.

Thus this book has been written setting out some of the history of what is still a relatively new industry, what the present situation is and what the future might hold. It looks at the various methods of delivery, starting from computer-based training through to training on the Internet, and emerging storage devices such as the digital video disc. Some technologies have disappeared into obscurity as new technologies have taken over; others have stood the test of time. Indeed, computer-based training is still extensively used, despite what some pundits say. Moreover, what matters is the learning that takes place, rather than whether training uses the latest technology or all the features of it.

In this book I also address the essentials of implementation and evaluation. Regrettably, these issues do not always receive the attention they deserve, and I hope that that message will come through. Technology-based training has on occasions failed to provide organisations with the undoubted benefits that this form of training can deliver. It has then been discarded and training has reverted to a less flexible and often more expensive delivery method. In most instances, failure has occurred because issues of implementation have not been considered, which gives the technologies an unjustified bad name. Properly implemented technology-based training will provide the benefits outlined in this book.

The issue of whether you should buy off-the-shelf or have specific courseware designed has also been covered, and I have outlined how you should go about the purchase of both types.

Finally, I have included a number of case studies with this text, and I am indebted to members of the Forum for Technology in Training for providing these studies. I would also like to express my sincere thanks to the vice-chairman of the Forum, Howard Hills, Head of Training Development at Lloyds TSB, for his invaluable support during the writing of this book.

Brian Tucker

The Forum for Technology in Training

The Forum for Technology in Training (formerly The National CBT Forum) was founded in 1982 with the aim of 'promoting performance improvement through the greater and more effective use of technology in training and development'. It is focused on the successful use of established technologies – such as computer-based training and interactive video, as well as the emerging multimedia and communication technologies – that are capable of making a positive contribution to training and development, and to distance, open and flexible learning.

Members of the Forum represent all areas in this field, and are drawn from a diversity of organisations, including major users, in most industry sectors, as well as in government and the armed forces, together with suppliers, academics, independent consultants and ancillary services.

The Forum, a company limited by guarantee, is a non-profit-making organisation, relying on the subscription of members to fund the meetings and to pay a part-time coordinator to deal with the administration. Its activities include the following:

- Meetings, usually five a year, to hear presentations on the latest in professional practice. Speakers include both members and guest speakers. These meetings are often hosted by members, giving an opportunity to see training methods in use.
- Perhaps the most important activity is the informal discussion and exchange of ideas that takes place between members, often after formal meetings and also as a result of the contacts made through membership of the Forum. These exchanges can help you to make the right decisions about emerging techniques and equipment, and about new applications.

The address of the Forum for communication and advice is as follows:

The Forum for Technology in Training
Orchard Chambers
4 Rocky Lane
Heswall
Wirral
Merseyside L60 0BY
Tel: 0151 342 8606
Fax: 0151 342 1660

Part I
Technology-based Training

1 What is Technology-Based Training?

The term 'technology-based training' is applied to training or learning which is undertaken using computer and/or communications technologies to enable learning to take place. The technology may be used for the delivery of the training, for testing (see Case Study 1, Chapter 9), for accreditation, or for tutor support by way of coaching or mentoring. It covers a wide range of training and learning experiences: from highly complicated flight simulators to basic drill and practice; from video conferencing to tutor support across an electronic mail (E-Mail) link; from using the latest multimedia personal computer (PC) to a simple 286 PC; from learning over the information superhighway to using a stand-alone PC.

Computers as learning tools have intrigued both the training industry and the computer industry almost since computers were invented. Computer technicians were the first to attempt to exploit the computer as such a tool because the trainers did not have the technical skills to carry out the complicated programming necessary with the early computers. Unfortunately, these earlier implementations often failed as good-quality learning experiences. The programmers could understand the power of the computer, but they had neither the necessary training skills, nor in some cases the screen design skills, to produce good training materials. Thus the early attempts at selling the concept of the computer as a learning/training tool were not well received. Even as higher-level computer languages became available, it was still the computer programmers that produced the training.

Technology-based training has progressed a long way since the early days of computer-based training in the 1960s and 1970s. Technology improvements have been rapid and so have the changes in training methods. However, the main changes have been the merging of video with computers, and later, the merging of communications with these technologies. The first step in this process was the introduction of interactive video. This enabled trainers to use the power of computer-based training with the ability of the interactive video disc to produce moving pictures and sound, thus creating stimulating and effective training.

The video at that time was analogue and the computer image was overlaid on the video picture. The increasing power of the computers and the compact-disc technologies led moves towards digitisation, and multimedia was born.

It was the phenomenal increase in the power of the PC that enabled the merger of computer and communications technologies. On-line systems with large mainframes had been a reality for some years. Now we have an information superhighway revolution which will, in the foreseeable future, give us the capability of delivering, accrediting and supporting learning/training anywhere in the world.

During this revolution in and merging of the technologies, there have been some technologies that have fallen by the wayside. Others, regrettably, still have a poor reputation – a hangover from the days when the courseware was provided by the wrong people. A similar problem occurred when interactive video became possible. Video companies suddenly became training producers, with little or no knowledge of training design or of the learning process.

Fortunately, this situation was soon rectified, and these problems are in the past. There are now specialists in each of the necessary disciplines working together to produce very good courseware, whether generic or bespoke. The United Kingdom has a reputation for good training, and for both screen and interactive design – a reputation that is justified. That doesn't mean that you won't find poor UK courseware or a number of excellent imports.

COMPUTER-BASED TRAINING

Computer-based training (CBT) is the generic term for training delivered, tested or managed by a computer, either mainframe or PC. It also covers a range of other terms that existed in the 1970s, such as, for example, the following:

- CBL Computer-based learning
- CBI Computer-based instruction
- CAL Computer-assisted learning
- CAT Computer-assisted training
- CAI Computer-assisted instruction
- CML Computer-managed learning
- CMT Computer-managed training
- CMI Computer-managed instruction

Fortunately, these other expressions have, in the main, fallen into disuse, and we are left with computer-based training. However, there is a further complication with the advent of multimedia, as this makes defining CBT more difficult.

At one stage, CBT meant any form of training delivered, administered or tested by computer, that did not include video in its presentation and/or the courseware was not held on a CD-ROM. The term is now generally used, however, to denote courseware that uses text and graphics only, whatever the storage medium used.

If we go back to the beginning of CBT we will see how this has developed and how it is different from multimedia. At the birth of CBT the delivery system was the mainframe computer and this was limited to the delivery of text in one font and monochrome. It could be very interactive and was ideal for the training of information technology (IT). It could also be used for administering tests and recording training completed against a training plan.

The advent of the PC, colour monitors and graphics brought a new dimension to the provision of training. Even though initially in only three colours, we saw programmes produced for electrical mechanics showing circuits on the screen with which the users could interact. With improved graphics packages, a better and wider range of colours, and the use of artists, the programmes became more alive. As the power of the computer increased, animation became a practical proposition. With the increase in the capacity of the hard disks, the addition of a limited amount of audio also enhanced the learning.

From the earliest days, the important benefits of computer-based training were that the training was interactive, available and self-paced. There were initial reservations about being 'taught' by machine, plus the added problem that few people were familiar with computers and many were wary of the new technology. Once users realised, however, that:

- they could not break the expensive equipment;
- the learning was much more individualised; and
- they could work at their own pace,

then their initial concerns melted away and the methodology took a hold.

So CBT can be courseware delivered by the PC using text, graphics, animation and limited audio, from data held on the hard disk. Many leading companies still use this medium for training their staff.

There is a temptation – that must be resisted – to use all the power and functionality of the available technologies because they are there, or because our competitors are using them. When computer technicians were the first to exploit computers as learning tools, their natural inclination was to use all the clever tricks they could think of. Yet the most important factor in developing computer-based training material was then, and still is, the learning process.

INTERACTIVE AUDIO

Language teachers, particularly those involved with language laboratories, were the first to recognise the benefits that could be gained from adding voice to computer courseware.

The early systems were effective but, in comparison with today's technologies, archaic. At that stage, digital recording and playback of voice had not come on the scene. These systems were restricted to analogue audio played from magnetic tape. It was possible, however, for the computer program to drive the tape machine, instructing it to play, pause or stop and to rewind or fast forward to a particular spot on the tape. The rewind and fast forward caused delays in the interactivity. However, this was acceptable at that time, as there was no alternative and people had nothing with which to compare it. A significant problem was that magnetic tape stretches the more it is played, which made finding the correct position when searching somewhat difficult and meant that spaces had to be left in the audio to allow for this contingency.

When digital storage of audio became possible, some use was made of this but audio takes a large amount of memory for a small amount of time, even at low-quality recording. Therefore, even with the improvements in technology giving larger-capacity hard disks in the PCs, limited use was made of this facility.

It was not until the advent of CD-ROM and compression techniques, that interactive audio became a really workable methodology. In fact, language training had already moved to interactive video when it became available. Sound could be recorded on the video disc on two channels, giving the opportunity of two languages. This was not the most economical use of the disc, but it was available before CD-ROM.

The ability to store more data both in main memory and on hard disk, and the advent of sound processing cards which could be slotted into the computer, opened up new horizons. The addition of the sound processing card also gave the facility to record the student's voice so that it could be played back later for comparison. This enhanced the learning and also gave the tutor the ability to give advice and guidance where needed.

There are many good language training programmes available today, covering language for beginners and for business. However, language training is not the only use for interactive audio. There are courses in existence covering human resource skills, such as interviewing. Here again, the ability to store the student's response for later discussion adds to the learning process.

It will be obvious to the reader that the current interactive audio programmes fall within the definition of multimedia and will be referenced as such in the second half of this book.

INTERACTIVE VIDEO

Interactive video (IV or IAV) started, like interactive audio, with computer programs driving linear video players. The same principles and difficulties applied to this method of delivery as with interactive audio. Neither method gave the interaction that we know and demand today, but at that time the standard was acceptable.

The introduction of the video disc that could store both video and sound gave the potential for true interactive video. Initially, there were two types of video disc, but it was the laserdisc that found favour with, and became the standard for, the training market. The other disc (JVC) became the standard for use in jukeboxes.

There were a number of factors which limited large-scale introduction of this medium. First, there was the cost of the equipment, which involved the purchase of a video disc player, replacing the computer monitor with a television monitor, and adding a card and software to the computer. These last items were necessary for the merging of text and video pictures on the screen. Secondly, there was the cost of producing programmes for internal use, and the non-availability of good – if any – generic courseware to run on the equipment.

It was a chicken and egg situation. The courseware suppliers did not want to invest in the production of high-cost courseware until there was a base of equipment in the marketplace. At the same time, the potential users of the technology did not want to invest in the equipment until there was courseware on the market. Thus only one company had the courage to produce generic material, while only one or two of the very large organisations, who could afford both the cost of the equipment and expensive generic courseware and the production cost of bespoke training, implemented this method of training. To make all this cost effective, a company needed a large volume of staff requiring the training, and so again it was only the large organisations with the necessary volume of staff that could justify the outlay. However, some of these companies were able to show some substantial cost savings.

As with some of the other media, the technology drove the training at the outset and there was a lot of what was sarcastically known as 'interrupted video' on the market, which consisted of linear video programmes that were transferred to video disc and were stopped occasionally for questions to be asked. This was not, and is not, interactivity. However, even with purpose-built interactive video, the interactivity seemed at first to be based on a linear process. It was only when the training designers became familiar with the capability of the medium that programmes of a high standard were produced.

The video disc not only gave the same facilities as the video tape player, – that is the ability to stop, pause, play, fast forward and fast reverse – but it also enabled the user to jump to a particular frame on the disc within a fraction of a second, and to hold a still frame on the screen. This was still analogue video, of course, and the marriage of this and digital text and graphics caused many problems, but the medium was very good and the added benefit of video and sound over CBT made training in other subjects, such as interpersonal skills, possible.

Interactive video also allowed users to simulate complex technical skills. For example, one course for schools and colleges covered the use of a gas chromatograph, which is a very expensive piece of equipment that students would not normally be able to see, let alone touch or practise using. In this instance, the programme gave them full use of the controls of the machine and did not restrict their use; they could even make serious mistakes which resulted in the destruction of the machine. In effect, it was true learning by discovery – not possible with the real thing!

Because the video was analogue, it was only possible to hold a still picture by playing the same frame again and again, which meant that it was not possible to play audio from the interactive video disc at the same time as holding the still picture. If there was a need for sound with the still picture the sound had to be stored on the computer hard disk, which required a sound-processing card to be installed in the computer, together with the relevant software. This method was not used a great deal, though, as shortly after the introduction of the first audio processing cards a system called 'Framestore' was introduced. Framestore digitised the frame and held it while the sound was processed from the interactive video disc. Once the ability to convert the analogue video to digital video in real time became available, then the problems of mixing text, graphics and video on the screen no longer existed and the digitised frame could be captured and held on screen while sound was played from the video disc.

Interactive video is still being used by many large organisations. While their equipment remains operational and their existing courseware relevant, they will continue to use this method of delivery. However, it is true to say that it would no longer be a wise investment choice for someone seeking to start using technology-based training today.

DIGITAL VIDEO INTERACTIVE

Digital video interactive (DVI) is not really another medium, but rather a different approach to the medium of interactive video. As its name implies, DVI uses digital video. The DVI process compresses the video and audio, and stores the compressed data on a CD-ROM. It then decompresses the data in real time for delivery on the screen. Because the video is compressed and decompressed it is possible to have full screen, full motion video.

One of the distinct advantages over the laserdisc is that with DVI it is possible to run the video at controlled variable speeds. With laserdisc it is only possible to play at normal speed or fast forward, fast backwards or frame by frame in either direction. The other advantage of DVI over laserdisc is that it has four audio channels which can be synchronised at the output stage.

An example of the use of variable speed video is in simulation. Hodos Creative Technology developed a train driving simulator for British Rail. Without any specially shot video they were able to simulate the driver's view of the progress of the train at variable speeds from too fast down to stop depending on the trainee's use of the controls. This could be achieved because the video can be run at any speed from 30 frames per second down to stop. The DVI process makes the production of this type of training much cheaper than using laserdisc. With laserdisc it would be necessary to have specially shot video, which would increase the cost beyond a practical proposition.

Digital video also allows a frame or frames to be altered by changing the pixels, a technique used in the film and video industry for special effects. Moreover, in one of the early applications of DVI a fish-eye lens was used on the camera that enabled a 360-degree picture to be taken. This technique produced a distorted picture, but the frames were altered to give the right perspective. The user was then able to turn left or right and see exactly what they would have seen had they been there, which included looking up and seeing the sky above them.

DVI was expected to take over from laserdisc and to be used by most organisations, but the process was never really popular. At the time, however, it was the only digital interactive video to give full screen, full motion video, and when it was bought by Intel it was thought that the technology would be embedded on the motherboard of every new PC that had an Intel processor. Yet today, few applications still exist that use this technology.

EXPERT SYSTEMS/ARTIFICIAL INTELLIGENCE

During the late 1980s we heard a great deal about how artificial intelligence and expert systems would revolutionise technology-based training. Once again, however, this did not happen, and one of the main reasons for this lack of success was that artificial intelligence required a huge amount of processing power. Had we not advanced to personal computers, but continued to run our training from mainframes, then this requirement would not have been a problem. Secondly, the programming of a course was expensive and very time consuming.

Expert systems held greater promise, as these systems were not so time consuming in production. However, obtaining and recording the knowledge from the expert was itself a time-consuming task. Thus, by comparison with other forms of technology-based training, expert systems took up a large amount of processing power and memory.

One of the benefits that this type of system provided was that once the knowledge was in the system, it was then possible for the trainee to learn by discovery. There was no forced route through the system, except in the learning of one skill. Nevertheless, the cost of producing courseware and the ratio of production time to hours of study were considerably higher for these systems than the cost and ratio for computer-based training. Therefore, benefit resulted only if the learning uptake and retention of knowledge was considerably better than for computer-based training.

A study was carried out for the then Department of Employment which compared the learning uptake of computer-based training and expert systems. Kingston University produced the shell for the expert system and Royal Insurance (UK) provided the courseware, the subject matter for which was motor insurance. There was already a computer-based-training course in existence, and this was now slightly modified so that it would have precisely the same training objectives as the expert system. The expert system was then produced and the knowledge obtained from the expert.

The new intake of trainees into the company were split into two selected groups to ensure that there would be no bias in the comparative exercises. Each group was given the opportunity to use both computer-based training and expert systems products so that they were familiar with both methodologies.

There was some prerequisite training that had to be undertaken and this was carried out using computer-based training. Both groups then studied the introductory module of the computer-based training course and then undertook the training by the method allocated to them. The training was completed in the same period of time for each method. All the trainees sat an immediate post-study test and a further test after a three-month period, both under strict examination conditions. None of the trainee were allowed to undertake and work within the field of motor insurance in the intervening period between tests.

The overall result of the exercise showed that there was no statistically significant difference in the results from the two tests. However, there was a marked preference for studying using computer-based training, as this was structured. The trainees had been used to and some found that the freedom to learn by discovery through the expert system left them a little confused about their place in the learning process.

One benefit that came out of the investigations into expert systems was that some of the features and advantages of expert systems were incorporated into learning design for other forms of technology-based learning, though this in itself probably hindered the adoption of expert systems.

There are some subjects that lend themselves to the artificial intelligence/ expert systems approach. The field of medicine is one of these. A course has recently been produced that uses artificial intelligence to help train general practitioners in the diagnosis and treatment of depression. Many days of effort were required to elicit the knowledge from the experts. The course deals with a child patient, accompanied by his mother. The child has a skin complaint, yet the root cause of the problem lies in the mother's state of depression. As the interview progresses banks of questions are made available to the GP, appropriate to the stage of the interview. Having completed the interview, the GP receives feedback on the diagnosis and the method by which he or she arrived at that diagnosis. The GP can then decide from a Windows-type application which product to prescribe, the dosage and frequency. The system can then provide additional feedback on the choice of drug and the level of dosage. This is a good example of the use of artificial intelligence being embedded into the courseware.

MULTIMEDIA

In the late 1960s to early 1970s, the term 'multimedia' meant training that involved the use of more than one delivery method. For example, a course that required the user to view a video, read a textbook and carry out tests on the computer. The term 'mixed media' is now used to describe this.

Today the term 'multimedia' has an entirely different meaning, but there does not seem to be one clear definition, for it is a combination of at least three of the following media: text, graphics, still pictures, animation, video, audio and data. What does tend to be a common factor in most definitions of multimedia products is that they use a compact disc as the storage medium.

Signe Hoffos of Multimedia Ventures defines multimedia in the *1996 Multimedia Yearbook* as: 'A system in which all the processing power is contained within a single box, and the entire presentation can be recorded on a single medium'. This is basically true, but there are still some people using external CD-ROM drives. Nonetheless, it is a good description because, with the ever increasing capacity of hard disks – currently four gigabytes is the maximum – there may be a tendency for courseware to be stored on the hard disk rather than on a CD-ROM.

In *Multimedia Design – A Newcomer's Guide*, the authors argue that four factors differentiate multimedia from other information presentation platforms or techniques, as follows:

1. The mix of media.
2. The use of digital technology.
3. The 'one unit' delivery platform.
4. Interaction.

Multimedia is not necessarily synonymous with training; indeed, it covers many disciplines, for example

- point-of-sale;
- publishing;
- entertainment;
- education; and
- training.

In fact, education and training are only a relatively minor part of the multimedia industry. Computer games probably accounts for most of the market.

The training industry can never put the same amount of investment into the production of multimedia, as the games industry does, nor can they hope to develop multimedia training courseware to the same technical level and standard. However, we, in the technology-based training industry, can learn a great deal from the games industry in terms of the use of graphics, screen design and, most important of all, interactivity, for the games industry knows how to attract the attention of users and how to retain their interest.

Multimedia not only covers a number of industries, but also has different processes or delivery methods, i.e. CD-ROM and compact disc interactive (CD-i), which will be discussed below.

CD-ROM

Compact disc read-only memory, (CD-ROM) is not a delivery method as such: it is a storage device. The disc is no different in size or appearance to the music CD, with which we are all familiar. The audio CD was devised to hold high-quality audio, whereas the CD-ROM was produced with the specific intention of storing high-volume digital data. In fact, they both hold data in exactly the same way, except that CD-ROM does not hold only audio data. Also, the CD-ROM disc requires a special drive, which are installed in most new PCs on the market – certainly in all multimedia PCs. For PCs without internal CD-ROM disc drives it is possible to purchase an external drive.

When it was first produced the storage capability of CD-ROM was many times greater than a hard disk, yet it had the advantage of the floppy disk in that it was portable, an advantage it retains. Nor does it take up much shelf storage space. However, its original advantage in capacity over the hard disks has disappeared, as technology has made large-capacity hard disks a reality: four gigabyte hard disks are available and capacity will continue to increase.

The introduction of the CD-ROM made multimedia available for the mass market. Before that, multimedia-type programs could only be produced with a videodisc and a large-capacity hard disk. What the CD has done is to bring down the cost of technology-based training material to make it accessible to a greater audience. The cost of a CD-ROM drive has also come down, which puts the conversion of a standard PC to a multimedia PC within the reach of even the smallest companies.

Nearly all home computers now have an internal quad-speed CD-ROM drive, and the latest models have eight-speed drives. Not surprisingly, the home multimedia PCs are often superior to the office multimedia PCs: home users do not have to justify upgrading or replacing their equipment, nor do they have to write off the cost over a period of time.

CD-ROM can store text, graphics, still pictures, video and audio for presentation on the PC's monitor in an interactive manner. However, the video is generally not full screen, full motion video, as was the case with interactive video and DVI and is the case with CD-i. Whether the training need requires the use of full screen, full motion video is a decision that only you can make.

CD-ROM is a storage medium and is not multimedia. The programmes could equally be stored on the hard disk, if only temporarily. Also CD-ROMs may only contain text, graphics and program code. One large financial institution has nothing on the hard disks at their training workstations other than the essential software to run the workstation. They hold their courses on back-up tape, loading it to the workstation when it is needed and removing it after use. Currently, this gives slightly faster access to the data.

However, both for ease of use and for storage, CD-ROM is a very good medium. It is used for many more applications than just training, and it is the entertainment sector that will keep this system alive for many years to come.

CD-ROM (XA)

While a standard CD-ROM disc can hold 650 megabytes of data – a greater capacity than was ever available on hard disk – it was not considered enough to provide good interactivity, particularly if it was necessary to store audio and/or video.

The first method of using CD-ROM for audio was to play the audio through a standard CD player interface, which could be plugged directly into a television monitor or loudspeaker. The computer could control the CD drive with the directions to stop, start, or go to a specific point. The disadvantage of this was that any computer code on the disc could only be read between audio sessions. Also, the audio storage was uneconomical, as it was high fidelity audio played back in an analogue format.

CD-ROM (XA) was therefore introduced to achieve three things:

1. Increased audio storage by compressing the audio.
2. The ability to use the disc to store computer code, which could be loaded at the same time as the audio.
3. The future possibility of playing video interleaved with audio, effectively at the same time.

It dates back to August 1991 when Philips and Sony agreed to a standard coding format for graphics, images and audio. For the authors of training material, this format enabled them to write good multimedia packages using a higher proportion of video and audio than had been available with the standard CD-ROM.

Apart from simplifying the combination of text, graphics and audio, this extended architecture was supposed to be a bridge between CD-ROM and

CD-i, but that regrettably never materialised. The Soundblaster card, the first and probably most used sound card, was introduced just after XA came on the market and was a better vehicle for interactive audio.

The ability to compress data – including audio and video – and decompress in real time, and under software control, has meant that the original need for CD-ROM (XA) has disappeared. Little courseware using this method is now sold. Those who installed the necessary hardware initially to gain the advantage of this method are the main users, and only a few of these have continued to use it. Certainly, the method would not be an option for those now moving into technology-based training for the first time.

However, CD-ROM (XA) played a significant part in introducing generic courseware to the CD-ROM PC. The first multimedia course available for sale purely in CD-ROM had originally been developed for British Telecom in the CD-ROM (XA) format.

COMPACT DISC INTERACTIVE

For CD-ROM and CD-ROM (XA), it is necessary to have a PC, a VGA monitor or better, and a CD-ROM player. For compact disc interactive (CD-i), the player has an on-board computer, and uses a video or television monitor and a pointing device of some description. The system does not require a keyboard. These points make CD-i an ideal delivery medium for the consumer market, for learning at home, and as a learning delivery method for those people who are still apprehensive of technology – though it is still daunting for those people who can't even use a video recorder.

CD-i gives full motion, full screen video, which many people consider to be an advantage over other CD storage devices, although it has not yet made the impact in the technology-based training industry that was originally expected. Conversion of training videos to this system is, however, gathering impetus, and it is accepted that the system does make a difference in how training videos are used in traditional training courses.

A training video on CD-i gives much greater flexibility to the trainer, since it provides the normal video controls plus the opportunity to jump back easily to a point in the video. The video is also broken into short sequences and has built-in questions for group discussion, which is an improvement on watching a full-length video and then discussing topics afterwards.

The fact that CD-i uses a player with its own on-board computer is what has stopped the system becoming a widely used distance-learning method with the larger companies. Such organisations already had an infrastructure of PCs with CD-ROM drives and/or interactive videodisc players, and they did not want to have to install hundreds and, in some cases, thousands of pieces of new equipment. Therefore they have stayed with the technology that is more compatible with their existing equipment.

However, what was perceived by the large organisations as a disadvantage may well have been an advantage to the small organisations. Small and medium-sized enterprises may not even have a computer, and where there is a computer, this may not have a CD-ROM drive or may be being used to capacity. Therefore, the relatively low cost of a CD-i player is an attraction. There would, of course, be the additional need to purchase a video or television monitor.

Although some of the material produced for this medium is not best used on an individual basis, it does allow a member of staff to take the training home for study in the peace and quiet of his or her own familiar environment. This is not currently happening with CD-ROM courses, despite the fact that there may be a multimedia PC available at home, and there are probably two reasons for this discrepancy.

First, the CD-ROM course would have to be loaded to the PC, which may not be allowed by the supplier and may, in any event, be beyond the capability of the staff member. Secondly, the home multimedia PC is probably the prize possession of the child in the family. Both reasons are disadvantages compared to CD-i, which just needs to be plugged into the aerial socket of the TV and the power supply.

The advantage of home study by employees would be of benefit to many large companies. Nevertheless, the fact that you cannot run a CD-ROM course on a CD-i player and vice versa prevents large organisations taking up this option.

At this point, however, we should note a recent report that Philips may well cease marketing CD-i players when digital video disc (DVD) is launched in 1997.

DIGITAL VIDEO DISC

Digital video disc (DVD) – now sometimes described as digital versatile disc – will have a capacity of 4.7Gb as against the 650Mb of the CD-ROM. The DVD movie, not a training tool, will be expensive for many reasons such as copy protection and the compression technology. However, DVD-ROM – a disc that will hold around eight times as much data as the current CD-ROM drive – is a different matter.

At the time of going to print, I would not rush out to buy one of these, for there are matters that still need to be resolved on this system. All the same, perhaps we can look forward to having DVD-i discs that will also run on a standard PC!

SIMULATION

When we talk of simulation and simulators everyone immediately thinks of aircraft simulators – highly complex pieces of machinery driven by equally complex computer programs. These simulators react to every change in the controls made by the trainee pilots. The trainee pilots see exactly what they would see out of the cockpit windows and the cockpit moves exactly as it would in reality. Yes, these are good examples of technology-based training, but do not fall within the range of day-to-day training that is used by the bulk of business and industry. Before leaving the aircraft industry, however, it is fair to say that not all aircraft simulators are very complex: some are provided from a multimedia PC on a standard monitor. It is a question of horses for courses, that is, only using the technology necessary to meet the training need.

Simulations, in fact, have many uses, including the following:

- Software products, such as word processing systems, databases, etc.
- Form filling.
- Office procedures.
- Industrial processes.
- Train and road driving.

If the procedure being taught is a computer procedure, then a very realistic simulation is relatively easy to produce. However, many of these training products do not allow you to make the mistakes that you will make in real life and are, therefore, not true simulations. If you accidentally press a wrong key it just asks you to try again. This does have the advantage that you are learning in a safe environment, without the concern about what will go wrong if you do press the wrong key. It does not, though, prepare you for the inevitable mistakes that you will make in the future – by which time, hopefully, your confidence should be greater. The type of simulation that restricts your interaction, sometimes only to the next correct response, is referred to as an emulator.

If the procedure being taught is keyboard entry, then it is a true simulation. There are many very good typing courses on the market, and training in office procedures can often be simulated effectively on a PC. It is when we move into the realm of industrial process that simulation becomes more difficult. Simulating the movement of sliders on control panels, pressing on–off switches, and so forth, is relatively easy. Turning knobs cannot be so realistically simulated, but can be done, and I have seen a combination lock on a safe well simulated by actually animating the numbers rather than the knob. Simulators have also been designed, for example, for power generation plants and nuclear plants, and have proved very successful in training operators.

VIRTUAL REALITY

This is a stage up from simulation. Most of us, when someone mentions virtual reality, visualise people walking around with complex headsets on, firing laser guns or waving swords about. This is certainly an application of virtual reality and, in some respects, has been the driving force that has made virtual reality a practical training option. In this form, virtual reality can in some cases be used in a training role – without the laser guns! In fact, aircraft simulators are virtual reality. You are using the controls of the cockpit, what you see out of the windscreen is what you would see in reality, and the way the plane reacts is as it would in reality.

There are some virtual reality applications on computer monitors. The navy use a virtual reality program to acquaint new intakes with the layout of a submarine. They can walk in any direction within the flat plane of 360 degrees. If they come to a lift or staircase they are taken down or up as the case may be. When they actually board the submarine, therefore, they are already fully conversant with the layout, do not have to waste time learning their way about, and can be effective more quickly.

British Gas use virtual reality on a PC for assessing engineers. In the past, to assess their engineers British Gas have used an actual street, with fictitious events played out by actors, and the assessor following the engineer around with a clipboard, noting everything that was said and done. The virtual reality programme provides this street on the computer. The engineer can go to any house in the street and ask questions of the resident, take meter readings of the level of gas in the air, and so on. He or she can make decisions, even to the extent of putting out cones and digging up the pavement to repair the fault. The engineer can also work without someone watching his or her every move, and so will work more realistically. The assessment is even more thorough as the computer can store every move, action and communication made by the engineer for review.

VIDEO CONFERENCING

Video conferencing uses video cameras and television monitors at each location and multiple-channel telephone links.

Video conferencing is used for training as well as for basic conferencing. In the early days it was not seen as a good medium for training, but rather as a multi-person to multi-person technology, with the people participating travelling to a special location where the equipment was set up and the broadband network existed. There are now video conferencing machines available that can be wheeled from room to room, and the system is becoming much more popular.

It is possible for video and multimedia programs to be transmitted across video conference links. These programs can then be used in a group situation, with participants discussing the response, this becoming input for the programs in return. The participants can then discuss the results of their response to a question before proceeding further.

However, the training use of video conferencing is mainly in the area of making the remote lecturer available to an audience across a wide geographical spread. Often an organisation has one or two real experts who cannot afford the time to attend courses right across the country. Their expertise is needed at their place of work. Thus to have them able to address a large dispersed audience, with personnel at the remote locations interacting and questioning the expert, is very cost effective.

Video conferencing is also very useful in a tutorial situation, with the tutor in one location able to communicate with students in a number of locations. The students can also interact with one another, making for effective learning. When people from different parts of an organisation, who normally never meet each other, interact in their learning experience, this enhances that experience.

DESK-TO-DESK CONFERENCING

Desk-to-desk conferencing is similar to video conferencing, but requires less bulky and less costly equipment. A small camera is mounted on the top of the PC monitor and a special card is installed in the computer. This form of conferencing is best for one-to-one location communication, although it can be used in a number of locations. The image of each person can be overlaid on the screen, so that the parties are in both voice and visual contact.

The chief benefit of this type of communication is that, with the addition of some software, the two locations can see the same screen and share the same application. Either party can mark areas of the screen and either party can remove such marking. If someone is using a multimedia training program and has some difficulty, they can contact their tutor/mentor, who may be the other side of the world, and discuss the problem. The tutor will be able to see the screen that is causing the student/trainee difficulty and talk them through their problem.

It is not always necessary to have the visual contact and a second telephone line for the voice contact can be used, with the other line handling the data communication. In some senses, the visual contact is an added extra that is more of a nicety than an essential. There are training situations where visual contact is beneficial. For example, if the tutor can see some of the trainee's body language, particularly the facial expressions, he or she will know whether the light has really dawned or whether the student is still unclear.

This methodology has been taken up by academia more than industry. Colleges and universities use the technique in cases where the student is remote from the college: for example, in teacher-training situations. Similarly, the appropriate tutor can be used for a particular course or training situation even if they are many miles away from the students or trainees.

SATELLITE BROADCASTING

Visual and audio messages are broadcast over a satellite link and the receiving stations have the benefit of seeing and hearing the people at the central broadcast location. This, however, has the disadvantage that it is not currently possible for the satellite link to be a two-way communication.

In effect, the remote sites can only be linked back to the central studio by telephone line. Depending on the number of remote sites connected to the system, it may not be possible to have all of these sites connected interactively. Some may have to be answered by an operator and have their questions relayed to the broadcasters. The satellite broadcast with a telephone link back to the broadcaster is referred to as interactive television.

This methodology has been to some extent superseded by video conferencing. But it does have the advantage that the video link is via satellite and does not need the broadband telephone links that are required by video conferencing.

NETWORKS/INTERNET/INTRANETS

The much vaunted information superhighway is not yet a reality. We do sometimes talk of highways, but Nigel Paine, Director of the Scottish Council for Educational Technology, was probably more correct when, in a paper presented in America, he said that we did not even have a 'super dirt-track'.

When we talk about the information superhighway, most of us think about the Internet. While the Internet is the most commonly known network, it is not the only one, although it is probably the most easily accessed and is the system used by thousands of organisations and hundreds of thousands of individuals worldwide. The Internet is actually a network of networks, which is accessed via a service provider, and it allows electronic communication across the world for the price of a local phone call.

Nevertheless, there are other networks. For example:

- MSN, the new Microsoft Network launched in August 1995 as part of Windows 95.
- Janet and SuperJanet, used by over 200 academic institutions.
- Company-dedicated networks, which have been in existence and use for many years to transmit voice and data.

- The telecommunication network, which allows us to transmit both data and voice.

This is not an exhaustive list, and as technology develops we will see new networks appearing, others merging, and some disappearing.

The information superhighway is an all-embracing term used to describe all the different networks and the interconnecting of these networks. When the superhighway arrives/emerges, it will be completely different from what we know now. There will be two main differences: first, it will be a managed network, whereas the present Internet just happens; and second, there will be greater bandwidth, which will allow faster transmission rates.

In addition to the Internet we have what are termed 'Intranets'. An intranet is a network specific to a group of users, which may be a company or a virtual organisation. Some companies/organisations have dedicated leased lines that have been used for transmission of voice and data across the organisation. Later they added E-Mail and are now beginning to use their intranet for transmission of information. The information on that intranet is only available to the organisation's staff and is not accessible by the public. These intranets generally do not have access to the Internet, but it is possible for this facility to exist without compromising the intranet.

While dedicated networks form intranets, it is possible to have an intranet using the Internet as a means of access. The information on that intranet will still be specific to the organisation, accessible only by them and not available to the public at large. A number of this form of intranet exist, particularly where an organisation has a small number of staff widely dispersed, making leased lines an impracticable solution.

The future of this technology is explored in the final chapter, but what can these networks do for training now?

One company is providing training material for teaching computer systems using the Microsoft Network. Some of the material is delivered across the network and some is provided in other forms of distance learning. Project work is set on the network and there is a bulletin board/coffee shop where the students can exchange messages and electronically discuss problems with their peers. There is tutor support at regular times of the day and communication by E-mail at any time. This company is based in the United Kingdom, but most of their students are based in the United States. They have now produced an Internet version of their courseware.

Universities are using a network to put students in communication with their remote tutors or the remote students in communication with their centrally based tutors. This is being handled in the manner discussed under desk-to-desk conferencing (see above).

There are projects running in the school environment where the schools are on-line to Anglia University. The system includes a number of applications. Two examples will help to show how these types of network help with learning:

1. The first application is in economics. Students are presented with a simulated coffee machine area. Whilst there, they are able to pick up on comments about the economy. They may follow up these comments and can ask questions, which will be answered by the financial institution that is sponsoring this programme. This is a novel way of learning that is appealing to the students undertaking this experiment.
2. The second application is in the science subjects, where some of the tuition is given over the network and the students can post questions which will be answered within one week, often by eminent scientists with whom they would normally never have had any contact.

The networks, the Internet and the intranets are mainly being used for interaction with tutors and experts. Some of the leased-line networks do have large bandwidths which would make it technically feasible to provide interactive training over their intranet. Whether they have the capacity to manage the extra traffic load without degrading the network for their existing users is debatable.

What is not happening at present is multimedia training, with video and audio, being delivered over a highway. Most, if not all, of the technology exists, but is not generally available, mainly due to the fact that the broadband networks are not in place. Currently, a large proportion of the population are still connected to the telephone system by a twisted pair of copper wires. Ideal for dealing with normal telephone calls and facsimiles, but not up to transferring the huge amounts of data necessary to provide interactive multimedia training.

Training material is not yet generally available, and this has been and still is very much another chicken and egg situation. Until there is a demand for the multimedia courseware on the highway, the supply will not be there; and if the courseware is not available, then there will be no demand. There are also problems that need to be resolved: for example, how to establish pricing and payment; and copyright and security issues.

One company has come up with a partial solution. They supply the multimedia course on a CD-ROM free of charge, but to use the course you have to go via the Internet to activate it. You are then charged for that usage. There are also organisations providing some form of interactive training from their web site, but this approach has some way to go yet.

ELECTRONIC PERFORMANCE SUPPORT SYSTEMS

An electronic performance support system (EPSS), otherwise known as a performance support system (PSS) or electronic performance support (EPS), is not in itself a training tool. However, it gives support as the individual is working and often embeds training within the system.

An EPSS supports the individual electronically and interactively at their workstation. When a person has a problem or comes across something that they have not dealt with before, they can call up the support. This is often at various levels, from basic help – much as exists with applications such as word processing – through to embedded computer-based training applicable to the particular problem area.

In a paper by Clay Carr, 'Performance support systems: a new horizon for expert systems', *AI Expert* **7**, (5), 44, he defines a performance support system as: 'a computer-based system that uses knowledge-based systems, hypertext, on-line reference, extensive databases, and allied technologies to provide support to performers on the job, where they need it, when they need it, in the form most useful to them'. This makes this truly just-in-time training. An early definition by Gloria Gery describes EPSS by its goal: 'the ultimate goal of an EPSS is to provide whatever is necessary to generate performance and learning *at the moment of need* ... and to implement that support *electronically.*'

Clay Carr also looks at the basic roles that an EPSS can fill, which he defines as follows:

- To act as a librarian. In this role, it helps the performer find, organize, and interpret the information required to carry out the task.
- To function as an advisor. It embodies and shares some specialized expertise that the performer needs to carry out the task.
- As an instructor. In this role, it trains the performer in some aspect of the work to be done. Just as the advisor role is closest to that of an expert system, the instructor role is an outgrowth of computer-based training (CBT).
- As a 'dofer'. When in this role, it does the work with or without assistance from the human performer.

An element of training/learning is involved in the first two roles. The third role is most definitely a training role. The fourth role offers the least training, particularly if the system is actually doing the work.

One of the benefits of EPSSs is that they take away the need to train people for the whole job up-front. Only the parts that are frequently used need to be taught, and those that occur infrequently can then be dealt with by the support system as they arise.

To be effective, performance support systems should be kept up-to-date on a regular basis, and should be able to identify where the person is in the process, so that context-sensitive help can be given.

2 The Benefits of Using TBT

The benefits of using technology-based training (TBT) are many and are achievable. The large financial institutions, and national and international companies, would not use these methods of training if they had not proved their worth. However, proving that the training produces a business benefit is not easy, although this has been carried out by some organisations (see Chapter 7).

The benefits of TBT can be split into two categories: those that have a direct benefit to the organisation, and those that are benefits to the learner. The latter are indirectly benefits to the organisation also, but are less easy to quantify. Some benefits are common to both learner and organisation. Let us now examine these benefits in more detail, with examples where possible.

THE ORGANISATIONAL BENEFITS OF TBT

In summary form, the organisational benefits of TBT are as follows:
- TBT offers a consistent message.
- Staff learn more through TBT compared to traditional training.
- Staff learn faster using TBT.
- Retention of knowledge is better.
- Learning can take place at a time and place best suited to the business needs.
- TBT can be used as reference material when a problem arises.
- TBT can be used for revision.
- TBT is often more cost effective than traditional training.
- TBT offers just-in-time training.
- TBT makes training possible when traditional training would be impractical or non-cost-effective.

We will now look in more detail at each of these benefits.

TBT OFFERS A CONSISTENT MESSAGE

This is seen as a very important factor by many organisations. The need for a consistent message will depend on the nature of the training that is being given, but for some subjects consistency is vital. Compliance with a legal requirement, or an operation which affects safety, are two obvious examples.

The benefit derives from the fact that the TBT course will always offer the same information in the same way and will check that the learner has understood the point. This will ensure not only that the message is consistent, but also that the quality and quantity of training is right as well.

Trainers can have their off days, can be diverted by questions, and cannot tailor their message to each individual participant. Learners on courses have periods of poor reception – some even drop off momentarily! TBT will put the message across as often as necessary, without ever tiring. It doesn't have off days, it can't be diverted, and it will patiently wait until the learner wakes up and continues with the training. Neither does it need to relieve the tedium of delivering the same course repeatedly by redesigning all or part of the course.

Large organisations with trainers in different parts of the country – or even the world – will be unable to deliver a totally consistent training message. But TBT can achieve this. Wherever and whenever the learner takes the training, the message will be the same.

One accountancy organisation developed a high-quality interactive video training course to train their specialist accountants in forty countries worldwide. By using this method they can be sure that an accountant in Africa will receive the same quality, quantity and level of training as an employee in the United Kingdom, and the organisation should therefore be able to apply consistent accountancy practices throughout all its branches.

STAFF LEARN MORE THROUGH TBT COMPARED TO TRADITIONAL TRAINING

Because we only take in a percentage of what we hear, we come away from a traditional learning experience with only a percentage of the knowledge we should have gained. Traditional types of learning experience seldom include post-training 'tests'. The trainer does not know how much each individual has learned and the individual is not aware of how his or her level of knowledge matches up to the expected level.

With TBT, the personal interactivity helps learners to take in the required knowledge. They are also tested to ensure that the required standard has been reached and, if not, are directed back to the topics where their knowledge is not up to the required level.

STAFF LEARN FASTER USING TBT

At first, this is difficult to understand. Why should learning from a machine – which we have already said will put the message across as many times as necessary – be quicker than traditional face-to-face training courses?

Trainer-centred training is tailored to the group, rather than the individual. This means that the learner will be presented with some material with which he/she is already proficient, whilst having to quiz the trainer further on any issues not fully understood.

With technology-based training, however, because there is a very personal involvement with course material, the learner has a much higher level of concentration than in a classroom situation. This has been observed with school children, when comparing their use of technology-based training with traditional teaching techniques. In TBT, the learner only studies in depth those parts of the course where they do not have prior knowledge, and move rapidly through those modules where they have some understanding. Moreover, in areas where they have no prior knowledge, they work through at their own pace. This has been proved to reduce training time by as much as a half, which is a very significant benefit and has proved to be the argument for technology-based training that carries greatest weight within large corporations.

Delayering, downsizing, re-engineering all add up to the same situation – there are fewer staff around than there used to be, and often with greater responsibilities! Covering for colleagues used to be a routine part of many people's responsibilities. Now organisations often have smaller work groups and individuals' workloads are higher, so dealing with anything for an absent colleague, other than immediate queries, is unlikely to happen. The junior management layer that many organisations have lost, and that would have been able to fill in for absent subordinates, is no longer available. Thus time away from the workplace is harder to justify and needs to be used more effectively than ever before.

RETENTION OF KNOWLEDGE IS BETTER

Few statistical exercises have been done in the United Kingdom to test knowledge over a period of time, but subjectively it is firmly believed that those who learn through TBT retain the knowledge for a longer period. Nevertheless, it is difficult to compare knowledge retention because, during the period between the immediate post-test and the second post-test, each individual will be exposed to different experiences in their day-to-day work and these experiences will affect the retention of knowledge.

US studies have proved conclusively that staff learn more and retain that knowledge for longer when using TBT as a learning tool. One study in the United Kingdom was carried out to ascertain whether there was any difference in knowledge retention between students using CBT and students using expert systems (see p. 10). At one branch office of the same company as the one featured in the study, ten trainees were trained on the job for ten weeks – the same period as the trainees in the main study – and then sat identical tests over the same period as the main sample (i.e. immediately post-test and again after three months). The on-the-job trained staff did not retain the knowledge as well as those in the main study, nor did they do as well in the immediate post-test. Although a sample of ten is not large enough to be of statistical significance, these results do appear to confirm that staff learn more when using technology-based training. Certainly the data reinforce earlier studies.

LEARNING CAN TAKE PLACE AT A TIME AND PLACE BEST SUITED TO THE BUSINESS NEEDS

The key aspect here is flexibility. Traditional courses, whether run in-house or externally, are inflexible. They can only be run on predetermined dates. By the time the member of staff has to attend the course, priorities may have changed and attendance is often cancelled, causing an unnecessary expense in unused course fees and a missed learning opportunity.

Technology-based training is flexible. TBT and other flexible learning materials, once purchased, are available most of the time. Learning can thus take place when there is a quieter time in the business day, immediately before the work period, or after work (i.e. at any time that causes the least disruption to the business). Even if priorities change, the learning session can be cancelled at short notice without incurring any financial penalties, and the learning opportunity remains available if required at a later date.

Some organisations have found that their staff are learning outside normal working hours and not interrupting the business at all. In one company the staff were, of their own accord, coming in early or staying on after their shift in order to study.

TBT CAN BE USED AS REFERENCE MATERIAL WHEN A PROBLEM ARISES

How often have you been on courses, come back to the workplace and tried to put the learning into practice, only to hit a problem at a later stage? You may have forgotten something you 'learned on the course', or perhaps the problem which has arisen was never discussed by the trainer. You can't go on the course again, so all that you can do is to refer to your notes, or to colleagues who were on the course, or, as a last resort, to the course instructor.

Technology-based training is generally available within the workplace, and it only take a few moments to search back to the appropriate part of the course and find the answer. The principle of electronic performance support means that, with computer systems, the technology-based training is embedded with the help usually provided on the F1 function key (see pages 21–2).

TBT CAN BE USED FOR REVISION

There are times when we would like to put a member of staff through a course again for revision purposes, but the time required and the cost prevent this. With technology-based training, however, only a small amount of time is necessary and little if any cost is incurred.

We may have someone returning to a job, perhaps as a result of changes in the organisation, following maternity leave, and so on. They therefore have some knowledge and need only to revise on some aspects of the work. To send them on a course will consume both time and money. Furthermore, much of the course material will be familiar to them, so that they are likely to become bored quickly and may then miss the vital part of the course.

With TBT, however, the necessary revision can be done very quickly, as the individual need only work through those areas where their knowledge is out of date. The ability to revise is also important with long-term life skills such as customer care, attitude to quality and interpersonal skills.

TBT IS OFTEN MORE COST EFFECTIVE THAN TRADITIONAL TRAINING

Many studies have been carried out and papers written on this subject. They all identify that TBT training is cost effective. Nobody has published a study that shows it to be more expensive! Frequently the studies have been carried out in big organisations where the advantage of having large numbers of staff to train makes the cost-effective equation better, since the set-up cost of TBT is spread over a large number of students. This factor is especially beneficial in the case of bespoke training where the cost of producing the courseware is high.

One of the problems faced by some of the larger organisations is that their traditional training is carried out in-house and no one really knows what the true cost is of that training. Conversely, there are many good examples of the cost effectiveness of TBT and other forms of open and flexible learning. A recent study of twelve companies in the United Kingdom, varying in size, showed cost advantages ranging from 12 per cent to as high as 90 per cent. Recent statistics from the United States show cost effectiveness in the region of 30 to 50 per cent.

There are a number of areas where savings can be made by using TBT rather than traditional training courses. Some of these areas we have already dealt with, such as:

- Reduced training time, because people learn quicker.
- Reduced time away from the job because there is no travel involved.

- Learning may take place outside working hours.
- Learning may take place in quiet periods.

Other areas of savings are as follows:

- Travel and accommodation for traditional courses can amount to as much as 20 per cent of the total training costs.
- Time away from the job, particularly where it is necessary to employ agency staff to cover for the members of staff being trained, is a significant cost. In other cases it may be that other staff have to work overtime to cover for their absent colleagues.
- Lost business opportunities can also be significant when looking at cost for traditional training, although it is not really possible to quantify business lost due to staff being away on training courses.

TBT OFFERS JUST-IN-TIME TRAINING

The optimum time to learn how to do something is when we are about to carry out that task. That is when motivation is highest and when most skill or knowledge can be transferred from the learning into work. If we can achieve training/learning that is timely, then we have the ideal situation. Much of what we learn concerns everyday, run-of-the-mill activities. Occasionally, however, there are those unusual or special cases that require different treatment, and it is in these cases that we need training readily available for when we encounter problems. Otherwise we spend valuable time trying to find out how to tackle the task, and waste production time on trial and error, possibly making expensive mistakes into the bargain, and certainly taking up other people's time asking for help.

Other situations also require just-in-time training. One leading insurance company ran week-long training courses for supervisors, but the demand for these courses was such that if someone was promoted to supervisor they were unlikely to get on a course before they had been in the job for six to nine months – plenty of time in which to make mistakes and acquire a lot of bad habits that are difficult to break later. The company then purchased a generic interactive video course. It was distributed to main branches and was available for study immediately, and sometimes before, an employee took on the role of supervisor. This was then backed up by a course at a later date.

It is also important from the employee's point of view that training support is providing:

- what they want;
- when they want it;
- where they want it; and
- how they want it.

Electronic performance support meets these requirements, and is the ideal example of just-in-time training.

TBT MAKES TRAINING POSSIBLE WHEN TRADITIONAL TRAINING WOULD BE IMPRACTICAL OR NON-COST-EFFECTIVE

Even large corporations are experiencing difficulty in finding the time to train. They are working under pressure, because business success appears to come to those organisations who work their people hardest. Comments made by line managers include: 'Time is money', 'I can't find the time to train', 'We can't afford the time to send people away'. Such comments are even more applicable to smaller businesses, where to send one person away is reducing their staff by a quarter or more.

Yet training is essential. As the old saying has it: 'If you think training is expensive, you should try ignorance.' Certainly, if it causes us to get things wrong and we lose a customer or two in consequence, ignorance can prove very expensive. So how do we resolve this problem? Technology-based training and other forms of open and flexible learning enable us to do the training in small, easily manageable periods of, say, an hour at a time, which begins to make training a possibility for even the smallest enterprise. Training and development is a vital stimulus for improvement in all organisations, for it enables:

- staff to perform their jobs better;
- organisations to increase their business performance; and
- companies to improve their competitiveness.

Staff will also be better motivated if they are trained, which will mean that they are more inclined to:

- help the business;
- give better customer care;
- take greater care in their work; and
- remain with the organisation longer.

THE LEARNER BENEFITS OF TBT

The learner benefits of TBT are as follows:

- Staff can study at their own pace.
- Staff learn more quickly.
- Staff can make mistakes in private.
- Staff need study only what they don't already know.
- Staff can learn by discovery.
- Staff do not have to leave the family to attend a course.

- Staff can often study at a time that suits them.
- Just-in-time training.
- Staff are being trained.

Let us look at each of these benefits individually.

STAFF CAN STUDY AT THEIR OWN PACE

From a learner's point of view, the ability to study at their own pace is of considerable benefit. With traditional training courses the pace rarely meets anyone's needs all of the time. The pace is either too slow or too fast, making learning difficult. If it is too slow, then boredom sets in and attention wanders. If it is too fast, the trainee either feels under pressure or switches off altogether. Even those who find the overall pace of the course about right will not necessarily find this to be the case for each individual section or session.

Achieving the right pace is difficult, even on a one-to-one basis. When the coach/trainer goes too fast, the learner may not be prepared to ask him or her to slow down. Or if the coach/trainer is overdeliberate and painstaking, the trainee may not be assertive enough to speak up and ask him or her to get on with it.

With technology-based training, however, the learner can proceed through the course at the rate that suits them. They are in total control. They can go back over points they are not sure of or gloss over those parts of the course with which they are already familiar. If the course has a built in pre-test this will indicate which parts of the course can be omitted or just skimmed through, and those parts which must be given extra attention.

Whether or not the overall training time with TBT is less than with traditional methods, the chief factor is the confidence that the trainee builds up through learning at his or her own pace, without being either pressured or bored.

STAFF LEARN MORE QUICKLY

Being free to choose when and what they learn – and to decide how best to use their own time – makes learning less stressful and more productive for most trainees.

STAFF CAN MAKE MISTAKES IN PRIVATE

This is one of the benefits that is rated highly by trainees. There is always the fear on a traditional training course of being made to look foolish by giving a wrong answer or asking a stupid question. Working on a technology-based training course by oneself – and knowing that the machine doesn't pass judgement – gives the trainee more confidence.

STAFF NEED STUDY ONLY WHAT THEY DON'T ALREADY KNOW

So often the training course, whether external or in-house, will include training elements that are already understood. No course will ever meet the trainee's needs precisely. Using technology-based training courses allows the trainees to omit those parts with which they are already familiar. Trainees may also choose to supplement a specific course with material from another course to help them with any areas of particular concern.

STAFF CAN LEARN BY DISCOVERY

Even in the most simple computer-based training course the trainee can try different answers – even wrong answers – to help them understand. With the better courses that use expert systems or artificial intelligence, the trainee can learn by discovery quite freely.

However, white people do tend to learn by discovery, when there is a need to learn a prescribed procedure or system in a methodical way, it is often easier to do this with a set structure to follow.

STAFF DO NOT HAVE TO LEAVE THE FAMILY TO ATTEND A COURSE

For some people, having to leave the family to attend a residential course is not convenient and can cause them worry or distress, which is not conducive to learning. The problem can be aggravated by any family crises, such as sickness, which coincides with the course. This problem does not occur with technology-based training, which can be carried out in the trainee's own environment and close to family and friends.

STAFF CAN OFTEN STUDY AT A TIME THAT SUITS THEM

While it is important that the study should be at a time convenient to the business (mentioned above as an organisation benefit), it is also essential from the employee's point of view that it should be at a time convenient to them. They will learn more and faster if they are studying at a time chosen by them, which, more often than not, will also be a time that fits in best with their work and will therefore be of benefit to the organisation as well. This might be within their own time, be that at break times or immediately before or after work.

JUST-IN-TIME TRAINING

Being able to receive training as and when the need arises is a great benefit to the individual. We have all experienced the problem of facing a difficult situation for which we don't have an answer. In such a case, to be able to get training as and when it is needed is important. We cannot learn enough on courses to cover all eventualities. In any event, we may have forgotten what we learned, because we didn't have the opportunity to put it into practice at the time. Just-in-time training gives the member of staff a feeling of support and is a comfort factor.

STAFF ARE BEING TRAINED

The knowledge that training is available to members of staff is important to them. Realising that you have been given a job to do, but feeling that you have not been properly trained for it, is a bad experience. There is always the fear that you will be criticised for failing to do the job adequately, or for making mistakes, when you have not been properly trained. Thus the fact that the organisation is providing training boosts the morale of staff, and good morale produces a better-motivated workforce.

3 Implementation

Implementation is a very important aspect of technology-based training, and it should be considered carefully before starting to use this method of training. If this is not done, then the training resources are not used properly, and, in consequence, technology-based training gains an unwarranted bad reputation that will make it difficult to reintroduce at a later stage.

You cannot just buy TBT resources, install them and expect them to work. Before implementing any technology-based training it is necessary to consider the following questions:

- Where is it going to be available?
- How you are going to sell it to line management?
- How you are going to sell it to the individual?
- How are people going to know that it is available?
- How it is going to be administered?
- How is it to be supported?

AVAILABILITY

In an ideal situation, everyone would have a multimedia workstation on their desk for their day-to-day work, which would allow them to switch to learning when they have a problem or when they have a slack period in their working day. However, we all know that this situation is still a long way in the future for most organisations. For a start, it assumes that all people work at desks, which is certainly not the case.

So there has to be a compromise, which may well mean that some of the benefits of this method of training are lost. For example, if you site the workstation in the training department, the individuals will feel that they are not studying in private and are being supervised. Needless to say, having the training material on the workstation on your desk also means that you lose some privacy.

Therefore you must give careful consideration to the siting of the learning workstation. It should be in a quiet part of the building where the trainee will not be distracted by noise or work going on around them. It should be somewhere where they can have some privacy. However, it should not be so remote that it is forgotten, nor too distant to be easily reached.

If you are installing more than one workstation at a site, then each one should be screened off from the others for privacy. If audio is to be used – either alone or as part of a video sequence – then the workstations must be sited so as not to distract other learners or people working nearby. Headsets can be used, of course, if it is not possible to isolate the workstations sufficiently, but in this case remember that it is a Health and Safety legislative requirement that the headset is cleaned and disinfected between use. Nevertheless, finding space to site workstations will not be easy in most organisations, where free space is at a premium, and headsets may well be part of the solution.

Finally, the workstation should be accessible. Its siting should not present any barriers, physical or otherwise, to its use. If it involves travel to another site, this will cut down on any study time and is likely to demotivate potential users.

SELLING TBT TO LINE MANAGEMENT

Training should be the responsibility of the line manager. In the past, training departments have assumed this part of the line manager's role. With on-site training available, however, the line manager can start to take on the responsibility for the training of his or her team. Managers will need to be convinced of the following facts:

- that technology based training works;
- that it is cost effective; and
- that there is a business benefit – particularly for their team, section or department.

If they are not convinced that technology-based training works or cannot perceive sufficient benefit, then they will not want their staff to use this method of training. Managers therefore need to be sold on the benefits of this method, such as the staff not being away from their jobs for long periods. Since they are also very much in tune these days with the need to improve the bottom line, they will need to be convinced that the training will be effective in increasing their organisation's profitability (see Chapter 7). If the line managers are able to see the business advantages, they will encourage their staff to undertake the training.

SELLING TBT TO THE INDIVIDUAL

If you have effectively sold the idea of technology-based training to the line managers, you can encourage them to sell it, in turn, to their staff. However, individual staff members must be able to see that using the technology will be beneficial to them and also that the training itself is relevant. If the training is irrelevant or out of date, then it will not be used and the methodology may be blamed for its non-use. Staff members are likely to revert to previous methods of learning, which will have less benefit both for them and for the organisation. Worse still, they may go back to no training at all (see Case Study 3 in Chapter 9).

Students should be encouraged to learn in periods of about an hour. Long sessions are not conducive to learning. If it is sold to the individuals as short spells of training, they are more likely to be encouraged to partake. The previous chapter described the benefits accruing to the learner and these benefits can be used to sell technology-based training to the individuals.

PUBLICISING TBT

There should be a well-publicised launch of the new method of training, which must be supported from the very top of the organisation. Top managers must do more than pay lip service to the initiative, and this is an occasion where leading by example will be most effective. Through pre-launch publicity, you may start to arouse curiosity and build expectations before the resources are actually made available, but make sure that you don't create false expectations or oversell the potential of the new training.

People must be made aware that technology-based training exists in their organisation, and it is equally important that they should know what courses are available and should be kept informed about new courses as they become available. On television and in the cinema we are told about the new programmes and films that are coming soon, and we should copy this strategy. Use posters on noticeboards and in the canteen, telling staff of the good things to come. Arrange for articles in the organisation's newsletter, circulars or house magazine. Issue a catalogue of the courses available and keep it updated. Don't be shy! (Further advice and ideas for launching TBT are given in the case studies in Chapter 9.)

Involve staff from different areas of the organisation in the evaluation of generic materials. If the course is going to be bespoke, then involve them in the project team that will develop the material. Use them as subject-matter experts. Ask them to check material/scripts. Involve them in testing the product. If it is seen that colleagues/peers are participating in the project, there will be greater acceptance of the course and greater ownership of the learning.

The line managers, of course, have to know what is available and the content of each course so that they can recommend a course when there is a need. Equally, the staff must also know what is available in case they wish to revise or study anew some particular topic. They may also be prompted to undertake training in order to improve their career prospects.

ADMINISTRATION OF TBT

It is important that an in-house technology-based training enthusiast has responsibility for the following aspects:

- the equipment;
- the booking of time on the workstation;
- the supporting material;
- ensuring that the trainee is comfortable about using the technology; and
- dealing with any problems the trainee may have with the equipment/methodology.

This is not an area that should be taken lightly.

If your organisation runs open-learning centres, then the open-learning staff would be an obvious choice for this new role after some additional training. If this is not the case, then who is to be responsible for the administration of the workstations and the courseware? Will it be a full-time post? Or will it be added to someone's existing role? If it is added to a person's present job, will they have sufficient time to fulfil the role properly? If it is being integrated into an existing post, then there has to be some recognition of the importance of the added task. All these points require urgent consideration and decision, but if you don't take the time to find and train the right person for this role, it may have serious repercussions for the use and effectiveness of technology-based training in your organisation.

SUPPORTING TBT

An essential element to be considered is how is the training going to be supported? It is all very well having remote learning, but the learner must never feel remote. There are considerable benefits to be gained from being able to study in private and at your own pace, but to feel that you are all alone in this learning experience can detract from the learning.

The learners should feel that they have any support and encouragement they need. If they have a problem with the equipment or the learning medium, then they should have someone they can turn to for advice. More importantly, they should have someone to support them in their learning – someone with whom they can discuss any problem they may have with the content of the training material, and who has a practical interest in whether they are able to put what they learn into practice.

The support does not necessarily have to be local, although this can be an advantage. It may involve a tutor/mentor at another site with whom they can communicate by telephone or E-mail. They should also be able – and indeed be encouraged – to communicate with their peers about what they have learnt, and to share and discuss problems. Again, this can be done by telephone, or electronically, or in face-to-face groups. Moreover, support from their own line manager is vital at every stage.

CASE STUDY

The following case study highlights the importance of getting the implementation of TBT right first time.

One company, in the financial sector, prior to using technology-based training as we now describe it, produced a number of courses using tape/slide as the medium. Equipment was purchased and sent to the branches, along with a certain amount of initial courseware. Subsequent courses were issued as they were produced.

Few people in the branches knew of the existence of the courseware and the methodology – not even the heads of departments and their supervisors. Surprisingly enough, the courses did not get used and the machines gathered dust. Usage in Head Office was better because they were aware of the existence of the material.

When the company decided to put all technical and procedural training on to computer-based training and some interpersonal skills training on to interactive video, they were determined not to repeat their earlier mistakes. They planned the implementation well in advance. Trainers in each location were instructed in the following details:

- How the equipment worked.
- Basic fault finding.
- The benefits of the media.
- The content of the courseware.
- How to support the learner.

The company ensured that within the management of each location there was someone already convinced of the benefits of the methodology – a champion of the method. Branches were well informed through circulars, newsletters and the house journal.

Initially, the system was successful and well received. The courseware was liked by those who had experienced this learning method. New courses were advertised in newsletters and circulars. After a few years, however, it appeared that all was not as well as it had at first seemed, and investigation revealed that in some locations the system was not being used to the extent that it should have been.

Further enquiries found that, again in some locations, the trainer originally selected to oversee and promote the centre had been moved on and no one had been appointed to continue to champion and administer the system. Bad habits had also crept in, particularly in the way the resources were used. Instead of the trainee spending an hour or so to study a topic and then being instructed to put this into practice to reinforce the learning, they were being sent into the learning resource centre to study *all* the courses relevant to their position in the organisation, which could take two or three days. Faced with this intense training – to which they had not necessarily subscribed – trainees were bored, unmotivated and unenthusiastic.

Fortunately, the management of the organisation in question were able to identify and correct their mistakes. The system is now working well and the technology-based learning centres are now used throughout the organisation by all types of staff.

4 How to Use TBT

Technology-based training has very many applications. It was originally seen as a distance-learning tool that would replace classroom training. This view was soon dispelled. As I have been at pains to stress, it is important that it is not seen simply as something that happens in isolation. TBT must be supported, and must be integrated with other forms of training.

TBT AS A DISTANCE-LEARNING TOOL

Technology-based training material can be used as a distance-learning tool, particularly when supported with printed workbooks or manuals that the learner can take away as an *aide-mémoire*. Mixing of training media is better than using one medium alone.

With distance learning, support from a mentor or coach is important as it will enable the learner to gain more out of this type of training. Remote training may make the trainee *feel* remote, and this must be prevented.

Technology-based training is often seen as a one-to-one training medium. However, there are significant advantages to working through some courses as a pair or in a small group, as this provokes discussion and enables group members to support and learn from one another. This is especially the case with interpersonal skills training, where benefit can be gained from discussion about why a particular action should or should not be taken. Equally, there are some subjects where the single user can reap the benefits of being able to make mistakes in private and learn at his or her own pace.

TBT AS PRE-COURSE WORK

Pre-course study is a good way of ensuring that everyone coming on a face-to-face course has roughly the same level of knowledge. If this is not the case, then you may spend time at the beginning of the course making sure that less knowledgeable participants are given some initial coaching before you can start training the whole group. This applies to all subjects, but is particularly relevant to interpersonal skills, where face-to-face training time is best used for practice. For example, on a supervisory skills course, time has to be spent in making sure that everyone is at the same level before you can start imparting the knowledge about the skills, such as the do's and don'ts of delegation. If this aspect has been dealt with as pre-course study in a technology-based training course, then the course director/tutor can immediately concentrate on syndicate exercises, role plays, simulations, and so forth.

TBT AS PART OF THE COURSE

TBT can be used with small groups; during a course it allows discussion, an advantage mentioned in Chapter 3. This will be of benefit in situations where there are no peers at an individual site to form a group for distance learning.

The added benefit from studying TBT course material within the main course is that with a tutor on hand, feedback discussions can take place straight away or shortly after the learning experience, helping to reinforce the learning. The material can also be used for individual practice following tutor sessions, again reinforcing the learning. This practice may be on systems or procedure.

Management type games/simulations on networked workstations provide good course work because, apart from the learning taking place in groups at the workstation, debriefings and feedback following the exercise can take place. It is a well-proved fact that feedback after management exercise is as valuable, if not more valuable, than the experience itself. However, these games/simulations can often only be used at a centre where groups can work together. Some management games are available for individual use.

One large financial institution uses technology-based training material on the management face-to-face training courses, as they find that the managers are happy to work together on these courses, rather than individually. Also, in their workplace they cannot, or do not, find the time to sit down and work through the technology-based training material.

TBT AS POST-COURSE WORK

This can be useful for learning reinforcement and/or work-based assessment, and particularly in situations where the possibility of putting the learning into practice straight away is remote. Work on the TBT material will help the later transfer of the skills into the workplace. For example, a course on disciplinary procedures could be followed up, using a technology-based training course, with practice in a safe environment where mistakes are not damaging to the company.

This type of practice, using multimedia, is especially helpful in cases where the individual will have little opportunity to employ the course skills. As soon as these skills and knowledge of procedures are needed in work situations, however, the immediate revision facility offered by TBT is an added bonus.

5 Generic Training

The term 'generic training' is used to describe training that is produced as a item for sale to a range of organisations. The opposite is 'bespoke training', which is specifically designed to meet the needs of, usually, large organisations. The situation can be compared to the clothing market, where you can buy ready made (off-the-peg) or made-to-measure (bespoke) clothes. Generic training is usually referred to as off-the-shelf training.

There are many similarities between buying training and buying clothing. The most obvious one is cost. If you go for bespoke in training, as with clothes, it is going to cost you more than buying an item that is ready-made. Similarly, you can have, say, a blazer and trousers both made-to-measure, or you can buy the blazer ready-made and have the trousers made to measure. With training you can buy both bespoke training and generic training, and it is quite possible to mix and match the two types of training to achieve the desired result.

We were familiar with generic training long before technology-based training came on to the market, although we never referred to it by that name. External or public formal training courses are generic, and we have used them as far back as I can remember.

WHY BUY GENERIC TRAINING?

This is rather like asking, 'Why reinvent the wheel?' If a course covering the subject topic at the right level already exists, why go to the expense of designing and producing the course for yourselves?

People, when looking at multimedia products, claim that generic material will not meet their training need and that it will not fit in with their company's culture. However, they are prepared to send people away on formal training courses, which rarely fit their training need completely and are certainly unlikely to meet their company's cultural needs and practices. Furthermore, whereas you can tailor flexible learning material, a formal training course can only be tailored if you can fill all the places. Then it is no longer a public course, and is probably costing you a lot more, anyway.

It is true that no piece of generic training material will exactly meet your training need, but if it will meet 90 per cent of that need, it will be considerably better than doing no training at all because the bespoke material is beyond your budget. Even large blue-chip companies, who might be assumed to prefer bespoke material, will use an off-the-shelf item if it closely matches their requirement. It comes down to an investment choice. If the lower cost of a generic course will produce, say, 70 per cent of the benefit of a bespoke course, but only costs 20 per cent of the latter, then it is clearly more cost-effective.

In addition, if only a small percentage of the target population needs training in a particular subject, then it is unlikely that a bespoke product will be cost-effective – it simply won't get sufficient usage. Again, it would be advisable to look for a generic product that closely approximates to your needs.

CUSTOMISING

There are various levels of tailoring or customising multimedia. These levels range from simply talking the student through the organisation's practices and pointing out where the training differs from company practice, to asking the supplier to customise the material for you.

First, most multimedia courses come with a booklet or workbook. These can be used in conjunction with an in-house leaflet that will advise the trainee of the differences in culture and procedures between the training and company practice, and, where necessary, which modules to skip because they are not relevant to the organisation. Another option is to customise the workbook – or, better still, ask the supplier to do this – so that it has the company logo on it and the differences are clearly set out in its pages. (See Case Study 5 in Chapter 9 for an example of a company which customised a workbook accompanying a generic course.)

Next, the course itself can be customised. Simply by the inclusion of the company logo at the start of the course, and noting the differences in leaflet or workbook, the student/trainee may feel that they are studying an in-house course rather than an off-the-shelf course. Rather than just having it 'badged', however, the course can be customised further by removing sections or otherwise amending it to meet the organisation's needs. Indeed, one of the ways to judge the quality of a generic course is to see how easy it is to add simple text or remove access to sections.

The ultimate customisation, or course, is to work with the generic producer when they are producing the course, and so ensure that it covers the areas you want it to cover (see Case Study 2 in Chapter 9). It can be made to look even more like an in-house course if you can get any photographs or video shot on your premises. An organisation's style of furnishing an office will be typical and will be recognised by the staff as their organisation's product. Other users will not know where it was shot.

For straightforward subjects such as training in word processing, generic courses are both highly suitable and perfectly acceptable to staff. In these cases, even customising a generic course is rarely necessary.

SUBJECT MATTER AVAILABLE ON THE MARKET

Generic courseware, as its name implies, will be in a range of fairly general subjects, such as:

- Literacy
- Numeracy
- Computer skills
- Telephone skills
- Book-keeping
- Accountancy/finance
- Tax and VAT
- Sales and marketing
- Supervisory and management skills.

However, there are many technology-based training courses available which are generic to a particular trade or profession, for example the power industry.

CHOOSING GENERIC COURSEWARE

There is a wealth of good generic flexible material available on the market at a wide range of prices. Your most difficult task may well be to find the product which best matches your needs. For example, there are numerous courses on appraisal and appraisal interviewing and it may therefore take a little time to make the choice, but you are advised to make the effort.

Do not take the first course that you find or that is offered to you by the salesman. Time spent in looking for alternatives will be time well spent (see Case Study 4 in Chapter 9). There is a catalogue of generic courseware in the second half of this book to assist you in finding the course best suited to your needs.

EVALUATING GENERIC COURSEWARE

We all have different criteria when evaluating training. Whatever these may be, it is important to focus on training objectives as outcomes. Thus, with generic material we need to decide the following:

- Is TBT the right medium for the particular training need?
- Is full screen, full motion video really necessary for the application?
- Indeed, is video necessary at all?
- Would a paper-based product do the job as well?
- Is the courseware interactive or is it a page-turning exercise?
- Is it interesting?
- Is there support material?
- Does it work?
- Does it have a bookmarking facility for easy return to the course?
- Does it have a course map?
- Does the student know where they are at any particular point in the programme?
- Do they know how long it should take?
- Does the content of the course fully cover the subject matter?
- Is the content accurate?
- Is the coverage of the content pitched at the right level?
- Is the content presented in a logical sequence?
- Can the content be accessed in different ways to cater for different learning styles?

If you are a trainer, then you should be looking at the teaching practice, the methods employed to ensure that learning takes place, and the overall structure of the course. The content of the course should be checked by the subject-matter expert. The best person to tell you whether the course is worthwhile is, of course, a participant, so ask them to help you in the evaluation. Ideally, find out what the participant, or user, actually learns or remembers from the course.

Ask the supplier to give you the names and contact details of other organisations using their products in general and this product in particular. Then talk to those organisations to see if they have found that the course fulfilled their expectations and needs.

6 Bespoke Training

IN-HOUSE OR EXTERNAL?

If you have decided that you require a bespoke course, you then need to decide: do you do this work in-house; if so, do you use your own staff or contracted staff; or do you place the work out to a supplier/producer.

The cost of employing a full-time multimedia design and production team is high. The benefits of having total control over the design and production have to be weighed against the high cost. Will there be sufficient work to justify setting up and maintaining a team in-house, including the ongoing costs? The team will incur a continuous cost irrespective of the business requirement for bespoke courses.

The advent of multimedia has made the use of totally in-house teams more difficult to justify. With computer-based training it was possible to train existing staff to become good designers and programmers. This required a range of products (to develop the range of skills) and internal coaching support. Now the design skills required are greater, with many different disciplines needed in the team. Invariably, this means that specialists would have to be recruited. Also, the range of products tends to be more restricted, which makes it more difficult to develop design skills.

Many large organisations have now outsourced the design and production of their technology-based training. They see this as a much more cost-effective and sensible way of handling this issue.

An alternative method, if you feel that you need to control the design and production of the courseware, is to contract freelance staff for the project. This involves a great deal of work in finding the right freelancers and more administration than with your own staff. Moreover, there is always the problem that the good freelance designers and production people will already be employed and that those who are available may not necessarily be the best people for the job. Again, therefore, the solution to these problems is to contract the whole job out to a supplier/producer who already has the staff with the necessary skills and will probably also have arrangements with freelance staff that they contract on a fairly regular basis.

47

CHOOSING A SUPPLIER

Using the analogy of clothing again, you need to choose your tailor with care. First, make sure that you are choosing a firm that is financially sound. You would like them both to complete the project, and be around to make any subsequent amendments. Second, as with self-employed freelance designers and producers, if the supplier is able to start your project immediately, is that because they are short of work, and if so, why is that?

You should get two or three quotations, and ask each bidder to provide a treatment for the courseware (i.e. a very brief outline of the course, the interaction, the hardware and software platforms, and so on). You wouldn't order a suit without first seeing the material to check its pattern, colour and quality; nor would you let the tailor have a totally free hand in the styling of the suit! So don't allow such leeway to a supplier of a bespoke course.

Ask also to see some of the work that the supplier has produced for other clients. Check whether this is of the standard you are expecting. And look at the quality of the work, not just at the glitzy presentation. At the same time, confirm that the supplier can provide all necessary support material, workbooks and instruction guides.

Talk to a cross-section of the supplier's previous customers. Find out what sort of job they did. For example:

- Did they complete on time?
- Did the cost keep rising?
- Did the programme work when it was delivered?
- Were there loads of bugs to sort out?
- Did they correct errors quickly?
- Was there a good working relationship?
- How effective was the final product?
- Would the customer be prepared to use the same supplier again?

DEFINING THE PROJECT

Defining the project to the supplier, whether internal or external, is extremely important. They need to know precisely what it is that you require, since they will be scheduling and costing the project on the basis of this definition. If you subsequently make changes because the project has not been thought through properly, then the cost will rise and the timescale will increase.

Be sure that you know precisely what your training need is and how you wish the project to be handled. Don't be persuaded by the supplier to deal with the subject matter in a different manner, unless you are quite sure that it provides a better solution to your problem. Some suppliers may be tempted to offer a different solution because it is easier, and possibly cheaper, for them to do it that way. If the solution to your training need can be adequately handled by CBT with graphics, then don't be persuaded to have video as well. Beware of the producer who is looking for an Academy Award – a good training product will usually be very simple.

SUBJECT-MATTER EXPERTS

Whether you have decided to produce the course in-house or to contract it out, you will have to provide the subject-matter expertise. Unless it is a broad management-skills-type training course, then it is your organisation that has the subject-matter knowledge, not the people producing the courseware. This expert knowledge will be required by the designers right from the start, as they commence their outline design. So time from the already-busy experts will be required at this stage and they must be accessible for questions as the work gets under way. The subject-matter experts will also have to check the scripts before the production stage.

Do not underestimate the time that will be required from your subject-matter experts. They are busy people and their time will need to be scheduled into the plan right from the start. They should be made aware of the need to set aside the time to check the scripts, and they must commit themselves to the schedule. If this is not done, then the supplier's schedule will be upset, and you cannot then automatically expect them to meet the production deadline. Sometimes it is possible for the programming to start before the program script has been checked. This is not good practice. If audio or video is involved, then the studios will have been booked and actors engaged, and delays or changes in the script at later stages can be very costly. Rebooking the studio and the actors is not easy and there will be inevitable delay, which will throw the whole timetable out and will not make you popular with the production company.

Using subject-matter experts from the branch staff or shop-floor staff, rather than from the head office, will help in making the product more acceptable to your staff generally. There will be a greater ownership of the finished product if the people know that it wasn't just produced by people in their remote Head Office.

PROJECT MANAGEMENT

The supplier, internal or external, will appoint a project manager for the job, but you need overall control and should have the overall project management role. Most of your liaison will be with the supplier's project manager who will have the day-to-day control of the design and production. However, you need to be sure that the timescale and various interim deadlines will be met, and you will therefore have to supervise closely the subject-matter experts and training staff within your own organisation.

There will be particular points in the schedule at which you must ensure that the work is on course. These interim deadlines tend to fall at the points in the schedule where your organisation will be involved; for example, at the end of the following phases:

- outline design;
- detailed design;
- scripting;
- production;
- testing;
- pilot exercise; and
- amendments.

These are, of necessity, broad headings. If there are a number of modules in the course, then there will be interim deadlines for each module. In this case, there will be a further stage of testing when all the modules are put together to ensure that they are coordinated.

Close contact between you and the supplier is obviously important. However, this does need to be controlled, since the supplier must be allowed room in which to work. Equally, too little contact could mean that you are unaware of any problems that may be arising.

At every stage in the process, the responsibility for ensuring an effective final product is one that is shared between client and producer. Clients who push too much of that responsibility on to the producer often end up with disappointing training resources. Remember – you understand the subject and your training need; the producer understands training design and production of TBT.

7 Evaluation

There is a necessity to prove that the training which is being undertaken will show a return on investment. Historically, training expenditure has often been spread across the years. Once CBT, interactive video and, more recently, CD-ROM came on the scene, the cost of the training was incurred at the beginning. The expenditure on courseware was high and a one-off payment. The fact that it would be used for many years with little or no ongoing cost was not immediately considered.

In some cases it was difficult to prove the return on investment because no one could tell what traditional training was costing. Certainly there was an overall budget, but no one had ever been asked to cost each course. Sometimes the in-house training centre was not a profit centre and therefore did not charge out its use, again making it difficult to put a price on this use. Training was thus rarely rigorously evaluated.

However, those organisations who were the early pioneers of technology-based training were able to provide figures that showed good cost benefits resulting from the investment in TBT. These companies were, in the main, big organisations that would be putting large numbers of people through the training. Hence the high upfront cost was spread over many people, and this brought down the cost per head.

At one leading insurance company an interactive video course was produced for insurance surveyors. The cost was high, but the number of potential trainees was small. In fact, the driving reason for producing the training was that there were never enough people to train at any one time. Most of the previous training had been on the basis of a trainee working with another surveyor and picking up the knowledge that way, which only led to bad habits being passed on from one surveyor to another. Thus, though the cost was high, as a member of general management said, if it only saved one major fire, the cost of the training would have been covered. Difficult to prove, unquestionably, but the important point to appreciate is that it was the business management making the statement and not the training management.

Cost benefit is important, and it is essential when calculating the costs and the benefits that the organisation has a full understanding of the effectiveness of any training. Cost savings that compromise the training, or cost overruns that don't produce significant additional benefit, must be resisted.

Whatever training methodology is being used, we should evaluate it on the following factors:

- Have the training objectives been met?
- Has the learning been put into practice?
- Has there been a business benefit? How has it affected the bottom line?

HAVE THE TRAINING OBJECTIVES BEEN MET?

It is relatively easy with technology-based training to test how far a student has learnt or developed skills and knowledge. Testing changes in underlying attitude is far harder.

The courseware may include tests/quizzes at the end of each module to ensure that the objectives of that module have been met by the student. If the student fails to meet the required level of learning, then he or she may try the module again and/or discuss the matter with their tutor or their peers. They may then retake the test to ensure that they now fully understand the module. The course may also include an overall test to establish how far the student has understood and mastered the complete subject.

If the subject matter is likely to be new to the students, an optional pre-test should be included. This will not only enable the learning to be structured to meet the needs of the student, but it can also be used in comparison with the end-of-course test results to ensure that learning has taken place. Adapting the training which an individual receives can have a major business impact. It reduces the time spent by that individual in learning a topic, but achieves the same performance output.

HAS THE LEARNING BEEN PUT INTO PRACTICE?

This is a harder assessment to make, as it involves the student in more time away from the work. Retaking the end-of-course test at the end of a given period following the training will indicate how much of what the student originally learned they now remember. Obviously, if the student has had the opportunity to put the knowledge they have gained into practical use, this will have consolidated their learning and the retention will be better.

If there is a good performance appraisal system in place, then there should be some check on the retention of knowledge and any change in behaviour. Few organisations put their students through further tests after, say, three to six months. However, the training should not have been carried out unless there was a need to put the learning into practice, which implies that there will be some evidence that learning has taken place and that the member of staff has been able to put this to effective use. This can best be measured by some form of workplace assessment, either by the manager or supervisor or by an external observer. There are two areas where this is already the norm.

LEGISLATION

There are some aspects of work where organisations are compelled to provide an assessment of workplace competency. These include companies selling life and pensions products, where the Personal Investment Authority can demand that competency is proven.

SAFETY

Where safety is important, then companies institute special tests and drills which role-play the safety procedure. Transport, petroleum, chemical and heavy engineering industries would typically check and recheck that staff could carry out tasks in a safe manner. The annual fire drill is a trivial example that applies to all organisations – not that a comprehensive training package would be needed, but some learning has to take place.

HAS THERE BEEN A BUSINESS BENEFIT?

Business benefit is much harder to quantify than straightforward knowledge or competency in the individual or the group. But unless there is a business benefit to training, then why is it being carried out?

We must have decided that the training was necessary, so what was the reason? If we know that, then evaluating whether we have achieved our objective is made much easier. If we decided that we needed to improve our customer service, this wasn't just because it was fashionable. It would have been because we wanted to improve our share of the market. So we must be able to measure whether we have achieved that improvement.

Some of the difficulties in proving the business benefit lie in the fact that organisations do not identify what performance measures they want to change – *and which training can directly affect* – before undertaking the training. This means that we do not have a benchmark against which to measure the evaluation. If we want to reduce the number of letters of complaint from customers, we need first to know how many we are getting now. Once the training has taken place, we can check the number of letters of complaint and see if there has been a reduction.

This is an essential point to note. If you are asked to evaluate a piece of training, the first question to ask of the business sponsor is: 'What performance measure do you wish to change and please can we see the last six months' scores?' The second question to ask – of yourself this time, and bearing in mind that the wrong people may be doing the task, that they may not know they have to do it and they may not want to do it – is: 'What impact on the score can the training have?' The training can have no impact on these issues without support from the business managers, especially bearing in mind that the processes may be too complex, that other parts of the organisation may work against improving the score (and do so unknowingly), or that customers may not value the change.

There are other factors outside our business that affect the desired business benefit. For example, we may undertake customer care programmes to increase our market share, but so may our main competitors. What we can't quantify is what would have happened had we not undertaken the training programme.

Some years ago, a building society wanted to reduce the number of bad debts they had and were looking at providing training for all their staff involved in making loans. They already knew their current bad debt situation and could use the same measures to quantify their position after the training had been completed. This would mean that they could evaluate the effectiveness of their training.

However, they were conscious that the result could be influenced by outside factors. Their competitors' reaction to bad debts could have an influence on the market as a whole. If a competitor relaxed its rules for lending money, then the 'dodgy' customers could well go to them. This would have an effect on the evaluation.

What we must not do is to allow these difficulties to discourage us from the evaluation process. To repeat, if we had a reason for setting up the training programme, then there must be a means of evaluating the outcome.

8 The Future

How technology will affect training in the future is something we would all like to know, and to some extent, of course, any reader of this book should be influencing the training of the future. Yet even those of us heavily involved in the technology-based side of the industry have been and still are concerned that technology should not be allowed to drive the training industry. The training need should be the first consideration; the second should be the decision on the best method to fulfil that need.

Many a technology-based training manager and technology-based training supplier has at some stage advised clients that 'TBT is not the right solution for your training need'. Professionals are careful to specify the most appropriate solution, and not simply the solution which is currently fashionable or popular with competitors.

Looking back to the 1970s and 1980s, hardware and software suppliers were able to drive change in the technology-based training industry. However, the advent of multimedia has seen a reduction in this aspect, mainly because training is only a small part of the multimedia industry, whereas it was a major part of the interactive video industry.

The advent of networks and the Internet will bring major changes in the way people learn in the future. It is likely to alter the whole pattern of learning and make lifetime learning a reality. The emphasis of the responsibility for learning will shift from the institutions to the individual.

Computer power and storage capacity are both continuing to increase at a phenomenal rate and prices are falling. Cable installation is moving apace. Telecommunication costs are reducing and available bandwidth is increasing.

When the local 'information superhighway' is available to many (if not all), and is capable of transferring video and enabling rapid interaction with data in another location, then high quality multimedia training will become available to large numbers of people. For many suppliers and users, this is a more attractive option than packaged multimedia in the shape of CD-ROMs. The key element which makes it more attractive is its economics. Users can pay as they use and this will cost less than alternative methods of learning. Suppliers do not have to worry about multiple users accessing the same package and can offer an economic single-user charge.

Multimedia in the shape of CD-ROM and DVD is unlikely to disappear for many years yet. When multimedia can be used over the 'highway', then we will see a decrease in the disc-based systems.

There is much talk of the benefits that the 'highway' will bring to training and learning, because many people will have the facilities in their homes for these functions. In the future, however, individuals may not have the computer power and storage in their own homes, but will be able to access this from a dumb machine linked to their television.

Indeed, there will be huge opportunities for people to learn. But if the telephone link and television is to be used for learning, when will an individual be able to use them? With hundreds of television channels, video on demand, home shopping, video games, and so on, when will this learning take place?

Some who speak about the future of learning on the superhighway predict changes in the education system, with less emphasis on the attendance at schools and universities and more emphasis on virtual-learning organisations. Others see the responsibility for learning moving to the individual, whether this is educational or vocational.

There is also some concern among experts in the field that there could be a division into haves and have-nots. In other words, that those who can afford to pay will be those who learn. The proposed solution to this dilemma is to place learning resources in community centres, perhaps using the local school to provide both further and higher education from a virtual campus. Multimedia workstations are already installed in main libraries and are proving very successful, not only for small to medium-sized enterprises, but also for individuals interested in improving their basic skills and therefore their suitability for employment.

There is little doubt that some of what the pundits are saying about the future of learning will take place. What is of concern, however, is whether the training available on the superhighway will be appropriate and effective. It is accepted that currently you can use the facility of book and resource libraries to learn whatever subject you wish and that the choice of the source of that learning is up to the individual. The system will be no different on the superhighway. In fact, this type of discovery learning is taking place on the Internet now. However, an employer will require the training undertaken by an individual to be along guidelines and up to the standard set by the company. Freedom for the individual to roam at will around the superhighway is unlikely to be acceptable if the company is paying for the training.

A recent survey of some fifty large organisations across most industrial sectors showed that:

- Few organisations had given any consideration to this method of training.

- Only 20 per cent would consider recognising training undertaken on the superhighway.
- There was considerable concern amongst organisations about: the accessibility to the superhighway; managing training on the superhighway; and security in using the superhighway.

Thus there will have to be significant cultural changes before this method of learning becomes the norm. However, our children are being brought up to be computer literate and will have undertaken some learning using the Internet – and they will be the managers of the future.

What does concern the industry at present is that, although the United Kingdom has an undoubted lead in the skills needed for design and production of good technology-based training material, and the people to provide the material for the superhighway, we must take the opportunity that is there to exploit the commercial benefit. The government has recognised the problems and has instituted a number of initiatives. They have a working group looking at the Superhighway for Interactive Training and the Information Society Initiative. In turn, we, in the training industry as a whole and the technology-based training industry in particular, must ensure that UK plc *does* benefit from the lead we now have in the skills and concepts for good interactive multimedia.

9 Case Studies

Case Study 1

Use of Computer-Based Testing to assist with Training Needs Analysis at NPI

NPI is one of the United Kingdom's leading pensions specialists. Established over 160 years ago, the company has built an enviable reputation for quality service.

An important part of customer service is the provision of quotations of likely pension amounts to policyholders who are thinking of retiring. Two existing members of staff in this area, Neil and John, felt that they and their colleagues would benefit from extra training. They were given approval by their manager to do something about this and they approached the Customer Service Training Department for advice on how to proceed.

Whilst the two people were brimming with ideas on what information they wanted to impart, the trainer assigned to help them, Tania, introduced them to the concept of training needs analysis. It was very important to find out what the trainees did not know to ensure that the training would be most effective. Given the nature of their jobs, interviewing the trainees did not seem likely to elicit the information needed, so it was decided to use the computer-based testing package recently purchased by the Training Department.

The two members of staff identified 30 sections of relevant training material and defined the objectives of what they would want to impart on each section, should the need be determined necessary. What proved to be the most difficult part of the whole training needs analysis was then encountered, namely, determining what questions to ask. Within a period of four weeks, 38 questions were assembled. These included multi-choice and multi-answer questions. To make the tests seem as real as possible, copies of computer enquiry screens were captured into the test as the source of data on which the trainees were required to perform calculations. The actual authoring of the questions within the package proved straightforward.

The test was piloted with two of the most experienced staff in the Customer

Service Division. This rehearsal resulted in the almost inevitable need to make some modifications, but a week later the full test was ready.

The next stage was approached with some trepidation as it was expected that some staff would be wary of the tests. Their concerns might include: How would the results be used? Would a record be put on to personal files? Neil and John took time to explain to everyone the reasoning behind the training initiative, and that the test had been designed to determine what the trainees did not know in order that training could be specifically targeted to their needs. The combination of this explanation, the user-friendly nature of the testing package and the incorporation of some humour into the questions resulted in staff saying how much they enjoyed taking the test.

Analysis of the test results proved to be much easier and so much more powerful than that which had been previously achieved using paper-based methods. The three members of staff involved were quickly able to identify which of the 30 sections were needed and could then concentrate their efforts on producing training material for them.

Each training course lasted three days, and five courses were delivered over a period of six weeks. To measure the effectiveness of the training, the test was repeated, but with the order of the questions randomised. The average score obtained increased from 72 per cent on the first test to 92 per cent on the post-training test.

All trainees appreciated the training and enjoyed the test. NPI's management team was also pleased with the initiative shown by the three people responsible for the work, who in fact won divisional and corporate quality awards for their achievement.

Case Study 2

Induction Training at Sun Life

In the first few days at work, new recruits form lasting impressions about an organisation's standards, culture and approach to customers. This is why effective induction is important – but normally it is hard to justify induction training for one member of staff at a time. Here John Wyatt, Training and Development Consultant at life and pensions company Sun Life, explains how his organisation is using a generic programme, called Induction, to prepare new people for work.

In January 1994, we took the technology plunge and set up an open-learning centre in one of our Bristol offices – not bad for a company which only a few years before had only two or three PCs in most departments. The centre has been so successful that we are planning to open another in London at the end of October and we have also started to use CD-ROM training systems within our nationwide branch network.

Open learning is flexible and it enables us to train a large number of people with the same material. However, you may think that induction training would not be a suitable subject for an open-learning course, because the process is different for every organisation. A year ago, I'd have agreed with you – but not now.

One multimedia producer has launched an induction programme which quite simply breaks new ground. It is a 'new style' multimedia training programme because it can be customised to meet the needs of individual organisations.

Induction comes with an easy-to-use 'toolkit' which enables you to add in details of your own organisation's mission, business strategy, principles, culture, policies, structure and even your company logo. This means that you can cost-effectively tailor the programme, so that your organisation ends up with its own personalised induction resource which can be used again and again – for a fraction of the price of producing a bespoke course.

There are four other modules in the programme, which cover Health and Safety Awareness (including first aid and fire procedures), Security and Confidentiality (including general security and computer security), Work Legislation (including the Data Protection Act, Financial Services Act and regulating bodies), and Essential Work Skills (such as customer care, effective use of the telephone and face-to-face communication).

The benefits of using the programme are that all users get the same positive message, in a high-quality format; the course can be adapted with company-specific information; as a trainer, you can concentrate on coaching and mentoring the trainees; and it helps to ensure that you have fulfilled your legal obligations.

As the programme is interactive, the trainee can choose their own path through the material and 'explore' at their own pace. The trainee can take part in simulations without fear of real-life consequences and if there is anything they haven't completely understood on any given point, they can go back over it as many times as they need to. The fact that the trainees are in control of what they see and hear helps reinforce their learning. To move around the programme and review different sections, the trainee simply moves the cursor around the screen and selects options with a mouse.

Induction comes complete with a tutor's guide and a user's workbook, which can be photocopied so that each user can keep his or her own copy. The CD-ROM disc contains enhanced video, graphics, animation, text and a wealth of clip art and clip audio that can be used for personalising the first module.

The Health and Safety Awareness module is particularly attractive because of the way the programme turns what is potentially a dry subject into an entertaining and fun way of learning. The Security Policy section is also particularly effective because it uses video to present scenarios and it gives the trainee a series of choices which they can go through to 'protect' their organisation and prevent various 'crimes' from happening.

Sun Life's relationship with the supplier stems back to Multimedia '93, when they saw two of the supplier's programmes, which were evaluated and subsequently purchased. They now have nine courses from the same supplier and actually worked with them in putting together the Induction programme. Sun Life provided some of the 'source material' and checked the supplier's scripts for factual accuracy.

They now have 15 copies of Induction, which are being used to train new people as they join. The programme's modular approach means that newcomers can concentrate on those areas where they have a training need. For example, people who have not had previous experience of working in a large office may need more details about health and safety than others who have.

The programme is used to communicate general information about the organisation, which is then reinforced by 'local' information from the newcomer's own manager. For example, details such as the name of the newcomer's health and safety officer or fire office r are given locally. Sun Life also continue to give out their own documents about their vision and corporate plan to new staff.

Induction gives everyone the same messages, regardless of their location. Staff near to Bristol or London can go into an open-learning centre to go through the programme; other staff further afield, such as Aberdeen or Belfast, can be loaned a portable CD-ROM system for this purpose. This means that Sun Life do not have to send people to Bristol for induction training, which is a distinct cost advantage.

The supplier customised the introductory module for Sun Life (an option, if other organisations want it) and they added in a video message from one of Sun Life's directors, who 'personally' welcomes new people to the company and explains the company's mission, strategy and culture. This has been very well received because it gives a clear indication of senior management's commitment to the induction process, and it also endorses the concept of learning via new technology.

Although the programme is geared towards newcomers to Sun Life, anyone can use it internally, or browse through any of the modules if they wish to. Even the company secretary has had a look at it. The response has been very positive from users. They think the programme is a first-class resource and they have learned a good deal from going through it.

Case Study 3

The Drive for Better Training at Vauxhall

Vauxhall Motors' plant in Luton has been supplementing face-to-face training with open-learning materials for over seven years. Two years ago, it set up its Guidelines Centre to give advice to employees on their personal development. Under Training Officer, Gary Seely, this centre now offers training opportunities to the Luton plant's 3,700 staff, 90 per cent of whom work in frequently changing shifts, and regularly provides 2,500 hours of training each month – and not just for Vauxhall staff, but for local unemployed people too.

When Gary took over as Training Officer about a year ago, his intention was to improve usage and to link training to the needs of the business. He set about making changes. 'Training is very important in a highly competitive industry such as ours,' said Gary. 'There was clearly great potential for the centre, but one of the main problems was lack of information. Few people knew what was here or how they could benefit. We rectified this by taking every opportunity to promote the facilities.'

He produced a 'prospectus' for the Guidelines Centre (which incorporates an open-learning centre), as well as frequent newsletters, and he agreed a regular slot in Vauxhall's in-house magazine. On top of this, he circulates a bi-monthly sheet which publicises any new purchases. Also, when staff complete their first open-learning programme, they receive a certificate recognising their achievement – plus a free T-shirt and baseball hat – which all helps to promote the centre within the plant.

The location of the centre was another of his initial problems. It is not based in the manufacturing plant and he found that workers were at first reluctant to enter what they saw as the 'management building'. What's more, the centre was laid out as a series of 'individual cubicles' for privacy in training. Gary simply removed the cubicles, so that staff could sit round the personal computers and go through the programmes in groups, which meant they didn't have to enter the building on their own. Once the trainees had been in, seen what was on offer and tried the programmes, they soon came back for more.

Gary also invested in new training resources, including all the Business Sense CD-ROM programmes. 'The thing that really promotes your open learning centre is the quality of the resources you have in it,' he said. 'If you come in for a training session at the end of a shift, you're tired and you don't want to waste time with boring programmes. We've found that people like to use these courses because they are enjoyable, interesting and relevant. They are used as a supplement to our existing tutor-led sessions and also as training programmes in their own right. The popularity of programmes such as these sells your centre more than any other promotion could ever hope to.'

Because of the set pattern of shifts, Gary found that even when the centre had become popular with workers, it was still very quiet in the mornings between 8 and 11 o'clock. He decided that he could maximise usage of the centre by opening it up to unemployed people during the quiet times and he discussed this proposal with the local Benefits Agency, who were very keen on the idea.

Gary told us: 'The open-learning resources are here, so somebody might as well make use of them when our staff can't. This has proved a useful way of helping local people to get up to speed with the latest training resources and it is one way that a large employer such as Vauxhall can put something back into the community.'

Case Study 4
Multimedia Training in Specsavers

Rapid growth and increased staff numbers enhanced the need for good communication on work performance at retail opticians group Specsavers. Director Steve Robinson has overhauled the group's appraisal process and introduced multimedia training in a new learning centre.

With 305 stores in the United Kingdom and Ireland and 3,500 employees, Specsavers is one of the leading firms in the retail ophthalmic industry. The group's success is based on its expertise in examining eyes and prescribing and supplying spectacles and contact lenses. It offers a large range, high quality and good value.

Based in Guernsey, the head office of Specsavers employs 260 people, making it one of the largest employers on the island. The group has grown so quickly that the number of head office staff has more than doubled in the last 18 months.

Rapid growth may please accountants but it can cause headaches for trainers, as roles and responsibilities change and new ones are created. This prompted two important developments at Specsavers.

The introduction of multimedia
Steve Robinson, Group Services Director, responsible for personnel and training, explained: 'Multimedia offered us a cost-effective way of providing high-quality training for our growing number of people. The benefits were so strong that we equipped our new head office learning centre with six dedicated multimedia PCs. The centre also has stand-up training facilities, video and audio facilities, and a library with reference and working sections for students taking professional qualifications.

'Our only problem initially was trying to find good-quality multimedia training programmes. We reviewed several from various suppliers and found that either the content was good although the multimedia delivery was poor, or vice versa.

Only one supplier got the balance right and successfully married the two elements.'

A new approach to appraisal
The second development occurred at much the same time. Steve had realised that the group's existing appraisal process was no longer meeting either organisational or individual needs. He decided to revamp the appraisal process. He explained: 'We wanted to establish an effective appraisal process, where people know how well they are doing, as this can be a powerful motivator. We implemented a number of changes to our existing appraisal mechanism, one of which was to encourage all managers, from senior supervisors to directors, to go through the generic CD-ROM course, Appraisal for Performance.'

After transforming the appraisal process, Steve instigated a series of half-day training sessions to explain the new approach and to show people how to book in and use the CD-ROM systems.

'Appraisal for Performance has proved to be very popular,' he said. 'People go through the initial self-assessment part of the programme, which tests their current knowledge and recommends which modules and sections they need to cover. They then continue at their own pace.'

'Feedback on the programme has been very positive so far, with experienced managers welcoming the chance to brush up on their skills.'

Extended use
Specsavers is now planning to equip all of its 305 retail stores with a multimedia PC, in order to provide staff training for a new EPOS (electronic point of sale) system. The PCs will also be used for management and staff development, and the group is evaluating two other CD-ROM programmes from the same supplier (Leading Teams and Coaching for Results) as a means of improving leadership and fostering teamwork within each store.

Steve explained: 'The benefit of improving a store manager's role as a team leader is that it cascades down into better performance from staff. In helping managers to improve their coaching skills, we are empowering them to further improve performance.'

Case Study 5

Multimedia training at Lloyds Bank

Lloyds Bank was a pioneer of open learning and it has produced a number of award-winning courses internally. Michael Dawson reports on why the bank is now using generic CD-ROM titles, which have been produced externally, as part of its core training programmes.

In the last four years, Lloyds Bank has increased its number of multimedia open-learning centres by 560 per cent. The Bank now has a network of over 130 centres in branches throughout the United Kingdom. Each centre offers a selection of 20 core training courses, which cover essential skills ranging from assertiveness to time management.

The open-learning centres are supported by the bank's Training Development Group (TDG), which is responsible for designing, developing, distributing, maintaining and supporting training throughout UK retail banking. This includes materials for face-to-face courses, delivered both regionally and centrally, distance-learning workbooks, computer-based training and open learning. Based in Guildford, the TDG employs around 40 staff, including project managers, analysts and designers who are actually involved in the development of new courses and the revision of existing training material. The bank also has a number of regional training teams and it conducts both management and technical training at its management centre in Kingswood.

'Lloyds Bank has been using technology for training for more than 25 years,' said Tim Drewitt, Assistant Manager, Open Learning at the TDG. 'We started in 1968 with audio tapes and we soon recognised the significance of bringing training as near as possible to the workplace.'

In the 1980s, Lloyds made a significant investment in interactive video systems for branch training, installing over 1,500 units. These were largely used for procedural training, such as cashiering and stocks and shares.

'At this time, all of the training material was produced in-house and this gave us experience in distance learning techniques,' said Tim Drewitt. 'We also began to develop computer-based training which was delivered using interactive video "trolleys" within the branches and, more recently, over the bank's mainframe computer system.

'Interactive video was an efficient means of delivering the training but we were looking for something more cost-effective. In an attempt to achieve this and provide a faster response to the changing training needs, we began to look more carefully at generic off-the-shelf training material, the idea being that we would save a lot of work if we could customise off-the-shelf products, rather than developing them from scratch ourselves.

'The problem was that our videodisc technology was a non-standard system, so generic material was not available for it and we could not run generic computer-based training courses through our branch computer system. We therefore looked for an alternative system that would give us access to generic material, and the solution was a multimedia platform, which included CD-ROM. This technology comes into its own when significant numbers need to be trained, as the cost per user comes down considerably.'

CD-ROM is an extension of CD audio, which stores digital video, text and graphics as well as sound on a compact disc. Users are shown lively scenarios and they 'interact' with a mouse to stop the action, skip over details or delve deeper into particular subjects, choose alternative responses, or receive constructive feedback on the implications of their choices. If there is anything they have not completely understood on any given point, they can go back over it as many times as they need to.

'In 1990, we had 20 multimedia open-learning centres around the United Kingdom, with nine courses available,' continued Tim Drewitt. 'Since then we have continued to expand the range of courses presented on CD-ROM, so that there are now 132 open-learning centres, including some at head office.'

Employees can use the open-learning centres to access the 20 core training courses voluntarily, or as part of a training programme prescribed by their managers. Guidance is always available from personnel or operations managers. The TDG has its own technical support team and it operates a telephone 'help desk' for solving any open-learning or technical problems. The courses are promoted within the bank's branches by posters, which highlight the details of the training that is available. Each open-learning centre is supplied with a handbook which explains the benefits of open learning and reviews each of the 20 core courses, outlining who they are for, how they should be used and how long each one takes to complete.

In 1995 there were two generic CD-ROM programmes on this core list, which were produced externally: Business Calls and Leading Teams. Business Calls aims to improve telephone skills and competence in dealing with customers and colleagues. It covers specialist skills for handling difficult calls and negotiating over the phone. Leading Teams covers the principles of leadership, including teamwork, motivation and discipline.

'These programmes have enabled us to train a large number of people very quickly,' said Tim Drewitt. 'Employees train at their own pace, in their own time and in their own workplace. They are free to ask questions and explore areas that might cause embarrassment in group situations. They can experiment freely in the simulation exercises without fear of real-life consequences.'

Business Calls was chosen as part of a major initiative by the bank to improve the quality of the telephone service it was offering to customers. This was achieved through reorganising the branches and the telephone system, as well as improving the skills of those individuals who would be answering the telephones and dealing with customers. In addition, the bank had set up a series of telephone enquiry teams in late 1993, in order to improve its telephone service to customers and to prepare for a national advertising campaign highlighting its commitment to answer the telephone in 'four rings'.

'Business Calls is comprehensive and well thought out,' said Tim Drewitt. 'We were able to make it even more appropriate to our needs by customising the beginning of the programme in order to direct users to what we considered to be the most relevant sections. We have also customised the training workbooks to make the messages consistent with those covered in our other forms of training.'

The decision to purchase Leading Teams was again triggered by reorganisation. The bank was moving towards a flatter structure and it wanted to make junior members of staff more responsible, so that quicker decisions could be taken. This meant that teamwork within the branches had to be improved and this prompted a need to provide supervisory and team-management skills to members of staff who had not previously been exposed to this form of training.

'Leading Teams is available as a stand-alone course, but it is also used as part of a new modular workshop programme called Supervisory Management, which integrates open learning with face-to-face training,' said Tim Drewitt.

The Supervisory Management programme is aimed at heads of department and first-line supervisors, such as 'number one' cashiers, office supervisors and individuals responsible for telephone service teams. It is also used by managers of individual branches, particularly those with a small number of staff, who want to improve their team-building skills.

'The combination of multimedia and face-to-face training has helped to make this an interesting and worthwhile programme for us,' continued Tim Drewitt. 'We intend to increase our use of this combination of training methods in the future.'

The Training Development Group has three other programmes from the same supplier – Business Words (for sharpening writing skills), Managing Tasks and Activities (which covers management, organisation, planning and control) and Business Meetings (which shows users how to be more effective at meetings) – and it is piloting a fourth programme called Business Communications, which develops personal and interpersonal skills.

Tim Drewitt summed up: 'These programmes have helped us meet our training objectives. They are very popular with trainees, as the programmes enable them to relate what they have learned to their work immediately. This not only reinforces the learning, but also benefits the bank itself.'

Case Study 6

A Catalogue of Training at Argos

What is the best way for a retailer to supplement its face-to-face management training? Andrea Gregory, Management Development Adviser at Argos, believes technology is the answer.

At Argos, a catalogue is delivered to the 600 managers at their head office in Milton Keynes. This is not the product catalogue that their customers are familiar with, but a management development handbook, which lists the 11 competencies Argos expects of its managers. Compiled by the Management Development Department, the handbook also provides a list of the training resources that are available to support each competence. These include face-to-face training courses, as well as other resources such as books, videos, audio tapes and technology-based training programmes.

Argos has a history of success with technology-based training, having won awards for a number of custom-made training programmes covering technical systems and procedures training. Now they are using technology to teach management skills – and are reaping the benefits of using 'off-the-shelf' as opposed to custom-made training solutions.

The key to this has been their investment in CD-ROM, a multimedia technology which has generated a considerable amount of interest in the training industry. It fares extremely well in a cost-benefit analysis against other forms of training and has proved to be a value-for-money means of providing effective training.

Programmes

Argos evaluated their first CD-ROM training programmes towards the end of 1993. There were two programmes, which covered business-writing skills and leadership skills. Some of the managers tried them out internally, liked them, and so Argos bought them. It was that simple.

They have found that people like to learn in different ways and not everyone learns best in the traditional face-to-face training environment. Hence the attraction of using technology. Andrea Gregory, explained: 'The beauty of the CD-ROM programmes is that they are not simply passive courses, where you have to absorb the training messages, they are "interactive". This can take a number of forms. Usually, you are asked questions and given the opportunity to decide on your own route through the programme. This is good, because you have to take part and you have to think. But you can go at your own pace. This process demands more from you, but you get more out of it.'

The two original programmes they purchased were Business Words and Leading Teams, both of which were published by a corporate-training specialist. These programmes proved to be of a high standard, and Argos have subsequently purchased seven other CD-ROM training programmes from this supplier: Appraisal for Performance; Business Meetings; Business Communications (interpersonal skills); Money Business 1 (cash flow); Money Business 2 (budgeting); Business Calls (telephone skills) and Managing Tasks and Activities (project management).

Although these programmes are mostly used to supplement their existing face-to-face training courses, Argos have found them so comprehensive that some are now being offered as an alternative to a course. For example, Argos no longer run their Finance for Non-Finance Managers course. They simply use Money Business 1 and 2 instead. The programmes all have a similar format, which makes it easy for staff to learn to use them. Also, help is always available from the main menu in each programme and keyboard skills are not necessary.

The user can start each programme with a short optional self-assessment quiz, which tests their current knowledge of the subject and asks about needs. The quiz is a sequence of scored multiple-choice questions. The programme analyses the results, recommends which modules and sections you need to cover, and gives approximate times for each module. Each user can store their own recommendations on a floppy disk and carry them from session to session.

At the beginning of each section in each programme, there is an exercise, observation or self-appraisal, which helps the user decide if they want to go on with the section. If they want to skip the section, they simply click on a button to go to the next section and the programme tells them whether this next section is recommended for them and how long it will take. It's very easy.

By taking part in scenarios, exercises and case studies as they unfold, the users learn by participating and it has been proven that this increases content retention.

All nine of the programmes are recommended in the management development handbook, which gives guidance on the training resources available to support each competence. If a manager wants more details about any of the training resources listed in the handbook, he or she can either contact a management development adviser or simply look up the details of the resource in a departmental directory, which gives more information about all resources mentioned.

To book the use of a CD-ROM programme, the manager contacts an administrator in the open-learning centre, who loads up the required programme so that it is ready to use when the manager comes in at the appointed time. Argos normally recommend that the managers spend no longer than a couple of hours on the CD-ROM programmes. They can supplement this by completing the activities in the accompanying workbooks. These workbooks are structured in the same way as the CD-ROM courses. At the beginning of each section, there is a summary of the content and a place to write your own notes. They reflect the key messages in the course, provide additional quiz questions, and ask the manager to link what he or she finds in the course to their own experience.

For Argos, the combination of face-to-face training supplemented by other training resources, such as CD-ROM, not only adequately covers the competency areas they want to develop, but it also improves the motivation and performance of the managers themselves. This is not only good for them, its good for the business too.

Case Study 7

TBT Open-Learning Material in the Newly Restructured British Gas

Tom Whitley, Training Officer at British Gas, describes how technology-based open-learning material is playing an increasing role in the newly restructured company.

In March 1994, British Gas began a two-year process of restructuring its gas business activities in Britain, from the existing 12-region structure into five stand-alone business units, each headed by a managing director. A sixth unit will provide common services for the transitional period.

This represents the most fundamental change in terms of organisation and culture in the UK gas business sector of British Gas for more than 40 years. A number of catalysts have led to the changes, but we are taking the opportunity to revitalise the organisation and our objective is to become leaner and more competitive. However, safety, reliability, price stability and quality service to our customers will remain paramount.

As you can imagine the response to these changes has resulted in a high and increasing demand for staff training, as the fledgling business units evolve from the old hierarchical structure. The majority of employees will see a difference in the way they work, and training has a role to play in helping them adapt to this. However, the way that training is organised has also changed as part of the restructuring.

Previously, each of the 12 national regions had its own training and development department. In the interest of business focus, these are now being integrated, so that in the future each business unit will have its own training and development facility within its own organisational structure. This will bring learning solutions closer to the needs of the business and it means that each training section will be able to respond faster to the development needs of each business unit.

The company as a whole is moving into a world where individuals are taking more responsibility for their own learning and, as trainers, we have to be more efficient and more flexible in the delivery of training to cope with this. In effect, it means that we must stretch the training budget over a wider number of training issues, without reducing the quality of the training.

Open learning holds the key to this. In the former south-eastern region, we have an open-learning library which has more than 400 training titles, including training videos, computer-based training programmes, interactive videos and CD-ROM programmes, as well as audio tapes and books. Hence we have access to a wide range of material and can choose the most appropriate medium for the training task.

Currently, around 15 per cent of our training is delivered through open learning. However, we are working to increase this and by the end of next year this figure should be up to 30 per cent. In three years' time, we expect that 80 per cent of our training will be done through some form of open or flexible learning, with line managers being responsible for delivery.

To achieve this objective, we need first to continue the task of identifying the training needs of the business units and thus ensure that open learning is the most appropriate solution. Secondly, we must choose the most effective media or platform for delivering the training. Thirdly, we have to choose the right courses from the wide range available both on the generic market and specific to the organisation.

Regarding the issue of media, we have been very impressed with the potential of CD-ROM as an open-learning technology. It has the advantages of interactive video, yet it can be more cost-effective in terms of both equipment and courseware. We also believe that we have found effective training programmes which can be run on this technology.

One of the issues highlighted by the restructuring was the need for our managers to understand the importance of the effective management of budgets at all levels – and the effect that going 'over budget' has on our business. To help meet this need, we have recently purchased multiple copies of two seven-hour CD-ROM training programmes which give a grounding in the essentials of business finance, and also have particularly good modules on preparing and using budgets, working with cash flow and managing working capital. The programmes, called Money Business 1 and Money Business 2, were produced by a company which publishes multimedia training courses. They allow users to make judgements, change figures in budgets and cash flow forecasts, and see the implications of large orders on working capital.

The programmes were initially reviewed by representatives from our finance department, who gave positive feedback. Now, copies are circulated, as required, around the local learning centres and district offices.

Our open-learning library currently has eight CD-ROM management training programmes, all of them from the same supplier, which have proved to be not only a reusable resource, but also highly effective and fun to use. The programmes are used as open learning tools for self-study and also for group discussions as part of wider courses incorporating a variety of delivery methods. Here the scenarios and quizzes used by the supplier to illustrate the learning points are particularly valuable.

Two of the programmes – Business Calls (for telephone skills) and Business Words (for writing skills) – have very broad appeal and are used by staff at all levels. They give a good grounding in essential skills for improving customer service and generally help to raise the overall standard of the competence of our staff. Three others – Leading Teams (for leadership skills), Managing Tasks and Activities (for organisation skills) and Business Communications (for interpersonal skills) – are used by managers and supervisors to improve specific skills that will be directly relevant in their jobs.

The supplier provides workbooks with each of its courses, which we photocopy (with their approval) and give to all staff who use the programmes. These have also been well received as they contain a wealth of information that can be used as ongoing reference material.

The programmes are either recommended to specific individuals working in the district offices or they are chosen by the individuals themselves from the open-learning library. Generally, staff are given time during the working day to go through the training programmes, and we normally recommend study in one-hour blocks for maximum concentration.

The results of the training are evaluated by line managers on an individual basis. So far, feedback has been very good. For example, with Business Words, we have seen a marked improvement in the effectiveness and precision of the writing skills of those individuals who have been through the programme.

British Gas knows where it is going and what needs to be done in order to get there. Our role as trainers is to provide the best possible training for staff in the new business units. To this end, we will continue to evaluate new programmes on CD-ROM, and on other emerging platforms, that will help us meet our training needs.

Case Study 8

The Effectiveness of Integration of Technology-Based Training with Traditional Methods at British Steel

Interactive Training Services is a central resource for British Steel plc. It is a production service to generate technology-based training (TBT) and multimedia courses based on training needs related to either companywide business objectives or more specific works-based objectives. As such, it acts as a centre of expertise to advise on the implementation and administration of open-learning systems and is part of the company's Training Services, which is a single-employer-status industry training organisation (ITO).

British Steel provides opportunities for its employees (currently over 40,000) to obtain qualifications as part of its further education policy. Steel making is both technology- and capital-intensive, and requires a highly skilled and competent workforce. NVQs are being introduced as a positive step which enhances the existing unit trainer philosophy to provide a system of external qualifications which confirms that employees are competent in the workplace. Moreover, British Steel has produced performance standards and assessment systems for each occupational group of employees. NVQs linked to these company standards are being developed in the main occupational areas.

A training programme was developed jointly by Interactive Training Services and the company training advisers to implement a network of workplace assessors that would support the introduction of an NVQ programme initially covering craft and production operators, and using TBT to increase the effectiveness and efficiency of the training process. The training of sufficient numbers of assessors who are competent to undertake assessments in the workplace proved essential for the following reasons:

- To guarantee the rigour of the assessment process and ensure that any shortfalls in competence would be identified and the appropriate training given.
- To support systems of NVQ accreditation which were being established in key occupational areas.
- The training of workplace assessors was made necessary by the decision to introduce schemes of training in support of the Government's Modern Apprenticeship initiative and by the commitment of businesses to attain Investors in People status.

The choice of a programme built around TBT materials was dictated by a need for:

- A cost-effective way of training in a relatively short space of time a large number of 'line' people (many of whom were employed on shift rotas) to operate as workplace assessors in addition to their normal duties.
- A flexible medium to minimise disruption to individuals and the operating requirements of a tightly manned company.
- A means of cascading the responsibility of training to others while at the same time maintaining the integrity of the means of assessor accreditation.
- The necessity to develop a unique system of training which could be run conveniently in-house.

The two relevant standards of competence set by the Training and Development Lead Body are:

D32 Assess candidate performance.
D33 Assess candidate performance using different sources of evidence.

The training course which was devised and implemented is in three parts:

Part 1 Workplace assessor multimedia programme (available as either laserdisc or CD-ROM MPEG).
Part 2 Attendance at a one-day practical session.
Part 3 Assessment at the workplace.

Part 1, the multimedia programme with supporting text materials, covers the key knowledge requirements of the training and takes approximately three hours to complete. It is completed by all course members at an open-learning resource centre before attending Part 2. The trainees can study in their own time or at a time suitable to their work schedule. The programme can be studied at the trainees' own pace and can be easily split over several sessions, as required. In order to be relevant to all trainees, the design is based around case studies in four business functions: craft, production, technical and administration.

Part 2 is designed as a practical 'hands-on' session to build on the knowledge gained from Part 1, and it gives trainees the confidence to be able to assess to the right depth and to be consistent. This one-day practical session includes: a review of the TBT materials in Part 1 that are used for reference and consolidation of knowledge; methods of assessment; conduct of assessments; and Awarding Body documentation. The course is practice-oriented and is designed to allow trainees to develop quickly the necessary skills of assessment specific to the situation in which they work.

Part 3 is the assessment of the course members to achieve full certification as an assessor. Only those who have satisfactorily completed Parts 1 and 2 of the programme will also be required to demonstrate these competences. This competence will be measured against the standards laid down by the Training and Development Lead Body (see above), and assessors achieving either or both of these D standards would be considered competent and externally certified accordingly.

The benefits to individuals can be covered in five main areas:

1. All the questions in the evaluation of Part 1 were rated above average by the trainees and there was a clear expressed preference for this as a delivery medium for the knowledge elements compared to traditional methods (this has also been shown in other research).
2. The main benefits of this medium are catered for in the design of the programme and include: instant feedback to aid learning, flexibility, repeatability, working at own pace, adaptability to different learning styles, use of examples relevant to own situation, private assessment practice to gain confidence, and suiting personal timetables.
3. The network of assessors will allow the awarding of NVQs which benefit the individual for personal motivation, for career enhancement and as a contribution towards productivity.
4. They will have gained a nationally recognised qualification through assessment of performance at the workplace that has been externally verified, and they will be confident that the standard is maintained through a communication network of internal verifiers.
5. Their being qualified will facilitate large numbers of others to achieve the same.

The development of the multimedia course facilitated benefits for Interactive Training Services in that:

1. The multimedia was fully evaluated in the context of assessing the effectiveness of this method for achieving the learning objectives. Both content and presentation were evaluated, as there is interaction between these. A straightforward statistical analysis of the results consistently showed that this course was achieving its objectives. This evaluation has been of use in the development of other programmes.
2. Using some of the latest technology increased the awareness amongst both training and line staff of the capabilities and advantages of multimedia in training.

The training facilitated benefits for the company in five areas:

1. The training package has provided the flexibility to train employees in a very relevant environment and provided the foundation of skills required to follow through the identified schemes across British Steel, helping the introduction of NVQs and the achievement of Investors in People status.
2. To date, a total of 332 employees have been trained as workplace assessors. It is not possible that this number could have been trained in the same timescale using other methods.
3. A comparison of costs, including external fees and employment figures, between, on the one hand, a three-day external course for the required number of assessors, and, on the other, the development of the TBT materials and in-house training for the same number, produces a net saving of £102,100 to the company.
4. As the training of the assessors was carried out internally, it also qualified for certification grants through local TECs.
5. To minimise costs to the businesses, delivery equipment was made available from Interactive Training Services on a loan basis.

As an employer, the benefits to the people in the company are:

1. An increase of awareness by assessors in the methods of collecting evidence to prove competence within their own workplace.
2. Personal satisfaction in achieving and receiving a certificate for a national qualification.
3. Also, all video shots in the video sections were filmed on company sites and involved company personnel as 'actors'. This contributed to the ownership of the programme by the trainees.

The infrastructure needed within a company to facilitate the achievement of an NVQ programme involves the investment of considerable time, effort and money. This course has enabled part of that infrastructure to be put in place as cost-effectively as possible, which encourages a more rapid introduction of the remainder of the programme and a wider application across the company.

With the assistance of networking groups, British Steel are now developing the most comprehensive and efficient means of assessment of candidates. Removing as much of the bureaucracy as possible will make NVQs more acceptable to line managers, and will also minimise resource requirements and, therefore, cost of implementation.

Case Study 9
IT Training in the Virtual Classroom

Server and database specialist Oracle Corporation have set up a European satellite training network to communicate with staff, resellers and clients. Described as an IDL (Interactive Distance Learning) network rather than as a more conventional business television system, the Oracle Channel will carry up to five hundred hours a year of courses aimed at Oracle staff and system users.

The decision to set up a network covering Europe, the Middle East and Africa follows the launch of an end-user-oriented network in the United States, which is being transmitted via commercial provider Westcott's network. However, Oracle's EMEA division channel will initially focus on an internal audience, reached through thirty-three sites located in Oracle offices throughout Europe, with a satellite footprint ranging from Dublin in the West to Oslo, Russia and Athens.

Technically, the European version of the channel, which started operation in April 1996, is also advanced. The turnkey satellite system and transmission arrangements, provided by Global Access, are all digital and use Scientific Atlanta PowerVu decoders allied to MPEG-2 uplinks. Digital transmission has fulfilled two roles. By maximising transponder usage (digital allows up to five channels per satellite responder, rather than just one), it cuts cost and frees uptime slots. It also allows Oracle to make its network interactive – a key feature of the distance-learning philosophy which is being employed.

Oracle Education already provides technology-based training, classroom training and training over the Internet. Believing that the IDL network should complement that activity, Oracle is choosing to run relatively long transmission – two- and four-hour events will be the norm – which consists of a mixture of video material, lectures and interaction carried out using five hundred One Touch numeric keypads. The One Touch system will also be used to allow course attendees to communicate with Bracknell studio (each keypad has a microphone) and for the collection of information about the audience.

Many of the courses themselves will be developed using materials devised by Oracle's San Francisco-based Worldwide Education Group and then tailored to European requirements.

Other transmissions, such as product and service launches, will be aimed at staff sectors within the organisation and specially developed for them. Examples of that kind of activity include: the future launch of a new telesales operation; communication with the two thousand Oracle consultants who spend most of their time working in client premises; and news on how the service systems and arrangements are changing.

However, Oracle Channel general manager, Mike Davies, is keen to point out that the service is a learning network, not a corporation television station: 'We will be using interaction every seven minutes, that's the thing that will stop it being television. People will concentrate because they want to get the answers right and interaction breaks up the programme and makes you part of it. It also gives us audience profiling information and lecturer feedback.' Mike Davies and his team already have 16 proven four-hour courses in place, and the experience gained in transmitting them live will help the unit produce presentations for other Oracle groups.

'We see this as a way to communicate across the division and cross international and cultural boundaries,' says Mike Davies. 'We are looking for commitment to programming. Although I am setting it up and running it, it's Oracle's channel and it should be open for people to use, and within six months we expect to be using the channel twelve to fifteen hours a week.'

Crucially, the channel also has to be at least Europewide. Although transmissions are currently in English, Mike Davies is aware that they will have to take linguistic and cultural differences into account. It is therefore no coincidence that the first two instructors being used are Danish.

Mike Davies originally examined the potential of a network based on videoconferencing technology. He opted for satellite in preference to video conferencing, first, because he estimated that transmission costs for video conferencing could have been up to seven times as high, and, secondly, because he considered the technology of satellite was more reliable.

Before the launch, Mike Davies and his colleagues had piloted course transmission to other offices and had confirmed Oracle's belief that 'everyone enjoys it and learns more . . . you can deliver a lot of information in a short time'.

The Bracknell studio facility, kitted out for a one-person operation (although, in practice, Mike Davies will probably employ two TV-trained personnel), is one of the keys to the whole operation. 'The only way to practice this kind of presentation is in the studio,' he says, 'and it's there for both broadcast and rehearsal. Content is all, and we are trying to make it easy for other users by taking their presentations, making them fit the TV medium and working together in the studio.'

In the long term, that's likely to be very important indeed. Although the European launch is focusing on the internal audience first, Oracle Education very successfully markets its courses through resellers and direct to clients. When a critical mass is achieved in Europe, the Oracle Channel would be able to support resellers wanting to sell their own educational packages.

In Mike Davies' words, it's an educational 'second wave' which progresses naturally from the establishment of Oracle Education as a global business within the corporation. One of the reasons for doing that was to develop educational business in each country so that Oracle becomes both a literal and metaphorical server company.

Index to Part I

access, 13, 56
accessibility, 34, 46, 57
accreditation, 3
administration, 33, 36, 38
aircraft simulators, 16, 17
analogue, 4, 6, 8, 13
Anglia University, 21
animation, 5, 11, 61
appraisal, 52, 64, 65
apprenticeships, 74
Argos, 68–70
artificial intelligence, 9, 10, 11, 31
assessment
  self 65, 69
  work-based, 65
  workplace, 63
Audio, 5, 6, 8, 11, 12, 13, 19, 21, 34, 49, 61, 64, 66, 69, 71
CD, 12
availability 33–4

bandwidth, 20, 21, 55
benchmark, 53
benefits, 5, 15, 22, 23, 24, 25, 29, 30, 33, 34, 35, 36, 37, 39, 40, 51, 52, 53, 54, 56, 61, 63, 64, 67, 68, 69, 75, 76
  business, 23, 34, 52, 53–4
  commercial, 57
  of using TBT, 23–32
  organisational, 23–9
  to learner, 29–32
body language, 18
bottom line, 34, 52
British Telecom, 14
British Gas, 71–3
British Rail, 13
British Steel, 17, 73–7
broadband, 19, 21

cable, 55
CBT, 3, 4–5, 7, 9, 10, 22, 26, 31, 37, 47, 49, 51

CD-i, 12, 13, 14–15
CD-ROM, 4, 6, 8, 11, 12, 13, 14, 15, 21, 51, 55, 56, 61, 62, 63, 65, 66, 67, 69, 70, 71, 72, 73, 74
CD-ROM drive, 11, 12, 14, 15
CD-ROM (XA), 13–14
clip art, 61
clip audio, 61
coaching, 3
compact disc interactive *see* CD-i
compact disc, 4, 11, 66
compression, 6, 8, 13, 14, 15
computer-based training *see* CBT
computer language, 3
consistent message, 23, 24
cost-effective, 18, 23, 27, 29, 34, 44, 47, 61, 64, 66, 74, 76
course map, 46
courseware, 4, 5, 7, 8, 9, 10, 11, 12, 14, 20, 21, 27, 36, 37, 45, 46, 47, 48, 49, 51, 52, 72
  bespoke 4, 7
  generic 4, 7, 45–6

Data Protection Act, 61
decompression, 8, 14
Department of Employment, 10
designer, 7, 47, 48, 49, 66
desk-to-desk conferencing, 18–19, 20
digital, 6, 7, 8, 9, 11, 12, 66, 71
  video disc *see* DVD
  video interactive *see* DVI
discovery learning, 87
distance learning, 29, 31, 39, 56
drill and practice, 3
DVD, 15, 56
DVD-i, 15
DVD movie, 15
DVD-ROM, 15
DVI, 8–9, 13

education, 11

81

electronic performance support systems *see* EPSS
E-mail, 3, 20, 36
embed training, 22
emulator, 16
entertainment, 11, 13
EPSS, 21–22
equipment, 5, 7, 8, 14, 17, 18, 36, 37, 72, 76
evaluation, 35, 46, 51–4, 75, 76
expert systems, 9–11, 22, 26, 31
extended architecture, 13

feedback, 10, 40, 65, 67, 72, 73, 75, 78
Financial Services Act, 61
flexible, 26, 27, 29, 43, 45, 61, 71, 72, 74
floppy disk, 12, 70
frame, 8, 9
framestore, 8
full motion, 8, 9, 13, 14, 45
full screen, 8, 9, 13, 14, 45
future, 55, 56, 57

gas chromatograph, 8
government, 57, 74
graphics, 5, 7, 8, 11, 12, 13, 49, 61, 66

hard disks, 5, 6, 8, 11, 12, 13
hardware, 14, 48, 55
headsets, 34
health and safety, 34, 61, 62
high fidelity audio, 13
highway, 21, 56

IAV *see* IV
implementation, 3, 33–8, 73, 77
increased business performance, 29
induction, 60, 61, 62
integrated, 36, 39, 71
integration, 73
Intel, 9
interact, 66
interactive, 5, 13, 21, 46, 57, 61, 69, 77
  audio, 5, 6, 14
  design, 4
  television, 19
  video *see* IV
interactivity, 6, 7, 12, 13, 24
Internet, 19, 20, 21, 55, 56, 77
interpersonal skills, 7, 37, 39, 40, 68, 69
intranet, 19, 20, 21
invest, 7
Investment, 8, 12, 44, 51, 66, 69, 76
IV, 3, 4, 6–7, 8, 9, 13, 24, 28, 37, 51, 55, 66, 72

Janet, 19

keyboard entry, 16
Kingston University, 10
knowledge, 9, 10, 22, 23, 24, 25, 26, 27, 39, 40, 41, 49, 51, 52, 53, 65, 70, 74, 75

language, 5, 6
laserdisc, 7, 8, 9, 74
learn faster, 23, 25, 31
learn more, 23, 24, 25, 26, 29, 30, 31
learning
  by discovery, 8, 9, 10, 29, 31
  experience, 3, 18, 24, 36, 40
  lifetime, 55
  styles, 46, 75
  centre, 36, 38, 60, 62, 63, 64, 66, 67, 70, 72
Libraries, 56, 64, 71, 72, 77
line management
  selling TBT to, 34–5
line manager, 29, 34, 35, 37, 72, 73, 77
linear video, 6, 7
Lloyds Bank, 65–8
lost business opportunities, 28
loudspeaker, 13

mainframes, 4, 9, 66
managed, 4, 20
management, 37, 40, 45, 49, 51, 60, 63, 65, 66, 68, 69, 70, 72
  training, 68, 72
manager, 25, 34, 35, 40, 45, 53, 54, 57, 59, 62, 65, 67, 68, 69, 70, 73
mentoring, 3
merging, 3, 4, 7, 20
Microsoft network, 19, 20
mixed media, 11
monitor, 5, 7, 13, 14, 15, 16, 17, 18
multimedia, 11–12
  customising, 44–5
  design, 11, 47
  PC, 3, 12, 15, 16, 64, 65
Multimedia Ventures, 11
Multimedia Yearbook, 11

Networks, 19–21, 55
NPI, 59
NVQ, 73–77

open learning, 61, 63, 65, 66, 67, 68, 71, 72, 73
  centre, 36, 60, 62, 63, 64, 66, 67, 70, 74, 75
Oracle, 77–9
outline design, 49, 50
own pace, 5, 25, 29, 30, 36, 39, 61, 65, 67, 69, 75

Philips, 13, 15
point-of-sale, 11

INDEX TO PART I

post-course work, 40–41
pre-course work, 39–40
privacy, 33, 34, 63
processing power, 9, 11
producer, 4, 44, 47, 49, 50, 61
production, 7, 9, 12, 47, 49, 50, 57, 73
  team, 47
project, 35, 47, 48
  management, 49, 67
  manager, 49, 66
publishing, 11

reinforcement, 40
retention of knowledge, 10, 23, 25, 52
revision, 23, 27, 41
Royal Insurance, 10

safe environment, 16, 41
satellite broadcasting, 19
scheduling, 48
script, 35, 49, 50, 62
security, 21, 57, 61
simulation, 8, 16, 17, 40, 61, 67
software, 7, 8, 13, 14, 16, 18, 48, 55
Sony, 13
sound, 3, 6, 7, 8, 66
  processing cards, 6, 8
Soundblaster, 14
Specsavers, 64–5
still picture, 8, 11, 12
storage, 5, 6, 11, 12, 13, 14, 55, 56
studio, 19, 49, 77, 78
Subject-matter, 10, 45, 46, 48, 49, 52
  expert, 35, 46, 49, 50
Sun Life, 60–62
superhighway, 3, 4, 19, 20, 21, 55, 56, 57
SuperJanet, 19
supervisor, 28, 37, 53, 65, 73
supplier, 7, 15, 44, 46, 48, 49, 50, 55, 62, 64, 65, 68, 72, 73
support, 3, 20, 21, 22, 26, 28, 29, 32, 36, 37, 39, 46, 47, 48, 54, 67, 68, 70, 74, 78

technical skills, 3, 12
Telecom, 14, 20, 55
test, 4, 5, 10, 11, 24, 25, 26, 30, 52, 53, 59, 60, 65, 70
testing, 3, 24, 35, 50, 52, 59–60
time away from the job, 27
timescale, 48–50
train driving simulator, 8
training
  bespoke, 27, 35, 43, 44, 47–50
  classroom, 39, 77
  computer-based *see* CBT
  face-to-face, 25, 40, 63, 68, 69, 70
  generic, 43–6
  in-house, 31, 47, 49, 51, 63, 66, 74, 76
  just-in-time, 22, 23, 28–9, 31–2
  management, 51
  manager, 55
  needs analysis, 59
  off-the-shelf, 43, 44, 66, 69
transmission rates, 20
treatment, 48

university, 10, 20, 21, 56

variable speeds, 8
Vauxhall Motors, 63–4
VGA, 14
video, 3, 4, 6, 7, 8, 9, 11, 12, 13, 14, 15, 17, 18, 19, 21, 34, 44, 46, 49, 55, 56, 61, 62, 64, 66, 76, 77
  conferencing, 3, 17–18
  disc, 3, 6, 7, 8
virtual campus, 56
virtual classroom, 77
virtual learning organisations, 56
virtual organisation, 20
virtual reality, 17

web site, 21
work legislation, 61
workbook, 39, 44, 48, 61, 66, 67, 70, 73

83

Part II
The Directory

Gower

The companion volume to this title, *Handbook of Management Games and Simulations*, is also availab[...] from Gower (see back of jacket for details). To order this book complete the details below and retur[...] this card to us.

Please send me:

.... copy/ies of *Handbook of Management Games and Simulations* 0 566 07753 1 @ £52.00
(Price includes post and packing)

WAYS TO PAY

.... Please invoice me/my company

.... Please charge £ .... to my
Access/Mastercard/American Express/Visa*
Circle which applies

Account No

Expiry Date ....

If you are using your personal credit card to order, please ensure you include details of your registered card address if it differs from that given opposite. We endeavour to despatch all orders within 14 days of receipt. If a title is not available, your order will be recorded and the book despatched as quickly as possible.

☐ *If you do not wish to receive offers of goods or services from any other organization, please tick here.*

ADDRESS DETAILS (BLOCK CAPITALS PLEASE)

Name ....

Job Title ....

Company ....

Address ....

....

.... Postcode ....

Tel No. ....

Signature ....

Date ....

If outside the UK please write your Company VAT/
IVA code here ....

Gower also has offices in Singapore • Sydney • Brookfield, VT, USA   *Code:* 13223

Gower   ## MANAGEMENT UPDATE

Gower is the leading publisher of business and management books in the UK and with over 400 titles i[...] print it is one of the largest in the world in this area. The range embraces handbooks, practica[...] management guides, reference works, personal skills books, audio manuals, and state-of-the-art studies in specialist areas of business activity. The subjects covered span from training, personnel and management development through manufacturing, sales and marketing to accountancy and finance.

We would be pleased to send you details of our publications in your chosen areas of interest. Just fill i[...] the section below and we will send you the relevant information.

Please send me information on the books and other materials you publish in the following subject areas:
(please write clearly)

....

....

Name ....

Job Title ....

Company ....

Address ....

....

.... Postcode ....

If you would like to receive e-mail on our new products, please give your e-mail address below, OR
include the names of any other colleagues in your company who would benefit from being on our mailing list:

....

....

☐ If you do not wish to receive information from other organizations, please tick here

Gower also has offices in Singapore • Sydney • Brookfield, VT, USA   *Code:* 13223

BUSINESS REPLY SERVICE
Licence No AT170

2

Gower Publishing
Gower House
Croft Road
ALDERSHOT
Hampshire
United Kingdom
GU11 3BR

BUSINESS REPLY SERVICE
Licence No AT170

2

Gower Publishing
Gower House
Croft Road
ALDERSHOT
Hampshire
United Kingdom
GU11 3BR

Introduction to Part II

CATEGORIES

The courses in this book cover a wide range of topics. Some are very generic, such as leadership skills, and others are generic to a specific industry. For this reason, the course entries have each been allocated a category, either by industry, such as Power Generation, or by subject, such as Accounting. For some categories it has been necessary to divide these further into subcategories: for example, the category Database Systems has 14 subcategories, including dBase, Excel and Supercalc. Part II therefore opens with a list in alphabetical sequence of the categories and subcategories amongst which the courseware is spread.

DIRECTORY

The directory section of this book has been designed to provide the reader with information about generic technology-based training courseware available on the market. It contains in excess of seven hundred entries, divided in alphabetical sequence by category, subcategory where applicable, and method of delivery.

Each entry gives information about the course under the following headings:

- *Title*   This is the title given to the course by the supplier.
- *Purpose*   This gives a broad indication of the purpose of the course.
- *Suitable for*   This gives an indication of the target audience for the course where this is known.
- *Prerequisites*   This indicates whether there is any prerequisite knowledge required or whether any other training should be carried out before starting this course.
- *Description*   This describes the course, its main learning points and its methodology.
- *Delivery method*   This states the delivery method (e.g. CBT or CD-i).
- *Minimum hardware requirement*   Where it is known, the minimum hardware

requirement is given. Where this information is lacking, please check carefully with the supplier.
- *Price* Where known, the price is given. In some cases, the price varies depending on the number purchased, so in some cases the price has been given as 'On application'.
- *Supplier* This gives the name, address and telephone number of the supplier.

The entries are of necessity brief and you are recommended to contact the supplier for further information. You are also recommended to view the courseware and evaluate its 'fitness for purpose' before purchase (see Part I, Chapter 5).

The delivery methods of the courses are different, with only a few courses offered in more than one delivery method.

INDICES

To make finding entries easier, there are three indices behind the directory section, as follows:

1. An alphabetical list of all course titles with page numbers. This will prove useful if you can remember the title of the course but not the category.
2. A list of course titles, with the page reference to the main entry, sorted alphabetically by delivery method. This you may find of assistance if you are constrained by the delivery method.
3. A list of courseware suppliers' names, addresses and telephone numbers with an alphabetical list of courseware titles with page number.

These indices will enable you to find courses by title, delivery method or supplier.

ATTENTION PRODUCERS!

Gower's *Handbook of Technology-Based Training* will be updated on a regular basis. Brian Tucker holds a database of technology-based training products and will include all of your generic training products on that database **at no charge**.

If you wish to update your entries in this *Handbook* or add new entries for the next edition, please send details of your products (product information sheets, catalogues or leaflets) to the address opposite:

Jonathan Norman
Project Director
Gower Publishing Limited
Gower House
Croft Road
Aldershot
Hampshire GU11 3HR
Tel: 01252 331551
Fax: 01252 344405
e-mail: gower@cityscape.co.uk

Alphabetical List of Categories and Subcategories

Accounting	97
Appraisal	100
Assertiveness	104
Balance sheets	105
Banking	107
Basic numeracy	109
Book-keeping	111
Budgeting and forecasting	113
Business functions	115
Business law	116
Business planning	116
Business strategy	117
Business writing	118
Capital spending	118
Change management	120
Chemical safety	120
Chromatography	121
Coaching and mentoring	123
Coatings	125
Communication skills	126
Communications technology	129
General	129
ISDN	131
Management	131
OSI	132
Security	132
TCP	133
X.25	134
X.400	134
Computer environments	135

Computer languages and programming	136
Basic	136
C	137
COBOL	140
GUI	140
IMS	142
Modelling	142
MultiTasking	143
Object-oriented technology	143
Oracle	145
Pascal	150
PowerBuilder	151
SQL	152
Sybase	153
Computer skills	153
General	153
Corel	157
DOS	158
E-mail	159
Freelance	164
Lotus	165
Office	167
Oracle	168
Organiser	169
OS/2	169
Powerpoint	170
Project	173
Schedule	174
Windows	174
Works	180
Computer systems	181
Conflict management	183
Construction	183
Contract negotiation and law	183
Costing	184
Counselling skills	184
Creativity and problem solving	185
Customer care	186
Data protection	191
Data storage	192
Database systems	192
Access	192
Approach	194

ALPHABETICAL LIST OF CATEGORIES AND SUBCATEGORIES

Dataease	195
DB2	195
dBase	196
Excel	196
IDMS	200
Lotus	200
Oracle	204
Quattro	209
RDBMS	210
SQL	210
Supercalc	213
Sybase	213
Delegation	214
Discipline interviewing	215
Economics	216
Electrical safety	217
Empowerment	219
English	220
Equal opportunities	221
European Union	222
Facilitation skills	223
Finance	224
Financial management	232
Financial services	233
Fire safety	238
Foreign languages (multiple language courses; see also separate languages)	239
French (see also Foreign languages)	240
German (see also Foreign languages)	241
Giving feedback and criticism	242
Graphics (see Computer skills)	
Harassment	243
Health and safety	243
High technology	246
Induction	247
Insurance practice	247
Internet	253
Interviewing skills	254
Investors in people	255
Italian (see also Foreign languages)	255
Japanese (see also Foreign languages)	256
Keyboard skills	257
Language skills	260

THE DIRECTORY

Leadership	261
Letter writing	263
Life assurance	264
Listening skills	266
Logistics	266
Management skills	267
Manual handling	278
Marketing strategy	278
Meetings	284
Mortgages	286
Motivation	286
Multimedia	288
Negotiation	288
Networking	290
General	290
LANS	291
Netware	292
Noise	294
Non-verbal communication	294
NVQ	294
Objective setting	295
Operating environments	295
Client	295
JCL	296
UNIX	297
PC applications (see Computer skills)	
Pensions	304
Personal	305
Personal finance	308
Personal skills	309
Plastics and polymers	309
Pneumatics	311
Power generation	311
Presentation skills	320
Production management	321
Project management	321
Protective equipment	325
Questioning skills	325
Reading skills	326
Recruitment and selection	326
Report writing	328
Research and development	329
Risk management	330

ALPHABETICAL LIST OF CATEGORIES AND SUBCATEGORIES

Sales management	330
Selling skills	332
Social care	335
Software maintenance	336
Spanish (see also Foreign languages)	337
Spreadsheets (see Database systems)	
Standards	338
Stock control	338
Street works	339
Stress management	340
Study skills	342
Team leadership and development	342
Telephone skills	345
Time management	347
Total quality	352
Training and development	356
Transport	357
VDU Safety	358
Web sites	359
Word processing	360
AmiPro	360
DisplayWrite	362
Word	362
WordPerfect	366
Working capital	371

Directory of Courses

Accounting

CBT

Title: **Business Accounting**
Purpose: To allow students to practise their foundation accounting skills more efficiently.
Suitable for: Students on foundation accounting course.
Prerequisites: Knowledge of the appropriate theory.
Description: Business Accounting is a tried and tested software teaching package for courses in accounting and book-keeping, which allows the student to concentrate on the key decisions as they practise.
Delivery method: CBT.
Minimum hardware requirement: 386 PC; 1Mb hard disk; 12.5 Mb RAM.
Price: £395.00 + VAT.
Source: Stanley Thornes (Publishers) Ltd, Ellenborough House, Wellington Street, Cheltenham, Gloucestershire GL50 1YW. Tel: 01242 228888

Title: **Do You Know Basic Accounting?**
Purpose: To act as a learning needs assessment which will be an aid to both learning and revision.
Suitable for: Anyone.
Prerequisites: A broad knowledge of basic accounting.
Description: A self-assessment tool consisting of about 300 multiple choice questions that will help you to develop your knowledge through repeated practice on questions covering all areas of the subject.
Delivery method: CBT and supporting text.
Minimum hardware requirement: IBM PC or compatible, 512k RAM.
Price: £165.00.
Source: Ivy Business Training Software plc, Ivy House, 233–235 Roehampton Lane, London SW15 4LB. Tel: 0181 780 1494

Title: **Do You Know Financial Accounting?**
Purpose: Is to act as a learning needs assessment which will be an aid to both learning and revision.
Suitable for: Anyone.
Prerequisites: A broad knowledge of financial accounting.
Description: A self-assessment tool consisting of about 300 multiple choice questions that will help you to develop your knowledge through repeated practice on questions covering all areas of the subject.
Delivery method: CBT and supporting text.
Minimum hardware requirement: IBM PC or compatible, 512k RAM.
Price: £165.00.
Source: Ivy Business Training Software plc, Ivy House, 233–235 Roehampton Lane, London SW15 4LB. Tel: 0181 780 1494

Title: **Do You Know How to Interpret Accounts?**
Purpose: Is to act as a learning needs assessment which will be an aid to both learning and revision.
Suitable for: Anyone.
Prerequisites: A broad knowledge of accounting.
Description: A self-assessment tool consisting of about 300 multiple choice questions that will help you to develop your knowledge through repeated practice on questions covering all areas of the subject.
Delivery method: CBT and supporting text.
Minimum hardware requirement: IBM PC or compatible, 512k RAM.
Price: £165.00.
Source: Ivy Business Training Software plc, Ivy House, 233–235 Roehampton Lane, London SW15 4LB. Tel: 0181 780 1494

Title: **Interactive Accounting Tutor**
Purpose: To teach more advanced aspects of financial accounting.
Suitable for: Those requiring advanced vocational training.
Prerequisites: Basic accounting knowledge.
Description: A modular course covering accounting standards, cash flow statements, incomplete records, partnership accounts, company accounts, group accounts and published accounts.
Delivery method: CBT.
Minimum hardware requirement: PC.
Price: On request.
Source: EQL International Ltd, Scottish Software Partner Centre, South Queensferry, West Lothian EH30 9TG. Tel: 0131 331 7371

Title: **Interactive Taxation Tutor**
Purpose: To teach the fundamentals of the main UK personal and business taxes.

Suitable for: Anyone requiring an understanding of UK taxation.
Prerequisites: None.
Description: The course covers the UK tax system, personal income tax, schedule D income tax, capital allowances, corporation tax, capital gains tax, value added tax, inheritance tax and self assessment.
Delivery method: CBT.
Minimum hardware requirement: PC.
Price: On request.
Source: EQL International Ltd, Scottish Software Partner Centre, South Queensferry, West Lothian EH30 9TG. Tel: 0131 331 7371

Title: **Understand Accounts**
Purpose: To familiarise users with accounting terminology and teach the analysis and interpretation of accounts.
Suitable for: Those needing to understand accounting terminology and the information contained in accounts.
Prerequisites: None.
Description: This course covers an introduction to accounts, balance sheet, profit and loss account, accounting fundamentals, profitability, cash and liquidity, business and gearing risk, investor ratios with an optional module on the use of tax information.
Delivery method: CBT.
Minimum hardware requirement: PC.
Price: On request.
Source: EQL International Ltd, Scottish Software Partner Centre, South Queensferry, West Lothian EH30 9TG. Tel: 0131 331 7371

Title: **Understand Management Accounting**
Purpose: To teach the principal concepts and techniques of management accounting.
Suitable for: Managers and accounting trainees.
Prerequisites: None.
Description: This course covers an introduction to costing, fixed overheads, budgeting, variance analysis, contribution analysis, investment appraisal, pricing and transfer pricing and wider considerations.
Delivery method: CBT.
Minimum hardware requirement: PC.
Price: On request.
Source: EQL International Ltd, Scottish Software Partner Centre, South Queensferry, West Lothian EH30 9TG. Tel: 0131 331 7371

CD-ROM

Title: **Accounting**

Purpose: To teach and support a complete introductory accounting course.

Suitable for: All business (or modular) students from HND level upwards.

Prerequisites: None.

Description: The course includes: Introduction to financial statements, introduction to book keeping, the final accounts of a sole trader, introduction to the accounts of a limited company, elementary interpretation of financial statements of manufacturing organisations, full absorption costing, budgeting and budgetary control, accounting for decision making.

Delivery method: CD-ROM.

Minimum hardware requirement: PC; 8Mb RAM; CD-ROM drive and sound card.

Price: £29.95 (inc. VAT) single user licence; multi-user licences from £650.00.

Source: Pitman Publishing, 128 Long Acre, London, WC2E 9AN. Tel: 0171 4472290

Appraisal

CBT

Title: **Managing the Reprimand**

Purpose: To teach you how to prepare for a reprimand and what strategies to use.

Suitable for: Team leaders and managers.

Prerequisites: None.

Description: The course looks at how to prepare and what strategies to use and discusses the tactics to use to achieve a satisfactory result.

Delivery method: CBT.

Minimum hardware requirement: PC.

Price: £175.00.

Source: Electrovision UK Ltd, Hamble Point Marina, School Lane, Hamble, Southampton SO31 4JD. Tel: 01703 452221

Title: **Performance Troubleshooting**

Purpose: To explain the factors that can cause performance problems.

Suitable for: Team leaders.

Prerequisites: None.

Description: Discusses the human performance system and looks at the working environment, the individual, the impact of work and the importance of feedback.

Delivery method: CBT.

Minimum hardware requirement: PC.

Price: £366.00.

Source: Electrovision UK Ltd, Hamble Point Marina, School Lane, Hamble, Southampton SO31 4JD. Tel: 01703 452221

CD-i
Title: **The Appraisal Interview**
Purpose: To aid a productive appraisal and show the basics of running one and giving feedback.
Suitable for: Appraisers and appraisees.
Prerequisites: None.
Description: Preparation, communication, objective setting and feedback; plus on-disc interview path to test the appraiser's learning.
Delivery method: CD-i.
Minimum hardware requirement: TV and CD-i player.
Price: Purchase: £1295.00 + carriage + VAT; 2-day hire: £195.00 + carriage + VAT.
Source: Melrose, 16 Bromells Road, London, SW4 0BL. Tel: 0171 627 8404

Title: **The Dreaded Appraisal**
Purpose: To teach both appraisor and appraisee the fundamentals of good appraisal interviews.
Suitable for: Everyone.
Prerequisites: None.
Description: This programme proves that an appraisal interview can be a positive experience for employer and employee, but only if both parties stick to the fundamentals. Key points are: create the right atmosphere with praise and encouragement; ask open questions and listen actively; face up to problems and stick to facts; invite self appraisal; agree action plan with measurable targets.
Delivery method: CD-i.
Minimum hardware requirement: CD-i player and television.
Price: £995.00; rental prices on request.
Source: Video Arts Ltd, Dumbarton House, 68 Oxford Street, London W1N 0LH. Tel: 0171 637 7288

CD-ROM
Title: **Appraisal for Performance**
Purpose: To teach definitions, objectives, preparation, communication skills, the actual interview and the follow-up.
Suitable for: Managers and supervisors.
Prerequisites: None.
Description: This 4-module course, which uses case studies throughout to show both good and bad practice, will give you better theoretical and practical knowledge of appraisal and the preparation and follow-up required.

Delivery method: CD-ROM.
Minimum hardware requirement: 486 PC, 8Mb RAM, 420Mb hard disk, CD-ROM drive, audio card.
Price: £1199.00.
Source: Xebec Multi Media Solutions Ltd, The Critchley Building, Bath Road, Woodchester, Stroud, Glos. GL5 5EY. Tel: 01453 835482

Title: **Appraisal Interviewing**
Purpose: To show you how to conduct appraisal interviews which will motivate your staff, and help them to spot their weaknesses and eradicate them.
Suitable for: Managers and supervisors.
Prerequisites: 'Essential Interviewing Skills'.
Description: This course will enable you to gather facts before the interview; prepare an interview plan; put the appraisee at ease; state the purpose of the interview; give positive feedback; focus on performance; help the appraisee identify problems and their solutions; identify training needs; summarise the action plan; build a follow-up action plan.
Delivery method: CD-ROM.
Minimum hardware requirement: 486 PC, 8Mb RAM, 420Mb hard disk, CD-ROM drive, audio card.
Price: £895.00.
Source: Training Direct, North Court, Edinburgh Gate, Harlow, Essex, CM20 2JE. Tel: 01279 623927

Title: **The Appraisal Interview**
Purpose: To teach you how to plan, conduct and evaluate appraisal interviews.
Suitable for: Supervisors and managers.
Prerequisites: None.
Description: This is an introductory course which will enable you to know what an appraisal interview means for the employee; what an appraisal interview means for the manager; how to prepare for and conduct a good appraisal interview; how to evaluate an employee's performance; and what forms and other practical aids to use to get better results.
Delivery method: CD-ROM.
Minimum hardware requirement: 486 PC, 8Mb RAM, 256 Colour VGA, sound card and 8Mb hard-disk space.
Price: £295.00.
Source: Ivy Business Training Software plc, Ivy House, 233–235 Roehampton Lane, London SW15 4LB Tel: 0181 780 1494

Title: **The Appraisal Interview**
Purpose: To teach the concept of appraisal interview and provide a structured method for carrying out the appraisal interview.

Suitable for: Business students, supervisors and managers at all levels.
Prerequisites: None.
Description: This course will help you learn what an appraisal interview actually is and what it means for both the employee and the manager. It covers how to conduct the interview, establishing the right environment, doing your homework, putting the interviewee at ease, ensuring the purpose is fully understood, and avoiding being either too casual or too interrogative.
Delivery method: CD-ROM.
Minimum hardware requirement: 386 PC; 6Mb hard disk; sound card; CD-ROM drive.
Price: £295.00.
Source: Comput-Ed Ltd, Long Lane, Dawlish EX7 0QR. Tel: 01626 889955

Interactive Video
Title: **Appraisal and Counselling**
Purpose: To give a complete understanding of the benefits of an appraisal system and the skills necessary to appraise and counsel effectively.
Suitable for: Managers and supervisors.
Prerequisites: None.
Description: This course will help managers and supervisors complete more accurate appraisals based on objective facts and as a result the staff will perform better and develop more fully.
Delivery method: Interactive video.
Minimum hardware requirement: Interactive video workstation.
Price: £2020.00.
Source: Training Direct, North Court, Edinburgh Gate, Harlow, Essex CM20 2JE. Tel: 01279 623927

Title: **Performance Review**
Purpose: To improve the skills used by a manager when conducting appraisal interviews.
Suitable for: Managers.
Prerequisites: None.
Description: This course allows you to work through the interactive interview, making decisions for the manager, testing your knowledge and observing the manager's and job-holder's action.
Delivery method: Interactive video.
Minimum hardware requirement: Interactive video workstation.
Price: £1135.00.
Source: Training Direct, North Court, Edinburgh Gate, Harlow, Essex CM20 2JE. Tel: 01279 623927

THE DIRECTORY

Assertiveness

CBT
Title: **Managing Assertiveness**
Purpose: To teach management techniques of assertiveness.
Suitable for: Managers.
Prerequisites: None.
Description: Introduces the four basic behavioural styles; covers management techniques including assertiveness techniques, responsive techniques, refusing requests, dealing with aggression and submission, and handling difficult situations.
Delivery method: CBT.
Minimum hardware requirement: PC.
Price: £348.00.
Source: Electrovision UK Ltd, Hamble Point Marina, School Lane, Hamble, Southampton SO31 4JD. Tel: 01703 452221

CD-i
Title: **Say What You Want**
Purpose: To help anyone recognise and develop their own assertiveness.
Suitable for: Everyone.
Prerequisites: None.
Description: The programme sets out a step-by-step route to becoming more assertive.
Delivery method: CD-i.
Minimum hardware requirement: TV and CD-i player.
Price: Purchase: £995.00 + carriage + VAT; 2-day hire: £165.00 + carriage + VAT.
Source: Melrose, 16 Bromells Road, London, SW4 0BL. Tel: 0171 627 8404

Title: **Straight Talking**
Purpose: To teach the art of assertiveness.
Suitable for: Everyone.
Prerequisites: None.
Description: This course demonstrates that assertiveness is simply a way of making sure that people and their views get noticed. The key points are: stick to relevant issues; establish a bottom line; use instant replay to maintain your position; invite others to help and negotiate as equals.
Delivery method: CD-i.
Minimum hardware requirement: CD-i player and television.
Price: £995.00; rental prices on request.
Source: Video Arts Ltd, Dumbarton House, 68 Oxford Street, London W1N 0LH. Tel: 0171 637 7288

CD-ROM
Title: **An Introduction to Assertiveness**
Purpose: To help you to distinguish between different behaviour patterns, and provide you with the skills you need to deal with them in yourself and in others.
Suitable for: Anyone.
Prerequisites: None.
Description: A course which will enable you to: know what is assertiveness; recognise and deal with passive/aggressive behaviour; recognise your own rights and those of others; develop assertiveness skills in yourself; recognise the importance of body language and how to cope with mixed messages; deal with conflict and criticism.
Delivery method: CD-ROM.
Minimum hardware requirement: 486 PC, 8Mb RAM, 420Mb hard disk, CD-ROM drive, audio card.
Price: £1135.00.
Source: Training Direct, North Court, Edinburgh Gate, Harlow, Essex CM20 2JE. Tel: 01279 623927

Title: **Say The Right Thing**
Purpose: To equip you with the necessary assertiveness skills.
Suitable for: Anyone.
Prerequisites: None.
Description: Assertiveness techniques are essential skills in the modern office. This product will equip you with these necessary skills. It includes some tricky situations for you to practise on and test yourself. Topics include giving and receiving criticism, how people behave, difficult situations and making requests.
Delivery method: CD-ROM.
Minimum hardware requirement: PC; 8Mb RAM; CD-ROM; sound card.
Price: £975.00.
Source: Electrovision UK Ltd, Hamble Point Marina, School Lane, Hamble, Southampton SO31 4JD. Tel: 01703 452221

Balance sheets

CBT
Title: **Business of Balance**
Purpose: To look at the two sides of the balance sheet and how trading can affect the balance.
Suitable for: Anyone.
Prerequisites: None.

Description: This course identifies what makes up a healthy business through the balance sheets and how they are interpreted.
Delivery method: CBT.
Minimum hardware requirement: PC.
Price: £299.00.
Source: Electrovision UK Ltd, Hamble Point Marina, School Lane, Hamble, Southampton SO31 4JD. Tel: 01703 452221

Title: **The Balance Sheet and Profit and Loss Account: Where Finance Begins**
Purpose: To explain the structure of these two well-know financial statements, examining the nature and significance of each item to be found in them.
Suitable for: Anyone.
Prerequisites: None.
Description: An introductory course with a study time of up to three hours. It covers: differences between sole traders, partnerships and companies; the balance sheet equation; the meanings of current and long term; the items on the two financial statement and their logical sequence; the connection between the two statements.
Delivery method: CBT and supporting text.
Minimum hardware requirement: IBM PC or compatible, 512k RAM.
Price: £165.00 per single copy; price for multiple copies on request.
Source: Ivy Business Training Software plc, Ivy House, 233–235 Roehampton Lane, London SW15 4LB. Tel: 0181 780 1494

Title: **Where do Balance Sheets and Profit and Loss Accounts Come From?**
Purpose: To give a detailed analysis of how the profit and loss account and the balance sheet are derived. If you know how they are produced, then you can dissect them for the valuable information.
Suitable for: Anyone with a basic understanding of the two financial statements.
Prerequisites: A basic understanding of financial statements.
Description: An intermediate course covering the concept of accounting transactions, the various heading under which items are classified and the purpose of a trial balance.
Delivery method: CBT with supporting text.
Minimum hardware requirement: IBM PC or compatible, 512k RAM.
Price: £165.00 single copy; price for multiple copies on request.
Source: Ivy Business Training Software plc, Ivy House, 233–235 Roehampton Lane, London SW15 4LB. Tel: 0181 780 1494

DIRECTORY OF COURSES

CD-ROM
Title: **How Money Works in Business**
Purpose: To take the mystery out of money and, during an exercise, introduce you to simple balance sheets and profit and loss accounts.
Suitable for: Managers.
Prerequisites: None.
Description: This course will give you an understanding of: where money comes from and where it goes; the profit and loss account; the balance sheet; cash flow; accounts receivable and accounts payable; how money works in business; financial statements; and the role of the accountant.
Delivery method: CD-ROM.
Minimum hardware requirement: 486 PC, 8Mb RAM, 420Mb hard disk, CD-ROM drive, audio card.
Price: £895.00.
Source: Training Direct, North Court, Edinburgh Gate, Harlow, Essex CM20 2JE. Tel: 01279 623927

Banking

CBT
Title: **Banking Law: The Banking–Customer Relationship**
Purpose: To explain the legal jargon as well as the rights and duties of bankers under the law. It also deals with the law relating to cheque transactions.
Suitable for: Anyone.
Prerequisites: None.
Description: This is an introductory course which is aimed at teaching the knowledge that is important to an understanding of the purposes, complexities and dynamics of banking law.
Delivery method: CBT and supporting text.
Minimum hardware requirement: IBM PC or compatible, 512k RAM.
Price: £165.00.
Source: Ivy Business Training Software plc, Ivy House, 233–235 Roehampton Lane, London SW15 4LB. Tel: 0181 780 1494

Title: **International Banking**
Purpose: To give an understanding of the foreign exchange markets, exchange rates and the services of importers and exporters in the finance of international trade.
Suitable for: Anyone.
Prerequisites: 'UK Domestic Banking'.
Description: This is an introductory course which will enable you to understand: how foreign exchange markets operate; the contracts used within these

markets; why exchange rates vary; floating and fixed exchange rate systems; Euromarkets; why foreign trade exists; letters of credit; bills of exchange; and the movement of funds internationally.
Delivery method: CBT and supporting text.
Minimum hardware requirement: IBM PC or compatible, 512k RAM.
Price: £165.00.
Source: Ivy Business Training Software plc, Ivy House, 233–235 Roehampton Lane, London SW15 4LB. Tel: 0181 780 1494

Title: **The Principles of Lending: How Banks Lend Money to Businesses**
Purpose: To set out the professional approach to lending decisions, emphasising the need for a balance between fact and judgement.
Suitable for: Anyone.
Prerequisites: None.
Description: This is an intermediate course which will enable you to understand: the history of bank lending; the general principles of lending; personal customer lending; the different types of loans available to businesses; how to evaluate a business as a lending proposition and the value of financial analysis in credit assessment and control.
Delivery method: CBT and supporting text.
Minimum hardware requirement: IBM PC or compatible, 512k RAM.
Price: £165.00.
Source: Ivy Business Training Software plc, Ivy House, 233–235 Roehampton Lane, London SW15 4LB. Tel: 0181 780 1494

Title: **UK Domestic Banking**
Purpose: To teach about the role and services offered by building societies and domestic clearing banks.
Suitable for: Anyone.
Prerequisites: 'Banking and Money: How They Work and What it Means to You'.
Description: This is an introductory course which will enable you to understand: how the modern UK banking system developed; how the bank clearing system operates; the main functions and activities of the Bank of England; the role of the Bank in managing the economy; the operation of the London money markets.
Delivery method: CBT and supporting text.
Minimum hardware requirement: IBM PC or compatible, 512k RAM.
Price: £165.00.
Source: Ivy Business Training Software plc, Ivy House, 233–235 Roehampton Lane, London SW15 4LB. Tel: 0181 780 1494

Basic numeracy

CBT

Title: **Do You Know Foundation Business Mathematics?**
Purpose: To act as a training needs analysis which will be an aid to both learning and revision.
Suitable for: Anyone.
Prerequisites: A broad knowledge of business mathematics.
Description: A self-assessment tool consisting of about 300 multiple-choice questions that will help you to develop your knowledge through repeated practice on questions covering all areas of the subject.
Delivery method: CBT and supporting text.
Minimum hardware requirement: IBM PC or compatible, 512k RAM.
Price: £165.00.
Source: Ivy Business Training Software plc, Ivy House, 233–235 Roehampton Lane, London SW15 4LB. Tel: 0181 780 1494

Title: **Introducing Numbers: Numbers and Fractions Made Easy**
Purpose: The first of a two-part course which teaches numeracy skills which are useful in all walks of life.
Suitable for: Anyone.
Prerequisites: Simple arithmetic competence.
Description: This is an introductory course which will enable you: to define whole numbers, a fraction and its parts – the numerator and denominator; and to know what common and decimal fractions are.
Delivery method: CBT and supporting text.
Minimum hardware requirement: IBM PC or compatible, 512k RAM.
Price: £165.00.
Source: Ivy Business Training Software plc, Ivy House, 233–235 Roehampton Lane, London SW15 4LB. Tel: 0181 780 1494

Title: **More Numbers: Ratios, Percentages and Charts Made Easy**
Purpose: The second of a two-part course which teaches numeracy skills that are useful in all walks of life.
Suitable for: Anyone.
Prerequisites: Simple arithmetic competence.
Description: This is an introductory/intermediate course which will enable you to understand: what a ratio is and how it can be used; what an average is; and how to calculate percentages; and how to choose appropriate tables, graphs and charts for presenting statistical information.
Delivery method: CBT and supporting text.
Minimum hardware requirement: IBM PC or compatible, 512k RAM.
Price: £165.00.

Source: Ivy Business Training Software plc, Ivy House, 233–235 Roehampton Lane, London SW15 4LB. Tel: 0181 780 1494

Title: **Numbusters**
Purpose: To provide basic numeracy training through a series of games.
Suitable for: Anyone.
Prerequisites: None.
Description: Providing basic numeracy training through a series of games.
Delivery method: CBT.
Minimum hardware requirement: PC.
Price: £49.00.
Source: Electrovision UK Ltd, Hamble Point Marina, School Lane, Hamble, Southampton SO31 4JD. Tel: 01703 452221

Title: **Presenting Numbers (DOS Version)**
Purpose: To teach the interpretation of charts and graphs.
Suitable for: Anyone.
Prerequisites: None.
Description: This course is aimed at people who need to interpret and present numerical information. It provides some of the classic tricks to look out for.
Delivery method: CBT.
Minimum hardware requirement: PC.
Price: £442.00.
Source: Electrovision UK Ltd, Hamble Point Marina, School Lane, Hamble, Southampton SO31 4JD. Tel: 01703 452221

Title: **Presenting Numbers (Windows Version)**
Purpose: To teach the interpretation of charts and graphs.
Suitable for: Anyone.
Prerequisites: None.
Description: This course is aimed at people who need to interpret and present numerical information. It provides some of the classic tricks to look out for.
Delivery method: CBT.
Minimum hardware requirement: PC with Windows.
Price: £617.00.
Source: Electrovision UK Ltd, Hamble Point Marina, School Lane, Hamble, Southampton SO31 4JD. Tel: 01703 452221

Title: **Working with Numbers**
Purpose: To teach the basics of numeracy.
Suitable for: Anyone.
Prerequisites: None.

Description: The course covers adding, subtracting, multiplying, dividing and percentages.
Delivery method: CBT.
Minimum hardware requirement: PC.
Price: £435.00.
Source: Electrovision UK Ltd, Hamble Point Marina, School Lane, Hamble, Southampton SO31 4JD. Tel: 01703 452221

Book-keeping

CBT

Title: **How to Master Book-Keeping (Part 1)**
Purpose: To enable you to understand practical book-keeping. This course covers trading, profit and loss accounts, books of prime entry and the concept of double entry.
Suitable for: Anyone.
Prerequisites: Basic arithmetic capability.
Description: This is an introductory course which will enable you to: identify and compare all elements of the trading account, profit and loss account and balance sheet; record transactions in double entry and sales transactions in three-column accounting format; use a chart of accounts; and post entries to and from sales and purchases day books.
Delivery method: CBT and supporting text.
Minimum hardware requirement: IBM PC or compatible, 512k RAM.
Price: £165.00.
Source: Ivy Business Training Software plc, Ivy House, 233–235 Roehampton Lane, London SW15 4LB. Tel: 0181 780 1494

Title: **How to Master Book-Keeping (Part 2)**
Purpose: This course builds on Part 1 and covers the cash book, wages and salaries ledgers, nominal accounts, posting to ledgers and the use of control accounts.
Suitable for: Anyone.
Prerequisites: Book-Keeping Part 1.
Description: This is an intermediate course which will enable you to: handle a 2- and 3-column analysed cash book; maintain and make up the petty cash book, handle bank reconciliations and enter salaries and wages; and make postings from books of prime entry to sales and purchase ledgers and general ledger.
Delivery method: CBT and supporting text.
Minimum hardware requirement: IBM PC or compatible, 512k RAM.
Price: £165.00.

Source: Ivy Business Training Software plc, Ivy House, 233–235 Roehampton Lane, London SW15 4LB. Tel: 0181 780 1494

Title: **How to Master Book-Keeping (Part 3)**
Purpose: This course builds on the previous two courses and will show you how to identify and correct errors through the journal, and how to prepare a trial balance.
Suitable for: Anyone.
Prerequisites: Book Keeping Parts 1 and 2.
Description: This intermediate course will enable you to use the trial case study to test your skill and accuracy in writing up a set of books to the trial balance, identifying and correcting errors in the trial balance and posting entries in a simulated computer environment.
Delivery method: CBT and supporting text.
Minimum hardware requirement: IBM PC or compatible, 512k RAM.
Price: £165.00.
Source: Ivy Business Training Software plc, Ivy House, 233–235 Roehampton Lane, London SW15 4LB. Tel: 0181 780 1494

Title: **Interactive Book-Keeping Tutor**
Purpose: To teach the principles and practices of double entry book-keeping.
Suitable for: Everyone needing a comprehensive knowledge of double entry book-keeping and basic accountancy.
Prerequisites: None.
Description: The topics covered include: double entry – balance sheets, balancing of accounts; double entry – profit and loss accounts; profit and loss account and balance sheet; nominal ledger and VAT; accruals and prepayments; wages and salaries; fixed assets and depreciation, and many other topics.
Delivery method: CBT.
Minimum hardware requirement: PC.
Price: On request.
Source: EQL International Ltd, Scottish Software Partner Centre, South Queensferry, West Lothian EH30 9TG. Tel: 0131 331 7371

Title: **Understanding Book-Keeping**
Purpose: To give a sound knowledge of the principles and practice of double entry book-keeping.
Suitable for: Anyone wishing to understand book-keeping.
Prerequisites: None.
Description: The package consists of nine separate modules and a workbook. Topics include: how money works in business; introduction to book-keeping and 'T' accounts; cash book; debtors, creditors and ledgers; books of prime

entry; three-column cash book; bank reconciliation statement and petty cash book; the trial balance; errors; and final accounts.
Delivery method: CBT.
Minimum hardware requirement: PC.
Price: £90.00 + VAT.
Source: Mobile Training Ltd, Green Acres, Sibford Gower, Banbury OX15 5RW. Tel: 01295 788115

Budgeting and forecasting

CBT
Title: **Budgeting Basics**
Purpose: To explain what a budget is and how it works.
Suitable for: Team leaders and managers.
Prerequisites: None.
Description: This course explains what a budget is and how the budgeting process works. It also looks at how organisations budget and gives an overview of accounting conventions relating to budgets.
Delivery method: CBT.
Minimum hardware requirement: PC.
Price: £326.00.
Source: Electrovision UK Ltd, Hamble Point Marina, School Lane, Hamble, Southampton SO31 4JD. Tel: 01703 452221

Title: **Managing Your Budget**
Purpose: To teach you how to manage your budget.
Suitable for: Team leaders and managers.
Prerequisites: None.
Description: Starts by looking at budget and management processes and reviewing your budgets. It also looks at ways of controlling costs and monitoring expenditure.
Delivery method: CBT.
Minimum hardware requirement: PC.
Price: £355.00.
Source: Electrovision UK Ltd, Hamble Point Marina, School Lane, Hamble, Southampton SO31 4JD. Tel: 01703 452221

Title: **Preparing Your Budget**
Purpose: To look at various budgeting formats and what groundwork needs to be done.
Suitable for: Team leaders and managers.
Prerequisites: None.

Description: This course looks at the various budgeting formats that companies use and what groundwork needs to be done before preparing a budget. It also looks at how to get the numbers right, presenting the final budget, and how to handle budget cuts.
Delivery method: CBT.
Minimum hardware requirement: PC.
Price: £380.00.
Source: Electrovision UK Ltd, Hamble Point Marina, School Lane, Hamble, Southampton SO31 4JD. Tel: 01703 452221

Title: **Resource Accounting and Budgeting**
Purpose: To teach accruals accounting procedures.
Suitable for: Anyone who works in the public sector and wants to know how finance works and how the new systems will impact their job.
Prerequisites: None.
Description: The course has five modules covering: basic principles; financial statements; resource planning and budgeting; financial management and control; measuring departmental performance. There is also an advanced section on financial statements.
Delivery method: CBT.
Minimum hardware requirement: 386 PC; 4Mb RAM; 12Mb hard disk.
Price: £425.00 single user; licence price on application.
Source: Unicorn Training, Copsham House, Broad Street, Chesham HP5 3EA. Tel: 01494 791064

CD-ROM

Title: **Budgeting**
Purpose: To demystify this aspect of finance for managers, who have no financial training, but need a good grasp of budgeting skills so they can manage with an awareness of the business's profitability.
Suitable for: Managers.
Prerequisites: 'How Money Works in Business'.
Description: This course will help you to understand: the need for budgeting; the budget as a management tool; the need to monitor expenditure; how to compare the figures; how to analyse data and take action.
Delivery method: CD-ROM.
Minimum hardware requirement: 486 PC, 8Mb RAM, 420Mb hard disk, CD-ROM drive, audio card.
Price: £895.00.
Source: Training Direct, North Court, Edinburgh Gate, Harlow, Essex CM20 2JE. Tel: 01279 623927

Title: **Money Business 2: Effective Budgeting**
Purpose: To help you make better business decisions as a result of a wider understanding and use of budgets.
Suitable for: First-line managers and supervisors.
Prerequisites: None.
Description: This course gives a comprehensive introduction to money in business, examining the way money works in business, budget preparation and groundwork, constructing a budget, and using a budget for control.
Delivery method: CD-ROM.
Minimum hardware requirement: 486 PC, 8Mb RAM, 420Mb hard disk, CD-ROM drive, audio card.
Price: £1199.00.
Source: Xebec Multi Media Solutions Ltd, The Critchley Building, Bath Road, Woodchester, Stroud, Glos. GL5 5EY. Tel: 01453 835482

Business functions

CBT
Title: **The Office Professional**
Purpose: To enable the user to practise discretion and judgement in a variety of situations.
Suitable for: Office support staff.
Prerequisites: None.
Description: This course covers, identifying needs, planning work, efficiency, working with colleagues, customers and managers, working in a team, and taking responsibility.
Delivery method: CBT.
Minimum hardware requirement: PC.
Price: £995.00.
Source: Electrovision UK Ltd, Hamble Point Marina, School Lane, Hamble, Southampton SO31 4JD. Tel: 01703 452221

CD-ROM
Title: **Business Functions**
Purpose: To teach and support a complete introductory course on the main functional business areas.
Suitable for: All business (or modular) students from HND level upwards.
Prerequisites: None.
Description: A detailed introduction to the five main business functions: production, marketing, personnel, design, and finance.
Delivery method: CD-ROM.
Minimum hardware requirement: PC; 8Mb RAM; CD-ROM drive and sound card.

Price: £29.95 (inc. VAT) single-user licence; multi-user licences from £650.00.
Source: Pitman Publishing, 128 Long Acre, London WC2E 9AN. Tel: 0171 4472290

Business law

CBT
Title: **Do You Know Business Law?**
Purpose: To act as a learning needs assessment which will be an aid to both learning and revision.
Suitable for: Anyone.
Prerequisites: A broad knowledge of business law.
Description: A self-assessment tool consisting of about 300 multiple-choice questions that will help you to develop your knowledge through repeated practice on questions covering all areas of the subject.
Delivery method: CBT and supporting text.
Minimum hardware requirement: IBM PC or compatible, 512k RAM.
Price: £165.00.
Source: Ivy Business Training Software plc, Ivy House, 233–235 Roehampton Lane, London SW15 4LB. Tel: 0181 780 1494

CD-ROM
Title: **Law**
Purpose: To teach and support a complete introductory course on law for business.
Suitable for: All business (or modular) students from HND level upwards.
Prerequisites: None.
Description: A detailed introduction to law for business.
Delivery method: CD-ROM.
Minimum hardware requirement: PC; 8Mb RAM; CD-ROM drive and sound card.
Price: £29.95 (inc. VAT) single-user licence; multi-user licences from £650.
Source: Pitman Publishing, 128 Long Acre, London WC2E 9AN. Tel: 0171 4472290

Business planning

CBT
Title: **Understanding Business Planning**
Purpose: This package gives an explanation of each stage of the business plan.
Suitable for: Management.
Prerequisites: None.

Description: The package consists of five separate modules and a workbook. Topics covered are: introduction, analysis, statement, strategy evaluation including implementation, and monitoring including corrective action.
Delivery method: CBT.
Minimum hardware requirement: PC.
Price: £90.00 + VAT.
Source: Mobile Training Ltd, Green Acres, Sibford Gower, Banbury OX15 5RW Tel: 01295 788115

Business strategy

CBT
Title: **Deciding on a Business Strategy: Your Capabilities Determine Your Choices**
Purpose: To assess the competitive environment, think strategically, and devise and implement a strategic plan.
Suitable for: Managers.
Prerequisites: None.
Description: This is an introductory course which will enable you to: produce a strategic plan and perform the steps in the process including an environmental appraisal; identify threats; perform an internal company appraisal and a SWOT analysis; implement a strategic plan; and perform a constant reappraisal.
Delivery method: CBT and supporting text.
Minimum hardware requirement: IBM PC or compatible, 512k RAM.
Price: £165.00.
Source: Ivy Business Training Software plc, Ivy House, 233–235 Roehampton Lane, London SW15 4LB. Tel: 0181 780 1494

Simulation
Title: **Global Operations**
Purpose: To teach business strategy and team working.
Suitable for: Middle through senior management.
Prerequisites: Line management experience.
Description: A total enterprise business simulation/game, replicating a manufacturing company. Involving market development, and capacity and financial planning, by teams of 4–5 in competition, with up to 8 teams.
Delivery method: Trainer uses computerised simulator.
Minimum hardware requirement: PC; 640Kb RAM and printer.
Price: Rental: £295.00; tutored from £800.00.
Source: Hall Marketing, Studio 11, Colman's Wharf, 45 Morris Road, London E14 6PA. Tel: 0171 537 2982

THE DIRECTORY

Business writing

CBT
Title: **Creative Writing Version 2.0**
Purpose: To teach creative writing to those who wish to write for pleasure or profit, or for business.
Suitable for: New and experienced writers, business people who wish to produce more effective press releases, etc.
Prerequisites: None.
Description: This course covers writing letters, fillers, slogans, magazine articles as well as many other topics.
Delivery method: CBT.
Minimum hardware requirement: 386PC; 4Mb RAM; 4Mb hard disk.
Price: £49.99 plus £2 p&p.
Source: Way Ahead Electronic Publishing, 27 Woodford Green, Bratton, Telford, Shropshire TF5 0NS. Tel: 01952 243153

Interactive video
Title: **Writing for Results**
Purpose: To teach you how to persuade, complain, respond to complaints and initiate action through the effective use of the written word.
Suitable for: Anyone.
Prerequisites: None.
Description: This four-module course shows users how to produce written communications which get the desired results. The modules cover: the basics, planning your writing, writing with style, and when the going gets tough.
Delivery method: Interactive video.
Minimum hardware requirement: Interactive video workstation.
Price: £4015.00.
Source: Training Direct, North Court, Edinburgh Gate, Harlow, Essex CM20 2JE. Tel: 01279 623927

Capital spending

CBT
Title: **Project/Investment Appraisal and Capital Spending: Compounding and Discounting**
Purpose: The second of a three-part series dealing with the six steps involved in preparing a capital budget.
Suitable for: Senior managers.
Prerequisites: The first in this series of courses.
Description: This is an advanced course which will enable you to: competently

perform discounting and compounding calculations; calculate the weighted average cost of capital; compute present values, internal rates of return and payback; state the advantages and disadvantages of NPV, IRR and payback.
Delivery method: CBT and supporting text.
Minimum hardware requirement: IBM PC or compatible, 512k RAM.
Price: £165.00.
Source: Ivy Business Training Software plc, Ivy House, 233–235 Roehampton Lane, London SW15 4LB. Tel: 0181 780 1494

Title: **Project/Investment Appraisal and Capital Spending: Making the Decision**
Purpose: The third of a three-part series dealing with the six steps involved in preparing a capital budget.
Suitable for: Senior managers.
Prerequisites: The first two in this series of courses.
Description: This is an advanced course which will enable you to: perform sensitivity analysis on your calculations and list important qualitative issues; compare the strengths and weaknesses of your assumptions; write up a formal capital spending proposal and convincingly defend it.
Delivery method: CBT and supporting text.
Minimum hardware requirement: IBM PC or compatible, 512k RAM.
Price: £165.00
Source: Ivy Business Training Software plc, Ivy House, 233–235 Roehampton Lane, London SW15 4LB. Tel: 0181 780 1494

Title: **Project/Investment Appraisal and Capital Spending: Projecting Cash Flows**
Purpose: The first of a three-part series dealing with the six steps involved in preparing a capital budget.
Suitable for: Senior managers.
Prerequisites: An understanding of management accounting.
Description: This is an advanced course which will enable you to compile a sensible list of relevant alternative investment options and prepare a cash flow forecast in each of its three parts: the investments; incremental income and expenses; and cash flow adjustments.
Delivery method: CBT and supporting text.
Minimum hardware requirement: IBM PC or compatible, 512k RAM.
Price: £165.00.
Source: Ivy Business Training Software plc, Ivy House, 233–235 Roehampton Lane, London SW15 4LB. Tel: 0181 780 1494

Change management

CBT
Title: **Management of Change**
Purpose: To teach how to manage change.
Suitable for: Managers.
Prerequisites: None.
Description: Introduces the reasons for change and how to plan for change. Discusses how change affects individuals and groups and how to get change accepted in a positive way.
Delivery method: CBT.
Minimum hardware requirement: PC.
Price: £348.00.
Source: Electrovision UK Ltd, Hamble Point Marina, School Lane, Hamble, Southampton SO31 4JD. Tel: 01703 452221

CD-i
Title: **Managing Change**
Purpose: To provide managers with the understanding and ability to implement change effectively.
Suitable for: Managers at any level, supervisors and team leaders involved in the change process.
Prerequisites: None.
Description: By watching the problems a small 'change' causes when brought into play, the film illustrates how the 'change' process affects an organisation and how to manage it.
Delivery method: CD-i.
Minimum hardware requirement: TV and CD-i player.
Price: Purchase: £995.00 + carriage + VAT; 2-day hire: £165.00 + carriage + VAT.
Source: Melrose, 16 Bromells Road, London SW4 0BL. Tel: 0171 627 8404

Chemical safety

CD-ROM
Title: **Chemical Safety**
Purpose: To be familiar with the nature and properties of chemicals, and to recognise the importance of safe working practices.
Suitable for: Those who come into or may come into contact with chemicals.
Prerequisites: None.
Description: The modules are: why chemical safety; chemical hazards; chemicals in the atmosphere; safe working and handling; basic first aid; and a self-test.
Delivery method: CD-ROM.

Minimum hardware requirement: 486 PC; 4Mb RAM; dual-speed CD-ROM drive; sound Card.
Price: On application.
Source: Instinct Training, Strawberry How Business Centre, Lorton Road, Cockermouth, Cumbria CA13 9XQ. Tel: 01900 827600

Chromatography

CBT
Title: **Atomic Absorption Spectrometry Softbook**
Purpose: To provide training in instrumental spectrometry and chromatography, giving practical interactive learning of both instrumental and chemical aspects of each technique.
Suitable for: Laboratory technicians and higher education students.
Prerequisites: A-level or higher chemistry.
Description: Presents the theory, instrumentation and practical analysis for each instrument. The user is shown how to prepare samples for analysis, how to use the instrument to carry out the analysis, and how to process the results.
Delivery method: CBT.
Minimum hardware requirement: 386 PC; 2MB RAM; 5MB hard disk.
Price: £345.00.
Source: Cognitive Solutions Ltd, 13 Herries Road, Glasgow G41 4DE. Tel: 0141 423 1060

Title: **Gas Chromatography Method Development Softbook**
Purpose: To provide training in instrumental spectrometry and chromatography, giving practical interactive learning of both instrumental and chemical aspects of each technique.
Suitable for: Laboratory technicians and higher education students.
Prerequisites: A-level or higher chemistry
Description: Presents the theory, instrumentation and practical analysis for each instrument. The user is shown how to prepare samples for analysis, how to use the instrument to carry out the analysis, and how to process the results.
Delivery method: CBT.
Minimum hardware requirement: 386 PC; 2MB RAM; 5MB hard disk.
Price: £345.00.
Source: Cognitive Solutions Ltd, 13 Herries Road, Glasgow G41 4DE. Tel: 0141 423 1060

Title: **Gas Chromatography Softbook**
Purpose: To provide training in instrumental spectrometry and chromatography,

giving practical interactive learning of both instrumental and chemical aspects of each technique.
Suitable for: Laboratory technicians and higher education students.
Prerequisites: A-level or higher chemistry.
Description: Presents the theory, instrumentation and practical analysis for each instrument. The user is shown how to prepare samples for analysis, how to use the instrument to carry out the analysis, and how to process the results.
Delivery method: CBT.
Minimum hardware requirement: 386 PC; 2MB RAM; 5MB hard disk.
Price: £345.00.
Source: Cognitive Solutions Ltd, 13 Herries Road, Glasgow G41 4DE. Tel: 0141 423 1060

Title: **High Performance Liquid Chromatography Softbook**
Purpose: To provide training in instrumental spectrometry and chromatography, giving practical interactive learning of both instrumental and chemical aspects of each technique.
Suitable for: Laboratory technicians and higher education students.
Prerequisites: A-level or higher chemistry.
Description: Presents the theory, instrumentation and practical analysis for each instrument. The user is shown how to prepare samples for analysis, how to use the instrument to carry out the analysis, and how to process the results.
Delivery method: CBT.
Minimum hardware requirement: 386 PC; 2MB RAM; 5MB hard disk.
Price: £345.00.
Source: Cognitive Solutions Ltd, 13 Herries Road, Glasgow G41 4DE. Tel: 0141 423 1060

Title: **Inductively Coupled Plasma Softbook**
Purpose: To provide training in instrumental spectrometry and chromatography, giving practical interactive learning of both instrumental and chemical aspects of each technique.
Suitable for: Laboratory technicians and higher education students.
Prerequisites: A-level or higher chemistry.
Description: Presents the theory, instrumentation and practical analysis for each instrument. The user is shown how to prepare samples for analysis, how to use the instrument to carry out the analysis, and how to process the results.
Delivery method: CBT.
Minimum hardware requirement: 386 PC; 2MB RAM; 5MB hard disk.
Price: £345.00.
Source: Cognitive Solutions Ltd, 13 Herries Road, Glasgow G41 4DE. Tel: 0141 423 1060

Title: **Mass Spectrometry Softbook**
Purpose: To provide training in instrumental spectrometry and chromatography, giving practical interactive learning of both instrumental and chemical aspects of each technique.
Suitable for: Laboratory technicians and higher education students.
Prerequisites: A-level or higher chemistry.
Description: Presents the theory, instrumentation and practical analysis for each instrument. The user is shown how to prepare samples for analysis, how to use the instrument to carry out the analysis, and how to process the results.
Delivery method: CBT.
Minimum hardware requirement: 386 PC; 2MB RAM; 5MB hard disk.
Price: £345.00.
Source: Cognitive Solutions Ltd, 13 Herries Road, Glasgow G41 4DE. Tel: 0141 423 1060

Coaching and mentoring

CBT

Title: **Coaching Skills**
Purpose: To teach coaching skills.
Suitable for: Team leaders and managers.
Prerequisites: None.
Description: This course teaches coaching skills to enable you to increase someone's competence by providing learning opportunities and giving guidance and feedback. Discusses assessing the learner, performance profiling, developing a plan, assessing competence and reviewing progress. Workbook supplied.
Delivery method: CBT.
Minimum hardware requirement: PC.
Price: £413.00.
Source: Electrovision UK Ltd, Hamble Point Marina, School Lane, Hamble, Southampton SO31 4JD. Tel: 01703 452221

Title: **Mentoring Skills**
Purpose: To develop successful mentoring relationships.
Suitable for: Team leaders and managers.
Prerequisites: None.
Description: The topics include: the mentoring relationship; where and how mentoring should be used; qualities of an effective mentor and protégé; key do's and don't's.
Delivery method: CBT.
Minimum hardware requirement: PC.
Price: £433.00.

Source: Electrovision UK Ltd, Hamble Point Marina, School Lane, Hamble, Southampton SO31 4JD. Tel: 01703 452221

CD-i

Title: **The Helping Hand**
Purpose: To teach the skills needed for successful coaching.
Suitable for: Managers.
Prerequisites: None.
Description: Managers need to decide which tasks a team member could take responsibility for and coach him or her accordingly. The key points are: identifying the need; planning the coaching programme; conducting the coaching in stages, and monitoring the results.
Delivery method: CD-i.
Minimum hardware requirement: CD-i player and television.
Price: £995.00; rental prices on request.
Source: Video Arts Ltd, Dumbarton House, 68 Oxford Street, London W1N 0LH. Tel: 0171 637 7288

CD-ROM

Title: **Coaching for Results**
Purpose: To give an in-depth awareness of the benefits of coaching in a variety of situations and gives the knowledge of how to coach successfully.
Suitable for: Managers and team leaders.
Prerequisites: None.
Description: This is a very practical training course which shows coaching sessions in action, with analysis from a coaching expert. It breaks down into five parts: cues to coach; your motivation; step by step; your behaviour; and coaches at work.
Delivery method: CD-ROM.
Minimum hardware requirement: 486 PC, 8Mb RAM, 420Mb hard disk, CD-ROM drive, audio card.
Price: £1199.00.
Source: Xebec Multi Media Solutions Ltd, The Critchley Building, Bath Road, Woodchester, Stroud, Glos. GL5 5EY. Tel: 01453 835482

Title: **Coaching for Success**
Purpose: To explain the chemistry of the coaching partnership and give practical, step-by-step guidance on the coaching process itself.
Suitable for: Anyone.
Prerequisites: None.
Description: This course will enable you to understand: how people learn through hands-on coaching; build the partnership and develop trust; the five-step

coaching process; how to foster continuous improvement; how to use mistakes as a learning aid; the need for regular feedback.
Delivery method: CD-ROM.
Minimum hardware requirement: 486 PC, 8Mb RAM, 420Mb hard disk, CD-ROM drive, audio card.
Price: £1135.00.
Source: Training Direct, North Court, Edinburgh Gate, Harlow, Essex CM20 2JE. Tel: 01279 623927

Title: **Coaching in the Workplace**
Purpose: To outline the benefits of coaching for the coach, the learner and the organisation. It provides the framework and skills needed to ensure that expertise is transferred within the workplace.
Suitable for: Anyone.
Prerequisites: None.
Description: This course covers: when you should coach; outcomes of effective coaching; determining performance needs; planning a coaching session; opening the session; exchanging views; closing and following up; supportive coaching; questioning techniques; giving positive feedback and corrective feedback.
Delivery method: CD-ROM.
Minimum hardware requirement: 486 PC, 8Mb RAM, 420Mb hard disk, CD-ROM drive, audio card.
Price: £1195.00.
Source: Intelligent Training Solutions, 29 Narrow Street, London E14 8DP. Tel: 0171 791 3000

Coatings

CD-ROM
Title: **Coatings for Life**
Purpose: To provide induction training for the surface coating industry.
Suitable for: New and existing staff, suppliers and customers, and the community.
Prerequisites: None.
Description: The course covers: the history of coatings; markets for coating products; performance specification; basic formulations; safety, health and the environment; how coatings are made; how coatings get to their customer; quality; how coatings are applied; and the industry and its responsibilities.
Delivery method: CD-ROM.
Minimum hardware requirement: 486PC; 8Mb RAM; CD-ROM drive; sound card.
Price: On application.

Source: British Coatings Federation Ltd, James House, Bridge Street, Leatherhead, Surrey KT22 7EP. Tel: 01372 360660

Communication skills

CBT
Title: **Encouraging Upward Communication**
Purpose: To introduce the benefits and the climate in which they will work best.
Suitable for: Team leaders.
Prerequisites: None.
Description: This course introduces the benefits of good upward communication and the climate in which they work best. It shows you how to set criteria, get the right information and how to encourage upward communication through individuals and meetings.
Delivery method: CBT.
Minimum hardware requirement: PC.
Price: £175.00.
Source: Electrovision UK Ltd, Hamble Point Marina, School Lane, Hamble, Southampton SO31 4JD. Tel: 01703 452221

Title: **Giving Clear Instructions**
Purpose: To provide the benefits of giving clear instructions.
Suitable for: Team leaders and managers.
Prerequisites: None.
Description: Discusses the benefits of giving clear instruction and what the characteristics of effective instructions are. Proposes a method of preparing instructions and an action plan for giving them.
Delivery method: CBT.
Minimum hardware requirement: PC.
Price: £175.00.
Source: Electrovision UK Ltd, Hamble Point Marina, School Lane, Hamble, Southampton SO31 4JD. Tel: 01703 452221

Title: **How to Communicate With Other People**
Purpose: To provide you with a practical guide for understanding individual behaviour. It is based on 'transactional analysis'.
Suitable for: Anyone in business.
Prerequisites: None.
Description: This is an introductory course which provides you with an opportunity to examine, and possibly change, your current approach to working with others, so as to increase your personal and managerial effectiveness.
Delivery method: CBT and supporting text.

Minimum hardware requirement: IBM PC or compatible, 512k RAM.
Price: £165.00.
Source: Ivy Business Training Software plc, Ivy House, 233–235 Roehampton Lane, London SW15 4LB. Tel: 0181 780 1494

Title: **Keeping Staff Informed**
Purpose: To identify the information that employees want.
Suitable for: Team leaders and managers.
Prerequisites: None.
Description: This course discusses the information that employees want and how this fits in with your management style. It looks at the day-to-day information needs and the quality that has to be maintained. It discusses the advantages and disadvantages of different information media types.
Delivery method: CBT.
Minimum hardware requirement: PC.
Price: £175.00.
Source: Electrovision UK Ltd, Hamble Point Marina, School Lane, Hamble, Southampton SO31 4JD. Tel: 01703 452221

CD-ROM
Title: **Business Communications**
Purpose: To sharpen up communication skills at every level of your organisation.
Suitable for: Everyone.
Prerequisites: None.
Description: This course uses case study examples covering a variety of business and disciplines, giving the course a very wide appeal. There are five modules covering: listening; questioning; non-verbal communication; putting your point across; and a practice module.
Delivery method: CD-ROM.
Minimum hardware requirement: 486 PC, 8Mb RAM, 420Mb hard disk, CD-ROM drive, audio card.
Price: £1199.00.
Source: Xebec Multi Media Solutions Ltd, The Critchley Building, Bath Road, Woodchester, Stroud, Glos. GL5 5EY. Tel: 01453 835482

Title: **Communication at Work**
Purpose: To help the user to understand the problems of communication and the ways in which successful communication can be achieved.
Suitable for: Everyone.
Prerequisites: None.
Description: Faults in communication can lie with us, with other people, with the medium and with the nature of the work situation (structure, culture, etc.) This course deals with all these aspects.

Delivery method: CD-ROM.
Minimum hardware requirement: 386 PC; 6Mb hard disk; sound card; CD-ROM drive.
Price: £295.00.
Source: Comput-Ed Ltd, Long Lane, Dawlish EX7 0QR. Tel: 01626 889955

Title: **Effective Communication**
Purpose: To show team leaders how to talk to groups and be sure the message is getting across, and how to listen to people, and get on with them.
Suitable for: Managers and supervisors.
Prerequisites: 'Building a Partnership'.
Description: This course will help you to understand why you should: plan your communications; keep people informed and avoid the 'grape vine'; explain your decisions and win support; get the team involved; listen; handle disciplinary issues with sensitivity; plus how to speak to individuals and how to deal with complaints and problems.
Delivery method: CD-ROM.
Minimum hardware requirement: 486 PC, 8Mb RAM, 420Mb hard disk, CD-ROM drive, audio card.
Price: £895.00.
Source: Training Direct, North Court, Edinburgh Gate, Harlow, Essex CM20 2JE. Tel: 01279 623927

Title: **Managing Information Overload: Getting the Message Across**
Purpose: To teach the practical skills and strategies needed to gain and keep readers' and listeners' attention. It also shows how to combine data and images in written presentations.
Suitable for: Managers.
Prerequisites: None.
Description: This course will help you to be a better communicator. The key training messages are how to attract attention; how to present your message on paper; how to present your message verbally and how to communicate with different audiences.
Delivery method: CD-ROM.
Minimum hardware requirement: 486 PC, 8Mb RAM, 420Mb hard disk, CD-ROM drive, audio card.
Price: £995.00.
Source: Training Direct, North Court, Edinburgh Gate, Harlow, Essex CM20 2JE. Tel: 01279 623927

Interactive video
Title: **Checking Understanding**
Purpose: To underline the importance of making sure that you understand the other person and that they understand you.
Suitable for: Anyone.
Prerequisites: None.
Description: This course is based on the game of Cluedo. You assume the role of a visitor to Foxton Hall. The various rooms provide you with feedback on progress and advice on where to go next; provide reference material about the communication process; test your understanding of the subject, etc.
Delivery method: Interactive video.
Minimum hardware requirement: Interactive video workstation.
Price: £1135.00.
Source: Training Direct, North Court, Edinburgh Gate, Harlow, Essex CM20 2JE. Tel: 01279 623927

Communications technology

General

CD-ROM
Title: **Basic Communications**
Purpose: To teach some broad technical knowledge about telecommunications today.
Suitable for: Anyone.
Prerequisites: None.
Description: This course has four modules: telecommunications overview; basic transmissions concepts; transmission technologies; transmission standards.
Delivery method: CD-ROM.
Minimum hardware requirement: 486PC; 8Mb RAM; CD-ROM drive; sound card.
Price: £650.00.
Source: Mindware Training Technologies Ltd, Block 2, International Business Centre, Plassey, Limerick, Ireland. Tel: (353) 6133 1430

Title: **Data Networks**
Purpose: To provide a comprehensive overview of data networks in terms of their architecture, implementation and associated controlling and communicating devices.
Suitable for: Anyone.
Prerequisites: None.
Description: This course has six modules: data network architectures; data

network controller; data communications devices; data communications protocols; packet switching networks; and mobile data networks.
Delivery method: CD-ROM.
Minimum hardware requirement: 486PC; 8Mb RAM; CD-ROM drive; sound card.
Price: £1300.00.
Source: Mindware Training Technologies Ltd, Block 2, International Business Centre, Plassey, Limerick, Ireland. Tel: (353) 6133 1430

Title: **Network Design**
Purpose: To describe the techniques used in the design of a network, including traffic analysis, and to detail suitable evaluation criteria for cable choice and general network performance.
Suitable for: Anyone.
Prerequisites: None.
Description: This course has eight modules covering: overview of design process; network design; traffic analysis and queues; cabling considerations; LAN considerations; practical design of networks; network design case study.
Delivery method: CD-ROM.
Minimum hardware requirement: 486PC; 8Mb RAM; CD-ROM drive; sound card.
Price: £1600.00.
Source: Mindware Training Technologies Ltd, Block 2, International Business Centre, Plassey, Limerick, Ireland. Tel: (353) 6133 1430

Title: **Overview of Networks**
Purpose: To provide a comprehensive description of network concepts, types, configurations, topologies, components, applications and integration.
Suitable for: Anyone.
Prerequisites: None.
Description: This course has five modules covering: network topology and concepts; mobile networks; local area networks; metropolitan area networks; and network integration.
Delivery method: CD-ROM.
Minimum hardware requirement: 486PC; 8Mb RAM; CD-ROM drive; sound card.
Price: £675.00.
Source: Mindware Training Technologies Ltd, Block 2, International Business Centre, Plassey, Limerick, Ireland. Tel: (353) 6133 1430

Title: **Voice Networks**
Purpose: To explain the principles of voice networks in terms of switching, signalling and performance, and to provide an outline of the range and extent of current related technologies.
Suitable for: Anyone.
Prerequisites: None.

Description: This course has eight modules covering: voice communication fundamentals; switching; signalling; transmission and line standards; private branch exchanges; alternative voice systems; public networks; ISDN.
Delivery method: CD-ROM.
Minimum hardware requirement: 486PC; 8Mb RAM; CD-ROM drive; sound card.
Price: £1575.00.
Source: Mindware Training Technologies Ltd, Block 2, International Business Centre, Plassey, Limerick, Ireland. Tel: (353) 6133 1430

ISDN

CBT
Title: **Introducing ISDN**
Purpose: To provide a comprehensive introduction to Integral Services Digital Network (ISDN).
Suitable for: People who need to know the basics of the operation and application of ISDN.
Prerequisites: None.
Description: The course has six lessons covering: ISDN overview; ISDN telecommunications services; subscriber access; the user's view; ISDN signalling; and ISDN networking.
Delivery method: CBT.
Minimum hardware requirement: PC.
Price: £750.00.
Source: Mindware Training Technologies Ltd, Block 2, International Business Centre, Plassey, Limerick, Ireland. Tel: (353) 6133 1430

Management

CD-ROM
Title: **Network Management**
Purpose: To describe those controls and structures that underpin network operation and management.
Suitable for: Those involved in network management.
Prerequisites: None.
Description: The control function is defined in terms of the integral role of service level agreements, report management and pricing policy. Structures are facilitated and determined by a network operation policy in line with the various legal and regulatory constraints. Also provides an overview of the problems and issues of network integration and open systems.
Delivery method: CD-ROM.
Minimum hardware requirement: 486PC; 8Mb RAM; CD-ROM drive; sound card.

Price: £1775.00.

Source: Mindware Training Technologies Ltd, Block 2, International Business Centre, Plassey, Limerick, Ireland. Tel: (353) 6133 1430

OSI

CBT

Title: **Introduction to OSI**

Purpose: To integrate a user's knowledge of networking with the development of the OSI reference model.

Suitable for: Technical staff.

Prerequisites: None.

Description: This course covers the OSI model, protocol functions, how the model works, and issues in OSI and ISDN, and finishes with a test.

Delivery method: CBT.

Minimum hardware requirement: PC.

Price: £520.00.

Source: Mindware Training Technologies Ltd, Block 2, International Business Centre, Plassey, Limerick, Ireland. Tel: (353) 6133 1430

Title: **OSI Model and Related Standards**

Purpose: To give in-depth training in this topic.

Suitable for: Technical staff.

Prerequisites: Knowledge of OSI basics.

Description: This course covers physical layer, data link layer, network layer, transport layer, session layer, presentation layer, application layer and the complete picture. The course finishes with a test, which is optional.

Delivery method: CBT.

Minimum hardware requirement: PC.

Price: £995.00.

Source: Mindware Training Technologies Ltd, Block 2, International Business Centre, Plassey, Limerick, Ireland. Tel: (353) 6133 1430

Security

CD-ROM

Title: **Network Security**

Purpose: To describe the threats and risks in network security and analyse appropriate counter-measures. Management principles and contingencies, security and law are also explored.

Suitable for: Anyone.

Prerequisites: None.

Description: This course has eight modules: introduction to IT security; risk management; overview of CRAMM; security in network environments; security in specific networks; security techniques and standards; security management; contingency planning.
Delivery method: CD-ROM.
Minimum hardware requirement: 486PC; 8Mb RAM; CD-ROM drive; sound card.
Price: £1600.00.
Source: Mindware Training Technologies Ltd, Block 2, International Business Centre, Plassey, Limerick, Ireland. Tel: (353) 6133 1430

TCP

CBT
Title: **TCP/IP Explained**
Purpose: To explain the major features of TCP/IP.
Suitable for: Technical staff.
Prerequisites: None.
Description: This course covers: an introduction to TCP/IP; addressing and routing; IP and ICMP; TCP and UDP; TCP/IP applications including TELNET/NVT/FTP/DNS/SMPT/NFS; network management; TCP/IP and OSI; and finishes with a course test.
Delivery method: CBT.
Minimum hardware requirement: PC.
Price: £750.00.
Source: Mindware Training Technologies Ltd, Block 2, International Business Centre, Plassey, Limerick, Ireland. Tel: (353) 6133 1430

Title: **Using TCP/IP**
Purpose: To give an understanding of TCP/IP for all UNIX users, using TCP/IUP applications.
Suitable for: UNIX users.
Prerequisites: None.
Description: The key learning points of this course are: Internet addressing; data transmission; subnets in a network; and TCP/IP application protocols.
Delivery method: CBT; also available via the Internet.
Minimum hardware requirement: Any PC capable of running Microsoft Windows.
Price: On application.
Source: Oracle Corporation UK Ltd, The Oracle Centre, The Ring, Bracknell, Berks RG12 1BW. Tel: 01344 860066

X.25

CBT

Title: **Advanced X.25**
Purpose: To provide training in the more technical aspects of X.25.
Suitable for: Technical staff.
Prerequisites: Basic knowledge of X.25.
Description: This course's contents include: X.25 physical layer; X.25 data link layer; packet structure; X.25 example; and an optional test.
Delivery method: CBT.
Minimum hardware requirement: PC.
Price: £680.00.
Source: Mindware Training Technologies Ltd, Block 2, International Business Centre, Plassey, Limerick, Ireland. Tel: (353) 6133 1430

Title: **X.25 and Related Protocols**
Purpose: To provide an overall appreciation of X.25.
Suitable for: Technical staff.
Prerequisites: None.
Description: This course covers topics including: introducing X.25; features of X.25; and related protocols, including PADs/X.75/X.32. The course finishes with an optional test.
Delivery method: CBT.
Minimum hardware requirement: PC.
Price: £520.00.
Source: Mindware Training Technologies Ltd, Block 2, International Business Centre, Plassey, Limerick, Ireland. Tel: (353) 6133 1430

X.400

CBT

Title: **X.400 Getting the Message**
Purpose: To provide an expert and practical appraisal and training in X.400.
Suitable for: Technical staff.
Prerequisites: None.
Description: This course covers topics including: introduction; X.400 background and infrastructures; overview of X.400; details of X.400 MTS service; details of X.400 IPM service, management; X.400 present and future; and an optional test.
Delivery method: CBT.
Minimum hardware requirement: PC.
Price: £850.00.

Source: Mindware Training Technologies Ltd, Block 2, International Business Centre, Plassey, Limerick, Ireland. Tel: (353) 6133 1430

Computer environments

CBT
Title: **UNIX System Administration Basics**
Purpose: To teach effective management skills for UNIX 5.4 systems.
Suitable for: UNIX users.
Prerequisites: None.
Description: This course teaches effective management skills for UNIX 5.4 systems.
Delivery method: CBT also available via the Internet.
Minimum hardware requirement: Any PC capable of running Microsoft Windows.
Price: On application.
Source: Oracle Corporation UK Ltd, The Oracle Centre, The Ring, Bracknell, Berks. RG12 1BW. Tel: 01344 860066

Title: **Writing Bourne Shell Scripts**
Purpose: To provide an understanding of Bourne Shell Scripts.
Suitable for: UNIX users.
Prerequisites: None.
Description: This course is designed for UNIX users wishing to create and use Bourne Shell Scripts to improve productivity.
Delivery method: CBT; also available via the Internet.
Minimum hardware requirement: Any PC capable of running Microsoft Windows.
Price: On application.
Source: Oracle Corporation UK Ltd, The Oracle Centre, The Ring, Bracknell, Berks. RG12 1BW. Tel: 01344 860066

Title: **Writing C Shell Scripts**
Purpose: To provide an understanding of C Shell Scripts.
Suitable for: UNIX users.
Prerequisites: None.
Description: This course includes topics on: C Shell features; variables; expression and arrays; programming commands; and debugging.
Delivery method: CBT; also available via the Internet.
Minimum hardware requirement: Any PC capable of running Microsoft Windows.
Price: On application.
Source: Oracle Corporation UK Ltd, The Oracle Centre, The Ring, Bracknell, Berks. RG12 1BW. Tel: 01344 860066

Title: **Writing Korn Shell Scripts**
Purpose: To provide an understanding of Korn Shell Scripts.
Suitable for: UNIX users.
Prerequisites: None.
Description: This course includes topics on: variables; programming; compound commands and debugging.
Delivery method: CBT; also available via the Internet.
Minimum hardware requirement: Any PC capable of running Microsoft Windows.
Price: On application.
Source: Oracle Corporation UK Ltd, The Oracle Centre, The Ring, Bracknell, Berks. RG12 1BW. Tel: 01344 860066

Computer languages and programming

Basic

CBT

Title: **Teach Yourself Basic**
Purpose: To teach you how to write a simple Basic program.
Suitable for: Trainee programmers.
Prerequisites: None.
Description: This package will enable you to write simple Basic programs. Introductory to the intermediate course. Workbook containing exercises supplied.
Delivery method: CBT.
Minimum hardware requirement: PC.
Price: £350.00.
Source: Electrovision UK Ltd, Hamble Point Marina, School Lane, Hamble, Southampton SO31 4JD. Tel: 01703 452221

Title: **Teach Yourself Basic**
Purpose: To teach you how to write a program in Basic.
Suitable for: Trainee programmers.
Prerequisites: None.
Description: Suitable for novices, this tutorial simulates Basic and allows you to write a program using techniques such as looping, counting and totalling. Report construction, storing, retrieving and reading data are covered, as is performing calculations and printing reports, etc.
Delivery method: CBT.
Minimum hardware requirement: PC.
Price: £75.00 (multiple copy price on application).
Source: Electrovision UK Ltd, Hamble Point Marina, School Lane, Hamble, Southampton SO31 4JD. Tel: 01703 452221

C

CBT

Title: **Advanced C**
Purpose: To teach advanced C programming.
Suitable for: Programmers and trainee programmers.
Prerequisites: Basic knowledge of C.
Description: This course covers: using dynamic data structures; using the C processor; compiling programs using make; debugging programs using Codeview; design issue; and case study.
Delivery method: CBT.
Minimum hardware requirement: PC.
Price: £795.00.
Source: Electrovision UK Ltd, Hamble Point Marina, School Lane, Hamble, Southampton SO31 4JD. Tel: 01703 452221

Title: **Advanced C Programming in Windows**
Purpose: To instruct C programmers who wish to move into Windows.
Suitable for: Intermediate Level C programmers.
Prerequisites: Functionally literate in Windows application environment.
Description: This course includes topics on: WinMain, WndProc; CreateDialog; compile an EXE; demonstrate I/O functions in a program; name variables, event driven and sequential programming concepts.
Delivery method: CBT.
Minimum hardware requirement: PC with Windows.
Price: £1995.00.
Source: Electrovision UK Ltd, Hamble Point Marina, School Lane, Hamble, Southampton SO31 4JD. Tel: 01703 452221

Title: **Advanced C++ Programming and Workshop**
Purpose: To provide a greater understanding of C++ programming.
Suitable for: System developers.
Prerequisites: 'An Introduction to C++ Programming and Workshop'.
Description: Following on from the introductory course this module focuses on the object-oriented aspects of C++ and, by using examples and workbook-based exercises, provides an environment in which these techniques can be practised. Covers: operator overloading; initialisation; inheritance; polymorphism and virtual functions; and I/O in C++ programs.
Delivery method: CBT; also available via the Internet.
Minimum hardware requirement: Any PC capable of running Microsoft Windows.
Price: On application.
Source: Oracle Corporation UK Ltd, The Oracle Centre, The Ring, Bracknell, Berks RG12 1BW. Tel: 01344 860066

Title: **C Fundamentals**
Purpose: To get you started with C.
Suitable for: Programmers and trainee programmers.
Prerequisites: The knowledge of at least one high-level language.
Description: This course covers: getting started with C; user interactions; programming constructs; data structures; functions; file handling; and case study.
Delivery method: CBT.
Minimum hardware requirement: PC.
Price: £795.00.
Source: Electrovision UK Ltd, Hamble Point Marina, School Lane, Hamble, Southampton SO31 4JD. Tel: 01703 452221

Title: **C Programming Level 1**
Purpose: To teach you how to write, compile and execute a basic C program.
Suitable for: Programmers and trainee programmers.
Prerequisites: None.
Description: A Windows-based course that sets out to teach the student how to write, compile and execute a basic C program. Topics include terminology, structure of C programs, C statements, data handling, operators, conditional branching and loops, user defined functions, and variables. Student manual supplied with the course.
Delivery method: CBT.
Minimum hardware requirement: PC with Windows.
Price: £1495.00 (multiple copy price on application).
Source: Electrovision UK Ltd, Hamble Point Marina, School Lane, Hamble, Southampton SO31 4JD. Tel: 01703 452221

Title: **C Programming Level 2**
Purpose: To teach you how to write, compile and execute a more advanced C program.
Suitable for: Programmers and trainee programmers.
Prerequisites: 'C Programming Level 1'.
Description: Students will be taught to use arrays, structures, pointer and file within C programs. Topics include arrays and C, structures and C, pointers and C, and input/output. A comprehensive student manual is supplied.
Delivery method: CBT.
Minimum hardware requirement: PC with Windows.
Price: £1495.00 (multiple copy price on application).
Source: Electrovision UK Ltd, Hamble Point Marina, School Lane, Hamble, Southampton SO31 4JD. Tel: 01703 452221

Title: **Introduction to C++ Programming and Workshop**
Purpose: To provide an introduction to the C++ programming language.

Suitable for: System developers.
Prerequisites: None.
Description: This course provides a practical hands-on introduction to the C++ programming language in an object-oriented environment by using a combination of tutorials and workbook-based exercises. The course contents include: overview of C++; functions; classes in C++; and memory management.
Delivery method: CBT; also available via the Internet.
Minimum hardware requirement: Any PC capable of running Microsoft Windows.
Price: On application.
Source: Oracle Corporation UK Ltd, The Oracle Centre, The Ring, Bracknell, Berks. RG12 1BW. Tel: 01344 860066

Title: **Object Oriented Programming in C++**
Purpose: To teach the use of OOP in C++.
Suitable for: Programmers and trainee programmers.
Prerequisites: Experience in C programming.
Description: This course covers: overview of OOP; key concepts of OOP – abstraction hierarchy and inheritance, polymorphism, and dynamic binding; features of C++ – class construct, scoping special functions, overloading; C++ library – streams, file I/O; OOP using C++; and case study.
Delivery method: CBT.
Minimum hardware requirement: PC.
Price: £795.00.
Source: Electrovision UK Ltd, Hamble Point Marina, School Lane, Hamble, Southampton SO31 4JD. Tel: 01703 452221

Title: **Teach Yourself C++ and OOP**
Purpose: To teach you how to use C++ and object-oriented programming.
Suitable for: Programmers and trainee programmers.
Prerequisites: The basics of C programming.
Description: This course covers C++ and object-oriented programming through a variety of tutorials and exercises. Student workbook included.
Delivery method: CBT.
Minimum hardware requirement: PC.
Price: £350.00.
Source: Electrovision UK Ltd, Hamble Point Marina, School Lane, Hamble, Southampton SO31 4JD. Tel: 01703 452221

Title: **Teach Yourself C Language**
Purpose: To teach you how to write simple program.
Suitable for: Programmers and trainee programmers.
Prerequisites: None.

Description: An introductory level course that will enable students to write simple C programs. Student workbook included.
Delivery method: CBT.
Minimum hardware requirement: PC.
Price: £350.00.
Source: Electrovision UK Ltd, Hamble Point Marina, School Lane, Hamble, Southampton SO31 4JD. Tel: 01703 452221

COBOL

CBT

Title: **Teach Yourself COBOL**
Purpose: To teach you how to write a simple COBOL program.
Suitable for: Trainee programmers.
Prerequisites: None.
Description: An introductory course which will enable you to write simple COBOL programs. Student workbook supplied.
Delivery method: CBT.
Minimum hardware requirement: PC.
Price: £350.00.
Source: Electrovision UK Ltd, Hamble Point Marina, School Lane, Hamble, Southampton SO31 4JD. Tel: 01703 452221

GUI

CBT

Title: **GUI Design**
Purpose: To support software developers in producing quality user interfaces.
Suitable for: Software developers.
Prerequisites: None.
Description: This course covers: what a GUI is; design considerations; elements of the interface layout; manipulating the interface language; and popular components of GUI.
Delivery method: CBT.
Minimum hardware requirement: PC.
Price: £795.00.
Source: Electrovision UK Ltd, Hamble Point Marina, School Lane, Hamble, Southampton SO31 4JD. Tel: 01703 452221

Title: **GUI Design Essentials**
Purpose: To teach the design and implementation of a graphical user interface (GUI).

Suitable for: Programmers and trainee programmers.
Prerequisites: Knowledge of Windows.
Description: Students design and implement a GUI for a group of astronomers. The project involves the application of HCI to develop a new interface. A discussion follows of a variety of interaction techniques in GUI design. Strategies for successful testing and implementation are then examined.
Delivery method: CBT.
Minimum hardware requirement: PC with Windows.
Price: £1995.00.
Source: Electrovision UK Ltd, Hamble Point Marina, School Lane, Hamble, Southampton SO31 4JD. Tel: 01703 452221

Title: **GUI Standards for Windows 3.x**
Purpose: To support applications developers creating Windows-based applications.
Suitable for: Applications developers.
Prerequisites: Knowledge of Windows.
Description: This course covers: an introduction to GUI design; designing applications windows; providing menus; handling user information; common dialogue boxes; and creating OLE interface.
Delivery method: CBT.
Minimum hardware requirement: PC with Windows.
Price: £795.00.
Source: Electrovision UK Ltd, Hamble Point Marina, School Lane, Hamble, Southampton SO31 4JD. Tel: 01703 452221

Title: **GUI Testing Essentials**
Purpose: To demonstrate a structured approach to using industry standard methods to perform a unit test on a GUI-based business application.
Suitable for: Programmers and trainee programmers.
Prerequisites: Knowledge of Windows.
Description: This course includes: test plans; expected results; test data generation and documentation. Emphasis is given to the scope of test conditions and steps included in the unit test plan. The course is platform independent but uses a Windows-based mode.
Delivery method: CBT.
Minimum hardware requirement: PC.
Price: £1995.00.
Source: Electrovision UK Ltd, Hamble Point Marina, School Lane, Hamble, Southampton SO31 4JD. Tel: 01703 452221

IMS

CBT

Title: **IMS/DB Programming**
Purpose: To explain the basic structure of the IMS database and PL/1 commands.
Suitable for: Applications programmers.
Prerequisites: COBOL.
Description: This course is intended for applications programmers who already have COBOL skills and who want to learn to program in the IMS environment. Student manual supplied.
Delivery method: CBT.
Minimum hardware requirement: PC.
Price: £1995.00 (multiple copy price on application).
Source: Electrovision UK Ltd, Hamble Point Marina, School Lane, Hamble, Southampton SO31 4JD. Tel: 01703 452221

Title: **IMS/DC Programming**
Purpose: To explore the IMS data communications environment and applications programming.
Suitable for: Applications developers.
Prerequisites: None.
Description: This course is available for COBOL or PL/1. It is intended for those who will be developing applications to run under the IMS/DC teleprocessing monitor. Student manual accompanies the course.
Delivery method: CBT.
Minimum hardware requirement: PC.
Price: £1995.00 (multiple copy price on application).
Source: Electrovision UK Ltd, Hamble Point Marina, School Lane, Hamble, Southampton SO31 4JD. Tel: 01703 452221

Modelling

CBT

Title: **Develop Basic Data Models**
Purpose: To introduce the fundamentals of data modelling.
Suitable for: Anyone.
Prerequisites: None.
Description: This course introduces the fundamentals of data modelling using entity-relationship models. Key learning points are: identify entities; develop an entity-relationship diagram; normalise the data model; model advanced relationships; and mapping an entity-relationship diagram.
Delivery method: CBT; also available via the Internet.

Minimum hardware requirement: Any PC capable of running Microsoft Windows.
Price: On application.
Source: Oracle Corporation UK Ltd, The Oracle Centre, The Ring, Bracknell, Berks. RG12 1BW. Tel: 01344 860066

Title: **Develop Basic Function Models**
Purpose: To introduce the fundamentals of function modelling.
Suitable for: Anyone.
Prerequisites: 'Develop Basic Data Models'.
Description: This course provides an introduction to function modelling concepts and terminology using standard CASE* method notation. The course covers: defining functions; developing and refining function models; function data usages; cross-checking the models; and the variables that impact business functions.
Delivery method: CBT; also available via the Internet.
Minimum hardware requirement: Any PC capable of running Microsoft Windows.
Price: On application.
Source: Oracle Corporation UK Ltd, The Oracle Centre, The Ring, Bracknell, Berks. RG12 1BW. Tel: 01344 860066

MultiTasking

CBT
Title: **Design MultiTasking Win32 Applications**
Purpose: To teach design and implementation of a multithread application.
Suitable for: Programmers and trainee programmers.
Prerequisites: Knowledge of Windows.
Description: Teaches the design and implementation of multithreading application, incorporating understanding of potential situations for multithreading/processing. Core API calls, communication, termination and synchronisation are discussed. Includes an application of multithreading/processing to the design of client/server applications.
Delivery method: CBT.
Minimum hardware requirement: PC with Windows.
Price: £1995.00.
Source: Electrovision UK Ltd, Hamble Point Marina, School Lane, Hamble, Southampton SO31 4JD. Tel: 01703 452221

Object-oriented technology

CBT
Title: **Introduction to Object Oriented Technology**
Purpose: To provide an introduction to object oriented technology.

Suitable for: System developers.
Prerequisites: None.
Description: This course provides an introduction to the concepts, benefits and implications of object oriented technology. It also covers such fundamental concepts as encapsulation, abstract data types, inheritance and polymorphism.
Delivery method: CBT; also available via the Internet.
Minimum hardware requirement: Any PC capable of running Microsoft Windows.
Price: On application.
Source: Oracle Corporation UK Ltd, The Oracle Centre, The Ring, Bracknell, Berks. RG12 1BW. Tel: 01344 860066

Title: **Object Oriented Analysis**
Purpose: To provide an understanding of the principles of object oriented analysis.
Suitable for: System developers.
Prerequisites: None.
Description: This practical course covers the principles involved in the analysis phase of the object oriented life cycle and is supported by a workbook-based case study.
Delivery method: CBT; also available via the Internet.
Minimum hardware requirement: Any PC capable of running Microsoft Windows.
Price: On application.
Source: Oracle Corporation UK Ltd, The Oracle Centre, The Ring, Bracknell, Berks. RG12 1BW. Tel: 01344 860066

Title: **Object Oriented Analysis**
Purpose: To teach the concepts of object oriented analysis.
Suitable for: IS managers and programmers.
Prerequisites: None.
Description: This course uses Booch method of analysis. It teaches topics including: evolution and advantages; classes; encapsulation; functional decomposition; polymorphism; designing class hierarchies; relationship annotations; and even class member access.
Delivery method: CBT.
Minimum hardware requirement: PC.
Price: £1495.00.
Source: Electrovision UK Ltd, Hamble Point Marina, School Lane, Hamble, Southampton SO31 4JD. Tel: 01703 452221

Title: **Object Oriented Design**
Purpose: To provide an understanding of the principles of object oriented design.
Suitable for: System developers.
Prerequisites: 'Object Oriented Analysis'.
Description: This course naturally follows on from object oriented analysis by

reviewing the object-modelling technique. It achieves this by covering the following topics: the functional model; relationship among models; organisational support; and systems design.
Delivery method: CBT; also available via the Internet.
Minimum hardware requirement: Any PC capable of running Microsoft Windows.
Price: On application.
Source: Oracle Corporation UK Ltd, The Oracle Centre, The Ring, Bracknell, Berks. RG12 1BW. Tel: 01344 860066

Title: **Object Oriented Design**
Purpose: To teach object oriented design.
Suitable for: Designers and trainee designers.
Prerequisites: Familiar with C syntax.
Description: This course addresses: the object oriented approach; components of OOD; the process of OOD, including identifying objects and classes; semantics; relationships; and completing and evaluating the design. Development issues and project management are also included.
Delivery method: CBT.
Minimum hardware requirement: PC.
Price: £795.00.
Source: Electrovision UK Ltd, Hamble Point Marina, School Lane, Hamble, Southampton SO31 4JD. Tel: 01703 452221

Oracle

CBT

Title: **Customise Applications with Oracle Terminal**
Purpose: To teach you how to use Oracle Terminal to customise applications.
Suitable for: Applications developers.
Prerequisites: None.
Description: This course provides an understanding of how to use Oracle Terminal to customise your applications, as well as providing the knowledge and references needed to apply these concepts to any solution, and is an ideal introduction for applications developers and other technical support staff.
Delivery method: CBT; also available via the Internet.
Minimum hardware requirement: Any PC capable of running Microsoft Windows.
Price: On application.
Source: Oracle Corporation UK Ltd, The Oracle Centre, The Ring, Bracknell, Berks. RG12 1BW. Tel: 01344 860066

Title: **Designer/2000 Forms Design and Generation**
Purpose: To show you how to use Designer/2000 to design and generate a forms-based application.

Suitable for: Both analysts and designers.
Prerequisites: None.
Description: Using extensive software simulation and advanced graphics, you are directed through the essential design tasks, from creating an initial application design to generating complex form application code.
Delivery method: CBT; also available via the Internet.
Minimum hardware requirement: Any PC capable of running Microsoft Windows.
Price: On application.
Source: Oracle Corporation UK Ltd, The Oracle Centre, The Ring, Bracknell, Berks. RG12 1BW Tel: 01344 860066

Title: **Designer/2000 Model Business Systems**
Purpose: To show you how to use Designer/2000 to perform the complete analysis of a business.
Suitable for: Both analysts and designers.
Prerequisites: None.
Description: Using advanced graphics and extensive software simulation, you will be guided through the essential business of modelling to prototyping databases and generating application code.
Delivery method: CBT; also available via the Internet.
Minimum hardware requirement: Any PC capable of running Microsoft Windows.
Price: On application.
Source: Oracle Corporation UK Ltd, The Oracle Centre, The Ring, Bracknell, Berks. RG12 1BW. Tel: 01344 860066

Title: **Designer/2000 Server Design and Generation**
Purpose: To give full details of how to design a database with server-based application logic.
Suitable for: Both analysts and designers.
Prerequisites: None.
Description: This course covers the essential design tasks from creating an initial design to generating database objects.
Delivery method: CBT; also available via the Internet.
Minimum hardware requirement: Any PC capable of running Microsoft Windows.
Price: On application.
Source: Oracle Corporation UK Ltd, The Oracle Centre, The Ring, Bracknell, Berks. RG12 1BW. Tel: 01344 860066

Title: **Developer/2000: Enhancing Applications with Graphics**
Purpose: To provide an understanding of the graphic component of Oracle Developer/2000.
Suitable for: Anyone involved in the production of professional applications in a client/server environment.

DIRECTORY OF COURSES

Prerequisites: None.
Description: This course covers the graphics component of Oracle Development/ 2000, so that forms and reports can be enhanced with graphical displays.
Delivery method: CBT; also available via the Internet.
Minimum hardware requirement: Any PC capable of running Microsoft Windows.
Price: On application.
Source: Oracle Corporation UK Ltd, The Oracle Centre, The Ring, Bracknell, Berks. RG12 1BW. Tel: 01344 860066

Title: **Developer/2000: Introduction to Oracle Forms 4.5**
Purpose: To provide a comprehensive introduction to Oracle Forms 4.5.
Suitable for: Anyone involved in the production of professional applications in a client/server environment.
Prerequisites: None.
Description: This course provides a comprehensive introduction to Oracle Forms 4.5 for anyone involved in the production of professional applications in a client/server environment.
Delivery method: CBT; also available via the Internet.
Minimum hardware requirement: Any PC capable of running Microsoft Windows.
Price: On application.
Source: Oracle Corporation UK Ltd, The Oracle Centre, The Ring, Bracknell, Berks. RG12 1BW. Tel: 01344 860066

Title: **Developer/2000: MS Windows Extensions with Forms**
Purpose: To provide an understanding of how to reuse specific functionality that already exists in packaged window applications.
Suitable for: Application developers and designer/developers.
Prerequisites: Knowledge of Developer/2000.
Description: This course teaches the student quick and easy methods for adding functionality to Developer/2000 applications by reusing specific functionality that already exists in packaged window applications.
Delivery method: CBT; also available via the Internet.
Minimum hardware requirement: Any PC capable of running Microsoft Windows.
Price: On application.
Source: Oracle Corporation UK Ltd, The Oracle Centre, The Ring, Bracknell, Berks. RG12 1BW. Tel: 01344 860066

Title: **Developer/2000: Oracle Advanced Forms 4.5**
Purpose: To provide an in-depth understanding of the advanced features of Forms 4.5.
Suitable for: Anyone involved in the production of professional applications in a client/server environment.
Prerequisites: 'Developer/2000: Introduction to Oracle Forms 4.5'.

Description: This course allows an in-depth understanding of the advanced features of Oracle Forms 4.5, including: advanced enhancements; menu exploration; trigger processing; forms intervals; and preparing the final application.
Delivery method: CBT; also available via the Internet.
Minimum hardware requirement: Any PC capable of running Microsoft Windows.
Price: On application.
Source: Oracle Corporation UK Ltd, The Oracle Centre, The Ring, Bracknell, Berks. RG12 1BW. Tel: 01344 860066

Title: **Developer/2000: Using Oracle Procedure Builder**
Purpose: To provide the hands-on experience to develop, debug and manage PL/SQL programs for client/server applications.
Suitable for: Anyone involved in the production of professional applications in a client/server environment.
Prerequisites: None.
Description: Working in real-world business scenarios, this course will provide the hands-on experience to develop, debug and manage PL/SQL programs for client/server applications.
Delivery method: CBT; also available via the Internet.
Minimum hardware requirement: Any PC capable of running Microsoft Windows.
Price: On application.
Source: Oracle Corporation UK Ltd, The Oracle Centre, The Ring, Bracknell, Berks. RG12 1BW. Tel: 01344 860066

Title: **Developer/2000: Using Oracle Reports 2.5**
Purpose: To provide an understanding of Oracle Reports 2.5.
Suitable for: Anyone involved in the production of professional applications in a client/server environment.
Prerequisites: None.
Description: This course covers: creating a report; enhancing a report; and specifying the report.
Delivery method: CBT; also available via the Internet.
Minimum hardware requirement: Any PC capable of running Microsoft Windows.
Price: On application.
Source: Oracle Corporation UK Ltd, The Oracle Centre, The Ring, Bracknell, Berks. RG12 1BW. Tel: 01344 860066

Title: **Developing Applications with Oracle Power Objects**
Purpose: To teach you to create powerful applications in an easy and efficient way.
Suitable for: System developers.
Prerequisites: Existing Oracle skills.

Description: Using this course will teach you how to create powerful applications in an easy and efficient way. The main topics are: overview; creating a database application; master detail relationships; creating and using classes; and creating reports.
Delivery method: CBT; also available via the Internet.
Minimum hardware requirement: Any PC capable of running Microsoft Windows.
Price: On application.
Source: Oracle Corporation UK Ltd, The Oracle Centre, The Ring, Bracknell, Berks. RG12 1BW. Tel: 01344 860066

Title: **Introduction to Personal Oracle**
Purpose: To introduce you to the concepts of Personal Oracle.
Suitable for: System developers.
Prerequisites: Existing Oracle skills.
Description: This course focuses on Personal Oracle database administration and data access by concentrating on: how to install Personal Oracle; database/password manager; user and session manager; database expander; backup and recovery tools; importing and exporting tools; and SQI*Plus & SQL*DBA.
Delivery method: CBT; also available via the Internet.
Minimum hardware requirement: Any PC capable of running Microsoft Windows.
Price: On application.
Source: Oracle Corporation UK Ltd, The Oracle Centre, The Ring, Bracknell, Berks. RG12 1BW. Tel: 01344 860066

Title: **Oracle 7 – Server Programming**
Purpose: To provide skills in PL/SQL and advanced SQL.
Suitable for: Programmers and trainee programmers.
Prerequisites: None.
Description: This course covers: introduction to PL/SQL programming; programming in PL/SQL; using subprograms and packages; creating triggers; using cursors; managing transactions; and locking.
Delivery method: CBT.
Minimum hardware requirement: PC.
Price: £795.00.
Source: Electrovision UK Ltd, Hamble Point Marina, School Lane, Hamble, Southampton SO31 4JD. Tel: 01703 452221

Title: **Oracle Online Mentor: Building Forms with Developer/2000**
Purpose: To provide a blend of technical instruction, background information and hands-on experience.
Suitable for: Applications designers and developers.
Prerequisites: None.
Description: This course provides a blend of technical instruction, background

information, hands-on experience, and a comprehensive set of reference manuals.
Delivery method: CBT; also available via the Internet.
Minimum hardware requirement: Any PC capable of running Microsoft Windows.
Price: On application.
Source: Oracle Corporation UK Ltd, The Oracle Centre, The Ring, Bracknell, Berks. RG12 1BW. Tel: 01344 860066

Title: **Oracle Online Mentor: Building Reports with Developer/2000**
Purpose: To provide a blend of technical instruction, background information and hands-on experience.
Suitable for: Applications designers and developers.
Prerequisites: None.
Description: This course provides a blend of technical instruction, background information, hands-on experience and a comprehensive set of reference manuals.
Delivery method: CBT; also available via the Internet.
Minimum hardware requirement: Any PC capable of running Microsoft Windows.
Price: On application.
Source: Oracle Corporation UK Ltd, The Oracle Centre, The Ring, Bracknell, Berks. RG12 1BW. Tel: 01344 860066

Title: **Using Oracle Forms (V4.0)**
Purpose: To provide a comprehensive introduction to Oracle Forms (V4.0).
Suitable for: Applications developers.
Prerequisites: None.
Description: This course provides an introduction to this powerful and sophisticated application development tool that operates in many different GUI environments. The course covers: creating a form; enhancing an application; accessing multiple tables; and triggers and routines.
Delivery method: CBT; also available via the Internet.
Minimum hardware requirement: Any PC capable of running Microsoft Windows.
Price: On application.
Source: Oracle Corporation UK Ltd, The Oracle Centre, The Ring, Bracknell, Berks. RG12 1BW. Tel: 01344 860066

Pascal

CBT
Title: **Teach Yourself Pascal**
Purpose: To teach you how to write a simple Pascal program.
Suitable for: Trainee programmers.
Prerequisites: None.

Description: An introductory course which will enable you to write simple Pascal programs and be familiar with the concepts of Pascal programming. Student workbook supplied.
Delivery method: CBT.
Minimum hardware requirement: PC.
Price: £350.00.
Source: Electrovision UK Ltd, Hamble Point Marina, School Lane, Hamble, Southampton SO31 4JD. Tel: 01703 452221

PowerBuilder

CBT

Title: **Getting Started with PowerBuilder**
Purpose: To introduce you to the applications development process in PowerBuilder.
Suitable for: Trainee programmers.
Prerequisites: None.
Description: This course covers: introduction to PowerBuilder; building windows and menus; adding functionality to the application; and completing and delivering an application.
Delivery method: CBT.
Minimum hardware requirement: PC with Windows.
Price: £795.00.
Source: Electrovision UK Ltd, Hamble Point Marina, School Lane, Hamble, Southampton SO31 4JD. Tel: 01703 452221

Title: **PowerBuilder: Creating Business Reports**
Purpose: To teach you how to produce business reports from PowerBuilder.
Suitable for: Programmers and trainee programmers.
Prerequisites: Familiarity with PowerBuilder.
Description: New course. Please phone for course outline.
Delivery method: CBT.
Minimum hardware requirement: PC with Windows.
Price: £795.00.
Source: Electrovision UK Ltd, Hamble Point Marina, School Lane, Hamble, Southampton SO31 4JD. Tel: 01703 452221

Title: **PowerBuilder: Creating MDI Applications**
Purpose: To teach you how to produce a simple course in PowerBuilder.
Suitable for: Application developers.
Prerequisites: None.
Description: This course covers: introduction to MDI; creating a database and tables; working with data; building an MDI menu; building MDI sheets;

manipulating data using DataWindows; creating a custom MDI application. Course also includes user and administration guides.
Delivery method: CBT.
Minimum hardware requirement: PC with Windows.
Price: £795.00.
Source: Electrovision UK Ltd, Hamble Point Marina, School Lane, Hamble, Southampton SO31 4JD. Tel: 01703 452221

SQL

CBT
Title: **Integrate Applications with SQL*Menu**
Purpose: To provide an introduction to SQL*Menu.
Suitable for: Applications developers.
Prerequisites: None.
Description: This course provides an introduction to SQL*Menu and covers: security; creating a menu; modifying a menu; and defining a default menu.
Delivery method: CBT; also available via the Internet.
Minimum hardware requirement: Any PC capable of running Microsoft Windows.
Price: On application.
Source: Oracle Corporation UK Ltd, The Oracle Centre, The Ring, Bracknell, Berks. RG12 1BW. Tel: 01344 860066

Title: **Using SQL*Forms (V3.0) I**
Purpose: To teach the essential skills needed to develop applications.
Suitable for: Applications developers.
Prerequisites: None.
Description: This course teaches the essential skills needed to develop applications using SQL*Forms (V3.0). It shows how triggers and packaged procedures are used to add to a form's power and versatility. Key learning points are: navigation in SQL*Forms; creating new forms; triggers for business functions; modifying existing forms; and writing the procedures to document forms.
Delivery method: CBT; also available via the Internet.
Minimum hardware requirement: Any PC capable of running Microsoft Windows.
Price: On application.
Source: Oracle Corporation UK Ltd, The Oracle Centre, The Ring, Bracknell, Berks. RG12 1BW. Tel: 01344 860066

Title: **Using SQL*Forms (V3.0) II**
Purpose: To teach you how to build complex applications.
Suitable for: Applications developers.
Prerequisites: 'Using SQL*Forms (V3.0) I'.

Description: This course builds upon the skills learnt in module I. It deals with: global variables; systems triggers; and multi-level forms. The key learning points are: create system variables; commit data through a join view; writing query triggers; maintaining totals; and controlling data transactions between forms.
Delivery method: CBT; also available via the Internet.
Minimum hardware requirement: Any PC capable of running Microsoft Windows.
Price: On application.
Source: Oracle Corporation UK Ltd, The Oracle Centre, The Ring, Bracknell, Berks. RG12 1BW. Tel: 01344 860066

Sybase

CBT

Title: **Sybase System 10 – Server Programming**
Purpose: To provide an introduction to server programming.
Suitable for: Programmers.
Prerequisites: None.
Description: This course covers: an introduction to server programming; organising code into batches; writing stored procedures; writing triggers; managing transactions and locking; row by row; processing with cursors. Also contains a T-SQL quick reference guide.
Delivery method: CBT.
Minimum hardware requirement: PC.
Price: £795.00.
Source: Electrovision UK Ltd, Hamble Point Marina, School Lane, Hamble, Southampton SO31 4JD. Tel: 01703 452221

Computer skills

General

CBT

Title: **Computing for the Terrified**
Purpose: To give all those with a fear of computers or who have had no experience with computers, a clear grasp of how the personal computer (PC) works and introduce some computer jargon.
Suitable for: Anyone.
Prerequisites: None.
Description: This is an introductory course which will enable you to: identify different types of computers; know how to use the keyboard; be conversant

with computer terminology; know what word-processing, database and spreadsheet software are.
Delivery method: CBT and supporting text.
Minimum hardware requirement: IBM PC or compatible, 512k RAM.
Price: £165.00.
Source: Ivy Business Training Software plc, Ivy House, 233–235 Roehampton Lane, London SW15 4LB. Tel: 0181 780 1494

Title: **Do You Know Information Technology?**
Purpose: Is to act as a training needs analysis which will be an aid to both learning and revision.
Suitable for: Anyone.
Prerequisites: A broad knowledge of information technology.
Description: A self-assessment tool consisting of about 300 multiple-choice questions that will help you to develop your knowledge through repeated practice on questions covering all areas of the subject.
Delivery method: CBT and supporting text.
Minimum hardware requirement: IBM PC or compatible, 512k RAM.
Price: £165.00.
Source: Ivy Business Training Software plc, Ivy House, 233–235 Roehampton Lane, London SW15 4LB. Tel: 0181 780 1494

Title: **InfoCheck**
Purpose: Performance-based skills assessment software to measure PC users' knowledge.
Suitable for: Use in the professional, corporate or academic sectors.
Prerequisites: None.
Description: Skills assessment software that can be used to determine skill levels and prescribe training based on test results. As a post-training tool, InfoCheck provides information that your training programme is effective. InfoCheck is available for MS Office, MS Professional and Lotus 1-2-3 software applications.
Delivery method: CBT.
Minimum hardware requirement: PC; 4MB RAM.
Price: Software shell £250.00. Testing sessions from £1.50 per test.
Source: InfoSource International, InfoSource House, 54 Marston Street, Oxford OX4 1JU. Tel: 0800 318923

Title: **PC Skills**
Purpose: To provide training and validation of skills learned in the area of office automation packages (Word-Processing, Spreadsheet, Presentation Manager, Data Base) in WIN 95, WIN 3.1, DOS and Macintosh platforms.
Suitable for: School age to adult, personal or business usage.
Prerequisites: None.

Description: These tutorials feature 'Learn, Practice and Skills Check' modes as well as a 'What's New?' feature which facilitates the upgrading of skills to the most current version. Dynamic graphics and interesting story lines keep the students' attention.
Delivery method: CBT.
Minimum hardware requirement: 386 PC; 10Mb hard disk, 2Mb RAM.
Price: £195–£495.00.
Source: QWIZ (UK) Ltd, QWIZ House, 219a Hatfield Road, St. Albans, Hertfordshire AL1 4SY. Tel: 01727 868600

Title: **Professor PC**
Purpose: To give an introduction to personal computers. Includes a free typing tutor.
Suitable for: Anyone.
Prerequisites: None.
Description: This course covers computer terminology, operating systems (DOS), environments (Windows) and the keyboard. It also shows common software types, e.g. word-processors, spreadsheets, and databases, without using a specific application.
Delivery method: CBT.
Minimum hardware requirement: PC.
Price: £49.95 (multiple copy price on application).
Source: Electrovision UK Ltd, Hamble Point Marina, School Lane, Hamble, Southampton SO31 4JD. Tel: 01703 452221

Title: **Seminar-On-A-Disk**
Purpose: A fully interactive, disk-based tutorial, blending colourful, effective lessons with a simulation of the application.
Suitable for: Anyone.
Prerequisites: None.
Description: Self-paced CBT providing lessons, quizzes and quiz summaries, a glossary and an index for all major PC applications, including those comprising MS Office, Professional and Lotus applications.
Delivery method: CBT.
Minimum hardware requirement: PC hard disk; 4MB RAM.
Price: £150.00 (bulk and bundle prices available on request).
Source: InfoSource International, InfoSource House, 54 Marston Street, Oxford OX4 1JU. Tel: 0800 318923

CD-ROM
Title: **How to Make Computers Work for You**
Purpose: To give an all-round introduction to PCs for beginners.
Suitable for: Anyone.

Prerequisites: None.
Description: This course covers all aspects of the PC including hardware, software, applications, Windows, DOS. It uses random quizzes and a comprehensive case study.
Delivery method: CD-ROM.
Minimum hardware requirement: 486 PC; 8Mb RAM; CD-ROM drive; sound card.
Price: £49.95.
Source: Electrovision UK Ltd, Hamble Point Marina, School Lane, Hamble, Southampton SO31 4JD. Tel: 01703 452221

Title: **How to Make Computers Work for You**
Purpose: This course goes back to basics to help people who have absolutely no knowledge of computers.
Suitable for: Everyone.
Prerequisites: None.
Description: This course is specifically designed to teach the novice about the fundamentals of personal computing. The key training messages being: simple explanations of key concepts (e.g. hardware, software, communications); detailed examinations of spreadsheets, word-processing, desk top publishing and databases.
Delivery method: CD-ROM.
Minimum hardware requirement: 486 PC, 8Mb RAM, 420Mb hard disk, CD-ROM drive, audio card.
Price: £499.00.
Source: Training Direct, North Court, Edinburgh Gate, Harlow, Essex, CM20 2JE. Tel: 01279 623927

Title: **Information Technology**
Purpose: To teach and support a complete introductory information technology course.
Suitable for: All business (or modular) students from HND level upwards.
Prerequisites: None.
Description: Covers: introduction to business IT; introduction to computer systems; the CPU; secondary storage devices and media; peripherals; operating systems and systems software; data storage and management; databases and database modelling; information systems and the organisation; data; communications; distributed systems and networks; the automated office and HCI.
Delivery method: CD-ROM.
Minimum hardware requirement: PC; 8Mb RAM; CD-ROM drive and sound card.
Price: £29.95 (inc. VAT) single-user licence; multi-user licences from £650.00.
Source: Pitman Publishing, 128 Long Acre, London, WC2E 9AN. Tel: 0171 4472290

DIRECTORY OF COURSES

Title: **Seminar-On-A-Disk: Multimedia Edition**
Purpose: A fully interactive, CD-ROM-based tutorial, blending colourful, effective lessons with audio and video in an environment that simulates the application.
Suitable for: Anyone.
Prerequisites: None.
Description: For MS Office, Professional and Upgrading to Windows 95, a self-paced computer-based CD-ROM training package for individual titles. Features include: 'Tip TV'; useful time-saving video tips; also provided are quizzes, a multimedia library and over 900 audio clips – all to reinforce the learning process. An optional tracker module documenting usage can be provided.
Delivery method: CD-ROM.
Minimum hardware requirement: 386PC; 4MB RAM; CD-ROM; sound card.
Price: £299.00 (discounts for bulk purchases; call for details).
Source: InfoSource International, InfoSource House, 54 Marston Street, Oxford OX4 1JU. Tel: 0800 318923

Interactive video
Title: **Using PCs for Windows**
Purpose: To introduce the use of IBM and compatible computers emphasising the practical uses of PCs.
Suitable for: Anyone.
Prerequisites: None.
Description: This course uses actual business examples throughout and gives plenty of practice using various applications through simulations.
Delivery method: Interactive video.
Minimum hardware requirement: Interactive video workstation.
Price: £2300.00.
Source: Training Direct, North Court, Edinburgh Gate, Harlow, Essex, CM20 2JE. Tel: 01279 623927

Corel

CBT
Title: **Perception of Corel Draw v4**
Purpose: To provide instruction on how to use Corel Draw v4.
Suitable for: Anyone.
Prerequisites: None.
Description: This course, which is suitable for novice to intermediate level users, uses realistic simulations to provide the instruction. The course includes drop-down menus, on-line search, on-line glossary and a very substantial manual.
Delivery method: CBT.
Minimum hardware requirement: PC.

Price: £119.00 (multiple copy price on application).
Source: Electrovision UK Ltd, Hamble Point Marina, School Lane, Hamble, Southampton SO31 4JD. Tel: 01703 452221

DOS

CBT

Title: **Perception Lite for MS DOS v6.2**
Purpose: To provide a very comprehensive training perception for MS DOS.
Suitable for: Anyone.
Prerequisites: None.
Description: This course covers new features, computer processes, input devices, RAM and ROM memory types and uses, shell, directories, and files and programmes.
Delivery method: CBT.
Minimum hardware requirement: PC.
Price: £75.00 (multiple copy price on application).
Source: Electrovision UK Ltd, Hamble Point Marina, School Lane, Hamble, Southampton SO31 4JD. Tel: 01703 452221

Title: **Perception of DOS v6.2**
Purpose: To provide a very comprehensive training perception for DOS.
Suitable for: Anyone.
Prerequisites: None.
Description: This course covers all the different kinds of memory including RAM and ROM, storing data, file types, directories, back-up, handling drives, SMARTDrive, Macros, and batch files.
Delivery method: CBT.
Minimum hardware requirement: PC.
Price: £119.00 (multiple copy price on application).
Source: Electrovision UK Ltd, Hamble Point Marina, School Lane, Hamble, Southampton SO31 4JD. Tel: 01703 452221

Title: **Professor DOS v6.2**
Purpose: To give comprehensive lessons on DOS and Smartguide to DOS.
Suitable for: Anyone.
Prerequisites: None.
Description: This course teaches: DOS commands; an understanding and use of the hard disk and shell; how to create batch files; how to customise the system; and how to use the tools available. Advanced lessons include using DOS on a network.
Delivery method: CBT.
Minimum hardware requirement: PC.

DIRECTORY OF COURSES

Price: £49.95 (multiple copy price on application).
Source: Electrovision UK Ltd, Hamble Point Marina, School Lane, Hamble, Southampton SO31 4JD. Tel: 01703 452221

Title: **Teach Yourself DOS v6.2**
Purpose: To guide you through the basis of DOS and file management.
Suitable for: Anyone.
Prerequisites: None.
Description: This course assumes no prior knowledge of DOS. Using simulation techniques, you are guided through the basics and some more advanced features of DOS.
Delivery method: CBT.
Minimum hardware requirement: PC.
Price: £75.00 (multiple copy price on application).
Source: Electrovision UK Ltd, Hamble Point Marina, School Lane, Hamble, Southampton SO31 4JD. Tel: 01703 452221

Title: **Understanding DOS v6.2**
Purpose: To provide a very comprehensive DOS tutorial, with some more advanced subjects.
Suitable for: Anyone.
Prerequisites: None.
Description: This course covers: DOS basics; directories and their management; files and file management; DOS shell; DOS utilities; virus checking; and error messages.
Delivery method: CBT.
Minimum hardware requirement: PC.
Price: £45.00 (multiple copy price on application).
Source: Electrovision UK Ltd, Hamble Point Marina, School Lane, Hamble, Southampton SO31 4JD. Tel: 01703 452221

E-mail

CBT

Title: **Lotus Notes for End Users**
Purpose: To teach organisational users how to create and maintain documents and mail in Notes.
Suitable for: Anyone.
Prerequisites: None.
Description: This course covers the basics of using Lotus Notes v3.30 and includes: managing workspace; views; create and work with documents; mail memos; file handling; address book and dial-up notes.
Delivery method: CBT.

Minimum hardware requirement: PC with Windows.
Price: £795.00.
Source: Electrovision UK Ltd, Hamble Point Marina, School Lane, Hamble, Southampton SO31 4JD. Tel: 01703 452221

Title: **Perception Lite for cc:Mail (Network)**
Purpose: To teach how to use cc:Mail (Network).
Suitable for: Anyone.
Prerequisites: None.
Description: This course uses glossaries, quizzes and quick search to help teach topics including Inbox and Post Office, mailing lists, archives, container and contents pages, message priority, forwarding and replying, message log, and bulletin boards.
Delivery method: CBT.
Minimum hardware requirement: PC.
Price: £395.00.
Source: Electrovision UK Ltd, Hamble Point Marina, School Lane, Hamble, Southampton SO31 4JD. Tel: 01703 452221

Title: **Perception Lite for Exchange (Office95)**
Purpose: To teach the use of Exchange (Office95).
Suitable for: Anyone.
Prerequisites: None.
Description: This course, which is suitable for both novice and intermediate users, covers: managing your messages; attaching objects; folders; address book; setting options; and storing messages.
Delivery method: CBT.
Minimum hardware requirement: PC with Windows 95.
Price: £75.00 (multiple copy price on application).
Source: Electrovision UK Ltd, Hamble Point Marina, School Lane, Hamble, Southampton SO31 4JD. Tel: 01703 452221

Title: **Perception Lite for Lotus Notes v3**
Purpose: To teach how to use Lotus Notes v3.
Suitable for: Anyone.
Prerequisites: None.
Description: This course uses: glossaries; quizzes and quick search to help teach topics, including Smart icons; NOTES Mail; delivery priorities; handling memos and documents; accessing NOTES database and workstations; search commands.
Delivery method: CBT.
Minimum hardware requirement: PC.
Price: £75.00 (multiple copy price on application).

DIRECTORY OF COURSES

Source: Electrovision UK Ltd, Hamble Point Marina, School Lane, Hamble, Southampton SO31 4JD. Tel: 01703 452221

Title: **Perception Lite for Mail/Schedule+**
Purpose: To teach the use of Mail/Schedule+.
Suitable for: Anyone.
Prerequisites: None.
Description: This course, which is suitable for both novice and intermediate users, covers: managing your messages; attaching objects; folders; address book; setting options; storing messages; working with appointments; project and task lists.
Delivery method: CBT.
Minimum hardware requirement: PC.
Price: £75.00 (multiple copy price on application).
Source: Electrovision UK Ltd, Hamble Point Marina, School Lane, Hamble, Southampton SO31 4JD. Tel: 01703 452221

Title: **Teach Yourself cc:Mail v2/Windows**
Purpose: To give a comprehensive coverage of cc:Mail.
Suitable for: Anyone.
Prerequisites: None.
Description: This course covers a range of topics including: logging in; processing incoming mail; sorting mail; sending mail; creating mailing lists and more.
Delivery method: CBT.
Minimum hardware requirement: PC with Windows.
Price: £395.00.
Source: Electrovision UK Ltd, Hamble Point Marina, School Lane, Hamble, Southampton SO31 4JD. Tel: 01703 452221

Title: **Teach Yourself Lotus Notes v3/Win**
Purpose: To teach how to use Lotus Notes v3/Win.
Suitable for: Anyone.
Prerequisites: None.
Description: This course uses drop-down menus, modular design, glossary, and quick search to facilitate learning. The topics covered include: Notes basics; using Notes mail; using Notes database; printing documents; customising Notes; managing documents; tables and Doclinks.
Delivery method: CBT.
Minimum hardware requirement: PC with Windows.
Price: £75.00 (multiple copy price on application).
Source: Electrovision UK Ltd, Hamble Point Marina, School Lane, Hamble, Southampton SO31 4JD. Tel: 01703 452221

Title: **Teach Yourself Mail/Schedule+**
Purpose: To teach how to use Mail/Schedule+.
Suitable for: Anyone.
Prerequisites: None.
Description: This course, suitable for novices and intermediate level, covers: Mail, including composing and sending messages, managing messages, objects, folders, and address book; and Schedule, including appointments, tasks and projects, and group scheduling.
Delivery method: CBT.
Minimum hardware requirement: PC with Windows.
Price: £75.00 (multiple copy price on application).
Source: Electrovision UK Ltd, Hamble Point Marina, School Lane, Hamble, Southampton SO31 4JD. Tel: 01703 452221

Title: **Training for cc:Mail v2**
Purpose: To train in the use of cc:Mail v2.
Suitable for: Anyone.
Prerequisites: None.
Description: This course, in addition to showing editing text, attaching messages, reading and organising mail, and searching and printing, also teaches Windows skills and cc:Mail basics.
Delivery method: CBT.
Minimum hardware requirement: PC with Windows.
Price: £79.95 (multiple copy price on application).
Source: Electrovision UK Ltd, Hamble Point Marina, School Lane, Hamble, Southampton SO31 4JD. Tel: 01703 452221

Title: **Training for Mail/Schedule+**
Purpose: To teach how to use Mail/Schedule+.
Suitable for: Anyone.
Prerequisites: None.
Description: The topics of this course include sending and receiving mail, attaching files to records, appointments management, planner and task list. The course also has a self-test disk.
Delivery method: CBT.
Minimum hardware requirement: PC with Windows.
Price: £79.95 (multiple copy price on application).
Source: Electrovision UK Ltd, Hamble Point Marina, School Lane, Hamble, Southampton SO31 4JD. Tel: 01703 452221

Title: **Understanding cc:Mail**
Purpose: To teach how to use cc:Mail.
Suitable for: Anyone.

Prerequisites: None.
Description: This course uses glossaries, quizzes and quick search to help teach topics including: Windows basics; sending; receiving; opening mail; attachments; editing text and attaching messages; reading and organising mail; searching and printing.
Delivery method: CBT.
Minimum hardware requirement: PC.
Price: £75.00 (multiple copy price on application).
Source: Electrovision UK Ltd, Hamble Point Marina, School Lane, Hamble, Southampton SO31 4JD. Tel: 01703 452221

Title: **Understanding Mail/Schedule+**
Purpose: To teach how to use Mail/Schedule+.
Suitable for: Anyone.
Prerequisites: None.
Description: This course uses true-to-life screens, summaries and quizzes to teach this topic from introduction to intermediate level. Mail topics include: sending; receiving; opening mail; attaching files to records; passwords; folders; creating personal groups. Schedule topics include: appointment management; using the planner; using task lists.
Delivery method: CBT.
Minimum hardware requirement: PC with Windows 95.
Price: £75.00 (multiple copy price on application).
Source: Electrovision UK Ltd, Hamble Point Marina, School Lane, Hamble, Southampton SO31 4JD. Tel: 01703 452221

CD-ROM
Title: **Discoverware Win 3.11 and Mail/Schedule+**
Purpose: To teach you Windows 3.11 and MS Mail/Schedule.
Suitable for: Anyone.
Prerequisites: None.
Description: This course, suitable for novice or intermediate users, gives instruction, and then lets you try it out using simulation. The course covers Windows overview, menus, dialogue boxes, applications basics, network group and MSMail/Schedule.
Delivery method: CD-ROM.
Minimum hardware requirement: PC; 8Mb RAM; CD-ROM drive; sound card.
Price: £99.00 (multiple copy price on application).
Source: Comput-Ed Ltd, Long Lane, Dawlish EX7 0QR. Tel: 01626 889955

Freelance

CBT

Title: **Perception Lite for Freelance (Win)**
Purpose: To teach the basics and more advanced topics of Freelance (Win).
Suitable for: Anyone.
Prerequisites: None.
Description: This course, which is suitable for novice to intermediate-level users, covers topics which include: basics of presentation; backgrounds; layouts; adding text; bullets; alignment styles; tables; organisation charts; data-driven charts; and advanced topics.
Delivery method: CBT.
Minimum hardware requirement: PC with Windows.
Price: £75.00 (multiple copy price on application).
Source: Electrovision UK Ltd, Hamble Point Marina, School Lane, Hamble, Southampton SO31 4JD. Tel: 01703 452221

Title: **Teach Yourself Freelance v2/Win**
Purpose: To teach how to use Freelance v2/Win.
Suitable for: Anyone.
Prerequisites: None.
Description: This course instructs using simulation of the actual software and contains topics including: creating quick charts; diagrams; planning a presentation; importing data; text charts; illustrations; and screen shows.
Delivery method: CBT.
Minimum hardware requirement: PC with Windows.
Price: £75.00 (multiple copy price on application).
Source: Electrovision UK Ltd, Hamble Point Marina, School Lane, Hamble, Southampton SO31 4JD. Tel: 01703 452221

Title: **Training for Freelance v2**
Purpose: To teach how to use Freelance v2.
Suitable for: Anyone.
Prerequisites: None.
Description: This course teaches all Freelance basics and shows you how to work on pages and with charts, and how to draw and edit objects, use the outliner and screen shows. The pack contains an additional self-test disk.
Delivery method: CBT.
Minimum hardware requirement: PC with Windows.
Price: £79.95 (multiple copy price on application).
Source: Electrovision UK Ltd, Hamble Point Marina, School Lane, Hamble, Southampton SO31 4JD. Tel: 01703 452221

Title: **Understanding Freelance v2**
Purpose: To teach how to use Freelance v2.
Suitable for: Anyone.
Prerequisites: None.
Description: This course, which includes on-line glossary, index, summaries and quizzes, contains topics including: Windows environment; creating a presentation; screen show, working with pages; object attributes; charts; drawing tools; symbols; printing; outliner; automatic build pages; and Smartmaster.
Delivery method: CBT.
Minimum hardware requirement: PC.
Price: £75.00 (multiple copy price on application).
Source: Electrovision UK Ltd, Hamble Point Marina, School Lane, Hamble, Southampton SO31 4JD. Tel: 01703 452221

CD-ROM
Title: **Discoverware Freelance v2/Win**
Purpose: To teach how to use Freelance v2/Win.
Suitable for: Anyone.
Prerequisites: None.
Description: This multimedia training course uses video, shows you how to do something, and then lets you try, using simulation exercises. Includes random quizzes.
Delivery method: CD-ROM.
Minimum hardware requirement: PC; 8Mb RAM; CD-ROM drive; sound card.
Price: £99.00.
Source: Comput-Ed Ltd, Long Lane, Dawlish EX7 0QR. Tel: 01626 889955

Lotus

CBT
Title: **Lotus Notes – Advanced Application Development**
Purpose: To teach the advanced aspects of building effective applications in Lotus Notes.
Suitable for: Anyone.
Prerequisites: 'Lotus Notes – Application Development'.
Description: This new course covers the advanced aspects of building applications in Lotus Notes. Please phone for course outline.
Delivery method: CBT.
Minimum hardware requirement: PC with Windows.
Price: £795.00.
Source: Electrovision UK Ltd, Hamble Point Marina, School Lane, Hamble, Southampton SO31 4JD. Tel: 01703 452221

Title: **Lotus Notes – Application Development**
Purpose: To teach the fundamentals of building effective applications in Lotus Notes.
Suitable for: Anyone.
Prerequisites: None.
Description: This course includes topics on differentiating between five types of Lotus Notes applications, using templates to build, create forms, field views, access control lists, design basic formulas including macros, and design help for the applications.
Delivery method: CBT.
Minimum hardware requirement: PC with Windows.
Price: £795.00.
Source: Electrovision UK Ltd, Hamble Point Marina, School Lane, Hamble, Southampton SO31 4JD. Tel: 01703 452221

Title: **Lotus Smartsuite**
Purpose: To teach the use of Lotus 1-2-3, AmiPro, Freelance, Approach and Organiser.
Suitable for: Everyone.
Prerequisites: None.
Description: This course can be used for classroom or distance learning.
Delivery method: CBT.
Minimum hardware requirement: 486 PC.
Price: £395.00.
Source: Intelligent Training Solutions, 29 Narrow Street, London E14 8DP. Tel: 0171 791 3000

Title: **Training for Smartsuite**
Purpose: To teach the use of Smartsuite.
Suitable for: Anyone.
Prerequisites: None.
Description: This pack includes training for Lotus v4, AmiPro v3, Approach, Freelance and cc:Mail. It also includes a self-test disk. Please see entries under 'Training for . . .' for further details on each of the components.
Delivery method: CBT.
Minimum hardware requirement: PC with Windows.
Price: £249.00 (multiple copy price on application).
Source: Electrovision UK Ltd, Hamble Point Marina, School Lane, Hamble, Southampton SO31 4JD. Tel: 01703 452221

Office

CBT

Title: **Microsoft Office**
Purpose: To teach the use of Word, Excel, Powerpoint, Access, Mail and Schedule.
Suitable for: Everyone.
Prerequisites: None.
Description: This course can be used for classroom or distance learning.
Delivery method: CBT.
Minimum hardware requirement: 486 PC.
Price: £395.00.
Source: Intelligent Training Solutions, 29 Narrow Street, London E14 8DP. Tel: 0171 791 3000

Title: **TutorPro for Microsoft Office**
Purpose: To teach the Microsoft Office suite of applications.
Suitable for: Anyone.
Prerequisites: None.
Description: TutorPro tutorials encourage you to learn by doing, using a friendly and humorous hands-on approach to help you understand and retain the material. Tutorpro provides a comprehensive simulation of the actual application. This means that you can learn without having access to the live application.
Delivery method: CBT.
Minimum hardware requirement: PC; 4Mb RAM; 12Mb hard disk.
Price: £225.00.
Source: Pan European Courseware Ltd, The Old Vicarage, Bishopswood, Chard, Somerset TA20 3RS. Tel: 01460 234232/234644

Title: **TutorPro for Word, Excel, PowerPoint, Mail/Schedule and Exchange**
Purpose: To teach a user of any of these applications how to use the many functions available to get the most benefit from the software.
Suitable for: Anyone.
Prerequisites: None.
Description: TutorPro tutorials encourage you to learn by doing, using a friendly and humorous hands-on approach to help you understand and retain the material. TutorPro provides a comprehensive simulation of the actual application. This means that you can learn without having access to the live application.
Delivery method: CBT.
Minimum hardware requirement: PC, 4MB RAM, 12MB hard disk.
Price: £79.00 per module for a single user.

Source: Pan European Courseware Ltd, The Old Vicarage, Bishopswood, Chard, Somerset TA20 3RS. Tel: 01460 234232/234644

CD-ROM
Title: **Discover Office 95**
Purpose: To provide training in Office 95.
Suitable for: Anyone.
Prerequisites: None.
Description: Covers an introduction to Office 95, helping you work, document management, new in Word, new in Excel, new in Powerpoint, new in Access, Schedule+ and putting it all together.
Delivery method: CD-ROM.
Minimum hardware requirement: 486 PC; 8Mb RAM; 8Mb disk space; CD-ROM drive; sound card.
Price: £99.00.
Source: Comput-Ed Ltd, Long Lane, Dawlish EX7 0QR. Tel: 01626 889955

Oracle

CBT
Title: **Navigate Oracle Applications (GUI)**
Purpose: To provide a basic understanding of the GUI and architecture of Oracle's SmartClient applications.
Suitable for: Anyone implementing, customising or using an Oracle Release 10SC application.
Prerequisites: None.
Description: This course will enable you to become familiar with the GUI and architecture of Oracle's SmartClient applications. The main concepts covered include: navigation through Oracle SmartClient applications; searching for data; tailoring data presentation; creating reports and programs; working with attachments; and description of the transition from character mode to Release 10SC.
Delivery method: CBT also available via the Internet.
Minimum hardware requirement: Any PC capable of running Microsoft Windows.
Price: On application.
Source: Oracle Corporation UK Ltd, The Oracle Centre, The Ring, Bracknell, Berks. RG12 1BW. Tel: 01344 860066

Title: **Using Oracle Office 2.1**
Purpose: To introduce the power and functionality of Oracle Office 2.1.
Suitable for: Anyone.
Prerequisites: None.
Description: This course will improve your time management skills and stream-

line your business communications through the use of Oracle's Office graphical environment. The course covers: access and navigation; sending and receiving a message; managing templates; storing messages; using a personal calendar; using a scheduler; using the remote access function; and customising.
Delivery method: CBT also available via the Internet.
Minimum hardware requirement: Any PC capable of running Microsoft Windows.
Price: On application.
Source: Oracle Corporation UK Ltd, The Oracle Centre, The Ring, Bracknell, Berks. RG12 1BW. Tel: 01344 860066

Organiser

CBT
Title: **Understanding Organiser**
Purpose: To teach you how to use Organiser.
Suitable for: Anyone.
Prerequisites: None.
Description: This course, which is suitable for novice to intermediate level, covers topics including: introduction to Windows; organiser screen; notebook; diary; planner; task management; appointments; navigation; reminders and much more.
Delivery method: CBT.
Minimum hardware requirement: PC with Windows.
Price: £75.00 (multiple copy price on application).
Source: Electrovision UK Ltd, Hamble Point Marina, School Lane, Hamble, Southampton SO31 4JD. Tel: 01703 452221

OS/2

CBT
Title: **Teach Yourself OS/2 v2.1**
Purpose: To teach the OS/2 environment and the additional features of v2.1.
Suitable for: Anyone.
Prerequisites: None.
Description: This course instructs by a simulation method and covers disk, file and directory management, and multitasking within OS/2.
Delivery method: CBT.
Minimum hardware requirement: PC with Windows or OS/2.
Price: £49.95 (multiple copy price on application).
Source: Electrovision UK Ltd, Hamble Point Marina, School Lane, Hamble, Southampton SO31 4JD. Tel: 01703 452221

THE DIRECTORY

Title: **Understanding OS/2 v2**
Purpose: To comprehensively teach the OS/2 environment.
Suitable for: Anyone.
Prerequisites: None.
Description: This course covers: the OS/2 environment; Windows management; objects drives folder; trees and paths; printing, work area folders and security; another command; shadows; program file association; command prompt; customising the desktop and more.
Delivery method: CBT.
Minimum hardware requirement: PC with Windows or OS/2.
Price: £75.00 (multiple copy price on application).
Source: Electrovision UK Ltd, Hamble Point Marina, School Lane, Hamble, Southampton SO31 4JD. Tel: 01703 452221

Powerpoint

CBT

Title: **Perception Lite for Powerpoint v4**
Purpose: To give a concise view of Powerpoint v4.
Suitable for: Anyone.
Prerequisites: None.
Description: This course is for novice to intermediate-user level. The topics include creating, editing, formatting a presentation, colour schemes, slides, handouts, masters, graphs, charts and tables, and running a presentation.
Delivery method: CBT.
Minimum hardware requirement: PC with Windows.
Price: £75.00 (multiple copy price on application).
Source: Electrovision UK Ltd, Hamble Point Marina, School Lane, Hamble, Southampton SO31 4JD. Tel: 01703 452221

Title: **Perception of Powerpoint v4**
Purpose: To teach the use of Powerpoint v4.
Suitable for: Anyone.
Prerequisites: None.
Description: This course includes topics covering: creating presentations; different views; formatting; colour schemes; slides masters; handouts; datasheet operations and much more.
Delivery method: CBT.
Minimum hardware requirement: PC with Windows.
Price: £119.00 (multiple copy price on application).
Source: Electrovision UK Ltd, Hamble Point Marina, School Lane, Hamble, Southampton SO31 4JD. Tel: 01703 452221

DIRECTORY OF COURSES

Title: **Perception of Powerpoint7 (Office95)**
Purpose: To teach the use of Powerpoint7 (Office95).
Suitable for: Anyone.
Prerequisites: None.
Description: This course includes topics covering: creating presentations; different views; formatting; colour schemes; slides masters; handouts; datasheet operations and much more.
Delivery method: CBT.
Minimum hardware requirement: PC with Windows 95.
Price: £119.00 (multiple copy price on application).
Source: Electrovision UK Ltd, Hamble Point Marina, School Lane, Hamble, Southampton SO31 4JD. Tel: 01703 452221

Title: **Teach Yourself Powerpoint v4/Win**
Purpose: To teach the use of Powerpoint v4/Win from introduction to strong intermediate-level users.
Suitable for: Anyone.
Prerequisites: None.
Description: This course covers topics including: the Powerpoint screen; opening and creating presentations; different views; text formatting; colour schemes; slide management and more.
Delivery method: CBT.
Minimum hardware requirement: PC with Windows.
Price: £75.00 (multiple copy price on application).
Source: Electrovision UK Ltd, Hamble Point Marina, School Lane, Hamble, Southampton SO31 4JD. Tel: 01703 452221

Title: **Training for Powerpoint v4**
Purpose: To teach the use of Powerpoint v4.
Suitable for: Anyone.
Prerequisites: None.
Description: This course covers topics including: a tour of the screen; slides and presentations; editing; wizards; templates; handouts; slide management and more. This pack includes a self-test disk.
Delivery method: CBT.
Minimum hardware requirement: PC with Windows.
Price: £79.95 (multiple copy price on application).
Source: Electrovision UK Ltd, Hamble Point Marina, School Lane, Hamble, Southampton SO31 4JD. Tel: 01703 452221

Title: **Understanding Powerpoint v4**
Purpose: To teach the use of Powerpoint v4 for introduction to intermediate level users.

171

Suitable for: Anyone.
Prerequisites: None.
Description: This course covers topics including: the Powerpoint screen; slides and presentations; wizards; zoom; editing moving and resizing objects; outline; speller; templates; adding pictures; undo; graphs; colours; handout master; printing; slide management; and autoshape.
Delivery method: CBT.
Minimum hardware requirement: PC with Windows.
Price: £75.00 (multiple copy price on application).
Source: Electrovision UK Ltd, Hamble Point Marina, School Lane, Hamble, Southampton SO31 4JD. Tel: 01703 452221

CD-ROM

Title: **Discoverware Powerpoint v4**
Purpose: To teach the use of Powerpoint v4.
Suitable for: Anyone.
Prerequisites: None.
Description: This course instructs and then lets you try, using a simulation. The topics include: Powerpoint concepts; creating slides; working with objects and text; visuals; masters; and overviews.
Delivery method: CD-ROM.
Minimum hardware requirement: PC; 8Mb RAM; CD-ROM drive; sound card.
Price: £99.00.
Source: Comput-Ed Ltd, Long Lane, Dawlish EX7 0QR. Tel: 01626 889955

Interactive video

Title: **PowerPoint 4 Basics**
Purpose: To teach you how to work with text and graphic elements to design an on-screen graphic presentation.
Suitable for: Anyone.
Prerequisites: None.
Description: This course is divided into lessons and will enable you to design good presentation material as well as knowing how to get the best results from PowerPoint.
Delivery method: Interactive video.
Minimum hardware requirement: Interactive video workstation.
Price: £2,300.00.
Source: Training Direct, North Court, Edinburgh Gate, Harlow, Essex CM20 2JE. Tel: 01279 623927

Project

CBT

Title: **Perception Lite for Project v4**
Purpose: To give a sound introduction to Project v4.
Suitable for: Anyone.
Prerequisites: None.
Description: This course is ideal for new users and right up to intermediate level. It has an easy-to-follow style. Details of the contents not available at the time of print. Please call for latest updates.
Delivery method: CBT.
Minimum hardware requirement: PC.
Price: £65.00 (multiple copy price on application).
Source: Electrovision UK Ltd, Hamble Point Marina, School Lane, Hamble, Southampton SO31 4JD. Tel: 01703 452221

Title: **Teach Yourself Project v4**
Purpose: To teach you how to use Project v4.
Suitable for: Anyone.
Prerequisites: None.
Description: This course covers: using quick preview; the project screen; organising your project; creating a project plan; entering detailed project information; establishing task relationships; viewing the project schedule; Gantt charts; PERT charts; and expanding/collapsing outlines.
Delivery method: CBT.
Minimum hardware requirement: PC with Windows.
Price: £75.00 (multiple copy price on application).
Source: Electrovision UK Ltd, Hamble Point Marina, School Lane, Hamble, Southampton SO31 4JD. Tel: 01703 452221

Title: **Training for Project Management**
Purpose: To give an overview of project management before looking at specific software training.
Suitable for: Anyone.
Prerequisites: None.
Description: This course provides an extremely useful generic tutorial for anyone requiring project management skills. It covers all the main elements of project management including: PERT charts; GANTT charts; critical path analysis; the need for documentation, etc.
Delivery method: CBT.
Minimum hardware requirement: PC with Windows.
Price: £69.95 (multiple copy price on application).

Source: Electrovision UK Ltd, Hamble Point Marina, School Lane, Hamble, Southampton SO31 4JD. Tel: 01703 452221

Schedule

CBT

Title: **Perception Lite for Schedule (Office95)**
Purpose: To teach the use of Schedule (Office95).
Suitable for: Anyone.
Prerequisites: None.
Description: This course, which is suitable for both novice and intermediate users, covers: managing your appointments; setting options; organising teams; personal time management; prioritising projects and tasks.
Delivery method: CBT.
Minimum hardware requirement: PC with Windows 95.
Price: £75.00 (multiple copy price on application).
Source: Electrovision UK Ltd, Hamble Point Marina, School Lane, Hamble, Southampton SO31 4JD. Tel: 01703 452221

Windows

CBT

Title: **Perception for Windows 95**
Purpose: To tutor in Windows 95 for both novices and intermediate users.
Suitable for: Anyone.
Prerequisites: None.
Description: This interactive course uses glossaries, quizzes and quick search. The topics covered include: the desktop; utilities and accessories; short cuts; task bar; explorer; briefcase; networks; MS Exchange; and system tools.
Delivery method: CBT and manual.
Minimum hardware requirement: PC with Windows 95.
Price: £119.00 (multiple copy price on application).
Source: Electrovision UK Ltd, Hamble Point Marina, School Lane, Hamble, Southampton SO31 4JD. Tel: 01703 452221

Title: **Perception Lite for Windows 3.1**
Purpose: To teach Windows 3.1 to novices and intermediate users.
Suitable for: Anyone.
Prerequisites: None.
Description: This friendly and highly interactive course covers: a tour of the screen; program manager; navigation; file management; applications setups; and tips for optimising Windows.

Delivery method: CBT.
Minimum hardware requirement: PC with Windows.
Price: £75.00 (multiple copy price on application).
Source: Electrovision UK Ltd, Hamble Point Marina, School Lane, Hamble, Southampton SO31 4JD. Tel: 01703 452221

Title: **Perception Lite for Windows 95**
Purpose: To tutor in Windows 95 for both novices and intermediate users.
Suitable for: Anyone.
Prerequisites: None.
Description: This interactive course uses glossaries, quizzes and quick search. The topics covered include: the desktop; utilities and accessories; short cuts; task bar; explorer; briefcase; networks; MS Exchange; and system tools.
Delivery method: CBT.
Minimum hardware requirement: PC with Windows 95.
Price: £75.00 (multiple copy price on application).
Source: Electrovision UK Ltd, Hamble Point Marina, School Lane, Hamble, Southampton SO31 4JD. Tel: 01703 452221

Title: **Perception of Windows 3.1**
Purpose: To teach Windows 3.1 to novices and intermediate users.
Suitable for: Anyone.
Prerequisites: None.
Description: This Windows-based course covers: installing; menus; file management; options; groups; multiple applications; desktop settings and much more.
Delivery method: CBT.
Minimum hardware requirement: PC with Windows.
Price: £119.00 (multiple copy price on application).
Source: Electrovision UK Ltd, Hamble Point Marina, School Lane, Hamble, Southampton SO31 4JD. Tel: 01703 452221

Title: **Professor Windows 3.1**
Purpose: To help you to understand the Windows environment, basic Windows and mouse skills.
Suitable for: Anyone.
Prerequisites: None.
Description: This course deals with: basic Windows and mouse skills; getting help; customising desktop; program Manager; File Manager; Windows printing and accessories. More advanced topics include networking capabilities and DDE.
Delivery method: CBT.
Minimum hardware requirement: PC with Windows.
Price: £49.95 (multiple copy price on application).

Source: Electrovision UK Ltd, Hamble Point Marina, School Lane, Hamble, Southampton SO31 4JD. Tel: 01703 452221

Title: **Teach Yourself Windows 3.1**
Purpose: To introduce the Windows environment.
Suitable for: Anyone.
Prerequisites: None.
Description: This course uses interactive instruction, quizzes, and an on-line glossary.
Delivery method: CBT.
Minimum hardware requirement: PC.
Price: £49.95 (multiple copy price on application).
Source: Electrovision UK Ltd, Hamble Point Marina, School Lane, Hamble, Southampton SO31 4JD. Tel: 01703 452221

Title: **Teach Yourself Windows 95**
Purpose: To provide an introduction to Windows 95 for novice and intermediate users.
Suitable for: Anyone.
Prerequisites: None.
Description: This course covers: the desktop; task bar; general accessories; tools; file manager; printers; property sheets; networks; MS Exchange; running other programs and a lot more.
Delivery method: CBT.
Minimum hardware requirement: PC with Windows 95.
Price: £75.00 (multiple copy price on application).
Source: Electrovision UK Ltd, Hamble Point Marina, School Lane, Hamble, Southampton SO31 4JD. Tel: 01703 452221

Title: **Training for Windows 3.1**
Purpose: To comprehensively teach Windows from novice through to a fairly advanced level.
Suitable for: Anyone.
Prerequisites: None.
Description: This course's topics include: basic Windows orientation; program manager; file manager; Windows printing; accessories; advanced concepts including networking.
Delivery method: CBT.
Minimum hardware requirement: PC with Windows.
Price: £79.95 (multiple copy price on application).
Source: Electrovision UK Ltd, Hamble Point Marina, School Lane, Hamble, Southampton SO31 4JD. Tel: 01703 452221

Title: **Training for Windows 95**
Purpose: To provide an in-depth coverage of the subject.
Suitable for: Anyone.
Prerequisites: None.
Description: This course features pre- and post-testing for accurate assessment of your skill level and progress. Topics include: networking; explorer; multiple applications and many more.
Delivery method: CBT.
Minimum hardware requirement: PC with Windows 3.1.
Price: £79.95 (multiple copy price on application).
Source: Electrovision UK Ltd, Hamble Point Marina, School Lane, Hamble, Southampton SO31 4JD. Tel: 01703 452221

Title: **Understanding Windows 3.1**
Purpose: To give a comprehensive introduction to Windows 3.1.
Suitable for: Anyone.
Prerequisites: None.
Description: This course covers an introduction to: the Windows environment; frames; scroll bars; group and program icons; adding new groups; file manager directory and file management; and the control panel.
Delivery method: CBT – DOS or Windows versions.
Minimum hardware requirement: PC.
Price: £75.00 (multiple copy price on application).
Source: Electrovision UK Ltd, Hamble Point Marina, School Lane, Hamble, Southampton SO31 4JD. Tel: 01703 452221

Title: **Understanding Windows 95**
Purpose: To introduce Windows 95 to new users and upgraders from Windows 3.1.
Suitable for: Anyone.
Prerequisites: None.
Description: This is an easy to follow interactive course. Topics include: network neighbourhood; explorer; taskbar; tilebar and menubar; multiple applications; file management; and view menu options.
Delivery method: CBT.
Minimum hardware requirement: PC with Windows 95.
Price: £75.00 (multiple copy price on application).
Source: Electrovision UK Ltd, Hamble Point Marina, School Lane, Hamble, Southampton SO31 4JD. Tel: 01703 452221

Title: **Understanding Windows for Workgroups 3.1**
Purpose: To teach the technical aspects of using Windows for Workgroups.
Suitable for: Technical staff.

Prerequisites: None.
Description: This course covers: network cards and connecting cables; Windows environment; file manager; print manager; control panel and main accessories; network activities and troubleshooting; sharing files; shared printers; diagnostics; system locks; memory problems; passwords; CD-ROM; and share resources.
Delivery method: CBT.
Minimum hardware requirement: PC with Windows.
Price: £75.00 (multiple copy price on application).
Source: Electrovision UK Ltd, Hamble Point Marina, School Lane, Hamble, Southampton SO31 4JD. Tel: 01703 452221

CD-ROM

Title: **Discoverware Learn Windows 3.11**
Purpose: To teach you the basics of working with Windows 3.11.
Suitable for: Anyone.
Prerequisites: None.
Description: Topics covered: Windows overview; Windows environment; program manager; file manager; control panel; main group; applications basics; networking concepts; and networking group.
Delivery method: CD-ROM.
Minimum hardware requirement: 486 PC; 8Mb RAM; 8Mb disk space; CD-ROM drive; sound card.
Price: £99.00.
Source: Comput-Ed Ltd, Long Lane, Dawlish EX7 0QR. Tel: 01626 889955

Title: **Discoverware Windows 95**
Purpose: To introduce Windows 95 to novice and intermediate users.
Suitable for: Anyone.
Prerequisites: None.
Description: This course demonstrates, instructs and allows you to try. It covers: a tour of Windows 95; new features and icons; program and file manager; document and files; programs; networking; accessories and more.
Delivery method: CD-ROM.
Minimum hardware requirement: PC with Windows 3.1; 8Mb RAM; CD-ROM drive; sound card.
Price: £99.00 (multiple copy price on application).
Source: Comput-Ed Ltd, Long Lane, Dawlish EX7 0QR. Tel: 01626 889955

Title: **Learn Windows 95**
Purpose: To introduce Windows 95.
Suitable for: Anyone.
Prerequisites: None.

Description: This course provides instruction, demonstration, exploration and hands-on learning.
Delivery method: CD-ROM.
Minimum hardware requirement: PC with Windows 3.1; 8Mb RAM; CD-ROM drive; sound card.
Price: £49.95 (multiple copy price on application).
Source: Electrovision UK Ltd, Hamble Point Marina, School Lane, Hamble, Southampton SO31 4JD. Tel: 01703 452221

Title: **Professor Windows 95**
Purpose: To provide a comprehensive introduction to Windows 95.
Suitable for: Anyone.
Prerequisites: None.
Description: This course covers: basics and new interface; plug and play; longer file names; and Exchange. It also includes Power user topics such as: integrated 32-bit networking; mobile computing; briefcase and more.
Delivery method: CD-ROM.
Minimum hardware requirement: PC with Windows 3.1; 8Mb RAM; CD-ROM drive; sound card.
Price: £49.95 (multiple copy price on application).
Source: Electrovision UK Ltd, Hamble Point Marina, School Lane, Hamble, Southampton SO31 4JD. Tel: 01703 452221

Title: **Using Personal Computers for Windows**
Purpose: To teach you the basics of PCs.
Suitable for: Everyone.
Prerequisites: None.
Description: This course introduces the use of personal computers. The course emphasises practical use with actual business examples and provides practice using various applications through simulations.
Delivery method: CD-ROM.
Minimum hardware requirement: Pentium 90; 16Mb RAM; Quad speed CD-ROM drive; sound card; MPEG card.
Price: £1499.00.
Source: Intelligent Training Solutions, 29 Narrow Street, London E14 8DP. Tel: 0171 791 3000

Title: **Using Windows**
Purpose: To teach the fundamentals of Windows.
Suitable for: Everyone.
Prerequisites: None.
Description: This course teaches the basic skills necessary to operate in the Windows graphical interface. It concentrates on the fundamental operations

that are necessary to run a Windows application. The intermediate course covers: File Manager; Write and Paintbrush, along with many other Windows accessories and utilities.
Delivery method: CD-ROM.
Minimum hardware requirement: Pentium 90; 16Mb RAM; Quad speed CD-ROM drive; sound card; MPEG card.
Price: £2599.00.
Source: Intelligent Training Solutions, 29 Narrow Street, London E14 8DP. Tel: 0171 791 3000

Interactive Video
Title: **Windows Basics 4×**
Purpose: To familiarise users with the appearance of the actual Windows software on screen as well as teaching how to use its facilities.
Suitable for: Anyone.
Prerequisites: None.
Description: This course provides the user with the basic skills and knowledge common to all Windows applications, concentrating on the operations necessary to run such applications.
Delivery method: Interactive video.
Minimum hardware requirement: Interactive video workstation.
Price: £1353.00.
Source: Training Direct, North Court, Edinburgh Gate, Harlow, Essex CM20 2JE. Tel: 01279 623927.

Title: **Windows Intermediate**
Purpose: To teach the user how to use: file manager; notepad; card file; calendar; and character map.
Suitable for: Anyone.
Prerequisites: 'Windows Basics'.
Description: This course follows on from Windows Basics and gives practical working to consolidate the learning.
Delivery method: Interactive video.
Minimum hardware requirement: Interactive video workstation.
Price: £2300.00.
Source: Training Direct, North Court, Edinburgh Gate, Harlow, Essex CM20 2JE. Tel: 01279 623927

Works

CBT
Title: **Perception Lite for Works v3**
Purpose: To teach the use of Works v3.

Suitable for: Anyone.
Prerequisites: None.
Description: This course for novice to intermediate-level user includes topics on: word-processor; spreadsheet; database; communications; command menus; toolbar; drawing program; integrating different document types; and using wizards.
Delivery method: CBT.
Minimum hardware requirement: PC with Windows.
Price: £75.00 (multiple copy price on application).
Source: Electrovision UK Ltd, Hamble Point Marina, School Lane, Hamble, Southampton SO31 4JD. Tel: 01703 452221

Title: **Perception of Works v3**
Purpose: To teach more advanced use of Works v3.
Suitable for: Anyone.
Prerequisites: None.
Description: This course includes topics on: word-processor; spreadsheet; database; communications; and with an in-depth coverage of all the features of each module.
Delivery method: CBT.
Minimum hardware requirement: PC with Windows.
Price: £119.00 (multiple copy price on application).
Source: Electrovision UK Ltd, Hamble Point Marina, School Lane, Hamble, Southampton SO31 4JD. Tel: 01703 452221

Computer systems

CBT
Title: **Distributed Computing Environment**
Purpose: To describe the concepts of DCE, what it is used for, and why there is a need for it.
Suitable for: Programmers and trainee programmers.
Prerequisites: Good knowledge of the client/server environment.
Description: This course covers topics which include: interoperability; platform support; interfaces; program design; security; and data encryption techniques.
Delivery method: CBT.
Minimum hardware requirement: PC.
Price: £1995.00.
Source: Electrovision UK Ltd, Hamble Point Marina, School Lane, Hamble, Southampton SO31 4JD. Tel: 01703 452221

Title: **Large Systems Overview**
Purpose: To inform those unfamiliar with large-systems terminology.
Suitable for: Those unfamiliar with large-systems terminology.
Prerequisites: PC background.
Description: This is an extremely informative course for those personnel who are unfamiliar with large-systems terminology, hardware and applications. It reviews the major concepts, history, interrelationships and components that exist in large-systems information management.
Delivery method: CBT.
Minimum hardware requirement: PC.
Price: £1295.00 (multiple copy price on application).
Source: Electrovision UK Ltd, Hamble Point Marina, School Lane, Hamble, Southampton SO31 4JD. Tel: 01703 452221

Title: **PCs to Supercomputers**
Purpose: To introduce computer hardware from PCs through mid-range systems and mainframes.
Suitable for: Those unfamiliar with large-systems terminology.
Prerequisites: PC background.
Description: This course explains terms and various operating systems, networking, etc., and how it all fits together. Invaluable for those unfamiliar with mid-range or mainframe environments.
Delivery method: CBT.
Minimum hardware requirement: PC.
Price: £1295.00 (multiple copy price on application).
Source: Electrovision UK Ltd, Hamble Point Marina, School Lane, Hamble, Southampton SO31 4JD. Tel: 01703 452221

Title: **Relational Database Concepts**
Purpose: To present a working knowledge of databases.
Suitable for: Applications programmers, database administrators, and power end users.
Prerequisites: None.
Description: This course presents a working knowledge of what databases are and the concepts and terminology that is used in their implementation. Discusses what constitutes good database design. Student manual supplied.
Delivery method: CBT.
Minimum hardware requirement: PC.
Price: £1595.00 (multiple copy price on application).
Source: Electrovision UK Ltd, Hamble Point Marina, School Lane, Hamble, Southampton SO31 4JD. Tel: 01703 452221

Conflict management

CD-ROM
Title: **Dealing with Conflict**
Purpose: To provide practical strategies for dealing with workplace conflict.
Suitable for: Team leaders and managers.
Prerequisites: None.
Description: The topics include: defining conflict clues; conflict habits; win-win approach; creativity; communicating effectively; options; evaluate and review.
Delivery method: CD-ROM.
Minimum hardware requirement: PC; 8Mb RAM; CD-ROM drive; sound card.
Price: £1195.00.
Source: Intelligent Training Solutions, 29 Narrow Street, London E14 8DP. Tel: 0171 791 3000

Construction

CBT
Title: **CDM – Getting It Right**
Purpose: To give an overview of the Construction (Design and Management) Regulations 1994.
Suitable for: Small to medium-sized construction companies, also students studying construction.
Prerequisites: None.
Description: The package explains in detail the responsibilities of all the duty holders under the regulations. It also explains the new documentation that is now required under CDM. The package concludes with the 'Construction Game'.
Delivery method: CBT.
Minimum hardware requirement: 386 PC; 4Mb RAM; 3Mb hard disk.
Price: £80.00 to CITB-registered companies and FE colleges; £100.00 to all others.
Source: Publications Department, CITB, Bircham Newton, Kings Lynn PE31 6RH. Tel: 01553 776677 or 01553 776651

Contract negotiation and law

CBT
Title: **Contract Law: What Contracts Are and How They Affect You**
Purpose: To give a comprehensive introduction to English contract law with a complete reference to case law and glossary of essential legal terminology.
Suitable for: Anyone.

Prerequisites: None.
Description: This is an introductory course specifically designed to cover most aspects of the professional CPE or first-year degree syllabus in English Contract Law. As such, it is a vocational examination-oriented programme which gives full reference to the case law relevant to each of the chapter headings of the course.
Delivery method: CBT and supporting text.
Minimum hardware requirement: IBM PC or compatible, 512k RAM.
Price: £165.00.
Source: Ivy Business Training Software plc, Ivy House, 233–235 Roehampton Lane, London SW15 4LB. Tel: 0181 780 1494

Costing

CBT
Title: **Do You Know Costing?**
Purpose: Is to act as a training needs analysis which will be an aid to both learning and revision.
Suitable for: Anyone.
Prerequisites: A broad knowledge of costing.
Description: A self-assessment tool consisting of about 300 multiple-choice questions that will help you to develop your knowledge through repeated practice on questions covering all areas of the subject.
Delivery method: CBT and supporting text.
Minimum hardware requirement: IBM PC or compatible, 512k RAM.
Price: £165.00.
Source: Ivy Business Training Software plc, Ivy House, 233–235 Roehampton Lane, London SW15 4LB. Tel: 0181 780 1494

Counselling skills

CD-ROM
Title: **The Counselling Interview**
Purpose: To enable you to carry out the counselling interview effectively.
Suitable for: Team leaders and managers.
Prerequisites: None.
Description: This course is in three main parts: general considerations; basic rules; and practical hints. It contains five simulations which will enable you to practise some counselling skills to reinforce the skills you have learned.
Delivery method: CD-ROM.

Minimum hardware requirement: 386 PC; 8Mb RAM; 6Mb hard-disk space; CD-ROM card; sound card.
Price: £295.00.
Source: Comput-Ed Ltd, Long Lane, Dawlish EX7 0QR. Tel: 01626 889955

Creativity and problem solving

CBT
Title: **Creative Thinking Techniques**
Purpose: To teach the concepts for creative thinking.
Suitable for: Team leaders and managers.
Prerequisites: None.
Description: Presents concepts for creative thinking, including spidergrams, reversals, bug listing and herringbones. You also learn how to run a creative session with other people.
Delivery method: CBT.
Minimum hardware requirement: PC.
Price: £175.00.
Source: Electrovision UK Ltd, Hamble Point Marina, School Lane, Hamble, Southampton SO31 4JD. Tel: 01703 452221

CD-i
Title: **Ideas Into Action**
Purpose: To encourage and develop team and individual creativity and innovation.
Suitable for: Everyone.
Prerequisites: None.
Description: A highly interactive programme packed full of creativity brain-teasers and mind-stretchers plus innovation tips.
Delivery method: CD-i
Minimum hardware requirement: TV and CD-i player.
Price: Purchase: £995.00 + carriage + VAT; 2-day hire: £165.00 + carriage + VAT.
Source: Melrose, 16 Bromells Road, London, SW4 0BL. Tel: 0171 627 8404

CD-ROM
Title: **Problem Solving**
Purpose: To provide a seven-step approach to problem solving and emphasise that 'problem-mindedness' should be increased whilst 'solution-mindedness' should be delayed.
Suitable for: Anyone.
Prerequisites: None.
Description: This is an introductory course which will enable you to understand: the seven-step solution to problem solving; the reason why each step is vital;

and the pitfalls involved in problem-solving. You will be able to be effective at problem solving and work with a problem-solving team.
Delivery method: CD-ROM.
Minimum hardware requirement: 486 PC; 8Mb RAM; 256 Colour VGA; sound card; and 8Mb hard-disk space.
Price: £295.00.
Source: Ivy Business Training Software plc, Ivy House, 233–235 Roehampton Lane, London SW15 4LB. Tel: 0181 780 1494

Title: **Problem Solving at Work**
Purpose: To provide you with a well-defined and structured method for reaching the best solution to any problem.
Suitable for: Team leaders and managers.
Prerequisites: None.
Description: This course uses a seven-step approach to problem solving; each of the steps is worked through by way of examples. Case studies are used to put into practical terms the seven-step approach.
Delivery method: CD-ROM.
Minimum hardware requirement: 386 PC; 8Mb RAM; 6Mb hard-disk space; CD-ROM card; sound card.
Price: £295.00.
Source: Comput-Ed Ltd, Long Lane, Dawlish EX7 0QR. Tel: 01626 889955

Title: **Turning Problems Into Opportunities**
Purpose: To provide a practical approach to turning problems around.
Suitable for: Managers.
Prerequisites: None.
Description: Topics include: analyse the problem; conceptualise; evaluate; implement; and then review the outcome.
Delivery method: CD-ROM.
Minimum hardware requirement: PC; 8Mb RAM; CD-ROM drive; sound card.
Price: £1195.00.
Source: Intelligent Training Solutions, 29 Narrow Street, London E14 8DP. Tel: 0171 791 3000

Customer care

CD-i
Title: **An Inside Job**
Purpose: To teach the art of meeting internal customer needs.
Suitable for: Everyone.
Prerequisites: None.

Description: This course reveals how the customer service chain stretches from those dealing with external customers right through the organisation. The key points are: identify your internal customers, consult internal customers and serve internal customers.
Delivery method: CD-i.
Minimum hardware requirement: CD-i player and television.
Price: £995.00; rental prices on request.
Source: Video Arts Ltd, Dumbarton House, 68 Oxford Street, London W1N 0LH. Tel: 0171 637 7288

Title: **How to Lose Customers Without Really Trying**
Purpose: To teach the art of keeping the customer satisfied.
Suitable for: Everyone.
Prerequisites: None.
Description: This course deals with five key points: put yourself in the customer's position; identify the customer's real need; acknowledge and involve the customer; accept responsibility, even if it is not your fault and, see it through until the customer is satisfied.
Delivery method: CD-i.
Minimum hardware requirement: CD-i player and television.
Price: £995.00, rental prices on request.
Source: Video Arts Ltd, Dumbarton House, 68 Oxford Street, London W1N 0LH. Tel: 0171 637 7288

Title: **If Looks Could Kill**
Purpose: To teach that behaviour is a useful tool people can change at will.
Suitable for: Everyone.
Prerequisites: None.
Description: How people behave when dealing with customers and colleagues can determine the success or failure of each interaction. The key points of this course are behaviour breeds behaviour, behaviour is a choice and that behaviour can be used to help a transaction.
Delivery method: CD-i.
Minimum hardware requirement: CD-i player and television.
Price: £995.00, rental prices on request.
Source: Video Arts Ltd, Dumbarton House, 68 Oxford Street, London W1N 0LH. Tel: 0171 637 7288

Title: **Keeping Customers Cool**
Purpose: To help the front line handle 'difficult' customers.
Suitable for: All front-line teams, salespeople and customer service people.
Prerequisites: None.

Description: A five-step practical approach to handling 'difficult' customers and turning the situation into a positive one.
Delivery method: CD-i.
Minimum hardware requirement: TV and CD-i player.
Price: Purchase: £995.00 + carriage + VAT; 2-day hire: £165.00 + carriage + VAT.
Source: Melrose, 16 Bromells Road, London, SW4 0BL. Tel: 0171 627 8404

Title: **No Complaints?**
Purpose: To teach the handling and preventing of complaints.
Suitable for: Everyone.
Prerequisites: None.
Description: This course is in two parts 'Complaints and the customer' and 'Complaints and quality management'. The key points are: listen and sympathise; ask the right questions; agree a course of action; check it is carried out; investigate – don't accuse; let staff find the solution; get departments networking, and agree and monitor targets.
Delivery method: CD-i.
Minimum hardware requirement: CD-i player and television.
Price: £995.00; rental prices on request.
Source: Video Arts Ltd, Dumbarton House, 68 Oxford Street, London W1N 0LH. Tel: 0171 637 7288

Title: **Telephone Behaviour**
Purpose: To teach the skills of good business telephone behaviour.
Suitable for: Everyone.
Prerequisites: None.
Description: This course deals with a range of techniques enabling anyone answering calls to represent an organisation professionally. The key points are introduce yourself; establish if it's convenient to proceed; control the call; record and repeat information; say what you are going to do, and do it.
Delivery method: CD-i.
Minimum hardware requirement: CD-i player and television.
Price: £995.00; rental prices on request.
Source: Video Arts Ltd, Dumbarton House, 68 Oxford Street, London W1N 0LH. Tel: 0171 637 7288

CD-ROM

Title: **Customer Fundamentals**
Purpose: To provide the ideal learning tool for anyone dealing with internal and external customers.
Suitable for: Everyone.
Prerequisites: None.

Description: The lessons are structured in three sections: confidence; creating the right impression; handling complaints.
Delivery method: CD-ROM.
Minimum hardware requirement: 486PC; 8Mb RAM; 10MB hard disk space.
Price: Single course £75.00; multiple course discount on request.
Source: Video Arts Ltd, Dumbarton House, 68 Oxford Street, London W1N OLH. Tel: 0171 637 7288

Title: **Exceeding Your Customers' Expectations**
Purpose: To help your organisation achieve a positive and responsive relationship based on the customers' expectations.
Suitable for: All persons with customer contact.
Prerequisites: None.
Description: This course will give you a better understanding of the customers' needs and a knowledge of strategies for good service. The key training messages are: definitions of customer service; how to give your company the edge; establishing customers' vital needs; and how to apply strategies to achieve excellence.
Delivery method: CD-ROM.
Minimum hardware requirement: 486 PC; 8Mb RAM; 420Mb hard disk; CD-ROM drive; audio card.
Price: £1195.00.
Source: Intelligent Training Solutions, 29 Narrow Street, London E14 8DP. Tel: 0171 791 3000

Title: **Front Line Customer Care – Challenges**
Purpose: To achieve success through outstanding customer care.
Suitable for: Everyone.
Prerequisites: None.
Description: Demanding situations require the best customer care. Students explore techniques for resolving complaints and turning angry customers into loyal customers. Two video simulations call upon all the student's customer care skills to reach a positive, successful conclusion.
Delivery method: CD-ROM.
Minimum hardware requirement: 486 PC; 8Mb RAM; CD-ROM drive; sound card.
Price: £699.00, including toolkit.
Source: Intelligent Training Solutions, 29 Narrow Street, London E14 8DP. Tel: 0171 791 3000

Title: **Front Line Customer Care – Handle with Care**
Purpose: To achieve success through outstanding customer care
Suitable for: Everyone.

Prerequisites: None.
Description: The CARE mnemonic (Contact-Analyse-Respond-Exceed) provides students with a map to make every customer interaction successful. Students see how personalised service is the key to meeting and beating customer expectations. A selection of brain-teasers consolidates knowledge and raises new questions for discussion.
Delivery method: CD-ROM.
Minimum hardware requirement: 486 PC; 8Mb RAM; CD-ROM drive; sound card.
Price: £699.00, including toolkit.
Source: Intelligent Training Solutions, 29 Narrow Street, London E14 8DP. Tel: 0171 791 3000

Title: **Front Line Customer Care – Prepare to Care**
Purpose: To achieve success through outstanding customer care.
Suitable for: Everyone.
Prerequisites: None.
Description: A comprehensive guide to appraisals, covering: definitions; objectives; preparation; communication skills; the actual interview; and the follow-up. Case studies are used throughout to show good and bad practice.
Delivery method: CD-ROM.
Minimum hardware requirement: 486 PC; 8Mb RAM; CD-ROM drive; sound card.
Price: £699.00, including toolkit.
Source: Intelligent Training Solutions, 29 Narrow Street, London E14 8DP. Tel: 0171 791 3000

Title: **Power to the Customer**
Purpose: To help you to establish excellent customer service by empowering your front-line staff to handle customer service issues.
Suitable for: Everyone who comes into contact with customers, and their managers.
Prerequisites: None.
Description: This course will give you the knowledge and confidence needed to deal with customers' requests responsibly and effectively.
Delivery method: CD-ROM.
Minimum hardware requirement: 486 PC; 8Mb RAM; 420Mb hard disk; CD-ROM drive; audio card.
Price: £1135.00.
Source: Training Direct, North Court, Edinburgh Gate, Harlow, Essex CM20 2JE. Tel: 01279 623927

Interactive video
Title: **Caring for Your Customer**
Purpose: To develop the attitudes and skills which will set you apart from your competitors.
Suitable for: Anyone.
Prerequisites: None.
Description: This three-module course will help you to: establish quality service as the standard expectation in your company; understand what constitutes quality service; and understand how stress is reduced when you know how to cope with difficult customer-related situations.
Delivery method: Interactive video.
Minimum hardware requirement: Interactive video workstation.
Price: £2880.00.
Source: Training Direct, North Court, Edinburgh Gate, Harlow, Essex CM20 2JE. Tel: 01279 623927

Title: **Everybody Has a Customer**
Purpose: To help you understand how the customer feels and to demonstrate the effects of both positive and negative attitudes towards the customer.
Suitable for: Everyone.
Prerequisites: None.
Description: This course will help you: to communicate better both internally and with customers; to better understand customer needs and how a higher company profile creates more sales opportunities.
Delivery method: Interactive video.
Minimum hardware requirement: Interactive video workstation.
Price: £2020.00.
Source: Training Direct, North Court, Edinburgh Gate, Harlow, Essex CM20 2JE. Tel: 01279 623927

Data protection

CBT
Title: **Handle with Care**
Purpose: To highlight the importance of data protection for employees.
Suitable for: Personal data users.
Prerequisites: None.
Description: A complete self-study course, introducing the user to the rationale for data protection and the everyday implications of handling data correctly. Topics include: background to data protection; the eight principles of data protection; subject access; and information security. Includes an assessment game 'The data trap' and a full learning management system.

Delivery method: CBT.
Minimum hardware requirement: 386 PC; 3Mb hard disk; 640Kb RAM.
Price: £595.00: unlimited workstation licence; £1950.00: unlimited network licence.
Source: Easy i Ltd, 42 The Square, Kenilworth, Warwickshire CV8 1EB. Tel: 01926 854111

Data storage

CBT
Title: **Data Warehousing**
Purpose: To give an overview of the emerging technique for storage and retrieval of data from heterogeneous sources.
Suitable for: Programmers and trainee programmers.
Prerequisites: Knowledge of relational concepts of distributed systems and GUI.
Description: Students will gain an overview of data warehousing and study the various components. Contains complete details on how to build, use and maintain a data warehousing system.
Delivery method: CBT.
Minimum hardware requirement: PC.
Price: £1995.00.
Source: Electrovision UK Ltd, Hamble Point Marina, School Lane, Hamble, Southampton SO31 4JD. Tel: 01703 452221

Database systems

Access

CBT
Title: **Perception Lite for Access v2**
Purpose: To teach the fundamentals of Access v2.
Suitable for: Anyone.
Prerequisites: None.
Description: This course is suitable for novice and intermediate users. The topics covered include: creating databases; field properties; query and form windows; creating queries; sorting; running reports; mail-merging wizard; and macros.
Delivery method: CBT.
Minimum hardware requirement: PC.
Price: £75.00 (multiple copy price on request).
Source: Electrovision UK Ltd, Hamble Point Marina, School Lane, Hamble, Southampton SO31 4JD. Tel: 01703 452221

DIRECTORY OF COURSES

Title: **Perception of Access 7 (Office 95)**
Purpose: To teach Access 7 (Office 95).
Suitable for: Anyone.
Prerequisites: None.
Description: This Windows 95-based course covers: the Access environment; creating a database; forms and queries; adding modifying and reading data; sorting; security; and applications.
Delivery method: CBT.
Minimum hardware requirement: PC with Windows 95.
Price: £119.00 (multiple copy price on request).
Source: Electrovision UK Ltd, Hamble Point Marina, School Lane, Hamble, Southampton SO31 4JD. Tel: 01703 452221

Title: **Perception of Access v2**
Purpose: To teach Access v2.
Suitable for: Anyone.
Prerequisites: None.
Description: This course covers: the Access environment; creating a database; forms and queries; adding, modifying and reading data; sorting; security; and applications.
Delivery method: CBT.
Minimum hardware requirement: PC.
Price: £119.00 (multiple copy price on request).
Source: Electrovision UK Ltd, Hamble Point Marina, School Lane, Hamble, Southampton SO31 4JD. Tel: 01703 452221

Title: **Teach Yourself Access v2/Win**
Purpose: To give an introduction to Access v2.
Suitable for: Anyone.
Prerequisites: None.
Description: This course uses simulation, chapter summaries and quizzes to reinforce the learning. The topics covered include: introduction to databases; various windows and views; field properties; data management; wizards; forms; queries; workgroups; importing/exporting files; macros and more.
Delivery method: CBT.
Minimum hardware requirement: PC with Windows 3.1.
Price: £75.00 (multiple copy price on request).
Source: Electrovision UK Ltd, Hamble Point Marina, School Lane, Hamble, Southampton SO31 4JD. Tel: 01703 452221

Title: **Understanding of Access v2**
Purpose: To introduce Access through to intermediate level.
Suitable for: Anyone.

Prerequisites: None.
Description: This course gives the user all the skills needed to perform the most popular applications of the product. Includes a comprehensive range of topics.
Delivery method: CBT.
Minimum hardware requirement: PC.
Price: £75.00 (multiple copy price on request).
Source: Electrovision UK Ltd, Hamble Point Marina, School Lane, Hamble, Southampton SO31 4JD. Tel: 01703 452221

CD-ROM
Title: **Discoverware Access v2**
Purpose: To give an introduction to Access v2.
Suitable for: Anyone.
Prerequisites: None.
Description: This course instructs you and then allows you to try it out, using a simulation. The topics covered include: database concepts; working with data; filtering; the Access environment; macros; modules; planning a database; tables; queries; and reports. It does not need Access to run.
Delivery method: CD-ROM.
Minimum hardware requirement: PC: 8Mb RAM; CD-ROM drive; sound card.
Price: £99.00.
Source: Comput-Ed Ltd, Long Lane, Dawlish EX7 0QR. Tel: 01626 889955

Approach

CBT
Title: **Understanding Approach v3**
Purpose: To give an introduction to Approach v3 and more detailed training in the use of this system.
Suitable for: Anyone.
Prerequisites: None.
Description: This course, which features on-line glossary, fast search, quizzes and summaries, has topics including: creating databases; working with databases; record management; creating reports; labels; and customisation.
Delivery method: CBT.
Minimum hardware requirement: PC.
Price: £75.00 (multiple copy price on request).
Source: Electrovision UK Ltd, Hamble Point Marina, School Lane, Hamble, Southampton SO31 4JD. Tel: 01703 452221

Dataease

CBT

Title: **Teach Yourself Dataease v4**
Purpose: To give both introductory and intermediate level training in the use of Dataease v4.
Suitable for: Anyone.
Prerequisites: None.
Description: This course uses simulations to assist the learning. The topics covered include: setting up a database; displaying and modifying data; reports; mailing labels; data entry forms; and menus.
Delivery method: CBT.
Minimum hardware requirement: PC.
Price: £75.00 (multiple copy price on application).
Source: Electrovision UK Ltd, Hamble Point Marina, School Lane, Hamble, Southampton SO31 4JD. Tel: 01703 452221

DB2

CBT

Title: **DB2 Application Programming (COBOL/PL1)**
Purpose: To teach how to write applications using SQL for the DB2 environment.
Suitable for: Programmers and trainee programmers.
Prerequisites: None.
Description: This course is intended for those involved with the development of DB2 applications in the CICS, IMS or TSO environments. A student manual is provided.
Delivery method: CBT.
Minimum hardware requirement: PC.
Price: £1995.00 (multiple copy price on application).
Source: Electrovision UK Ltd, Hamble Point Marina, School Lane, Hamble, Southampton SO31 4JD. Tel: 01703 452221

Title: **DB2 Design and Administration**
Purpose: To provide a practical insight into the design and implementation of efficient relational databases and related DB2 objects.
Suitable for: Database administration personnel and application developers.
Prerequisites: None.
Description: This course gives a practical insight into the design and implementation of efficient relational databases and related DB2 objects. Supplied with a comprehensive student manual.
Delivery method: CBT.

Minimum hardware requirement: PC.
Price: £1995.00 (multiple copy price on application).
Source: Electrovision UK Ltd, Hamble Point Marina, School Lane, Hamble, Southampton SO31 4JD. Tel: 01703 452221

Title: **DB2 Essentials**
Purpose: To provide an understanding of the concepts and terminology used in the implementation of a DB2 system.
Suitable for: First-time users of DB2.
Prerequisites: None.
Description: This course comes with a student manual.
Delivery method: CBT.
Minimum hardware requirement: PC.
Price: £1295.00 (multiple copy price on application).
Source: Electrovision UK Ltd, Hamble Point Marina, School Lane, Hamble, Southampton SO31 4JD. Tel: 01703 452221

dBase

CBT
Title: **Training for dBase IV (v1.1 to 1.5)**
Purpose: To give both introductory and intermediate level training in all the main features of dBase IV.
Suitable for: Anyone.
Prerequisites: None.
Description: This course includes topics such as: working with databases; edit; browse; data queries; reports; dot prompt; dBase programming (very basic); and SQL.
Delivery method: CBT.
Minimum hardware requirement: PC.
Price: £69.95 (multiple copy price on application).
Source: Electrovision UK Ltd, Hamble Point Marina, School Lane, Hamble, Southampton SO31 4JD. Tel: 01703 452221

Excel

CBT
Title: **Perception Lite for Excel v5**
Purpose: To teach the use of Excel v5.
Suitable for: Anyone.
Prerequisites: None.
Description: This course which is for novice to intermediate level, includes topics

on: cells; control bar; workbooks and worksheets; calculation; data types; formulae; formatting; charts; graphics; searching; advanced features; and sharing data.
Delivery method: CBT.
Minimum hardware requirement: PC with Windows.
Price: £75.00 (multiple copy price on application).
Source: Electrovision UK Ltd, Hamble Point Marina, School Lane, Hamble, Southampton SO31 4JD. Tel: 01703 452221

Title: **Perception of Excel 7 (Office95)**
Purpose: To give in-depth instruction in the use of Excel 7 (Office95).
Suitable for: Anyone.
Prerequisites: None.
Description: This course covers: creating a worksheet; formatting data; formulas; drag/drop editing; multiple worksheets; charts; macros; and graphics.
Delivery method: CBT.
Minimum hardware requirement: PC with Windows 95.
Price: £119.00 (multiple copy price on application).
Source: Electrovision UK Ltd, Hamble Point Marina, School Lane, Hamble, Southampton SO31 4JD. Tel: 01703 452221

Title: **Perception of Excel v5**
Purpose: To give in-depth instruction in the use of Excel v5.
Suitable for: Anyone.
Prerequisites: None.
Description: This course contains exercises at intro to advanced level in the comprehensive student manual. The CBT covers: creating a worksheet; formatting data; formulas; drag/drop editing; multiple worksheets; charts; macros; and graphics.
Delivery method: CBT.
Minimum hardware requirement: PC with Windows.
Price: £119.00 (multiple copy price on application).
Source: Electrovision UK Ltd, Hamble Point Marina, School Lane, Hamble, Southampton SO31 4JD. Tel: 01703 452221

Title: **Teach Yourself Excel v5/Windows**
Purpose: To teach you how to use Excel v5.
Suitable for: Anyone.
Prerequisites: None.
Description: This course covers: creating worksheets; entering and formatting data; formulas; drag and drop editing; multiple worksheets; find and replace; charts; macros; and graphics.
Delivery method: CBT.

Minimum hardware requirement: PC with Windows.
Price: £75.00 (multiple copy price on application).
Source: Electrovision UK Ltd, Hamble Point Marina, School Lane, Hamble, Southampton SO31 4JD. Tel: 01703 452221

Title: **Training for Excel v5**
Purpose: To teach you how to use Excel v5.
Suitable for: Anyone.
Prerequisites: None.
Description: This course, which covers introductory to intermediate level, includes: introduction; basic skills; selecting commands; toolbar; labels and numbers; cells and ranges; formulas; charts; macros and more. The pack also includes a comprehensive self-test.
Delivery method: CBT.
Minimum hardware requirement: PC with Windows.
Price: £79.95 (multiple copy price on application).
Source: Electrovision UK Ltd, Hamble Point Marina, School Lane, Hamble, Southampton SO31 4JD. Tel: 01703 452221

Title: **Understanding Excel v5**
Purpose: To teach the use of Excel v5.
Suitable for: Anyone.
Prerequisites: None.
Description: This course, which uses summaries, quizzes and true-to-life screens, has topics which include: introduction to spreadsheets; introduction to the Excel screen; selecting commands; toolbar; icons; labels and numbers; cells and ranges; formulas; recalculation; formatting; charts; editing; macros; and multiple worksheets.
Delivery method: CBT.
Minimum hardware requirement: PC.
Price: £75.00 (multiple copy price on application).
Source: Electrovision UK Ltd, Hamble Point Marina, School Lane, Hamble, Southampton SO31 4JD. Tel: 01703 452221

CD-ROM
Title: **Discoverware Excel v5**
Purpose: To teach you how to use Excel v5.
Suitable for: Anyone.
Prerequisites: None.
Description: This course instructs and then lets you try it for yourself, using simulation exercises. The topics covered include: workbook and worksheets; working with data; formulas and functions; formatting; ranges; charts; and printing.

Delivery method: CD-ROM.
Minimum hardware requirement: PC; 8Mb RAM; CD-ROM drive; sound card.
Price: £99.00.
Source: Comput-Ed Ltd, Long Lane, Dawlish EX7 0QR. Tel: 01626 889955

Title: **Excel for Windows**
Purpose: To teach the fundamentals of Excel.
Suitable for: Everyone.
Prerequisites: None.
Description: The basic course covers the basic concepts of spreadsheets and how to create spreadsheets in Excel. The intermediate course covers: using formulas; formatting; printing; styles; consolidation; graphics; data management; and macro capabilities.
Delivery method: CD-ROM.
Minimum hardware requirement: Pentium 90; 16Mb RAM; Quad speed CD-ROM drive; sound card; MPEG card.
Price: £2599.00.
Source: Intelligent Training Solutions, 29 Narrow Street, London E14 8DP. Tel: 0171 791 3000

Interactive video
Title: **Using Excel 4 for Windows**
Purpose: To give the user a full understanding of all Excel's main features.
Suitable for: Anyone.
Prerequisites: None.
Description: This 12-lesson course allows you to learn with the actual Excel 4 for Windows software and gives access to comprehensive self-paced tuition.
Delivery method: Interactive video.
Minimum hardware requirement: Interactive video workstation.
Price: £3680.00.
Source: Training Direct, North Court, Edinburgh Gate, Harlow, Essex CM20 2JE. Tel: 01279 623927

Title: **Using Excel 5 for Windows**
Purpose: To give the user a full understanding of all Excel 5's main features. There are two courses: Excel Basics and Excel Intermediate.
Suitable for: Anyone.
Prerequisites: None.
Description: The Basics course covers the basic concepts of spreadsheets and how to create these in Excel. The Intermediate course builds on the skills acquired through Excel Basics and covers: using formulas; formatting; printing styles; consolidation; graphics; data management; and macro capabilities.
Delivery method: Interactive video.

Minimum hardware requirement: Interactive video workstation.
Price: £2300.00 each course.
Source: Training Direct, North Court, Edinburgh Gate, Harlow, Essex CM20 2JE. Tel: 01279 623927

IDMS

CBT
Title: **IDMS**
Purpose: To provide a working knowledge of IDMS.
Suitable for: Applications programmers and designers.
Prerequisites: None.
Description: Students will gain a working knowledge of the IDMS system. The first part of the course can be used by anyone requiring an overview of IDMS. Student manual supplied.
Delivery method: CBT.
Minimum hardware requirement: PC.
Price: £1995.00 (multiple copy price on application).
Source: Electrovision UK Ltd, Hamble Point Marina, School Lane, Hamble, Southampton SO31 4JD. Tel: 01703 452221

Lotus

CBT
Title: **Perception Lite for Lotus v5 (Win)**
Purpose: To teach you how to use Lotus v5.
Suitable for: Anyone.
Prerequisites: None.
Description: This course presents concise training for novice to intermediate user level. The topics covered include: worksheets; editing; entering data; moving around; formatting; formulae; multiple worksheets; charts; styles; smart icons; and graphics.
Delivery method: CBT.
Minimum hardware requirement: PC with Windows.
Price: £75.00 (multiple copy price on application).
Source: Electrovision UK Ltd, Hamble Point Marina, School Lane, Hamble, Southampton SO31 4JD. Tel: 01703 452221

Title: **Perception of Lotus v5 (Windows)**
Purpose: To give in-depth training on how to use Lotus v5 for Windows.
Suitable for: Anyone.
Prerequisites: None.

Description: This course gives in-depth training. The topics covered include: smart icons; worksheet Windows; entering data and formulae; moving and copying; all you need to know about charts and many other topics.
Delivery method: CBT.
Minimum hardware requirement: PC with Windows.
Price: £119.00 (multiple copy price on application).
Source: Electrovision UK Ltd, Hamble Point Marina, School Lane, Hamble, Southampton SO31 4JD. Tel: 01703 452221

Title: **Teach Yourself Lotus v3.1/DOS**
Purpose: To teach you how to use Lotus v3.1/DOS.
Suitable for: Anyone.
Prerequisites: None.
Description: This very detailed course guides the novice user from scratch through the various levels of complexity of Lotus. Each section uses simulation to test skills learned. Topics covered include: setting up spreadsheet; entering text data and formulas; formatting; combining worksheets; macros and more.
Delivery method: CBT.
Minimum hardware requirement: PC.
Price: £75.00 (multiple copy price on application).
Source: Electrovision UK Ltd, Hamble Point Marina, School Lane, Hamble, Southampton SO31 4JD. Tel: 01703 452221

Title: **Teach Yourself Lotus v5/Win**
Purpose: To teach you how to use Lotus v5/Win.
Suitable for: Anyone.
Prerequisites: None.
Description: This course has a visual on-line glossary and quick search index, as well as easy to use pull-down menus. Topics covered include: creating a spreadsheet; entering and formatting data; cells and ranges; drag and drop editing; multiple worksheets; charts; graphics; and macros. There is a summary and quiz at the end of each section.
Delivery method: CBT.
Minimum hardware requirement: PC with Windows.
Price: £75.00 (multiple copy price on application).
Source: Electrovision UK Ltd, Hamble Point Marina, School Lane, Hamble, Southampton SO31 4JD. Tel: 01703 452221

Title: **Training for Lotus v2.4 to 3.4/DOS**
Purpose: To teach you how to use Lotus v2.4 to 3.4 / DOS.
Suitable for: Anyone.

Prerequisites: None.
Description: This is a useful package that covers all the DOS versions of Lotus from 2.4 through to 3.4+. It teaches all the basics of Lotus including: working with worksheets; databases and data tables; graphics; and keyboard macros.
Delivery method: CBT.
Minimum hardware requirement: PC.
Price: £69.95 (multiple copy price on application).
Source: Electrovision UK Ltd, Hamble Point Marina, School Lane, Hamble, Southampton SO31 4JD. Tel: 01703 452221

Title: **Training for Lotus v5**
Purpose: To teach you how to use Lotus v5.
Suitable for: Anyone.
Prerequisites: None.
Description: This course teaches all Lotus basics, plus: formatting a worksheet; working with charts; macros; and multiple documents. It also teaches intermediate topics. It includes an additional disk that enables you to test your knowledge.
Delivery method: CBT.
Minimum hardware requirement: PC with Windows.
Price: £79.95 (multiple copy price on application).
Source: Electrovision UK Ltd, Hamble Point Marina, School Lane, Hamble, Southampton SO31 4JD. Tel: 01703 452221

Title: **Understanding Lotus v5**
Purpose: To teach you how to use Lotus v5.
Suitable for: Anyone.
Prerequisites: None.
Description: This course, which covers introduction through to strong intermediate level, uses on-line glossary, fast search, quizzes and summaries to aid the learning. The topics covered include from getting started to multiple spread sheets, smarticons and graphs.
Delivery method: CBT.
Minimum hardware requirement: PC with Windows.
Price: £75.00 (multiple copy price on application).
Source: Electrovision UK Ltd, Hamble Point Marina, School Lane, Hamble, Southampton SO31 4JD. Tel: 01703 452221

CD-ROM
Title: **Discoverware Lotus v5**
Purpose: To teach you how to use Lotus v5 without needing to have Lotus loaded.
Suitable for: Anyone.

Prerequisites: None.
Description: This course uses video and instructs, and then lets you try using a simulation exercise. It has variable user level, bookmark and random quizzes.
Delivery method: CD-ROM.
Minimum hardware requirement: PC; 8Mb RAM; CD-ROM drive; sound card.
Price: £99.00.
Source: Comput-Ed Ltd, Long Lane, Dawlish EX7 0QR. Tel: 01626 889955

Title: **Lotus 1-2-3 for Windows**
Purpose: To teach the fundamentals of Lotus 1–2–3.
Suitable for: Everyone.
Prerequisites: None.
Description: The basic course introduces the fundamentals of Lotus 1–2–3, including the basic concepts of spreadsheets and how to create spreadsheets in Lotus. The intermediate course covers: formulas; formatting; printing; styles; 3D worksheets; consolidation; graphics; data management; and macro capabilities.
Delivery method: CD-ROM.
Minimum hardware requirement: Pentium 90; 16Mb RAM; Quad speed CD-ROM drive; sound card; MPEG card.
Price: £2599.00.
Source: Intelligent Training Solutions, 29 Narrow Street, London E14 8DP. Tel: 0171 791 3000

Interactive video

Title: **Using Lotus 1–2–3 for Windows Release 4**
Purpose: To teach the fundamentals and many of the advanced features of the Windows version of Lotus 1–2–3.
Suitable for: Anyone.
Prerequisites: None.
Description: There are two courses. The basic course covers the basic concepts of spreadsheets and how to create these in Lotus 1–2–3. The intermediate course builds on the skills acquired in the basic course and covers: using formulas; formatting; printing styles; 3-D worksheets; consolidation; graphics; data management; and macro capabilities.
Delivery method: Interactive video.
Minimum hardware requirement: Interactive video workstation.
Price: £2300.00 each course.
Source: Training Direct, North Court, Edinburgh Gate, Harlow, Essex CM20 2JE. Tel: 01279 623927

Oracle

CBT

Title: **Administer the Oracle 7.1 Database I**
Purpose: To provide a comprehensive introduction to administering the Oracle 7.1 Database.
Suitable for: Database administrators.
Prerequisites: None.
Description: This course covers: SQL*DBA; prepare to create a database; creating a database; startup and shutdown; and manage database storage.
Delivery method: CBT; also available via the Internet.
Minimum hardware requirement: Any PC capable of running Microsoft Windows.
Price: On application.
Source: Oracle Corporation UK Ltd, The Oracle Centre, The Ring, Bracknell, Berks. RG12 1BW. Tel: 01344 860066

Title: **Administer the Oracle 7.1 Database II**
Purpose: To guide you through the major functions to be performed by an Oracle 7 database administrator.
Suitable for: Database administrators.
Prerequisites: 'Administer the Oracle 7.1 Database I'.
Description: Using product simulation, this course follows on from module I to guide you through the major functions to be performed. The key learning points are: control database usage; audit the database; manage locking; manage data integrity; and backup and recovery.
Delivery method: CBT; also available via the Internet.
Minimum hardware requirement: Any PC capable of running Microsoft Windows.
Price: On application.
Source: Oracle Corporation UK Ltd, The Oracle Centre, The Ring, Bracknell, Berks. RG12 1BW. Tel: 01344 860066

Title: **Advanced Oracle Forms 4.5**
Purpose: To teach advanced techniques.
Suitable for: Programmers and trainee programmers.
Prerequisites: None.
Description: This is a new course. Please telephone for course outline.
Delivery method: CBT.
Minimum hardware requirement: PC.
Price: £795.00.
Source: Electrovision UK Ltd, Hamble Point Marina, School Lane, Hamble, Southampton SO31 4JD. Tel: 01703 452221

DIRECTORY OF COURSES

Title: **Backup and Recovery with Server Manager**
Purpose: To enable you to practice the concepts of database backup and recovery.
Suitable for: Database administrators.
Prerequisites: None.
Description: This backup and recovery simulator will allow you to practice the concepts of database backup and recovery using server manager in scenarios that emulate real-life situations.
Delivery method: CBT; also available via the Internet.
Minimum hardware requirement: Any PC capable of running Microsoft Windows.
Price: On application.
Source: Oracle Corporation UK Ltd, The Oracle Centre, The Ring, Bracknell, Berks. RG12 1BW. Tel: 01344 860066

Title: **Configure the Multi-Threaded Server**
Purpose: To teach the essentials required to maximise utilisation of available resources.
Suitable for: Database administrators.
Prerequisites: None.
Description: This course covers the essentials required to maximise utilisation of available resources. The key learning points are: Using SQL*Net and Oracle 7; the advantages of the multi-threaded server; configuring the multi-threaded server; and managing the multi-threaded server.
Delivery method: CBT; also available via the Internet.
Minimum hardware requirement: Any PC capable of running Microsoft Windows.
Price: On application.
Source: Oracle Corporation UK Ltd, The Oracle Centre, The Ring, Bracknell, Berks. RG12 1BW. Tel: 01344 860066

Title: **Fundamentals of Oracle Forms 4.5**
Purpose: To introduce you to the basics of creating a form application in Oracle Forms 4.5.
Suitable for: Programmers and trainee programmers.
Prerequisites: None.
Description: This course introduces you to the basics of creating a form application in Oracle Forms 4.5. It covers key aspects of developing an application, including: working with default blocks; using items and triggers; and creating custom menus.
Delivery method: CBT.
Minimum hardware requirement: PC.
Price: £795.00.
Source: Electrovision UK Ltd, Hamble Point Marina, School Lane, Hamble, Southampton SO31 4JD. Tel: 01703 452221

Title: **Introduction to Oracle Networking**
Purpose: To provide a broad view of how Oracle Enterprise Networking products assist you.
Suitable for: Database administrators.
Prerequisites: None.
Description: This course gives you the opportunity of taking a broad view of how Oracle's Enterprise Networking products help you to give users transparent access to Oracle databases in a variety of networked environments.
Delivery method: CBT; also available via the Internet.
Minimum hardware requirement: Any PC capable of running Microsoft Windows.
Price: On application.
Source: Oracle Corporation UK Ltd, The Oracle Centre, The Ring, Bracknell, Berks. RG12 1BW. Tel: 01344 860066

Title: **Oracle 7 – Advanced Administration**
Purpose: To teach advanced administration of Oracle 7.
Suitable for: Database administrators.
Prerequisites: 'Oracle 7 – Basic Administration'.
Description: This course covers: the structure of Oracle; improving data access; recovering data; improving server performance; memory allocation; tuning I/O; reducing contention; managing distributed databases; global database names; table snapshots and more.
Delivery method: CBT.
Minimum hardware requirement: PC.
Price: £795.00.
Source: Electrovision UK Ltd, Hamble Point Marina, School Lane, Hamble, Southampton SO31 4JD. Tel: 01703 452221

Title: **Oracle 7 – An Overview**
Purpose: To introduce you to Oracle 7.
Suitable for: Managers, application developers and database administrators.
Prerequisites: None.
Description: This course gives an overview of Oracle 7. The course structure is: introduction; applications development in Oracle 7; distributed processing; database administration.
Delivery method: CBT.
Minimum hardware requirement: PC.
Price: £795.00.
Source: Electrovision UK Ltd, Hamble Point Marina, School Lane, Hamble, Southampton SO31 4JD. Tel: 01703 452221

Title: **Oracle 7 – Basic Administration**
Purpose: To teach basic administration of Oracle 7.

Suitable for: 3GL programmers and database administrators.
Prerequisites: Previous experience in any RDBMS.
Description: Designed for 3Gl programmers and database administrators working on any RDBMS, who are moving to database administration of Oracle 7. The course covers: the architecture of Oracle; installation and start-up; managing tablespaces and data files; managing tables and views; securing the server; and backing up data.
Delivery method: CBT.
Minimum hardware requirement: PC.
Price: £795.00.
Source: Electrovision UK Ltd, Hamble Point Marina, School Lane, Hamble, Southampton SO31 4JD. Tel: 01703 452221

Title: **Oracle 7 – SQL Programming**
Purpose: To teach SQL programming in Oracle 7.
Suitable for: Programmers and trainee programmers.
Prerequisites: None.
Description: The emphasis of this course is on providing skills to do the following tasks in Oracle 7: create, alter and delete database objects; perform queries on a database; manage tables; and manipulate data in a database.
Delivery method: CBT.
Minimum hardware requirement: PC.
Price: £795.00.
Source: Electrovision UK Ltd, Hamble Point Marina, School Lane, Hamble, Southampton SO31 4JD. Tel: 01703 452221

Title: **Oracle 7 – New Features for DBAs**
Purpose: To help you to increase the productivity and response times.
Suitable for: Database administrators.
Prerequisites: None.
Description: In this course, you learn how to increase the productivity and response time of the database, using the enhanced features of release 7.3 of the Oracle 7 Server.
Delivery method: CBT; also available via the Internet.
Minimum hardware requirement: Any PC capable of running Microsoft Windows.
Price: On application.
Source: Oracle Corporation UK Ltd, The Oracle Centre, The Ring, Bracknell, Berks. RG12 1BW. Tel: 01344 860066

Title: **Oracle 7.1 Architecture**
Purpose: To provide a basic understanding of the Oracle 7 Database System.
Suitable for: Database administrators and system designers.
Prerequisites: None.

Description: This course provides a basic understanding of the Oracle 7 Database System through the following topics: overview of Oracle 7 architecture; defining the database structure; accessing and updating data; and logging transactions.
Delivery method: CBT; also available via the Internet.
Minimum hardware requirement: Any PC capable of running Microsoft Windows.
Price: On application.
Source: Oracle Corporation UK Ltd, The Oracle Centre, The Ring, Bracknell, Berks. RG12 1BW. Tel: 01344 860066

Title: **Tune the Oracle 7.1 Database**
Purpose: To teach you how to fine-tune the various resources to ensure efficient running.
Suitable for: Database administrators.
Prerequisites: None.
Description: Oracle 7 is both sophisticated and highly flexible insomuch as various resources can be fine-tuned to ensure the database is running efficiently. The key learning points are: tuning methodology; tuning SQL statements and applications; tune memory allocation; tune input/output; and minimise contention.
Delivery method: CBT; also available via the Internet.
Minimum hardware requirement: Any PC capable of running Microsoft Windows.
Price: On application.
Source: Oracle Corporation UK Ltd, The Oracle Centre, The Ring, Bracknell, Berks RG12 1BW. Tel: 01344 860066

Title: **Using Oracle Enterprise Manager**
Purpose: To provide hands-on experience of using the Oracle Enterprise Manager.
Suitable for: Database administrators.
Prerequisites: None.
Description: This course will give you hands-on experience using Oracle's Enterprise manager to administer, diagnose and monitor the Oracle environment from a single integrated console.
Delivery method: CBT; also available via the Internet.
Minimum hardware requirement: Any PC capable of running Microsoft Windows.
Price: On application.
Source: Oracle Corporation UK Ltd, The Oracle Centre, The Ring, Bracknell, Berks. RG12 1BW. Tel: 01344 860066

Title: **Using Oracle Reports 2.5**
Purpose: To teach you how to use Oracle report 2.5.
Suitable for: Programmers and trainee programmers.

Prerequisites: None.
Description: This is a new course. Please telephone for course outline.
Delivery method: CBT.
Minimum hardware requirement: PC.
Price: £795.00.
Source: Electrovision UK Ltd, Hamble Point Marina, School Lane, Hamble, Southampton SO31 4JD. Tel: 01703 452221

Title: **Using Oracle7 Workgroup Server I**
Purpose: To introduce the principles of Oracle7 Workgroup Server.
Suitable for: System developers.
Prerequisites: Existing Oracle skills.
Description: The key points of this introductory course are: client/server components; managing relational databases; workgroup/2000 tools; and installation and setup and connectivity.
Delivery method: CBT; also available via the Internet.
Minimum hardware requirement: Any PC capable of running Microsoft Windows.
Price: On application.
Source: Oracle Corporation UK Ltd, The Oracle Centre, The Ring, Bracknell, Berks. RG12 1BW. Tel: 01344 860066

Title: **Using Oracle7 Workgroup Server II**
Purpose: To build on the knowledge gained in the first module.
Suitable for: System developers.
Prerequisites: 'Using Oracle7 Workgroup Server I'.
Description: This course covers the major Oracle Workgroup/2000 database management and administration tools. The course includes: managing a database; migration issues; and advantages of the Oracle7 Server.
Delivery method: CBT; also available via the Internet.
Minimum hardware requirement: Any PC capable of running Microsoft Windows.
Price: On application.
Source: Oracle Corporation UK Ltd, The Oracle Centre, The Ring, Bracknell, Berks. RG12 1BW. Tel: 01344 860066

Quattro

CBT
Title: **Understanding Quattro Pro v5**
Purpose: To teach you how to use Quattro Pro v5.
Suitable for: Anyone.
Prerequisites: None.
Description: This course takes you from the introductory stage through to a strong intermediate stage. It features on-line glossary, fast search, quizzes,

summaries, etc. The topics include from getting started to multiple spreadsheets, formulas, macros and more.
Delivery method: CBT.
Minimum hardware requirement: PC with Windows.
Price: £75.00 (multiple copy price on application).
Source: Electrovision UK Ltd, Hamble Point Marina, School Lane, Hamble, Southampton SO31 4JD. Tel: 01703 452221

RDBMS

CBT
Title: **RDBMS Fundamentals**
Purpose: To teach RDBMS.
Suitable for: Applications developers and database designers new to RDBMS.
Prerequisites: None.
Description: This course covers: introducing databases; using relational databases; interpreting data – entities and relationships; using E/R diagrams; simplifying data; storing and retrieving data; and ensuring integrity of data.
Delivery method: CBT.
Minimum hardware requirement: PC.
Price: £1995.00.
Source: Electrovision UK Ltd, Hamble Point Marina, School Lane, Hamble, Southampton SO31 4JD. Tel: 01703 452221

SQL

CBT
Title: **Advanced SQL**
Purpose: To further expand the knowledge learnt in the introductory course.
Suitable for: Everyone involved in the design, building and maintenance of Oracle databases and applications.
Prerequisites: 'An Introduction to SQL'.
Description: The course is complemented by an extensive workbook of exercises that build upon the material learnt in the course. The key topics are: using the select statement; advanced functions; aggregated functions; using subqueries; joins and transactions; and using tables and views.
Delivery method: CBT; also available via the Internet.
Minimum hardware requirement: Any PC capable of running Microsoft Windows.
Price: On application.
Source: Oracle Corporation UK Ltd, The Oracle Centre, The Ring, Bracknell, Berks. RG12 1BW. Tel: 01344 860066

DIRECTORY OF COURSES

Title: **Develop Applications with PL/SQL (V2.0)**
Purpose: To introduce the fundamentals of PL/SQL to those new to the subject, but with an understanding of SQL.
Suitable for: Anyone with an understanding of SQL.
Prerequisites: An understanding of SQL.
Description: PL/SQL allows you to combine the power of SQL with procedural control to improve the performance of key applications. The topics include: variables and constraints; using SQL statements within PL/SQL; and using control structures and cursors.
Delivery method: CBT; also available via the Internet.
Minimum hardware requirement: Any PC capable of running Microsoft Windows.
Price: On application.
Source: Oracle Corporation UK Ltd, The Oracle Centre, The Ring, Bracknell, Berks. RG12 1BW. Tel: 01344 860066

Title: **Develop Reports with SQL*Report Writer (V1.1)**
Purpose: To teach you how to develop reports using SQL*Report Writer (V1.1).
Suitable for: Applications developers.
Prerequisites: None.
Description: This practical course covers all aspects involved in producing a report in SQL*Report Writer. It covers in detail: creating a basic tabular report; break reports; summaries and text objects; run time parameters; and the production of special purpose forms.
Delivery Method: CBT; also available via the Internet.
Minimum hardware requirement: Any PC capable of running Microsoft Windows.
Price: On application.
Source: Oracle Corporation UK Ltd, The Oracle Centre, The Ring, Bracknell, Berks. RG12 1BW. Tel: 01344 860066

Title: **Introduction to SQL**
Purpose: To provide a thorough knowledge of SQL.
Suitable for: Everyone involved in the design, building and maintenance of Oracle databases and applications.
Prerequisites: None.
Description: This comprehensive skills-building course teaches the essentials of Oracle's implementation of ANSI-SQL, and how to use it from SQL*Plus– Oracle's ad hoc querying environment.
Delivery method: CBT; also available via the Internet.
Minimum hardware requirement: Any PC capable of running Microsoft Windows.
Price: On application.
Source: Oracle Corporation UK Ltd, The Oracle Centre, The Ring, Bracknell, Berks. RG12 1BW. Tel: 01344 860066

Title: **SQL Data Management**

Purpose: To provide a practical grasp of SQL commands for manipulating data.

Suitable for: Programmers and trainee programmers.

Prerequisites: None.

Description: An introductory-level course, aimed to give the student a practical grasp of SQL commands for manipulating data. It also teaches commands to define tables, views and indexes. A comprehensive student manual accompanies the course.

Delivery method: CBT.

Minimum hardware requirement: PC.

Price: £1295.00 (multiple copy price on application).

Source: Electrovision UK Ltd, Hamble Point Marina, School Lane, Hamble, Southampton SO31 4JD. Tel: 01703 452221

Title: **SQL Queries**

Purpose: To describe simple to advanced queries to SQL.

Suitable for: Programmers and trainee programmers.

Prerequisites: None.

Description: Describes SQL querying, from simple 'one column, one table' queries to advanced joining and merging of data from multiple tables. Topics include: relational concepts; simple queries; selecting rows function and grouping; and joining and merging tables.

Delivery method: CBT.

Minimum hardware requirement: PC.

Price: £1295.00 (multiple copy price on application).

Source: Electrovision UK Ltd, Hamble Point Marina, School Lane, Hamble, Southampton SO31 4JD. Tel: 01703 452221

Title: **SQL/DS Essentials**

Purpose: To introduce SQL/DS essentials.

Suitable for: Programmers and trainee programmers.

Prerequisites: None.

Description: An introductory level course covering the SQL/DS environment, SQL and QMF. Teaches structure, commands and security features. Comprehensive manual accompanies the course.

Delivery method: CBT.

Minimum hardware requirement: PC.

Price: £1295.00 (multiple copy price on application).

Source: Electrovision UK Ltd, Hamble Point Marina, School Lane, Hamble, Southampton SO31 4JD. Tel: 01703 452221

Supercalc

CBT
Title: **Teach Yourself Supercalc 5**
Purpose: To teach you how to use Supercalc 5.
Suitable for: Anyone.
Prerequisites: None.
Description: This course covers: setting up a spreadsheet; adding and modifying data; linking spreadsheets; graphs and macros.
Delivery method: CBT.
Minimum hardware requirement: PC.
Price: £75.00 (multiple copy price on application).
Source: Electrovision UK Ltd, Hamble Point Marina, School Lane, Hamble, Southampton SO31 4JD. Tel: 01703 452221

Sybase

CBT
Title: **Overview of Sybase System 10**
Purpose: To teach the features of System 10 and provide basic task skills.
Suitable for: Application developers new to System 10.
Prerequisites: None.
Description: This course provides the skills needed to create, maintain and query database objects using T-SQL. A set of reference tools is provided for performing support during real-life applications development.
Delivery method: CBT.
Minimum hardware requirement: PC.
Price: £795.00.
Source: Electrovision UK Ltd, Hamble Point Marina, School Lane, Hamble, Southampton SO31 4JD. Tel: 01703 452221

Title: **Sybase System 10 – Advanced Admin**
Purpose: To provide the advanced skills for system Administration.
Suitable for: Database administrators.
Prerequisites: 'Sybase System 10 – System Administration'.
Description: Provides skills to: recover databases on SQL server; kill suspended processes on SQL server; monitor space, memory and other SQL server activities; configure SQL server and improve its performance; add remote servers, and access databases on them.
Delivery method: CBT.
Minimum hardware requirement: PC.
Price: £795.00.

Source: Electrovision UK Ltd, Hamble Point Marina, School Lane, Hamble, Southampton SO31 4JD. Tel: 01703 452221

Title: **Sybase System 10 – System Administration**
Purpose: To provide the necessary skills for system administration.
Suitable for: Database administrators.
Prerequisites: None.
Description: This course provides skills to: install, start and shut down SQL server; create and maintain database devices, databases, segments, and mirrored devices; grant and revoke permissions and roles and audit SQL server; back up data on SQL server.
Delivery method: CBT.
Minimum hardware requirement: PC.
Price: £795.00.
Source: Electrovision UK Ltd, Hamble Point Marina, School Lane, Hamble, Southampton SO31 4JD. Tel: 01703 452221

Title: **Sybase System 10 – T-SQL Programming**
Purpose: To introduce T-SQL programming.
Suitable for: Programmers new to Sybase System 10.
Prerequisites: None.
Description: This course covers an introduction to: T-SQL programming; managing database objects; performing simple queries; performing complex queries; and manipulating data. It also contains a T-SQL quick reference guide.
Delivery method: CBT.
Minimum hardware requirement: PC.
Price: £795.00.
Source: Electrovision UK Ltd, Hamble Point Marina, School Lane, Hamble, Southampton SO31 4JD. Tel: 01703 452221

Delegation

CBT
Title: **Do or Delegate?**
Purpose: To teach the concepts of delegation.
Suitable for: Team leaders and managers.
Prerequisites: None.
Description: Discusses why you should delegate and what should be delegated. The course covers what should be delegated and how to choose which person to delegate a task to.
Delivery method: CBT.
Minimum hardware requirement: PC.

Price: £175.00.

Source: Electrovision UK Ltd, Hamble Point Marina, School Lane, Hamble, Southampton SO31 4JD. Tel: 01703 452221

CD-ROM

Title: **Delegation**

Purpose: To help you to sharpen your delegation skills and to get a picture of your own attitudes.

Suitable for: Managers and supervisors.

Prerequisites: None.

Description: This course provides the concepts of delegation and will help you to: know what to delegate and to whom; use delegation to achieve your objectives; know what happens when you fail to delegate; know the barriers to delegation; support once a task has been delegated; and deal with problems.

Delivery method: CD-ROM.

Minimum hardware requirement: 486 PC; 8Mb RAM; 420Mb hard disk; CD-ROM drive; audio card.

Price: £895.00.

Source: Training Direct, North Court, Edinburgh Gate, Harlow, Essex CM20 2JE. Tel: 01279 623927

Discipline interviewing

CD-ROM

Title: **Grievance and Disciplinary Interviewing**

Purpose: To give you all the guidance you need and a chance to practise what you have learnt.

Suitable for: Managers.

Prerequisites: 'Essential Interviewing Skills'.

Description: This course will help you to recognise the need for: grievance or disciplinary procedures; gathering facts; reviewing grievance or disciplinary procedures; choosing an appropriate place and time; establishing objectives; documenting the interview and monitoring progress.

Delivery method: CD-ROM.

Minimum hardware requirement: 486 PC; 8Mb RAM; 420Mb hard disk; CD-ROM drive; audio card.

Price: £895.00.

Source: Training Direct, North Court, Edinburgh Gate, Harlow, Essex CM20 2JE. Tel: 01279 623927

Title: **The Discipline Interview**

Purpose: To enable you to carry out the discipline interview effectively.

Suitable for: Team leaders and managers.
Prerequisites: None.
Description: This course will help you, whether it is a quiet word without a great deal of fuss, or a serious matter which must be resolved without fail, so the informal warning and the formal disciplining are covered. The topics covered include: preparation; the face-to-face interview; and ongoing measures.
Delivery method: CD-ROM.
Minimum hardware requirement: 386 PC; 8Mb RAM; 6Mb hard-disk space; CD-ROM card; sound card.
Price: £295.00.
Source: Comput-Ed Ltd, Long Lane, Dawlish EX7 0QR. Tel: 01626 889955

Economics

CBT
Title: **Do You Know Economics?**
Purpose: To act as a learning needs assessment which will be an aid to both learning and revision.
Suitable for: Anyone.
Prerequisites: A broad knowledge of economics.
Description: A self-assessment tool consisting of about 300 multiple choice questions that will help you to develop your knowledge through repeated practice on questions covering all areas of the subject.
Delivery method: CBT and supporting text.
Minimum hardware requirement: IBM PC or compatible, 512k RAM.
Price: £165.00.
Source: Ivy Business Training Software plc, Ivy House, 233–235 Roehampton Lane, London SW15 4LB. Tel: 0181 780 1494

CD-ROM
Title: **Economics**
Purpose: To teach and support a complete introductory economics course.
Suitable for: All business (or modular) students from HND level upwards.
Prerequisites: None.
Description: The course is divided up into parts including: the economic problem; demand; supply; price and market mechanism; market structures; factor prices and markets; national income and aggregate demand; money and national income; the IS/LM model; the external sector; inflation; macroeconomics policy.
Delivery method: CD-ROM.
Minimum hardware requirement: PC; 8Mb RAM; CD-ROM drive and sound card.
Price: £29.95 (inc. VAT) single-user licence; multi-user licences from £650.

Source: Pitman Publishing, 128 Long Acre, London WC2E 9AN. Tel: 0171 4472290

Title: **The McGraw-Hill Interactive Guide to World Business and Economics**
Purpose: To help users gain in-depth, comparative economic, business and life-style information on over 220 countries worldwide and manipulate that data into graphs, charts and maps.
Suitable for: Marketers, researchers, consultants, importers/exporters, sales managers, geographers and students.
Prerequisites: None.
Description: There are 17 core areas of information: World of Information guides (2 years); country map; key facts; industry; investment and companies; labour force; import and export; agriculture; armed forces; communications and media; energy; education; population and welfare; sex and age; economic indicators; transport; natural resources.
Delivery method: CD-ROM.
Minimum hardware requirement: 386 PC; CD-ROM drive; 3Mb hard disk; 4Mb RAM.
Price: £85.00 + VAT (standalone); £149.00 + VAT (network).
Source: McGraw-Hill Publishing Co, Shoppenhangers Road, Maidenhead, Berks. SL6 2QL. Tel: 01628 23432

Electrical safety

CD-ROM
Title: **Electrical Safety**
Purpose: To identify potential hazards caused by careless use.
Suitable for: Persons who use electrically powered equipment or tools.
Prerequisites: None.
Description: The modules of this course are: what is electricity; dangers of electricity; safe use of electrical equipment; electric shocks and first aid; and a self-test.
Delivery method: CD-ROM.
Minimum hardware requirement: 486 PC; 4Mb RAM; dual speed CD-ROM drive; sound card.
Price: On application.
Source: Instinct Training, Strawberry How Business Centre, Lorton Road, Cockermouth, Cumbria CA13 9XQ. Tel: 01900 827600

Title: **Electricity at Work**
Purpose: To explain the implications of the regulations for electrical safety at

work and outline the duties and responsibilities of everyone affected by the legislation.
Suitable for: Those responsible for electrical safety at work.
Prerequisites: None.
Description: The modules are: legal aspects; dangers of electricity; some terms explained; safe systems of work; outline of safe systems; checklist; users quick checklist; and a self-test.
Delivery method: CD-ROM.
Minimum hardware requirement: 486 PC; 4Mb RAM; Dual speed CD-ROM drive; sound card.
Price: On application.
Source: Instinct Training, Strawberry How Business Centre, Lorton Road, Cockermouth, Cumbria CA13 9XQ. Tel: 01900 827600

Title: **Safety Rules – Acceptors**
Purpose: To provide comprehensive training in the Electrical and Mechanical Safety Rules.
Suitable for: Persons nominated to receive and clear safety documents at power station sites.
Prerequisites: None.
Description: The course modules are: introduction; policy, philosophy and principles; general provisions; safety rules; permit to work; access certificate; safety document procedures; and an assessment. A score of 93 per cent or more must be achieved in order to pass.
Delivery method: CD-ROM.
Minimum hardware requirement: 486 PC; 4Mb RAM; dual speed CD-ROM drive; sound card.
Price: On application.
Source: Instinct Training, Strawberry How Business Centre, Lorton Road, Cockermouth, Cumbria CA13 9XQ. Tel: 01900 827600

Title: **Safety Rules – Issuers**
Purpose: To provide comprehensive training in the Electrical and Mechanical Safety Rules.
Suitable for: Persons nominated to issue and transfer safety documents at power station sites.
Prerequisites: None.
Description: The modules of this course are: introduction; policy, philosophy and principles; general provisions; permit; safety document procedures; legislation: persons involved; safety rules; access certificate; and assessment. A score of 93 per cent or better must be achieved in order to pass.
Delivery method: CD-ROM.

Minimum hardware requirement: 486 PC; 4Mb RAM; dual speed CD-ROM drive; sound card.
Price: On application.
Source: Instinct Training, Strawberry How Business Centre, Lorton Road, Cockermouth, Cumbria CA13 9XQ Tel: 01900 827600

Title: **Safety Rules – Safety Controllers**
Purpose: To provide comprehensive training in the Electrical and Mechanical Safety Rules.
Suitable for: Persons responsible for ensuring that adequate precautions are taken to provide safety from the system.
Prerequisites: None.
Description: The modules of this course are: introduction; policy, philosophy and principles; general provisions; permit; safety document procedures; legislation: persons involved; safety rules; access certificate; and assessment. A score of 93 per cent or better must be achieved in order to pass.
Delivery method: CD-ROM.
Minimum hardware requirement: 486 PC; 4Mb RAM; dual speed CD-ROM drive; sound card.
Price: On application.
Source: Instinct Training, Strawberry How Business Centre, Lorton Road, Cockermouth, Cumbria CA13 9XQ. Tel: 01900 827600

Empowerment

CBT

Title: **Empowerment**
Purpose: To explain the concept of empowerment.
Suitable for: Managers.
Prerequisites: None.
Description: This course covers the key issues of empowerment such as: decision making process; information sharing; evaluating performance; motivating; and developing individuals. Student workbook supplied with the course.
Delivery method: CBT.
Minimum hardware requirement: PC.
Price: £413.00.
Source: Electrovision UK Ltd, Hamble Point Marina, School Lane, Hamble, Southampton SO31 4JD. Tel: 01703 452221

CD-i

Title: **The Empowering Manager**
Purpose: To help managers adapt existing skills to a new, empowered environment.
Suitable for: New managers and existing managers/team leaders and supervisors.
Prerequisites: None.
Description: The film follows a formula for successful empowerment using the mnemonic POWER: participative; open; willing to let go; enabling; results driven.
Delivery method: CD-i.
Minimum hardware requirement: TV and CD-i player.
Price: Purchase – £995.00 + carriage + VAT. 2 day hire – £165.00 + carriage + VAT.
Source: Melrose, 16 Bromells Road, London SW4 0BL. Tel: 0171 627 8404

English

CD-ROM

Title: **Basic Skills – English**
Purpose: To provide the fundamentals of a language.
Suitable for: Anyone.
Prerequisites: None.
Description: Basic Skills provide the fundamentals of a language in a fun and easy-to-use way. Chapters are: alphabet; numbers; currency; weather; times; calendar; basic phrases. British and American English are included on the same disc.
Delivery method: CD-ROM.
Minimum hardware requirement: PC; 8Mb RAM; CD-ROM; sound card.
Price: £39.00.
Source: Electrovision UK Ltd, Hamble Point Marina, School Lane, Hamble, Southampton SO31 4JD. Tel: 01703 452221

Title: **Business English Activities**
Purpose: To teach business English.
Suitable for: Anyone.
Prerequisites: None.
Description: This six-disc course teaches business English. The topics cover: introductions; the office; phones; appointments; presentations; travel; hotels; market research; entertaining; negotiating; tests and exercises.
Delivery method: CD-ROM.
Minimum hardware requirement: PC; 8Mb RAM; CD-ROM; sound card.

Price: £399.00.
Source: Electrovision UK Ltd, Hamble Point Marina, School Lane, Hamble, Southampton SO31 4JD. Tel: 01703 452221

Title: **Expressions – English**
Purpose: To provide practical language training.
Suitable for: Anyone.
Prerequisites: None.
Description: This course provides practical language training by concentrating on various scenarios: airport, train, eating out, etc. The CD also has practice, speaking test, playback and various exercises.
Delivery method: CD-ROM.
Minimum hardware requirement: PC; 8Mb RAM; CD-ROM; sound card.
Price: £69.00.
Source: Electrovision UK Ltd, Hamble Point Marina, School Lane, Hamble, Southampton SO31 4JD. Tel: 01703 452221

Equal opportunities

CBT

Title: **Equal Opportunities**
Purpose: To teach the student about the moral and business motives for equal opportunities; the terminology and legislation involved.
Suitable for: Management and employees within companies with or without an equal opportunities policy.
Prerequisites: None.
Description: The course is available with two options: one for a company with their own policy, their policy would be incorporated; the other for a company wishing to introduce a policy, the CBT offers advice, guidelines and checklists.
Delivery method: CBT.
Minimum hardware requirement: 486PC; CD-ROM; 4Mb RAM; 12Mb hard disk.
Price: Available on application.
Source: CBL Technology Ltd, St Katherine's House, Mansfield Road, Derby DE1 3TQ. Tel: 01332 205800

Title: **Equal Opportunities at Work**
Purpose: To explain what equal opportunities legislation is and how to avoid breaking the law.
Suitable for: Managers and employees.
Prerequisites: None.
Description: Based on case law and created in association with the Commission for Racial Equality and the Equal Opportunities Commission. The programme

covers the basic principles and provides an easy reference on both procedural and legal aspects of implementing an equal opportunities policy.
Delivery method: CBT.
Minimum hardware requirement: 386 PC; 128Kb RAM; 2.5Mb hard disk.
Price: Licences – single: £99.00; network: £500–£3500.00.
Source: MLS Ltd, 26 Warwick Road, London SW5 9UD. Tel: 0171 373 9489

Title: **Understanding Equal Opportunities**
Purpose: To increase awareness and understanding of equal opportunities policies with all staff.
Suitable for: Induction training; management and supervisory training; sales and customer service training.
Prerequisites: None.
Description: This package enables you to tackle modules about the law, and about the different elements of discrimination and prejudice, as well as the benefits of equal opportunities policies and more. A learning management system is included in the package, enabling you to assess staff and keep full training records of their performance.
Delivery method: CBT.
Minimum hardware requirement: 386 PC; 3Mb hard disk; 640Kb RAM.
Price: £595.00: unlimited workstation licence; £1950.00: unlimited network licence.
Source: Easy i Ltd, 42 The Square, Kenilworth, Warwickshire CV8 1EB. Tel: 01926 854111

European Union

CBT
Title: **Doing Business in Europe**
Purpose: To give an overview of the business environment in the member states of the Community.
Suitable for: Anyone.
Prerequisites: 'The European Community: Its History and Institutions'.
Description: This is an introductory course which will enable you to understand: the practical implications of 'convergence' as the test for implementing Economic and Monetary Union; some of the different attitudes to conducting business in other Community countries.
Delivery Method: CBT and supporting text.
Minimum Hardware Requirement: IBM PC or compatible, 512k RAM.
Price: £165.00.
Source: Ivy Business Training Software plc, Ivy House, 233–235 Roehampton Lane, London SW15 4LB. Tel: 0181 780 1494

DIRECTORY OF COURSES

Title: **Euroquest**
Purpose: To increase awareness of European legislation and improve knowledge of the EC and its operation within the European business environment.
Suitable for: Anyone.
Prerequisites: None.
Description: Changes in the EC have a great impact on this country. British companies face opportunities to expand their markets into Europe and threats to their survival from increased competition. This course provides the information that is essential to managers and their staff.
Delivery method: CBT.
Minimum hardware requirement: PC.
Price: £145.00.
Source: Marketing Department, The Chartered Insurance Institute, 20 Aldermanbury, London EC2V 7HY. Tel: 0171 417 4427

Title: **The European Community: Its History and Institutions**
Purpose: To give a general foundation knowledge of the growth and development of the European Community and its institutions in an easily understood format.
Suitable for: Anyone.
Prerequisites: None.
Description: This is an introductory course which will enable you to understand the aims of the EC; be familiar with the Community framework; be aware of the legal implications and know the history and expansion of the Community.
Delivery method: CBT and supporting text.
Minimum hardware requirement: IBM PC or compatible, 512k RAM.
Price: £165.00.
Source: Ivy Business Training Software plc, Ivy House, 233–235 Roehampton Lane, London SW15 4LB. Tel: 0181 780 1494

Facilitation skills

CBT
Title: **Facilitation Skills**
Purpose: To describe what facilitation is.
Suitable for: Team leaders and managers.
Prerequisites: None.
Description: The course explores a powerful approach to team development – facilitation. It describes what facilitation is and explains how it differs from other team approaches. The student learns how to recognise and use different facilitation models, how to observe, listen to and interpret what a team is doing, and how to use key intervention techniques.
Delivery method: CBT.

223

Minimum hardware requirement: PC.
Price: £413.00.
Source: Electrovision UK Ltd, Hamble Point Marina, School Lane, Hamble, Southampton SO31 4JD. Tel: 01703 452221.

Finance

CBT
Title: **An Introduction to Financial Futures**
Purpose: To cover the structure of the market, LIFFE conventions, hedging and trading.
Suitable for: Anyone.
Prerequisites: None.
Description: This is an introductory/intermediate course which will give you a sound foundation in the concepts of futures trading.
Delivery method: CBT and supporting text.
Minimum hardware requirement: IBM PC or compatible, 512k RAM.
Price: £165.00.
Source: Ivy Business Training Software plc, Ivy House, 233–235 Roehampton Lane, London SW15 4LB. Tel: 0181 780 1494

Title: **An Introduction to Traded Options**
Purpose: To give a detailed overview of how the International Traded Options Market works and teach you the basics of dealing in options.
Suitable for: Anyone.
Prerequisites: Some familiarity with money markets and share dealing.
Description: This is an introductory course which will enable you to know how and when to buy and sell call and put options; how to hedge with options; and how to trade index options.
Delivery method: CBT and supporting text.
Minimum hardware requirement: IBM PC or compatible, 512k RAM.
Price: £165.00.
Source: Ivy Business Training Software plc, Ivy House, 233–235 Roehampton Lane, London SW15 4LB. Tel: 0181 780 1494

Title: **Analysing Financial Statements: How Successful Are We?**
Purpose: To train you to evaluate a company's past performance; compare its performance to other companies; and get some idea of what future performance may be.
Suitable for: People needing to analyse company performance.
Prerequisites: A grasp of the concepts of financial statements and maths.

Description: An advanced course which will enable you to perform ratio analysis, interpret the results and to understand the major categories of ratios.
Delivery method: CBT with supporting text.
Minimum hardware requirement: IBM PC or compatible, 512k RAM.
Price: £165.00 single copy; price for multiple copies on request.
Source: Ivy Business Training Software plc, Ivy House, 233–235 Roehampton Lane, London SW15 4LB. Tel: 0181 780 1494

Title: **Banking and Money: How They Work and What it Means to You**
Purpose: To teach about the banking system and how banks create spending power.
Suitable for: Anyone.
Prerequisites: None.
Description: This is an introductory course which will enable you to understand the background of banking and money.
Delivery method: CBT and supporting text.
Minimum hardware requirement: IBM PC or compatible, 512k RAM.
Price: £165.00.
Source: Ivy Business Training Software plc, Ivy House, 233–235 Roehampton Lane, London SW15 4LB. Tel: 0181 780 1494

Title: **Cash Flow Statements: The Naked Truth About Financial Performance**
Purpose: To show how to compile and analyse cash flow statements.
Suitable for: People with a sound understanding of profit and loss accounts and balance sheets.
Prerequisites: A sound understanding of the two financial statements.
Description: This intermediate to advanced course covers: what a cash flow statement is and how it differs from the profit and loss account and the balance sheet; the difference between cash and profit; the concepts of working capital, cash generation and cash absorption; the difference between cash and working capital approaches to cash flow analysis.
Delivery method: CBT and supporting text.
Minimum hardware requirement: IBM PC or compatible, 512k RAM.
Price: £165.00 single copy; price for multiple copies on request.
Source: Ivy Business Training Software plc, Ivy House, 233–235 Roehampton Lane, London SW15 4LB. Tel: 0181 780 1494

Title: **Corporate Finance: Projecting Profits and Cash Flow**
Purpose: To teach the principles and their related techniques which are valuable for decision making in most business enterprises.
Suitable for: Decision makers.
Prerequisites: A sound understanding of managerial accounting.

Description: An advanced course which will enable you to: competently perform and interpret ratio analysis on the operating performance, liquidity and financial strengths of an organisation; prepare a cash flow and profit projection, taking into account qualitative factors; and perform sensitivity analysis.
Delivery method: CBT and supporting text.
Minimum hardware requirement: IBM PC or compatible, 512k RAM.
Price: £165.00.
Source: Ivy Business Training Software plc, Ivy House, 233–235 Roehampton Lane, London SW15 4LB. Tel: 0181 780 1494

Title: **Corporate Finance: The Cost of Capital**
Purpose: To teach the important topic of the firm's cost of capital and how to finance investments.
Suitable for: Decision makers.
Prerequisites: The other two courses in this series.
Description: This advanced course consists of three lessons which cover the important topics of how to calculate a firm's cost of capital, which is the discount rate used in corporate financial situations and which has far-reaching consequences. The course concludes with a section on mergers and acquisitions and how to finance investments.
Delivery method: CBT and supporting text.
Minimum hardware requirement: IBM PC or compatible, 512k RAM.
Price: £165.00.
Source: Ivy Business Training Software plc, Ivy House, 233–235 Roehampton Lane, London SW15 4LB. Tel: 0181 780 1494

Title: **Corporate Finance: The Creation of Value**
Purpose: Addresses the concept of the 'creation of value'. Value is created or added when profits are increased, risks reduced or greater efficiencies produced.
Suitable for: Decision makers.
Prerequisites: 'Corporate Finance: Projecting Profits and Cash Flow'.
Description: An advanced course that will enable you to calculate present and future values and payback, and to explain the capital budgeting process.
Delivery method: CBT and supporting text.
Minimum hardware requirement: IBM PC or compatible, 512k RAM.
Price: £165.00.
Source: Ivy Business Training Software plc, Ivy House, 233–235 Roehampton Lane, London SW15 4LB. Tel: 0181 780 1494

Title: **Do You Know Management Accounting?**
Purpose: To act as a learning needs assessment which will be an aid to both learning and revision.

Suitable for: Anyone.
Prerequisites: A broad knowledge of management accounting.
Description: A self-assessment tool consisting of about 300 multiple-choice questions that will help you to develop your knowledge through repeated practice on questions covering all areas of the subject.
Delivery method: CBT and supporting text.
Minimum hardware requirement: IBM PC or compatible, 512k RAM.
Price: £165.00.
Source: Ivy Business Training Software plc, Ivy House, 233–235 Roehampton Lane, London SW15 4LB. Tel: 0181 780 1494

Title: **Documentary Collections**
Purpose: To provide a complete understanding of documentary collections as used in banking and international trade.
Suitable for: Bankers/executives/staff involved with international trade: freight forwarders, company export department executives, etc.
Prerequisites: Three months' work in or with international trade documentation.
Description: Eight chapters: methods of payment in international trade; the parties to a collection; the collection cycle; financial documents; commercial documents; protesting and noting; international terms of trade incoterms; uniform rules for collections; and final test.
Delivery method: CBT.
Minimum hardware requirement: 386PC; 1Mb RAM; 6Mb hard disk.
Price: £600.00 + VAT; discount for volume purchases.
Source: Investment Education plc, 20 Dickinson Street, Manchester M1 4LF. Tel: 0161 228 2400

Title: **FPA (Financial Performance Assessment)**
Purpose: To teach practical business finance from the fundamentals of finance, through analysis and key performance ratios, to strategic issues.
Suitable for: All levels of management, from new graduates to senior executives.
Prerequisites: None.
Description: Fifteen modules, covering the financial statements, analysis, investment appraisal, performance ratios and strategic measures.
Delivery method: CBT; users can import their own audio and video files.
Minimum hardware requirement: 386 PC, 4MB RAM and 10MB hard disk.
Price: Personal user version: £400.00; learning centre version: £1200.00.
Source: Intellexis International Ltd, Lyric House, 149 Hammersmith Road, London W14 0QL. Tel: 0171 371 4444

Title: **Global Custody: A Practical Overview**
Purpose: To train anyone working in the global custody area or working with global custodians.

Suitable for: Staff or new managers working in or with investments and securities, especially those in the back-office area.
Prerequisites: A general awareness of securities.
Description: Thirteen chapters covering: introduction; legal requirements; services and custody relationships; payment and communication systems; procedures for purchases and sales; settlement operations, dividends and interest; taxation; corporate actions overview; cross-border proxy voting; cash management; stock borrowing and lending; record keeping; reporting and valuations; and final test.
Delivery method: CBT.
Minimum hardware requirement: 386PC; 1Mb RAM; 6Mb hard disk.
Price: £1900.00 + VAT; discount for volume purchases.
Source: Investment Education plc, 20 Dickinson Street, Manchester M1 4LF. Tel: 0161 228 2400

Title: **Making The Money Go Round**
Purpose: To look at what makes the money go round in a company and how a business is financed.
Suitable for: Anyone.
Prerequisites: None.
Description: This course has four sections: the money-go-round; financing the business; the statement of funds; and managing the money-go-round.
Delivery method: CBT.
Minimum hardware requirement: PC.
Price: £299.00.
Source: Electrovision UK Ltd, Hamble Point Marina, School Lane, Hamble, Southampton SO31 4JD. Tel: 01703 452221

Title: **Pushing for Profit**
Purpose: To put profit into perspective.
Suitable for: Anyone.
Prerequisites: None.
Description: This course puts profit into perspective and looks at costs and revenue. It also covers the trading statement and the profit and loss account.
Delivery method: CBT.
Minimum hardware requirement: PC.
Price: £299.00.
Source: Electrovision UK Ltd, Hamble Point Marina, School Lane, Hamble, Southampton SO31 4JD. Tel: 01703 452221

Title: **The Balancing Act**
Purpose: To introduce business finance.
Suitable for: Anyone.

Prerequisites: None.
Description: The course has five modules covering: the language of finance; profit and loss; cash flow; the balance sheet; and improving financial performance.
Delivery method: CBT.
Minimum hardware requirement: 386 PC; 4Mb RAM; 12Mb hard disk.
Price: £295.00 single user; licence price on application.
Source: Unicorn Training, Copsham House, Broad Street, Chesham, HP5 3EA. Tel: 01494 791064

Title: **The SFA Rules: A Management and Staff Training Programme**
Purpose: To provide a detailed review of the SFA rules for managers and staff under SFA regulation.
Suitable for: Managers and staff in organisations subject to SFA regulation.
Prerequisites: None.
Description: Sixteen chapters covering: introduction; membership; general rules; types of clients; disclosure and consent requirements; client relations; regulated business; publicising and promoting business; dealing rules, conflicts of interest; illegal practices; self-monitoring and rule enforcement; rule enforcement by SFA; safe custody; client money; corporate finance; and final test.
Delivery method: CBT.
Minimum hardware requirement: 386PC; 1Mb RAM; 6Mb hard disk.
Price: £1900.00 + VAT; discount for volume purchases.
Source: Investment Education plc, 20 Dickinson Street, Manchester M1 4LF. Tel: 0161 228 2400

Title: **Trade Tutor**
Purpose: To teach the use of letters of credit, collections and international trade commercial and financial documents (invoices, bills of lading, insurance documents, bills of exchange, etc.).
Suitable for: Bank staff working in trade finance, and administrative and sales staff involved in import or export.
Prerequisites: None.
Description: Course has 24 sections divided into three modules: hazards of international trade; how collections work; and how letters of credit work. Each module finishes with a test.
Delivery method: CBT.
Minimum hardware requirement: 386 PC; 4Mb RAM; 50Mb hard disk.
Price: £1750.00 + p&p.
Source: Mantissa Ltd, 1 Cresswell Park, London SE3 9RD. Tel: 0181 297 0441

Title: **Understanding Business Finance**
Purpose: An introduction to the principles of business finance.
Suitable for: Non-financial managers.

Prerequisites: None.
Description: The package consists of five separate modules and a workbook. Topics covered are: how money works in business; the profit and loss account; the balance sheet; the cash flow forecast and working capital control; interpreting published accounts.
Delivery method: CBT.
Minimum hardware requirement: PC.
Price: £90.00 + VAT.
Source: Mobile Training Ltd, Green Acres, Sibford Gower, Banbury OX15 5RW. Tel: 01295 788115

Title: **Understanding Management Accounting**
Purpose: To introduce and demonstrate the principles of management accounting showing how each technique can be applied to the day-to-day work.
Suitable for: Managers.
Prerequisites: None.
Description: The package consists of nine separate modules and a workbook. Topics covered are: introduction to management accounting; full costing; marginal costing; project appraisal; working capital; cash management; budgetary control; standard costing; interpretation.
Delivery method: CBT.
Minimum hardware requirement: PC.
Price: £90.00 + VAT.
Source: Mobile Training Ltd, Green Acres, Sibford Gower, Banbury OX15 5RW. Tel: 01295 788115

CBT (tutor led)

Title: **Practical Finance**
Purpose: To familiarise and gain an understanding of financial and management accounting at a practical and strategic level in business.
Suitable for: New managers and graduates.
Prerequisites: None.
Description: A one-day event in which all concepts are practically illustrated in a visual 'hands-on' experience using the Executive business simulation. A very practical way of learning, with the emphasis on application rather than theory.
Delivery method: CBT activity with tutor-led discussion and instruction.
Minimum hardware requirement: 386 PC.
Price: From £650.00 per day for 12 delegates.
Source: April Training Executive Ltd, Tarvin Road, Frodsham, Cheshire WA6 6XN. Tel: 01928 735868

CD-ROM

Title: **Improving Profitability**
Purpose: To look at profitability, trading profit, fixed assets and working capital, and business performance through a case study.
Suitable for: Managers involved in managing resources.
Prerequisites: 'How Money Works in Business'.
Description: This course, which gets you to run your own market stall, will help you to understand: profitability as 'return on investment'; the four factors which effect trading profit; fixed assets and working capital; the need to monitor business performance; and the trends and potential problems.
Delivery method: CD-ROM.
Minimum hardware requirement: 486 PC, 8Mb RAM, 420Mb hard disk, CD-ROM drive, audio card.
Price: £895.00.
Source: Training Direct, North Court, Edinburgh Gate, Harlow, Essex CM20 2JE. Tel: 01279 623927

Title: **Money Business 1: Managing Cash**
Purpose: To help you make better business decisions as a result of a better understanding of the financial implications.
Suitable for: First-line managers and supervisors.
Prerequisites: None.
Description: This course gives a comprehensive introduction to money in business, examining the way money cycles around a business, money traps and working capital, and explains the impact of business decisions on cash flow. It also shows how to manage stock, creditors and debtors effectively.
Delivery method: CD-ROM.
Minimum hardware requirement: 486 PC, 8Mb RAM, 420Mb hard disk, CD-ROM drive, audio card.
Price: £1199.00.
Source: Xebec Multi Media Solutions Ltd, The Critchley Building, Bath Road, Woodchester, Stroud, Glos. GL5 5EY. Tel: 01453 835482

Title: **Quantitative Method**
Purpose: To teach and support a complete introductory quantitative methods course.
Suitable for: All business (or modular) students from HND level upwards.
Prerequisites: None.
Description: Contents include: basic mathematics; the use of models, the mathematics of finance; linear programming; introduction to calculus; introduction to descriptive statistics; and descriptive statistics – averages and dispersion, time series, index numbers, probability, probability distribution, simulation, decision analysis, sampling theory, estimation and confidence limits.

Delivery method: CD-ROM.
Minimum hardware requirement: PC; 8Mb RAM; CD-ROM drive and sound card.
Price: £29.95 (inc. VAT) single-user licence; multi-user licences from £650.
Source: Pitman Publishing, 128 Long Acre, London WC2E 9AN. Tel: 0171 4472290

Simulation
Title: **Financial Analysis**
Purpose: To introduce financial concepts for a financial appreciation course.
Suitable for: Trainees, functional specialists, supervisors, junior through middle management.
Prerequisites: None.
Description: A simulation/game for teams of 4–5, involving preparing a financial plan covering basic financial reports and measures.
Delivery method: Teams use computerised simulator.
Minimum hardware requirement: PC; 640Kb RAM and printer.
Price: Rental: £195.00; purchase: £495.00; tutored from £500.00.
Source: Hall Marketing, Studio 11, Colman's Wharf, 45 Morris Road, London E14 6PA. Tel: 0171 537 2982

Financial management

CBT
Title: **Do You Know Financial Management?**
Purpose: To act as a training needs analysis which will be an aid to both learning and revision.
Suitable for: Anyone.
Prerequisites: A broad knowledge of financial management.
Description: A self-assessment tool consisting of about 300 multiple-choice questions that will help you to develop your knowledge through repeated practice on questions covering all areas of the subject.
Delivery method: CBT and supporting text.
Minimum hardware requirement: IBM PC or compatible, 512k RAM.
Price: £165.00.
Source: Ivy Business Training Software plc, Ivy House, 233–235 Roehampton Lane, London SW15 4LB. Tel: 0181 780 1494

Financial services

CBT

Title: **Advanced Financial Planning Certificate**
Purpose: To practise the skills required to pass the AFPC examination.
Suitable for: Those taking the AFPC examinations.
Prerequisites: None.
Description: There are four modules, each containing four case studies: taxation and trusts; personal investment planning; pensions; business financial planning.
Delivery method: CBT.
Minimum hardware requirement: 486 PC; 8Mb RAM; 25Mb hard disk space per module.
Price: £150.00 per module.
Source: Marketing Department, The Chartered Insurance Institute, 20 Aldermanbury, London EC2V 7HY. Tel: 0171 417 4427

Title: **Financial Planning Certificate – Paper 1**
Purpose: To help those taking the first paper of the FPC to prepare and revise for the examination.
Suitable for: Those taking the FPC examinations.
Prerequisites: Study of the subject.
Description: Covers: regulatory framework; conduct of business; compliance rules; monitoring/enforcement; legal requirements; taxation; national insurance; financial needs; client information and financial. Includes 148 questions covering the above.
Delivery method: CBT.
Minimum hardware requirement: PC.
Price: £250.00.
Source: Marketing Department, The Chartered Insurance Institute, 20 Aldermanbury, London EC2V 7HY. Tel: 0171 417 4427

Title: **Financial Planning Certificate – Paper 2**
Purpose: To help those taking the second paper of the FPC to prepare and revise for the examination.
Suitable for: Those taking the FPC examinations.
Prerequisites: Study of the subject.
Description: Covers: protection products – comparing products and providers; pension products – comparing products and providers; savings and investment products – comparing products and providers; arranging a mortgage; mortgage products – comparing products and providers. Multiple-choice test disk containing questions based on the above.
Delivery method: CBT.

Minimum hardware requirement: PC.
Price: £250.00.
Source: Marketing Department, The Chartered Insurance Institute, 20 Aldermanbury, London EC2V 7HY. Tel: 0171 417 4427

Title: **Financial Planning Certificate – Paper 3**
Purpose: To help those taking the second paper of the FPC to prepare and revise for the examination.
Suitable for: Those taking the FPC examinations.
Prerequisites: Study of the subject.
Description: Covers four different case studies containing a combination of simulated interview situations and tutorials. Each case study comprises: case history; case interview; assessing client needs; presenting the recommendations and referrals; and reviewing.
Delivery method: CBT.
Minimum hardware requirement: PC.
Price: £250.00.
Source: Marketing Department, The Chartered Insurance Institute, 20 Aldermanbury, London EC2V 7HY. Tel: 0171 417 4427

Title: **FPC3**
Purpose: To teach the student about the syllabus of the FPC3 exam.
Suitable for: Sales staff and employees within companies dealing with financial sales. Covers all requirements for FPC standards.
Prerequisites: None.
Description: The course covers the exam technique involved in the FPC3 exam and the three question types involved.
Delivery method: CBT.
Minimum hardware requirement: 486PC; CD-ROM; 4Mb RAM; 10Mb hard disk.
Price: Available on application.
Source: CBL Technology Ltd, St Katherine's House, Mansfield Road, Derby DE1 3TQ. Tel: 01332 205800

Title: **General Investment and Financial Services Knowledge**
Purpose: The second of a nine-part series which aims to give new entrants to the industry a thorough foundation knowledge for the purposes of the Financial Planning Certificate Part 1.
Suitable for: New entrants to the financial planning industry.
Prerequisites: None.
Description: This is an intermediate course which will enable you to understand the economic conditions, the investors, the providers and the products.
Delivery method: CBT and supporting text.
Minimum hardware requirement: IBM PC or compatible, 512k RAM.

Price: £165.00.
Source: Ivy Business Training Software plc, Ivy House, 233–235 Roehampton Lane, London SW15 4LB. Tel: 0181 780 1494.

Title: **Products Related to Life Assurance**
Purpose: The fourth of a nine-part series which aims to give new entrants to the industry a thorough foundation knowledge for the purposes of the Financial Planning Certificate Part 1.
Suitable for: New entrants to the financial planning industry.
Prerequisites: None.
Description: This is an intermediate course which will enable you to understand the general principles of life assurance and the mechanics, benefits and related taxation.
Delivery method: CBT and supporting text.
Minimum hardware requirement: IBM PC or compatible, 512k RAM.
Price: £165.00.
Source: Ivy Business Training Software plc, Ivy House, 233–235 Roehampton Lane, London SW15 4LB. Tel: 0181 780 1494.

Title: **Products Related to Mortgage Arrangements**
Purpose: The eighth of a nine-part series which aims to give new entrants to the industry a thorough foundation knowledge for the purposes of the Financial Planning Certificate Part 1.
Suitable for: New entrants to the financial planning industry.
Prerequisites: None.
Description: This is an intermediate course which will enable you to understand the general principles of mortgage arrangements and the mechanics, benefits and related taxation.
Delivery method: CBT and supporting text.
Minimum hardware requirement: IBM PC or compatible, 512k RAM.
Price: £165.00.
Source: Ivy Business Training Software plc, Ivy House, 233–235 Roehampton Lane, London SW15 4LB. Tel: 0181 780 1494

Title: **Products Related to Pensions: Occupational Pensions**
Purpose: The sixth of a nine-part series which aims to give new entrants to the industry a thorough foundation knowledge for the purposes of the Financial Planning Certificate Part 1.
Suitable for: New entrants to the financial planning industry.
Prerequisites: None.
Description: This is an introductory course which will enable you to understand the general principles of occupational pensions and the mechanics, benefits and related taxation.

Delivery method: CBT and supporting text.
Minimum hardware requirement: IBM PC or compatible, 512k RAM.
Price: £165.00.
Source: Ivy Business Training Software plc, Ivy House, 233–235 Roehampton Lane, London SW15 4LB. Tel: 0181 780 1494

Title: **Products Related to Pensions: Personal Pensions**
Purpose: The seventh of a nine-part series which aims to give new entrants to the industry a thorough foundation knowledge for the purposes of the Financial Planning Certificate Part 1.
Suitable for: New entrants to the financial planning industry.
Prerequisites: None.
Description: This is an introductory course which will enable you to understand the general principles of personal pensions and the mechanics, benefits and related taxation.
Delivery method: CBT and supporting text.
Minimum hardware requirement: IBM PC or compatible, 512k RAM.
Price: £165.00.
Source: Ivy Business Training Software plc, Ivy House, 233–235 Roehampton Lane, London SW15 4LB. Tel: 0181 780 1494

Title: **Products Related to Pensions: The State Pension**
Purpose: The fifth of a nine-part series which aims to give new entrants to the industry a thorough foundation knowledge for the purposes of the Financial Planning Certificate Part 1.
Suitable for: New entrants to the financial planning industry.
Prerequisites: None.
Description: This is an introductory course which will enable you to understand the general principles of state pensions and the mechanics, benefits and related taxation.
Delivery method: CBT and supporting text.
Minimum hardware requirement: IBM PC or compatible, 512k RAM.
Price: £165.00.
Source: Ivy Business Training Software plc, Ivy House, 233–235 Roehampton Lane, London SW15 4LB. Tel: 0181 780 1494

Title: **Regulatory and Compliance Knowledge**
Purpose: The first of a nine-part series which aims to give new entrants to the industry a thorough foundation knowledge for the purposes of the Financial Planning Certificate Part 1.
Suitable for: New entrants to the financial planning industry.
Prerequisites: None.
Description: This is an introductory course which will enable you to understand

DIRECTORY OF COURSES

the 1986 Financial Services Act, the FSA regulations, and the key compliance issues.
Delivery method: CBT and supporting text.
Minimum hardware requirement: IBM PC or compatible, 512k RAM.
Price: £165.00.
Source: Ivy Business Training Software plc, Ivy House, 233–235 Roehampton Lane, London SW15 4LB. Tel: 0181 780 1494

Title: **Self-Assessment for FPC 1**
Purpose: To allow you to test yourself prior to the examination. It will help you to get to know your areas of strength and weakness, and enable you to plan your revision accordingly.
Suitable for: Persons in the financial planning industry.
Prerequisites: Study of core syllabus for FPC 1.
Description: This is a self-assessment test with nearly 500 multiple-choice questions which you can group in line with parts of the syllabus or alternatively over the whole range.
Delivery method: CBT and supporting text.
Minimum hardware requirement: IBM PC or compatible, 512k RAM.
Price: £165.00.
Source: Ivy Business Training Software plc, Ivy House, 233–235 Roehampton Lane, London SW15 4LB. Tel: 0181 780 1494

Title: **Self-Assessment for FPC 2**
Purpose: To allow you to test yourself prior to the examination. It will help you to get to know your areas of strength and weakness and enable you to plan your revision accordingly.
Suitable for: Persons in the financial planning industry.
Prerequisites: Study of core syllabus for FPC 2.
Description: This is a self-assessment test with over 400 multiple-choice and true/false questions which you can group in line with parts of the syllabus or alternatively over the whole range.
Delivery method: CBT and supporting text.
Minimum hardware requirement: IBM PC or compatible, 512k RAM.
Price: £165.00.
Source: Ivy Business Training Software plc, Ivy House, 233–235 Roehampton Lane, London SW15 4LB. Tel: 0181 780 1494

Title: **Taxation and Social Security Knowledge**
Purpose: The third of a nine-part series which aims to give new entrants to the industry a thorough foundation knowledge for the purposes of the Financial Planning Certificate Part 1.
Suitable for: New entrants to the financial planning industry.

Prerequisites: None.
Description: This is an introductory course which will enable you to understand personal taxation, capital gains tax, inheritance tax, VAT, business tax, National Insurance contributions and social security benefits.
Delivery method: CBT and supporting text.
Minimum hardware requirement: IBM PC or compatible, 512k RAM.
Price: £165.00.
Source: Ivy Business Training Software plc, Ivy House, 233–235 Roehampton Lane, London SW15 4LB. Tel: 0181 780 1494

Title: **Unit Trusts, Investment Trusts, Bonds, PEPs, Annuities, Single Premium Endowments**
Purpose: The ninth of a nine-part series which aims to give new entrants to the industry a thorough foundation knowledge for the purposes of the Financial Planning Certificate Part 1.
Suitable for: New entrants to the financial planning industry.
Prerequisites: None.
Description: This is an introductory/intermediate course which will enable you to understand the general principles of unit trusts, investment trusts, PEPs, bonds, annuities and single premium endowments, and the mechanics, benefits and related taxation.
Delivery method: CBT and supporting text.
Minimum hardware requirement: IBM PC or compatible, 512k RAM.
Price: £165.00.
Source: Ivy Business Training Software plc, Ivy House, 233–235 Roehampton Lane, London SW15 4LB. Tel: 0181 780 1494

Fire safety

CBT
Title: **Fire Instructions and Fire Precautions**
Purpose: To teach you what you should do in the event of fire and methods of fire prevention.
Suitable for: Everyone.
Prerequisites: None.
Description: This is an introductory course which will enable you to know: the main features of fire precautions; where alarm points and fire appliances are; what to do to prevent fires; what action to take if a fire occurs; the correct extinguisher to use for the appropriate fire; and how to recognise and deal with bomb threats.
Delivery method: CBT and supporting text.
Minimum hardware requirement: IBM PC or compatible, 512k RAM.

Price: £165.00.
Source: Ivy Business Training Software plc, Ivy House, 233–235 Roehampton Lane, London SW15 4LB. Tel: 0181 780 1494

Foreign languages

CD-ROM

Title: **Basic Skills – French and German and Spanish**
Purpose: To provide the fundamentals of a language.
Suitable for: Anyone.
Prerequisites: None.
Description: Basic Skills provides the fundamentals of a language in a fun and easy to use way. Chapters are: alphabet; numbers; currency; weather; times; calendar; basic phrases. French, German and Spanish included on the same disc.
Delivery method: CD-ROM.
Minimum hardware requirement: PC; 8Mb RAM; CD-ROM; sound card.
Price: £39.00.
Source: Electrovision UK Ltd, Hamble Point Marina, School Lane, Hamble, Southampton SO31 4JD. Tel: 01703 452221

Title: **The Hotel Europa Series, France/Deutschland/España**
Purpose: To help students learn business languages.
Suitable for: Anyone.
Prerequisites: None.
Description: The Hotel Europa series of multimedia CD-ROMs provides the ideal package for business people and vocational language students who want to have a good working knowledge of French, German or Spanish. Studying at their own comfortable pace, learners can develop their listening skills and become fluent in speaking the language.
Delivery method: CD-ROM.
Minimum hardware requirement: 386SX PC; 4Mb RAM; 5Mb hard disk; CD-ROM with audio output and recording facilities.
Price: Licences: single – £69.00.
Source: MLS Ltd, 26 Warwick Road, London SW5 9UD. Tel: 0171 373 9489

Title: **Up to Standard Series: French/German**
Purpose: To help students to achieve NVQ levels 1 and 2.
Suitable for: Students taking business vocational language studies.
Prerequisites: None.
Description: The complete multimedia language programme for business and vocational language learning. Structured to fit the National Language Stan-

dards and Qualifications. Each unit contains three sections, two dialogues, and a section to 'check your progress'. In addition to the dialogues available on screen at all times, there are notes on culture and vocabulary, and tips on using the package.
Delivery method: CD-ROM.
Minimum hardware requirement: 386SX PC; 4Mb RAM; 5Mb hard disk; CD-ROM with audio output and recording facilities.
Price: Licences: single – £150.00; site – £950.00.
Source: MLS Ltd, 26 Warwick Road, London SW5 9UD. Tel: 0171 373 9489

Interactive video
Title: **Connections**
Purpose: To teach foreign languages. There are five courses: French, German, Spanish, Italian and Japanese.
Suitable for: Beginners or intermediate-level learners.
Prerequisites: None.
Description: These courses teach spoken language, with little or no teacher intervention. They give control and access to authentic foreign language video material and a wealth of support opportunities.
Delivery method: Interactive video.
Minimum hardware requirement: Interactive video workstation.
Price: £2595.00 per language, except Japanese which is £3595.00.
Source: Training Direct, North Court, Edinburgh Gate, Harlow, Essex CM20 2JE. Tel: 01279 623927

French

CBT
Title: **French Mistress**
Purpose: To provide a highly successful aid to learning French.
Suitable for: Anyone.
Prerequisites: None.
Description: This course provides a highly successful aid to modern language learning in vocabulary and grammar, with a variety of learning modes and test modes. All words and phrases are displayed complete with accents and special characters. In addition to the vast vocabulary supplied, the program also allows you to add your own lessons.
Delivery method: CBT.
Minimum hardware requirement: PC.
Price: £45.00.
Source: Electrovision UK Ltd, Hamble Point Marina, School Lane, Hamble, Southampton SO31 4JD. Tel: 01703 452221

CD-ROM

Title: **Expressions – French**
Purpose: To provide practical language training.
Suitable for: Anyone.
Prerequisites: None.
Description: This course provides practical language training by concentrating on various scenarios – airport, train, eating out, etc. The CD also has practice, speaking test, playback and various exercises.
Delivery method: CD-ROM.
Minimum hardware requirement: PC; 8Mb RAM; CD-ROM; sound card.
Price: £69.00.
Source: Electrovision UK Ltd, Hamble Point Marina, School Lane, Hamble, Southampton SO31 4JD. Tel: 01703 452221

Title: **Think and Talk French**
Purpose: To teach you to think and talk French.
Suitable for: Anyone.
Prerequisites: None.
Description: Lively dialogue and engrossing scenes, using sound effects, music and other audio cues, make this an interesting training course. Eight CDs are contained in this pack, which has a 10,000-word dictionary and enough training to aim at a vocabulary in excess of 1,000 words.
Delivery method: CD-ROM.
Minimum hardware requirement: PC; 8Mb RAM; CD-ROM; sound card.
Price: £159.00.
Source: Electrovision UK Ltd, Hamble Point Marina, School Lane, Hamble, Southampton SO31 4JD. Tel: 01703 452221

German

CBT

Title: **German Master**
Purpose: To provide a highly successful aid to learning German.
Suitable for: Anyone.
Prerequisites: None.
Description: This course provides a highly successful aid to modern language learning in vocabulary and grammar. Provides a variety of learning modes and test modes. All words and phrases are displayed complete with accents and special characters. In addition to the vast vocabulary supplied, the program also allows you to add your own lessons.
Delivery method: CBT.
Minimum hardware requirement: PC.

Price: £45.00.
Source: Electrovision UK Ltd, Hamble Point Marina, School Lane, Hamble, Southampton SO31 4JD. Tel: 01703 452221

CD-ROM
Title: **Expressions – German**
Purpose: To provide practical language training.
Suitable for: Anyone.
Prerequisites: None.
Description: This course provides practical language training by concentrating on various scenarios – airport, train, eating out, etc. The CD also has practice, speaking test, playback and various exercises.
Delivery method: CD-ROM.
Minimum hardware requirement: PC; 8Mb RAM; CD-ROM; sound card.
Price: £69.00.
Source: Electrovision UK Ltd, Hamble Point Marina, School Lane, Hamble, Southampton SO31 4JD. Tel: 01703 452221

Title: **Think and Talk German**
Purpose: To teach you to think and talk German.
Suitable for: Anyone.
Prerequisites: None.
Description: Lively dialogue and engrossing scenes using sound effects, music and other audio cues, make this an interesting training course. Eight CDs are contained in this pack, which has a 10,000-word dictionary and enough training to aim at a vocabulary in excess of 1,000 words.
Delivery method: CD-ROM.
Minimum hardware requirement: PC; 8Mb RAM; CD-ROM; sound card.
Price: £159.00.
Source: Electrovision UK Ltd, Hamble Point Marina, School Lane, Hamble, Southampton SO31 4JD. Tel: 01703 452221

Giving feedback and criticism

CBT
Title: **The Power of Positive Criticism**
Purpose: To teach you how to use positive criticism.
Suitable for: Team leaders and managers.
Prerequisites: None.
Description: Teaches you how to use positive criticism in three stages; planning, delivery, and follow up.
Delivery method: CBT.

Minimum hardware requirement: PC.
Price: £199.00.
Source: Electrovision UK Ltd, Hamble Point Marina, School Lane, Hamble, Southampton SO31 4JD. Tel: 01703 452221

Harassment

CBT
Title: **Sexual Harassment: Define it, Deal With it**
Purpose: To identify types of sexual harassment and discuss ways of preventing it and dealing with complaints.
Suitable for: Everyone.
Prerequisites: None.
Description: This is an introductory course which will enable you to: understand what constitutes sexual harassment; have some clear ideas how to prevent it; be aware of the legal ramifications of harassment; be aware of how to make and deal with a complaint; know where to go for help within and outside your organisation.
Delivery method: CBT and supporting text.
Minimum hardware requirement: IBM PC or compatible, 512k RAM.
Price: £165.00.
Source: Ivy Business Training Software plc, Ivy House, 233–235 Roehampton Lane, London SW15 4LB. Tel: 0181 780 1494

Health and safety

CBT
Title: **An Introduction to Safety In The Office**
Purpose: To teach you the basic, common sense elements of office safety with a view to helping you to observe good safety practice and to recognise and deal with the most frequent hazards.
Suitable for: All office staff.
Prerequisites: None.
Description: This is an introductory course which will enable you to know: the sensible rules that help avoid accidents in the office; which type of fire extinguisher to use for different fires; how to recognise and deal with common hazards in the office; and the broad provisions of the Health and Safety at Work Act.
Delivery method: CBT and supporting text.
Minimum hardware requirement: IBM PC or compatible, 512k RAM.
Price: £165.00.

Source: Ivy Business Training Software plc, Ivy House, 233–235 Roehampton Lane, London SW15 4LB. Tel: 0181 780 1494

Title: **Health and Safety at Work**
Purpose: To draw your attention to danger points, show you how to avoid them.
Suitable for: Anyone.
Prerequisites: None.
Description: This is an introductory course which will enable you to know: the principles of safe conduct and best practice with regard to the main health and safety issues to be found in places of work; know how to work safely and use preventative safety measures; when to report accidents; and how to ensure that your actions do not endanger yourself or others.
Delivery method: CBT and supporting text.
Minimum hardware requirement: IBM PC or compatible, 512k RAM.
Price: £165.00.
Source: Ivy Business Training Software plc, Ivy House, 233–235 Roehampton Lane, London SW15 4LB. Tel: 0181 780 1494

Title: **Safety for Women: Confronting Danger**
Purpose: To help women identify potential risks and prepare for contingencies, with guidance on what to do if 'the worst' occurs.
Suitable for: Everyone – as it is also important for men to study this course.
Prerequisites: None.
Description: This is an introductory course which will enable you to: be proficient in recognising potentially dangerous situations before it is too late; prepare for the worst by rehearsing over and over again – even if just in your mind – what you would do in case of trouble; handle yourself and cope in hazardous and dangerous circumstances.
Delivery method: CBT and supporting text.
Minimum hardware requirement: IBM PC or compatible, 512k RAM.
Price: £165.00.
Source: Ivy Business Training Software plc, Ivy House, 233–235 Roehampton Lane, London SW15 4LB. Tel: 0181 780 1494

Title: **Safety in Excavations**
Purpose: Aimed at improving the knowledge of operatives put to work in excavations. To highlight safe practices and hazardous situations.
Suitable for: Those who work in excavations. Also for young site engineers and students studying construction in Further Education colleges.
Prerequisites: None.
Description: The package covers the following areas: health and safety hazards; ground conditions; support methods; inspection check lists; plus an end-of-test course.

Delivery method: CBT.
Minimum hardware requirement: 386 PC; 400Kb RAM; 2.5Mb hard-disk space.
Price: £80.00 to CITB registered companies and FE colleges; £100.00 to all others.
Source: Publications Department, CITB, Bircham Newton, Kings Lynn PE31 6RH.
Tel: 01553 776677 or 01553 776651

Title: **Scaffold Inspection**
Purpose: To assist in learning the basics of scaffolding and hazard spotting.
Suitable for: Managers and supervisors.
Prerequisites: None.
Description: It presents basic information in a clear, concise manner, making it easy to understand general scaffolding principles. The package has a question-and-answer session to enable self-testing on the information presented.
Delivery method: CBT.
Minimum hardware requirement: 386 PC; 2.5Mb disk space; 400Kb RAM.
Price: £80.00: CITB companies and FE colleges; £100.00 to all other purchasers.
Source: Publications Department, CITB, Bircham Newton, Kings Lynn PE31 6RH.
Tel: 01553 776677 or 01553 776651

CD-i
Title: **The Newcomers**
Purpose: Health and safety induction course.
Suitable for: Newcomers to the workplace or organisation as part of induction training. Also suitable for supervisors.
Prerequisites: None.
Description: The story follows five newcomers around for a day uncovering a minefield of unsafe working practices. Will the story have a happy ending?
Delivery method: CD-i.
Minimum hardware requirement: TV and CD-i player.
Price: Purchase: £995.00 + carriage + VAT; 2-day hire: £165.00 + carriage + VAT.
Source: Melrose, 16 Bromells Road, London SW4 0BL. Tel: 0171 627 8404

CD-ROM
Title: **Management of Health and Safety at Work**
Purpose: To explain the requirements and implications of the regulations and to encourage a more systematic approach to health and safety management.
Suitable for: Employers and managers responsible for health and safety.
Prerequisites: None.
Description: The modules cover: European overview; risk assessment; health and safety arrangements; health surveillance; health and safety assistance; procedures for serious and imminent danger; information for employees; co-operation and co-ordination; persons working in host employers' undertaking; capabilities and training; employees' duties; temporary workers; self-test.

Delivery method: CD-ROM.
Minimum hardware requirement: 486 PC; 4Mb RAM; Dual speed CD-ROM drive; sound card.
Price: On application.
Source: Instinct Training, Strawberry How Business Centre, Lorton Road, Cockermouth, Cumbria CA13 9XQ. Tel: 01900 827600

Title: **Safe Working at Heights**
Purpose: To provide training in safe practices when working at heights.
Suitable for: All persons who work at high levels.
Prerequisites: None.
Description: The course aims to encourage the adoption of safe practices while working at heights and provides instruction in the correct use of access and safety equipment. The modules are: ladders; step ladders; scaffolding; trestles; roof work; and a self-test.
Delivery method: CD-ROM.
Minimum hardware requirement: 486 PC; 4Mb RAM; dual speed CD-ROM drive; sound card.
Price: On application.
Source: Instinct Training, Strawberry How Business Centre, Lorton Road, Cockermouth, Cumbria CA13 9XQ. Tel: 01900 827600

Title: **Safety Rules – Contractors**
Purpose: To provide comprehensive training in the electrical and mechanical safety rules.
Suitable for: Contractors' employees.
Prerequisites: None.
Description: This a shorter version of the 'Safety Rule – Acceptors' course.
Delivery method: CD-ROM.
Minimum hardware requirement: 486 PC; 4Mb RAM; dual speed CD-ROM drive; sound card.
Price: On application.
Source: Instinct Training, Strawberry How Business Centre, Lorton Road, Cockermouth, Cumbria CA13 9XQ. Tel: 01900 827600

High technology

Simulation
Title: **TECHNIQUE – High Technology**
Purpose: To teach business strategy and team working in companies that design, produce and sell high-technology products in multiple markets.
Suitable for: Middle through senior management.

Prerequisites: Line management experience.
Description: A total enterprise business simulation/game. Involving product design and positioning, setting up manufacturing facilities and financial planning by teams of 4–5 in competition, with up to 4 teams.
Delivery method: Trainer uses computerised simulator.
Minimum hardware requirement: PC; 640Kb RAM and printer.
Price: Tutored from £2500.00.
Source: Hall Marketing, Studio 11, Colman's Wharf, 45 Morris Road, London E14 6PA. Tel: 0171 537 2982

Induction

CD-ROM
Title: **Induction**
Purpose: To provide induction training for new entrants.
Suitable for: New entrants.
Prerequisites: None.
Description: The main modules of this course are: health and safety; security; legislation; customer care; telephone skills; writing skills; and the basics of interpersonal skills. You can add or remove modules yourself, using the built in toolkit.
Delivery method: CD-ROM.
Minimum hardware requirement: PC; 8Mb RAM, CD-ROM drive; sound card.
Price: £1299.00.
Source: Xebec Multi Media Solutions Ltd, The Critchley Building, Bath Road, Woodchester, Stroud, Glos. GL5 5EY. Tel: 01453 835482

Insurance practice

CBT
Title: **Accounting and Finance for Managers in Insurance**
Purpose: To give managers a good understanding of costing, budgetary control and relevant taxation.
Suitable for: Managers and those studying ACII subject 940 Accounting and Finance for Managers in Insurance.
Prerequisites: None.
Description: This course covers costing, budgetary control and taxation. You will work through practical examples of the different forms of accounts and accounting principles.
Delivery method: CBT.
Minimum hardware requirement: PC.

Price: £125.00.
Source: Marketing Department, The Chartered Insurance Institute, 20 Aldermanbury, London EC2V 7HY. Tel: 0171 417 4427

Title: **Business Interruption Insurance**
Purpose: To provide a comprehensive introduction to this class of business.
Suitable for: Those studying ACII subject 640 Business Interruption Insurance.
Prerequisites: None.
Description: The course looks at the history and covers risk assessment and claims. It covers the syllabus of the ACII subject 640 Business Interruption Insurance.
Delivery method: CBT.
Minimum hardware requirement: IBM or compatible PC.
Price: £125.00 + VAT.
Source: Marketing Department, The Chartered Insurance Institute, 20 Aldermanbury, London EC2V 7HY. Tel: 0171 417 4427

Title: **Certificate of Insurance Practice – Testing**
Purpose: To assist those taking CIP to prepare and revise for the examinations.
Suitable for: Those studying CII's Certificate of Insurance Practice.
Prerequisites: Study of the subjects.
Description: Subjects covered are: insurance; practice; legal aspects of insurance; introduction to commercial general insurance; and introduction to personal general insurance.
Delivery method: CBT.
Minimum hardware requirement: PC.
Price: £50.00 each.
Source: Marketing Department, The Chartered Insurance Institute, 20 Aldermanbury, London EC2V 7HY. Tel: 0171 417 4427

Title: **Contract Law and Insurance**
Purpose: To introduce the legal principles governing insurance contracts.
Suitable for: Those studying for the ACII subject 520 Contract Law and Insurance.
Prerequisites: None.
Description: This is a comprehensive introduction to the law of contract in general and its application to insurance in particular. It covers: law and legal systems; formation of a contract; contents of a contract; discharge and privity; insurance contracts; consumer protection; principles of agency; types of agent.
Delivery method: CBT.
Minimum hardware requirement: PC.
Price: £170.00 + VAT.
Source: Marketing Department, The Chartered Insurance Institute, 20 Aldermanbury, London EC2V 7HY. Tel: 0171 417 4427

DIRECTORY OF COURSES

Title: **Insurance Practice**
Purpose: To provide an introduction to insurance practice.
Suitable for: Those studying CII's Certificate of Insurance Practice.
Prerequisites: None.
Description: This course covers: what is meant by risk; the different types of risk; the different forms of cover available; and how insurance is transacted.
Delivery method: CBT (both DOS and Windows versions available).
Minimum hardware requirement: PC.
Price: £175.00.
Source: Marketing Department, The Chartered Insurance Institute, 20 Aldermanbury, London EC2V 7HY. Tel: 0171 417 4427

Title: **Introduction to Commercial General Insurances**
Purpose: To provide an introduction to commercial general insurances.
Suitable for: Those studying CII's Certificate of Insurance Practice.
Prerequisites: None.
Description: Covers: the insurance market; risk improvement and loss prevention; basic insurance principles; an introduction to property insurance; engineering insurance; business interruption insurance; liability insurance; commercial vehicle insurance; and reinsurance.
Delivery method: CBT.
Minimum hardware requirement: PC.
Price: £175.00.
Source: Marketing Department, The Chartered Insurance Institute, 20 Aldermanbury, London EC2V 7HY. Tel: 0171 417 4427

Title: **Introduction to Personal General Insurances**
Purpose: To provide an introduction to personal general insurances
Suitable for: Those studying CII's Certificate of Insurance Practice.
Prerequisites: None.
Description: Covers: the personal insurance marketplace; household insurance; travel insurance; private motor insurance; personal accident insurance; personal health insurance; life assurance; pensions; and reinsurance.
Delivery method: CBT.
Minimum hardware requirement: PC.
Price: £175.00.
Source: Marketing Department, The Chartered Insurance Institute, 20 Aldermanbury, London EC2V 7HY. Tel: 0171 417 4427

Title: **Legal Aspects of Insurance**
Purpose: To provide an introduction to the legal aspects of insurance.
Suitable for: Those studying CII's Certificate of Insurance Practice.
Prerequisites: None.

Description: This course covers: the legal system; legal personalities; agents; torts; contracts; utmost good faith; insurance interest; proximate cause; indemnity; subrogation; and contribution.
Delivery method: CBT.
Minimum hardware requirement: PC.
Price: £175.00.
Source: Marketing Department, The Chartered Insurance Institute, 20 Aldermanbury, London EC2V 7HY. Tel: 0171 417 4427

Title: **Modern Business Practice**
Purpose: To provide an introduction to modern business practice.
Suitable for: Those studying CII's Certificate of Insurance Practice.
Prerequisites: None.
Description: Covers: communication within an organisation; marketing and promotional management; communication methods; reports of business meetings; communication skills; the role of accounting; the accounting equation; the balance sheet; annual reports; budgeting; use and development of IT; computers in the office; and telecommunications.
Delivery method: CBT.
Minimum hardware requirement: PC.
Price: £175.00.
Source: Marketing Department, The Chartered Insurance Institute, 20 Aldermanbury, London EC2V 7HY. Tel: 0171 417 4427

Title: **Motor Insurance**
Purpose: To give an in-depth understanding of motor insurance.
Suitable for: Anyone working in motor insurance and those studying for the ACII subjects 610 Private and 615 Commercial Motor Insurance.
Prerequisites: None.
Description: The package may be studied in its entirety or selected disks may be used to improve knowledge in specific areas. It covers: the history of motor insurance; the Road Traffic Act 1988; other legislation; private car insurance; motor cycles; commercial vehicle insurance; motor claims; fleet rated risks.
Delivery method: CBT.
Minimum hardware requirement: IBM or compatible PC.
Price: £125.00 + VAT.
Source: Marketing Department, The Chartered Insurance Institute, 20 Aldermanbury, London EC2V 7HY. Tel: 0171 417 4427

Title: **Practice of Reinsurance**
Purpose: To provide an introduction to the practice of reinsurance
Suitable for: Those studying ACII subject 835 Practice of Reinsurance.
Prerequisites: 'Principles of Reinsurance'.

DIRECTORY OF COURSES

Description: Covers: analysing reinsurance business; underwriting a reinsurance programme; reinsurance claims; reinsurance accounting; reinsurance statistics; market networking; and computer systems.
Delivery method: CBT.
Minimum hardware requirement: PC.
Price: £125.00.
Source: Marketing Department, The Chartered Insurance Institute, 20 Aldermanbury, London EC2V 7HY. Tel: 0171 417 4427

Title: **Principles of Reinsurance**
Purpose: To provide an introduction to the principles of reinsurance.
Suitable for: Those studying ACII subject 830 Principle of Reinsurance.
Prerequisites: None.
Description: Covers: the nature and purpose of reinsurance; methods of reinsurance; types of treaty; classes of business; types of reinsurer; the intermediary or broker; retrocession; the law relating to reinsurance; and reinsurance treaty wordings.
Delivery method: CBT.
Minimum hardware requirement: PC.
Price: £125.00.
Source: Marketing Department, The Chartered Insurance Institute, 20 Aldermanbury, London EC2V 7HY. Tel: 0171 417 4427

Title: **Property Insurance Risk Assessment and Control**
Purpose: To give the user a thorough knowledge of the fundamentals of property insurance, predominantly fire, special perils, theft and arson.
Suitable for: Newcomers to the property insurance industry and those studying for the ACII subject 620 Property Insurance Risk.
Prerequisites: None.
Description: This comprehensive course covers: the background to property insurance; property risks arising from occupation and from natural hazards; risk protection and control-building design to control fire; methods of fire fighting; risk inspection.
Delivery method: CBT.
Minimum hardware requirement: IBM or compatible PC.
Price: £125.00 + VAT.
Source: Marketing Department, The Chartered Insurance Institute, 20 Aldermanbury, London EC2V 7HY. Tel: 0171 417 4427

Title: **Risk and Insurance**
Purpose: To give a comprehensive explanation of the ACII subject 510 Risk and Insurance.
Suitable for: Those studying for ACII and the Lloyd's Market Certificate.

Prerequisites: None.
Description: Covers: the nature of risk and uncertainty; risk assessment techniques; the ways in which risk is measured; the nature of insurance; the structure of the insurance market; the way insurance operates.
Delivery method: CBT.
Minimum hardware requirement: PC.
Price: £170.00 + VAT.
Source: Marketing Department, The Chartered Insurance Institute, 20 Aldermanbury, London EC2V 7HY. Tel: 0171 417 4427

Title: **Risk Management**
Purpose: To provide an in-depth knowledge of the principles and practice of risk management.
Suitable for: Those studying for ACII subject 655 Risk Management.
Prerequisites: None.
Description: This course covers: analysis and probability; risk and loss control; and risk transfer decisions.
Delivery method: CBT.
Minimum hardware requirement: PC.
Price: £125.00.
Source: Marketing Department, The Chartered Insurance Institute, 20 Aldermanbury, London EC2V 7HY. Tel: 0171 417 4427

Title: **The Business Environment**
Purpose: To provide an introduction to the general environment in which a business must operate.
Suitable for: Anyone new to the insurance or finance sector and those studying for ACII subject 530 The Business Environment.
Prerequisites: None.
Description: This course covers the syllabus of the ACII subject 530 The Business Environment, including: the economic environment; the financial environment; the operational environment; and the legal environment.
Delivery method: CBT.
Minimum hardware requirement: IBM or compatible PC.
Price: £170.00 + VAT.
Source: Marketing Department, The Chartered Insurance Institute, 20 Aldermanbury, London EC2V 7HY. Tel: 0171 417 4427

Title: **The Reinsurance Market**
Purpose: To provide an introduction to the reinsurance market.
Suitable for: Those studying ACII subject 840 The Reinsurance Market.
Prerequisites: 'Principles of Reinsurance'.
Description: Covers: the various world markets, including London, USA, Canada,

continental Europe and Japan; the interrelationship of the world markets; government regulations; financial aspects – accounting, investment and taxation.
Delivery method: CBT.
Minimum hardware requirement: PC.
Price: £125.00.
Source: Marketing Department, The Chartered Insurance Institute, 20 Aldermanbury, London EC2V 7HY. Tel: 0171 417 4427

Title: **The Single Insurance Market and You**
Purpose: To show insurance intermediaries throughout the EU how to make maximum use of the opportunities for cross-border sales.
Suitable for: Insurance intermediaries.
Prerequisites: None.
Description: The course not only deals with opportunities for cross-border sales, but also demonstrates the likely pitfalls due to anomalies in European insurance legislation as it currently stands.
Delivery method: CBT.
Minimum hardware requirement: PC.
Price: £95.00.
Source: Marketing Department, The Chartered Insurance Institute, 20 Aldermanbury, London EC2V 7HY. Tel: 0171 417 4427

Internet

CBT

Title: **Getting the most out of the Internet**
Purpose: To teach individuals and companies how to use the Internet effectively and efficiently.
Suitable for: Anyone.
Prerequisites: None.
Description: Topics include: user groups; shopping; security issues; how to promote your business; product support and much more. It includes high-level treatment of Internet terminology and technology, with a client-side look at the Internet as a resource.
Delivery method: CBT.
Minimum hardware requirement: PC.
Price: £1995.00.
Source: Electrovision UK Ltd, Hamble Point Marina, School Lane, Hamble, Southampton SO31 4JD. Tel: 01703 452221

CD-ROM
Title: **Perception of the Internet**
Purpose: To provide a very comprehensive training perception of the Internet.
Suitable for: Anyone.
Prerequisites: None.
Description: This course will help you to understand the technology and terminology of the Internet; its uses and how you can benefit from using the Internet.
Delivery method: CD-ROM.
Minimum hardware requirement: 486 PC; 8Mb RAM; CD-ROM drive; sound card.
Price: £119.00 (multiple copy price on application).
Source: Electrovision UK Ltd, Hamble Point Marina, School Lane, Hamble, Southampton SO31 4JD. Tel: 01703 452221

Title: **Surf the Internet**
Purpose: To introduce you to the Internet and instruct you how to do something on the Internet.
Suitable for: Anyone.
Prerequisites: None.
Description: This course lets you try out simulation exercise of the material that is taught and uses random quizzes to let you check your understanding.
Delivery method: CD-ROM.
Minimum hardware requirement: 486 PC; 8Mb RAM; CD-ROM drive; sound card.
Price: £99.00.
Source: Electrovision UK Ltd, Hamble Point Marina, School Lane, Hamble, Southampton SO31 4JD. Tel: 01703 452221

Interviewing skills

CBT
Title: **Interviewing Skills**
Purpose: To introduce successful interviewing techniques.
Suitable for: Anyone.
Prerequisites: None.
Description: This course covers the correct use of questioning and the importance of listening, and looks at the different types of interview and how to apply the techniques taught to each.
Delivery method: CBT.
Minimum hardware requirement: PC.
Price: £348.00.
Source: Electrovision UK Ltd, Hamble Point Marina, School Lane, Hamble, Southampton SO31 4JD. Tel: 01703 452221

CD-ROM

Title: **Essential Interviewing Skills**

Purpose: To teach you the basic interviewing skills which are the bedrock of good communication.

Suitable for: Managers.

Prerequisites: None.

Description: This course will help you to: establish interview objectives; draw up a plan; listen actively; observe reactions and body language; ask the right questions; give information; control the interview; and build rapport.

Delivery method: CD-ROM.

Minimum hardware requirement: 486 PC, 8Mb RAM, 420Mb hard disk, CD-ROM drive, audio card.

Price: £895.00.

Source: Training Direct, North Court, Edinburgh Gate, Harlow, Essex CM20 2JE. Tel: 01279 623927

Investors in people

CD-ROM

Title: **CAPITA**

Purpose: To help businesses undertake the process leading to the design and implementation of effective human resources policies and procedures, and attainment and retention of Investors in People accreditation.

Suitable for: Organisations implementing effective training systems as part of the IiP process.

Prerequisites: None.

Description: Interactive performance support system, comprising advice and guidance, planning tools, databases, templates of documents, a glossary and many other interactive features.

Delivery method: CD-ROM or diskettes and user guide.

Minimum hardware requirement: 486PC; 8Mb RAM; 10Mb hard disk.

Price: Price on application.

Source: Dean Associates, 9 The South West Centre, Troutbeck Road, Sheffield S7 2QA. Tel: 0114 258 1171

Italian

CBT

Title: **Italian Tutor**

Purpose: To provide a highly successful aid to learning Italian.

Suitable for: Anyone.

Prerequisites: None.

Description: This course provides a highly successful aid to modern language learning in vocabulary and grammar. Provides a variety of learning modes and test modes. All words and phrases are displayed complete with accents and special characters. In addition to the vast vocabulary supplied, the program also allows you to add your own lessons.

Delivery method: CBT.

Minimum hardware requirement: PC.

Price: £45.00.

Source: Electrovision UK Ltd, Hamble Point Marina, School Lane, Hamble, Southampton SO31 4JD. Tel: 01703 452221

CD-ROM

Title: **Think and Talk Italian**

Purpose: To teach you to think and talk Italian.

Suitable for: Anyone.

Prerequisites: None.

Description: Lively dialogue and engrossing scenes, using sound effects, music and other audio cues, make this an interesting training course. Eight CDs are contained in this pack, which contains a 10,000-word dictionary and enough training to aim at a vocabulary in excess of 1,000 words.

Delivery method: CD-ROM.

Minimum hardware requirement: PC; 8Mb RAM; CD-ROM; sound card.

Price: £159.00.

Source: Electrovision UK Ltd, Hamble Point Marina, School Lane, Hamble, Southampton SO31 4JD. Tel: 01703 452221

Japanese

CD-ROM

Title: **Japanese – Kana Kun**

Purpose: To provide a fun way to learn Kana.

Suitable for: Anyone.

Prerequisites: None.

Description: A fun CD teaching: Kana tables; Kana matching game; Kana cards; and writing Kana characters. Vocabulary modules teach words; word game tests your knowledge; word typer types words using a virtual Kana keyboard, which keeps track of your performance; and Kana cartoon module teaches sentences.

Delivery method: CD-ROM.

Minimum hardware requirement: PC; 8Mb RAM; CD-ROM; sound card.

Price: £65.00.

Source: Electrovision UK Ltd, Hamble Point Marina, School Lane, Hamble, Southampton SO31 4JD. Tel: 01703 452221

Title: **Japanese – Kantaro**
Purpose: To provide a fun way to learn Kanji.
Suitable for: Anyone.
Prerequisites: None.
Description: Learn through pictures, morph animations and games; 200 Kanji supported; read full Japanese text with hypertext help; click-and-drag exercise to replace Kana with Kanji; increases in difficulty; also covers numbers, calendar and times; examples of usage with pronunciation.
Delivery method: CD-ROM.
Minimum hardware requirement: PC; 8Mb RAM; CD-ROM; sound card.
Price: £249.00.
Source: Electrovision UK Ltd, Hamble Point Marina, School Lane, Hamble, Southampton SO31 4JD. Tel: 01703 452221

Keyboard skills

CBT
Title: **Mavis Beacon Teaches Typing/Windows**
Purpose: To teach touch typing.
Suitable for: Anyone.
Prerequisites: None.
Description: A well-known and popular typing course which includes exercises, tests and some games.
Delivery method: CBT.
Minimum hardware requirement: PC with Windows 3.1.
Price: £39.95 (multiple copy price on application).
Source: Electrovision UK Ltd, Hamble Point Marina, School Lane, Hamble, Southampton SO31 4JD. Tel: 01703 452221

Title: **Typequick for DOS**
Purpose: To teach touch typing.
Suitable for: Anyone.
Prerequisites: None.
Description: This course is ideal for those who are serious about learning to type. The tutorial does not allow you to advance beyond your current level of proficiency.
Delivery method: CBT.
Minimum hardware requirement: PC.
Price: £54.00 (multiple copy price on application).

Source: Electrovision UK Ltd, Hamble Point Marina, School Lane, Hamble, Southampton SO31 4JD. Tel: 01703 452221

Title: **Typequick for Windows**
Purpose: To teach touch typing.
Suitable for: Anyone.
Prerequisites: None.
Description: This course is ideal for those who are serious about learning to type. The tutorial does not allow you to advance beyond your current level of proficiency.
Delivery method: CBT.
Minimum hardware requirement: PC with Windows 3.1.
Price: £54.00 (multiple copy price on application).
Source: Electrovision UK Ltd, Hamble Point Marina, School Lane, Hamble, Southampton SO31 4JD. Tel: 01703 452221

Title: **Typequick Skill Evaluator**
Purpose: To evaluate the speed and accuracy of typists.
Suitable for: Anyone.
Prerequisites: None.
Description: This is a testing product that has tests of varying length and complexity or you can devise your own.
Delivery method: CBT.
Minimum hardware requirement: PC with Windows 3.1.
Price: £285.00.
Source: Electrovision UK Ltd, Hamble Point Marina, School Lane, Hamble, Southampton SO31 4JD. Tel: 01703 452221

Title: **Typing Instructor/DOS**
Purpose: To teach touch typing.
Suitable for: Anyone.
Prerequisites: None.
Description: This popular course starts at the beginning with the correct posture, hand placement and touch-typing techniques. You can choose from a wide variety of practice exercises designed to improve your speed and accuracy. There is also a game to test your skills.
Delivery method: CBT.
Minimum hardware requirement: PC.
Price: £49.95 (multiple copy price on application).
Source: Electrovision UK Ltd, Hamble Point Marina, School Lane, Hamble, Southampton SO31 4JD. Tel: 01703 452221

DIRECTORY OF COURSES

Title: **Typing Tutor for DOS**
Purpose: To give you the basics of touch typing.
Suitable for: Anyone.
Prerequisites: None.
Description: This course is a good general purpose typing tutor for different levels. It gives the basics of touch typing, but if speed is important, use of constant feedback gives a prescribed route through the course to increase speed and accuracy.
Delivery method: CBT.
Minimum hardware requirement: PC.
Price: £45.00 (multiple copy price on application).
Source: Electrovision UK Ltd, Hamble Point Marina, School Lane, Hamble, Southampton SO31 4JD. Tel: 01703 452221

Title: **Typing Tutor for Windows**
Purpose: To teach touch typing.
Suitable for: Anyone.
Prerequisites: None.
Description: This is a Windows-based course that uses sophisticated pre-testing and feedback mechanisms to help you reach your goals whatever the level. Continuous feedback is given and you can adjust your own goals as you progress.
Delivery method: CBT.
Minimum hardware requirement: PC with Windows 3.1.
Price: £75.00 (multiple copy price on application).
Source: Electrovision UK Ltd, Hamble Point Marina, School Lane, Hamble, Southampton SO31 4JD. Tel: 01703 452221

Title: **Typing Tutor/DOS**
Purpose: To teach touch typing.
Suitable for: Anyone.
Prerequisites: None.
Description: This course is suitable for all. The tutorial determines your current typing speed, aims to get you typing without looking at the keyboard, monitors speed and accuracy, and records your progress.
Delivery method: CBT.
Minimum hardware requirement: PC.
Price: £49.95 (multiple copy price on application).
Source: Electrovision UK Ltd, Hamble Point Marina, School Lane, Hamble, Southampton SO31 4JD. Tel: 01703 452221

THE DIRECTORY

CD-ROM

Title: **Mavis Beacon Teaches Typing/CD-ROM**
Purpose: To teach touch typing.
Suitable for: Anyone.
Prerequisites: None.
Description: This multimedia version of the Mavis Beacon course contains audio analysis and dictates letters. Personalised lessons, and use of games and progress charts help to maintain interest.
Delivery method: CD-ROM.
Minimum hardware requirement: PC; 8Mb RAM; CD-ROM drive and sound card.
Price: £49.95 (multiple copy price on request).
Source: Electrovision UK Ltd, Hamble Point Marina, School Lane, Hamble, Southampton SO31 4JD. Tel: 01703 452221

Title: **Multimedia Typing Instructor**
Purpose: To teach touch typing.
Suitable for: Anyone.
Prerequisites: None.
Description: This course has variable user levels, multiple tests and reporting facilities. The use of good graphics and activities hold your interest.
Delivery method: CD-ROM.
Minimum hardware requirement: PC; 8Mb RAM; CD-ROM drive and sound card.
Price: £49.95 (multiple copy price on request).
Source: Electrovision UK Ltd, Hamble Point Marina, School Lane, Hamble, Southampton SO31 4JD. Tel: 01703 452221

Language skills

CBT

Title: **Grammar Quiz**
Purpose: To test your knowledge and aid learning.
Suitable for: Anyone.
Prerequisites: None.
Description: This quiz provides an entertaining way of simultaneously testing your knowledge and learning more about the correct use of grammar. The questions are grouped into four separate quizzes: punctuation; spelling; word use; and spot the mistake.
Delivery method: CBT.
Minimum hardware requirement: PC.
Price: £99.00.
Source: Electrovision UK Ltd, Hamble Point Marina, School Lane, Hamble, Southampton SO31 4JD. Tel: 01703 452221

Leadership

CBT
Title: **Leadership Skills**
Purpose: To teach the principles of effective leadership.
Suitable for: Team leaders and managers.
Prerequisites: None.
Description: Presents the different leadership styles and then addresses this in more detail, using case studies. Teaches the principles of effective leadership and how to implement them successfully.
Delivery method: CBT.
Minimum hardware requirement: PC.
Price: £348.00.
Source: Electrovision UK Ltd, Hamble Point Marina, School Lane, Hamble, Southampton SO31 4JD. Tel: 01703 452221

Title: **Leadership: Do You Have What it Takes?**
Purpose: To help you to assess your leadership ability and potential. Using questionnaires, you will learn whether you can manage and delegate, and your likely behaviour as a manager.
Suitable for: Potential leaders.
Prerequisites: None.
Description: This is an introductory course which will enable you to: use practical approaches as a leader in managing change situations; analyse yourself and others in terms of leadership; understand how people set about the process of managing; and learn to delegate the right tasks to the right people at the right time.
Delivery method: CBT and supporting text.
Minimum hardware requirement: IBM PC or compatible, 512k RAM.
Price: £165.00.
Source: Ivy Business Training Software plc, Ivy House, 233–235 Roehampton Lane, London SW15 4LB. Tel: 0181 780 1494

Title: **Supervisory and Managerial Leadership: From Analysis to Action**
Purpose: To assess how effective you are as a leader and to know how other people rate you as a leader.
Suitable for: Potential leaders.
Prerequisites: None.
Description: This introductory course enables you to assess yourself on the seven widely acknowledged key areas of strength, or to have others assess you using anonymously completed software-based questionnaires.
Delivery method: CBT and supporting text.
Minimum hardware requirement: IBM PC or compatible, 512k RAM.

Price: £165.00.
Source: Ivy Business Training Software plc, Ivy House, 233–235 Roehampton Lane, London SW15 4LB. Tel: 0181 780 1494

Title: **The Effective Leader**
Purpose: To discuss the characteristics of an effective leader.
Suitable for: Team leaders and managers.
Prerequisites: None.
Description: This course discusses the leader as an organiser, planner, motivator and co-ordinator. It also discusses the different leadership styles. Student workbook accompanies this course.
Delivery method: CBT.
Minimum hardware requirement: PC.
Price: £413.00.
Source: Electrovision UK Ltd, Hamble Point Marina, School Lane, Hamble, Southampton SO31 4JD. Tel: 01703 452221

CD-ROM
Title: **Developing Leadership Styles**
Purpose: To outline the powerful skills you need to develop to become a capable and respected leader.
Suitable for: Team leaders and managers.
Prerequisites: None.
Description: A range of styles is presented which can be used to encourage staff, reviving motivation, productivity and relationships. Each style is examined in detail. Consequential effects, both positive and negative, are given significant focus. The course also includes a section offering suggestions for matching a style to a situation.
Delivery method: CD-ROM.
Minimum hardware requirement: 386 PC; 8Mb RAM; 6Mb hard-disk space; CD-ROM card; sound card.
Price: £295.00.
Source: Comput-Ed Ltd, Long Lane, Dawlish EX7 0QR. Tel: 01626 889955

Title: **Leading Teams**
Purpose: To provide hands-on solutions to such problems as lack of enthusiasm, disinterest in work and incorrect management style.
Suitable for: Team leaders and managers.
Prerequisites: None.
Description: This four-module course can be tailored to specific needs by adding a toolkit package. It will enable you to know: the techniques you should be using; how the team approach to management will increase productivity,

motivation and commitment; and how to maximise a team environment in your workplace.
Delivery method: CD-ROM.
Minimum hardware requirement: 486 PC; 8Mb RAM; 420Mb hard disk, CD-ROM drive, audio card.
Price: £1199.00.
Source: Xebec Multi Media Solutions Ltd, The Critchley Building, Bath Road, Woodchester, Stroud, Glos. GL5 5EY. Tel: 01453 835482

Title: **Styles of Leadership**
Purpose: To examine the pros and cons of five different management styles and whether a constant or flexible approach is more successful.
Suitable for: Team leaders.
Prerequisites: None.
Description: This is an introductory course which will enable you to: tell the difference between autocratic and democratic styles; state the pluses and minuses of the different approaches; note the benefits and downside of involving the staff in decision making; see how potential conflict can be avoided by challenging people to be innovative and involved.
Delivery method: CD-ROM.
Minimum hardware requirement: 486 PC; 8Mb RAM; 256 Colour VGA; sound card; and 8Mb hard-disk space.
Price: £295.00.
Source: Ivy Business Training Software plc, Ivy House, 233–235 Roehampton Lane, London SW15 4LB. Tel: 0181 780 1494

Letter writing

CBT
Title: **Effective English for Business Letters**
Purpose: To enable the acquisition of good practice in business letter writing.
Suitable for: Those responsible for designing business letters.
Prerequisites: An understanding of the basic concepts, i.e. nouns and verbs.
Description: Covers: punctuation; spelling; meaning; word selection; sentence length; good English practice (e.g. subject + verb agreement).
Delivery method: CBT.
Minimum hardware requirement: PC; 256Kb RAM.
Price: £70.00 plus VAT (£82.25) including postage.
Source: Dean Associates, 9 The South West Centre, Troutbeck Road, Sheffield S7 2QA. Tel: 0114 258 1171.

Title: **The Letters Game**

Purpose: To help all employees improve their letter-writing skill and enhance the image of your organisation.

Suitable for: Everyone.

Prerequisites: None.

Description: The package covers all aspects of effective letter-writing from grammar, layout and style to writing letters of complaint, sales letters and debt collection letters. In addition, the package also contains a workbook including sample letters, layouts and glossary.

Delivery method: CBT.

Minimum hardware requirement: 386 PC; 3Mb hard disk; 640Kb RAM.

Price: £595.00: unlimited workstation licence; £1950.00: unlimited network licence.

Source: Easy i Ltd, 42 The Square, Kenilworth, Warwickshire CV8 1EB Tel: 01926 854111

CD-ROM

Title: **Business Words**

Purpose: To increase people's confidence in writing and to make their communication effective.

Suitable for: Anyone.

Prerequisites: None.

Description: The course stresses that business letters should generate appropriate action and emphasises the effect of letters on their readers through case study scenarios. Self-assessment quizzes help you to concentrate on strengthening weaker areas.

Delivery method: CD-ROM.

Minimum hardware requirement: 486 PC; 8Mb RAM; 420Mb hard disk; CD-ROM drive; audio card.

Price: £1199.00.

Source: Xebec Multi Media Solutions Ltd, The Critchley Building, Bath Road, Woodchester, Stroud, Glos. GL5 5EY. Tel: 01453 835482

Life assurance

CBT

Title: **Business Insurance**

Purpose: To provide a useful introduction to key person and partnership/co-shareholder insurance.

Suitable for: Anyone.

Prerequisites: Basic knowledge of life assurance.

Description: The course deals with this increasingly important class of business. It covers key person and partnership/co-shareholder insurance in detail.
Delivery method: CBT.
Minimum hardware requirement: PC.
Price: £95.00.
Source: Marketing Department, The Chartered Insurance Institute, 20 Aldermanbury, London EC2V 7HY. Tel: 0171 417 4427

Title: **Life and Disability Underwriting**
Purpose: To provide an introduction to life underwriting with a look at basic medical disorders.
Suitable for: Anyone new to assurance or reassurance and those studying for the ACII subject 555 Life and Disability Underwriting.
Prerequisites: None.
Description: The program covers: structure of a life office; life assurance documentation; methods of obtaining medical evidence; methods of rating; methods of assessing degrees of extra mortality and morbidity; the major disorders that affect the various systems of the body; their significance in life and permanent health underwriting and underwriting case studies.
Delivery method: CBT.
Minimum hardware requirement: IBM or compatible PC.
Price: £125.00 + VAT.
Source: Marketing Department, The Chartered Insurance Institute, 20 Aldermanbury, London EC2V 7HY. Tel: 0171 417 4427

Title: **Product Modules – Life, Investments and Pensions**
Purpose: To provide a comprehensive introduction to various life, investment and pensions products.
Suitable for: Anyone, but useful for those studying for FPC.
Prerequisites: None.
Description: There are eight modules covering: term assurance; whole of life; sickness insurance; regular premium investments; annuities; lump-sum investments; trust and estate planning; state provision; personal pensions; and occupational pensions. There are also two testing disks: life assurance and investments (covering modules 1–7); and pensions (covering modules 8–10).
Delivery method: CBT.
Minimum hardware requirement: PC.
Price: £50.00 each module and test; or £250.00 the set.
Source: Marketing Department, The Chartered Insurance Institute, 20 Aldermanbury, London EC2V 7HY. Tel: 0171 417 4427

Listening skills

CBT
Title: **Active Listening**
Purpose: To introduce the concept of active listening.
Suitable for: Anyone.
Prerequisites: None.
Description: In addition to explaining the concepts of active listening it also covers the consequences if you don't listen properly. Identifies common listening traps and suggests techniques for overcoming them.
Delivery method: CBT.
Minimum hardware requirement: PC.
Price: £175.00.
Source: Electrovision UK Ltd, Hamble Point Marina, School Lane, Hamble, Southampton SO31 4JD. Tel: 01703 452221

Interactive video
Title: **Active Listening**
Purpose: To teach the vital skills of listening. Even the best questioning techniques are virtually useless if the person using them doesn't know how to listen.
Suitable for: Anyone.
Prerequisites: None.
Description: This course gives information and training on the techniques of listening. You see listening skills in action and are given tips on how to develop them. You are asked to: identify listening skills being used; put your new-found skills to work interviewing two 'personalities'.
Delivery method: Interactive video.
Minimum hardware requirement: Interactive video workstation.
Price: £1135.00.
Source: Training Direct, North Court, Edinburgh Gate, Harlow, Essex CM20 2JE. Tel: 01279 623927

Logistics

CD-ROM
Title: **Introduction to Logistics**
Purpose: To introduce the concepts of logistics and supply chain management.
Suitable for: New managers and managers who need to understand the concepts of logistics.
Prerequisites: None.
Description: The course provides understanding in the following areas: the scope

of logistics; the supply chain; the cost/service relationship; logistics and the marketing mix; the financial impact of logistics; trade-offs; inventory; order- and forecast-driven demand; lead time; decoupling points; and added value.
Delivery method: CD-ROM.
Minimum hardware requirement: 486 PC; 4Mb RAM; CD-ROM drive and sound card.
Price: £995.00.
Source: Logistics Training International Ltd, Development House, Newton Road, Heather, Coalville, Leicestershire LE67 2RD. Tel: 01530 262666

Management skills

Business game
Title: **Marsgame**
Purpose: To encourage the development of business management skills.
Suitable for: Managers and supervisors
Prerequisites: None.
Description: An interactive computer-controlled business game primarily concerned with intellectual, analytical and decision-making skills. Covers: purchasing; pricing; promotion; finance; stock control; and credit control. Teams of 4–6 members each.
Delivery method: Computer-controlled business game.
Minimum hardware requirement: 286 PC; 640K RAM.
Price: £395.00 plus VAT.
Source: Daedal Training Ltd, 309 High Street, Orpington, Kent BR6 0NN. Tel: 01689 873637

Title: **The Cheese Market**
Purpose: To provide an introduction to running a business.
Suitable for: Ideal for those with little or no understanding of how a business works.
Prerequisites: None.
Description: The game helps people learn about the factors that affect business success. The game can be used with competing teams, or individuals can use it in a self-study mode.
Delivery method: Computer-controlled business game.
Minimum hardware requirement: 286 PC; 640K RAM.
Price: £195.00 plus VAT.
Source: Daedal Training Ltd, 309 High Street, Orpington, Kent BR6 0NN. Tel: 01689 873637

CBT

Title: **Hope and Glory**
Purpose: To provide an involving and exciting introduction to the nature and tasks of business management.
Suitable for: Managers, supervisors, team leaders and MBA students.
Prerequisites: None.
Description: A practical illustration of the key theories and concepts of business and management. Contents include: finance; marketing; selling; manufacturing; purchasing; decision making; creativity; problem solving; project management; negotiating time management; delegation; communication; and team building.
Delivery method: CBT and textbook.
Minimum hardware requirement: 386 PC; 1Mb RAM.
Price: £95.00.
Source: Simulation Training Ltd, The New Hall, Methwold, Thetford, Norfolk IP26 4NR. Tel: 01366 728215

Title: **Introduction to Management**
Purpose: To introduce management to the new manager.
Suitable for: New managers and supervisors.
Prerequisites: None.
Description: This course covers: the responsibilities of the manager, the relationships the manager will have with other work groups; and the key roles of the manager. It also discusses work planning and scheduling.
Delivery method: CBT.
Minimum hardware requirement: PC.
Price: £348.00.
Source: Electrovision UK Ltd, Hamble Point Marina, School Lane, Hamble, Southampton SO31 4JD. Tel: 01703 452221

Title: **Management 2000**
Purpose: To provide an introduction to the key tasks of management and a detailed assessment of the management skill, influence and teamwork of each participant.
Suitable for: Managers, supervisors, team leaders and MBA students.
Prerequisites: None.
Description: A relocation project in which teams: select a suitable site; plan and manage a relocation project; deal with various 'people problems' amongst the project team; and deal with an in-tray of outstanding tasks. Feedback is by way of 12 models dealing with: change; time management; control; leadership; delegation; teamwork; conflict; communications; assertiveness; quality and effectiveness.
Delivery method: CBT with facilitation and support.

Minimum hardware requirement: 386 PC; 1Mb RAM.
Price: On application.
Source: Simulation Training Ltd, The New Hall, Methwold, Thetford, Norfolk IP26 4NR. Tel: 01366 728215

Title: **MENTA**
Purpose: To provide a detailed assessment of the management skill of the user and to develop a training plan for him/her.
Suitable for: Managers, supervisors, team leaders and MBA students.
Prerequisites: None.
Description: Designed to help users to analyse their own training needs and plan their own personal development. The course employs artificial intelligence techniques in order to assess what an individual knows about management and then to guide him/her through the possibilities for improvement. Contents: planning; organising; controlling; leading; motivating; and communicating.
Delivery method: CBT.
Minimum hardware requirement: 386 PC; 1Mb RAM; 2Mb hard-disk space; printer.
Price: £495.00.
Source: Simulation Training Ltd, The New Hall, Methwold, Thetford, Norfolk IP26 4NR. Tel: 01366 728215

Title: **Perform! Managing to Win**
Purpose: To teach managers how to create direction, plan for the future and manage staff more effectively in order to ensure the best results possible for the business or organisation.
Suitable for: Anyone in a junior, middle or senior management role, within any size of business or organisation.
Prerequisites: None.
Description: This course covers all the areas businesses need to concentrate on in order to achieve that sometimes elusive 100 per cent performance.
Delivery method: CBT.
Minimum hardware requirement: 386PC; 4Mb RAM; 4Mb hard disk.
Price: £79.99 plus £2.00 p&p.
Source: Way Ahead Electronic Publishing, 27 Woodford Green, Bratton, Telford, Shropshire TF5 0NS. Tel: 01952 243153

Title: **Setting Objectives**
Purpose: To teach the benefits of setting objectives.
Suitable for: Team leaders and managers.
Prerequisites: None.
Description: Participants learn how to recognise different types of objectives,

give priority to the objectives, and follow a step-by-step guide to an objective setting action plan which is realistic and measurable.
Delivery method: CBT.
Minimum hardware requirement: PC.
Price: £413.00.
Source: Electrovision UK Ltd, Hamble Point Marina, School Lane, Hamble, Southampton SO31 4JD. Tel: 01703 452221

Title: **Superskills**
Purpose: To raise the trainee's awareness of the key elements that make a good supervisor, team leader or first-line manager.
Suitable for: New first-line managers.
Prerequisites: None.
Description: An interactive package that will provide the user with an opportunity to develop an understanding of their new role, whilst introducing practical tips and guidelines. Topics covered: the role of the supervisor; goal setting procedures and planning; problem solving; motivation, manipulation and incentivising; managing yourself and the group.
Delivery method: CBT.
Minimum hardware requirement: 386 PC; 3Mb hard disk; 640Kb RAM.
Price: £595.00: unlimited workstation licence; £1950.00: unlimited network licence.
Source: Easy i Ltd, 42 The Square, Kenilworth, Warwickshire CV8 1EB. Tel: 01926 854111

Title: **SWOT**
Purpose: To teach SWOT analysis.
Suitable for: Team leaders and managers.
Prerequisites: None.
Description: Identifying strengths, weaknesses, opportunities and threats starts by discussing what a SWOT is and then discusses the four elements. Looks at how to follow up on the elements of a SWOT and how to do a SWOT by yourself or with a group.
Delivery method: CBT.
Minimum hardware requirement: PC.
Price: £175.00.
Source: Electrovision UK Ltd, Hamble Point Marina, School Lane, Hamble, Southampton SO31 4JD. Tel: 01703 452221

Title: **Tycoon**
Purpose: To provide practice in management skills using a simulation exercise.
Suitable for: Managers, supervisors, team leaders and MBA students.
Prerequisites: None.

Description: Each team represents a typical manufacturing company, competing against other teams in a typical market. Decisions include: marketing; pricing; factory capacity and productivity; bank borrowings; staffing levels; wage rates and industrial relations. Results include: profit and loss account; balance sheet; cash flow; key ratios; and indices of performance.
Delivery method: CBT with facilitation.
Minimum hardware requirement: 386 PC; 1Mb RAM.
Price: £495.00.
Source: Simulation Training Ltd, The New Hall, Methwold, Thetford, Norfolk IP26 4NR. Tel: 01366 728215

CD-ROM

Title: **Building a Partnership**
Purpose: To explain the critical first steps in building a partnership where both sides of a team know what they are aiming to achieve.
Suitable for: Managers and supervisors.
Prerequisites: None.
Description: This course will enable you to understand: why both parties must know what is expected of them; how to establish a trusting relationship; how to offer clear support in a partnership; how to set realistic expectations; how to handle the first meeting; how to show confidence in your partner; and how to make everyone feel good about the new team.
Delivery method: CD-ROM.
Minimum hardware requirement: 486 PC; 8Mb RAM; 420Mb hard disk; CD-ROM drive; audio card.
Price: £895.00.
Source: Training Direct, North Court, Edinburgh Gate, Harlow, Essex CM20 2JE. Tel: 01279 623927

Title: **Business Management**
Purpose: To give a comprehensive overview of business management.
Suitable for: Managers.
Prerequisites: None.
Description: This course has eight modules covering: the business environment; organisations and change; information requirements; corporate mission and strategy; organisation development; finance and investment; marketing and personnel; operational strategies; and IT.
Delivery method: CD-ROM.
Minimum hardware requirement: 486PC; 8Mb RAM; CD-ROM drive; sound card.
Price: £2075.00.
Source: Mindware Training Technologies Ltd, Block 2, International Business Centre, Plassey, Limerick, Ireland. Tel: (353) 6133 1430

Title: **Developing People**

Purpose: To show you how to develop your staff to fulfil their and your potential, both as individuals and as team members.

Suitable for: Managers and supervisors.

Prerequisites: 'Building a Partnership'.

Description: This course will help you to: manage your own time; look after new staff; monitor progress; delegate responsibility; keep the team informed; train for change; motivate staff; use training effectively; and allocate work.

Delivery method: CD-ROM.

Minimum hardware requirement: 486 PC; 8Mb RAM; 420Mb hard disk; CD-ROM drive; audio card.

Price: £895.00.

Source: Training Direct, North Court, Edinburgh Gate, Harlow, Essex CM20 2JE. Tel: 01279 623927

Title: **Management Techniques**

Purpose: To provide an insight into the management environment from the perspective of changes, conflict and culture.

Suitable for: Managers.

Prerequisites: None.

Description: This course has eight modules covering: competencies and planning; team development and motivation; communications and influencing; meetings and presentations; resourcing and staff appraisal; reorganisation; culture and image; external and internal boundaries.

Delivery method: CD-ROM.

Minimum hardware requirement: 486PC; 8Mb RAM; CD-ROM drive; sound card.

Price: £2175.00.

Source: Mindware Training Technologies Ltd, Block 2, International Business Centre, Plassey, Limerick, Ireland. Tel: (353) 6133 1430

Title: **Managing Information Overload: Taking in Information Effectively**

Purpose: To teach the practical skills needed to avoid information overload and develop your ability to process large amounts of information quickly and competently.

Suitable for: Managers.

Prerequisites: None.

Description: This course will help you to make better use of your time. The key training messages being: how memory works; how to make things easy to remember; how to read more quickly; and how to maximise understanding.

Delivery method: CD-ROM.

Minimum hardware requirement: 486 PC; 8Mb RAM; 420Mb hard disk; CD-ROM drive; audio card.

Price: £995.00.

Source: Training Direct, North Court, Edinburgh Gate, Harlow, Essex CM20 2JE. Tel: 01279 623927

Title: **Organisational Behaviour**
Purpose: To teach and support a complete introductory course on organisational behaviour.
Suitable for: All business (or modular) students from HND level upwards.
Prerequisites: None.
Description: A detailed introduction to organisational behaviour.
Delivery method: CD-ROM.
Minimum hardware requirement: PC; 8Mb RAM; CD-ROM drive and sound card.
Price: £29.95 (inc. VAT) single-user licence; multi-user licences from £650.
Source: Pitman Publishing, 128 Long Acre, London WC2E 9AN. Tel: 0171 4472290

Interactive video
Title: **Focus on Management**
Purpose: To show you how to manage yourself, the task, the team and the individual.
Suitable for: Managers.
Prerequisites: None.
Description: This two-module course will enable you to: build a committed and productive team; know how to use better decision-making skills; balance conflicting demands; and gain an insight into your own strengths and weaknessess.
Delivery method: Interactive video.
Minimum hardware requirement: Interactive video workstation.
Price: £2020.00.
Source: Training Direct, North Court, Edinburgh Gate, Harlow, Essex CM20 2JE. Tel: 01279 623927

Simulation
Title: **Business Awareness**
Purpose: To widen appreciation and knowledge of the key business functions of finance, marketing, production and personnel.
Suitable for: Managers, supervisors and graduates.
Prerequisites: None.
Description: A very practical event where delegates experience running a business – making all the responsible decisions, seeing the results of their actions, and experiencing the importance of cross-function activities.
Delivery method: Business simulation with tutor-led discussion and input.
Minimum hardware requirement: 386 PC.
Price: From £650.00 per day for 12 delegates.

Source: April Training Executive Ltd, Tarvin Road, Frodsham, Cheshire WA6 6XN. Tel: 01928 735868

Title: **CISCO – Contract Business**
Purpose: To teach business strategy and team working in companies that bid for contracts and design custom solutions for clients.
Suitable for: Middle through senior management.
Prerequisites: Line management experience.
Description: A total enterprise business simulation/game replicating a contracting company, and involving bidding, resourcing, capacity and financial planning by teams of 4–5 in competition, with up to 4 teams.
Delivery method: Trainer uses computerised simulator.
Minimum hardware requirement: PC; 640Kb RAM and printer.
Price: Tutored from £2500.00.
Source: Hall Marketing, Studio 11, Colman's Wharf, 45 Morris Road, London E14 6PA. Tel: 0171 537 2982

Title: **INTEX – Industrialising Nation**
Purpose: To teach business strategy and team working in companies that are operating in a rapidly industrialising nation environment.
Suitable for: Middle through to senior management.
Prerequisites: Line management experience.
Description: A total enterprise business simulation/game, involving trading, setting up local manufacturing, staffing, product offering and financial planning by teams of 4–5 in competition, with up to 4 teams.
Delivery method: Trainer uses computerised simulator.
Minimum hardware requirement: PC; 640Kb RAM and printer.
Price: Tutored from £2500.00.
Source: Hall Marketing, Studio 11, Colman's Wharf, 45 Morris Road, London E14 6PA. Tel: 0171 537 2982

Title: **Management Experience**
Purpose: To teach: the tactical management and control of a company; business objectives and measures; basic finance and marketing; operational control and forecasting; decision-making; and team working.
Suitable for: Junior through middle management.
Prerequisites: Line management experience.
Description: A total enterprise business simulation/game replicating a manufacturing company, and involving marketing, operational and financial decisions by teams of 4–5 in competition, with up to 8 teams.
Delivery method: Trainer uses computerised simulator.
Minimum hardware requirement: PC; 640Kb RAM and printer.
Price: Rental: £295.00; fully tutored from £1200.00.

Source: Hall Marketing, Studio 11, Colman's Wharf, 45 Morris Road, London E14 6PA. Tel: 0171 537 2982

Title: **Strategic Management**
Purpose: To gain experience and knowledge in the development and implementation of strategic planning.
Suitable for: Department/group managers and project managers.
Prerequisites: Managerial experience
Description: Participants set objectives against which decisions must be made, results assessed and action taken to achieve these targets. The course examines the inter-relationship of the functions and commercial measurements against which companies are assessed, and includes marketing concepts, planning and presentation skills.
Delivery method: Business simulation with tutor instruction and discussion.
Minimum hardware requirement: 386 PC.
Price: From £650.00 per day for 12 delegates.
Source: April Training Executive Ltd, Tarvin Road, Frodsham, Cheshire WA6 6XN. Tel: 01928 735868

Title: **SYCOPS – Systems Company Operations**
Purpose: To teach: business objectives and measures; basic finance and marketing; operational control and forecasting; decision-making; and team working.
Suitable for: Trainees, functional specialists, supervisors, junior through middle management.
Prerequisites: Some basic business appreciation.
Description: A total enterprise business simulation/game replicating a company selling systems involving hardware and software, and taking in marketing, operational and financial decisions by teams of 4–5 in competition, with up to 8 teams.
Delivery method: Trainer uses computerised simulator.
Minimum hardware requirement: PC; 640Kb RAM and printer.
Price: Rental: £295.00; purchase: POA; fully tutored from £800.00.
Source: Hall Marketing, Studio 11, Colman's Wharf, 45 Morris Road, London E14 6PA. Tel: 0171 537 2982

Title: **TEAMSKILL – Production Management**
Purpose: To teach production management.
Suitable for: Trainees, functional specialists, supervisors, junior through middle management.
Prerequisites: Some basic production knowledge.
Description: A simulation/game replicating the production operation of a manu-

facturing company, and involving purchasing, scheduling, machine purchase, etc., decisions by teams of 4–5.
Delivery method: Trainer uses computerised simulator.
Minimum hardware requirement: PC; 640Kb RAM and printer.
Price: Fully tutored from £1200.00.
Source: Hall Marketing, Studio 11, Colman's Wharf, 45 Morris Road, London E14 6PA. Tel: 0171 537 2982

Title: **The Casino Challenge**
Purpose: To teach: business objectives and measures; basic finance and marketing; operational control and forecasting; decision-making; and team working.
Suitable for: Trainees, functional specialists, supervisors, junior through middle management.
Prerequisites: Some basic business appreciation.
Description: A total enterprise business simulation/game replicating a casino company, and involving marketing, operational and financial decisions by teams of 4–5 in competition, with up to 8 teams.
Delivery method: Trainer uses computerised simulator.
Minimum hardware requirement: PC; 640Kb RAM and printer.
Price: Rental: £195.00; purchase: £795.00; fully tutored from £800.00.
Source: Hall Marketing, Studio 11, Colman's Wharf, 45 Morris Road, London E14 6PA. Tel: 0171 537 2982

Title: **The Executive Challenge**
Purpose: To teach: business objectives and measures; basic finance and marketing; operational control and forecasting; decision-making; and team working.
Suitable for: Trainees, functional specialists, supervisors, junior through middle management.
Prerequisites: Some basic business appreciation.
Description: A total enterprise business simulation/game replicating a company, and involving marketing, operational and financial decisions by teams of 4–5 in competition, with up to 8 teams.
Delivery method: Trainer uses computerised simulator.
Minimum hardware requirement: PC; 640Kb RAM and printer.
Price: Rental: £195.00; purchase: £795.00; fully tutored from £800.00.
Source: Hall Marketing, Studio 11, Colman's Wharf, 45 Morris Road, London E14 6PA. Tel: 0171 537 2982

Title: **The Management Challenge**
Purpose: To teach: business objectives and measures; basic finance and mar-

keting; operational control and forecasting; decision making; and team working.
Suitable for: Trainees, functional specialists, supervisors, junior through middle management.
Prerequisites: Some basic business appreciation.
Description: A total enterprise business simulation/game replicating a manufacturing company, and involving marketing, operational and financial decisions by teams of 4–5 in competition, with up to 8 teams.
Delivery method: Trainer uses computerised simulator.
Minimum hardware requirement: PC; 640Kb RAM and printer.
Price: Rental: £195.00; purchase: £795.00; fully tutored from £800.00.
Source: Hall Marketing, Studio 11, Colman's Wharf, 45 Morris Road, London E14 6PA. Tel: 0171 537 2982

Title: **The Retail Challenge**
Purpose: To teach: business objectives and measures; basic finance and marketing; operational control and forecasting; decision making; and team working.
Suitable for: Trainees, functional specialists, supervisors, junior through middle management.
Prerequisites: Some basic business appreciation.
Description: A total enterprise business simulation/game replicating a retail company, and involving marketing, operational and financial decisions by teams of 4–5 in competition, with up to 8 teams.
Delivery method: Trainer uses computerised simulator.
Minimum hardware requirement: PC; 640Kb RAM and printer.
Price: Rental: £195.00; purchase: £795.00; fully tutored from £800.00.
Source: Hall Marketing, Studio 11, Colman's Wharf, 45 Morris Road, London E14 6PA. Tel: 0171 537 2982

Title: **The Service Challenge**
Purpose: To teach: business objectives and measures; basic finance and marketing; operational control and forecasting; decision making; and team working.
Suitable for: Trainees, functional specialists, supervisors, junior through middle management.
Prerequisites: Some basic business appreciation.
Description: A total enterprise business simulation/game replicating a services company, and involving marketing, operational and financial decisions by teams of 4–5 in competition, with up to 8 teams.
Delivery method: Trainer uses computerised simulator.
Minimum hardware requirement: PC; 640Kb RAM and printer.
Price: Rental: £195.00; purchase: £795.00; fully tutored from £800.00.

Source: Hall Marketing, Studio 11, Colman's Wharf, 45 Morris Road, London E14 6PA. Tel: 0171 537 2982

Title: **UMIX – Functional Interaction**
Purpose: To teach about the flows of material, information and money in a company, with: business objectives and measures; finance and marketing; operational control and forecasting; decision making; and team working.
Suitable for: Junior through middle management.
Prerequisites: None.
Description: A total enterprise business simulation/game replicating a manufacturing company, and involving teams of 4–5 managing their own functional area.
Delivery method: Trainer uses computerised simulator.
Minimum hardware requirement: PC; 640Kb RAM and printer.
Price: Rental: £295.00; fully tutored from £1200.00.
Source: Hall Marketing, Studio 11, Colman's Wharf, 45 Morris Road, London E14 6PA. Tel: 0171 537 2982

Manual handling

CD-ROM
Title: **Safe Manual Handling**
Purpose: To explain the basic principles of correct manual handling and the injuries which can be caused by poor lifting techniques.
Suitable for: All employees.
Prerequisites: None.
Description: The modules are: introduction; reducing the risk; your back; good handling techniques; team lifting; pushing and pulling; and a self-test.
Delivery method: CD-ROM.
Minimum hardware requirement: 486 PC; 4Mb RAM; dual speed CD-ROM drive; sound card.
Price: On application.
Source: Instinct Training, Strawberry How Business Centre, Lorton Road, Cockermouth, Cumbria CA13 9XQ. Tel: 01900 827600

Marketing strategy

Business model
Title: **Marketing Essentials**
Purpose: To teach and give experience in the concepts of marketing.
Suitable for: Anyone.

Prerequisites: None.
Description: A very practical course where participants receive instruction followed by practical experience in marketing audits and preparation of a marketing plan. They gain a better understanding of the market mix and segmentation and how to apply these to taking over the marketing department of a company, which they run within the interactive business simulation.
Delivery method: Tutor instruction and discussion based on a business model.
Minimum hardware requirement: 386 PC.
Price: From £650.00 per day for 12 delegates.
Source: April Training Executive Ltd, Tarvin Road, Frodsham, Cheshire WA6 6XN. Tel: 01928 735868

CBT

Title: **Business Acumen Marketing**
Purpose: To teach all aspects of marketing from researching ideas for businesses and new products, to advertising, public relations and selling skills.
Suitable for: Anyone in a marketing role of any kind, in any size of company, charity or other organisation.
Prerequisites: None.
Description: This complete course consists of six modules: market research; the marketing mix; advertising and sales promotion; selling skills; public relations; and the role of the computer. Also includes case studies, interactive tests and checklists, with feedback and scores, glossaries and useful marketing material templates.
Delivery method: CBT.
Minimum hardware requirement: 386PC; 4Mb RAM; 7Mb hard disk.
Price: £69.99 plus £2 p&p.
Source: Way Ahead Electronic Publishing, 27 Woodford Green, Bratton, Telford, Shropshire TF5 0NS. Tel: 01952 243153

Title: **Marketing Essentials for Everyone in Business**
Purpose: To give you a sound understanding of the principles of marketing as well as some important techniques and skills.
Suitable for: Anyone.
Prerequisites: None.
Description: This is an introductory course which will enable you: to structure and use an analytical marketing model; identify market segments and subsegments; use the four elements of the marketing mix in formulating a marketing strategy; obtain and use internal as well as external market research information.
Delivery method: CBT and supporting text.
Minimum hardware requirement: IBM PC or compatible, 512k RAM.
Price: £165.00.

Source: Ivy Business Training Software plc, Ivy House, 233–235 Roehampton Lane, London SW15 4LB. Tel: 0181 780 1494

Title: **Marketing for Profit**
Purpose: To identify the key elements of the marketing mix; to analyse them, using appropriate techniques; and to show how the process can be applied to products and services to meet marketing objectives.
Suitable for: Marketing staff.
Prerequisites: None.
Description: Tutorials which explore in detail all the variables involved in optimising a company's profitability in this area: the product (or service); pricing; promotion (communicating with the customer); and distribution. Case studies simulate real-life situations and trainees explore the likely results of the decisions they make.
Delivery method: CBT.
Minimum hardware requirement: PC; 512Kb RAM.
Price: £395.00 + VAT. Copies are available on 30 days' approval.
Source: Bourne Training Systems Ltd, Bourne House, Sandy Lane, Romsey, Hampshire SO51 0PD. Tel: 01794 523301

Title: **Marketing Planning**
Purpose: To identify the logical steps in the preparation of a marketing plan and to produce a marketing plan relevant to their products (or service) and the marketplace.
Suitable for: Anyone. As an introduction to newcomers to marketing planning, and as a refresher course to more experienced managers.
Prerequisites: None.
Description: Tutorials which provide an in-depth study of the marketing planning process. Case studies are used to give trainees practice in the skills of marketing planning. The course is cross-referenced to, and supported by, a course companion, based on Professor McDonald's highly acclaimed work in marketing planning.
Delivery method: CBT.
Minimum hardware requirement: PC; 512Kb RAM.
Price: £395.00 + VAT. Copies are available on 30 days' approval.
Source: Bourne Training Systems Ltd, Bourne House, Sandy Lane, Romsey, Hampshire SO51 0PD. Tel: 01794 523301

Title: **Successful Marketing – Deciding on Product, Price, Promotion and Distribution**
Purpose: To understand the four elements of the marketing mix, which is one element of a dynamic marketing model. In a case study, you will explore the 'fit' of the elements in the mix.

Suitable for: Anyone.
Prerequisites: 'Marketing Essentials for Everyone in Business'.
Description: This is an introductory course which will enable you: to use the four elements to devise an effective marketing mix within the overall marketing model; and to use the product life cycle to analyse both products and market segments.
Delivery method: CBT and supporting text.
Minimum hardware requirement: IBM PC or compatible, 512k RAM.
Price: £165.00.
Source: Ivy Business Training Software plc, Ivy House, 233–235 Roehampton Lane, London SW15 4LB. Tel: 0181 780 1494

Title: **The Marketing Executive: Do We Need a Sales Force?**
Purpose: To examine the relationship between the sales force and product policy, pricing, distribution and advertising.
Suitable for: Senior sales managers.
Prerequisites: The other three courses in this series.
Description: This is an introductory course which will enable you: to analyse where a product lies in its life cycle, and to analyse the product, pricing, distribution and advertising policies for a product with respect to its phase in a life cycle.
Delivery method: CBT and supporting text.
Minimum hardware requirement: IBM PC or compatible, 512k RAM.
Price: £165.00.
Source: Ivy Business Training Software plc, Ivy House, 233–235 Roehampton Lane, London SW15 4LB. Tel: 0181 780 1494

Title: **The Mathematics of Profit: Pricing and Discounts**
Purpose: To increase your quantitative marketing skills by teaching you how to calculate prices and discounts in the most typical marketing situations.
Suitable for: Anyone.
Prerequisites: An understanding of the fundamental concepts in marketing.
Description: This is an introductory course which will enable you to: calculate the selling price of an item when the desired mark-up on cost or margin on sales is known; calculate the selling price at the manufacturing, wholesaling and retailing levels; assess the impact of price barriers; and convert mark-ups to margins and vice versa.
Delivery method: CBT and supporting text.
Minimum hardware requirement: IBM PC or compatible, 512k RAM.
Price: £165.00.
Source: Ivy Business Training Software plc, Ivy House, 233–235 Roehampton Lane, London SW15 4LB. Tel: 0181 780 1494

Title: **The Mathematics of Survival: Costs and Breakeven**
Purpose: To understand some important quantitative analytical tools that are invaluable in any application of marketing principles to real-life situations.
Suitable for: Anyone.
Prerequisites: An understanding of the fundamental concepts in marketing.
Description: An introductory course which will enable you to: calculate contribution and total costs; know how to construct a graph that shows total, variable and fixed costs, revenue and contribution; calculate breakeven and target analysis in term of units and monetary values.
Delivery method: CBT and supporting text.
Minimum hardware requirement: IBM PC or compatible, 512k RAM.
Price: £165.00.
Source: Ivy Business Training Software plc, Ivy House, 233–235 Roehampton Lane, London SW15 4LB. Tel: 0181 780 1494

CD-ROM
Title: **Marketing**
Purpose: To teach and support a complete introductory course on marketing.
Suitable for: All business (or modular) students from HND level upwards.
Prerequisites: None.
Description: A detailed introduction to marketing.
Delivery method: CD-ROM.
Minimum hardware requirement: PC; 8Mb RAM; CD-ROM drive and sound card.
Price: £29.95 (inc. VAT) single-user licence; multi-user licences from £650.
Source: Pitman Publishing, 128 Long Acre, London WC2E 9AN. Tel: 0171 4472290

Interactive video
Title: **An Introduction to Marketing**
Purpose: To gain an understanding of the basic marketing process. It looks at all factors which influence why and how people buy, and explores the basics of market research, forecasting and planning.
Suitable for: Anyone.
Prerequisites: None.
Description: This three-module course develops a common understanding and language of marketing throughout an organisation. All people will perceive the impact that their function has on the marketing effort.
Delivery method: Interactive video.
Minimum hardware requirement: Interactive video workstation.
Price: £2020.00.
Source: Training Direct, North Court, Edinburgh Gate, Harlow, Essex CM20 2JE. Tel: 01279 623927

Title: **Practical Marketing**
Purpose: This course illustrates clearly that the role of marketing extends far beyond those whose job titles include the word itself, and how key areas of the business relate to each other.
Suitable for: Anyone.
Prerequisites: None.
Description: This two-part course gives an understanding of the theory of marketing and how the key business areas fit together through extensive use of case studies.
Delivery method: Interactive video.
Minimum hardware requirement: Interactive video workstation.
Price: £2020.00.
Source: Training Direct, North Court, Edinburgh Gate, Harlow, Essex CM20 2JE. Tel: 01279 623927

Simulation
Title: **Product Launch**
Purpose: To introduce marketing concepts.
Suitable for: Trainees, functional specialists, supervisors, junior through middle management.
Prerequisites: None.
Description: A simulation/game replicating the product life cycle, and involving pricing, promotion and production decisions by teams of 4–5.
Delivery method: Teams use computerised simulator.
Minimum hardware requirement: PC; 640Kb RAM and printer.
Price: Rental: £125.00; purchase: £295.00; tutored from £500.00.
Source: Hall Marketing, Studio 11, Colman's Wharf, 45 Morris Road, London E14 6PA. Tel: 0171 537 2982

Title: **Sales Mix**
Purpose: To introduce marketing concepts with a team formation dimension.
Suitable for: Trainees, functional specialists, supervisors, junior through middle management.
Prerequisites: None.
Description: A simulation/game replicating pricing and promotion, but with defined responsibilities and measures, for teams of 4–5.
Delivery method: Teams use computerised simulator.
Minimum hardware requirement: PC; 640Kb RAM and printer.
Price: Rental: £125.00; purchase: £295.00; tutored from £500.00.
Source: Hall Marketing, Studio 11, Colman's Wharf, 45 Morris Road, London E14 6PA. Tel: 0171 537 2982

Title: **SMART – Service Marketing**
Purpose: To teach marketing strategy and team working in service companies.
Suitable for: Middle through senior management.
Prerequisites: Line management experience.
Description: A total enterprise business simulation/game, involving running a hotel by teams of 4–5 in competition, with up to 4 teams.
Delivery method: Trainer uses computerised simulator.
Minimum hardware requirement: PC; 640Kb RAM and printer.
Price: Rental: £295.00; purchase: £1195.00; tutored from £1200.00.
Source: Hall Marketing, Studio 11, Colman's Wharf, 45 Morris Road, London E14 6PA. Tel: 0171 537 2982

Meetings

CBT

Title: **Managing Meetings**
Purpose: To teach you how to manage meetings.
Suitable for: Team leaders and managers.
Prerequisites: None.
Description: Takes you through all aspects of planning and conducting a successful meeting. Includes: controlling a meeting; making statements; asking questions; handling conflict; and other tactics for success.
Delivery method: CBT.
Minimum hardware requirement: PC.
Price: £348.00.
Source: Electrovision UK Ltd, Hamble Point Marina, School Lane, Hamble, Southampton SO31 4JD. Tel: 01703 452221

CD-i

Title: **Meetings, Bloody Meetings**
Purpose: To make meetings more productive.
Suitable for: Managers and team leaders.
Prerequisites: None.
Description: The key points of this course are: plan the meeting in advance; prepare and circulate a precise agenda; allocate sufficient time to each item on the agenda; structure and control the meeting, and summarise and record decisions.
Delivery method: CD-i.
Minimum hardware requirement: CD-i player and television.
Price: £995.00; rental prices on request.
Source: Video Arts Ltd, Dumbarton House, 68 Oxford Street, London W1N 0LH. Tel: 0171 637 7288

DIRECTORY OF COURSES

Title: **More Bloody Meetings**
Purpose: To deal with the 'people' side of a meeting.
Suitable for: Managers and team leaders.
Prerequisites: None.
Description: This course is about getting people to work together. The key points are: unite the group and control aggression; focus the group and keep to the point, and mobilise the group, getting everyone involved.
Delivery method: CD-i.
Minimum hardware requirement: CD-i player and television.
Price: £995.00; rental prices on request.
Source: Video Arts Ltd, Dumbarton House, 68 Oxford Street, London W1N 0LH. Tel: 0171 637 7288

CD-ROM
Title: **Business Meetings**
Purpose: To make your organisation's meetings more positive and effective. It stresses that every individual can make a positive contribution to a meeting and everybody shares responsibility for its success.
Suitable for: Anyone who leads meetings.
Prerequisites: None.
Description: This course is organised in six modules: preparing to attend a meeting; preparing to lead a meeting; participating in a meeting; leading in a meeting; follow-up; and minutes.
Delivery method: CD-ROM.
Minimum hardware requirement: 486 PC, 8Mb RAM, 420Mb hard disk, CD-ROM drive, audio card.
Price: £1199.00.
Source: Xebec Multi Media Solutions Ltd, The Critchley Building, Bath Road, Woodchester, Stroud, Glos. GL5 5EY. Tel: 01453 835482

Interactive video
Title: **Effective Meetings**
Purpose: To give you more confidence in meetings and the ability to participate more effectively.
Suitable for: Anyone.
Prerequisites: None.
Description: This course is in five sections allowing you: to explore your own feelings about meetings and shows the effects those feelings have on meetings you attend; to understand the need for planning and preparation; to deal with the initial meeting and the follow-up meeting; and the last section is available to provide help and advice to you.
Delivery method: Interactive video.
Minimum hardware requirement: Interactive video workstation.

Price: £2020.00.
Source: Training Direct, North Court, Edinburgh Gate, Harlow, Essex CM20 2JE. Tel: 01279 623927

Mortgages

CBT
Title: **Generic Mortgages**
Purpose: To teach the student about generic mortgages and the home-buying process.
Suitable for: Sales staff and employees within companies dealing with mortgages. Covers all requirements for FPC standards.
Prerequisites: None.
Description: The course has three modules: what is a mortgage – a general overview on mortgages; generic mortgages – detailed training on the different mortgage schemes and loan types available; the home-buying process – a step-by-step guide to the process of buying a home, through four types of mortgage loan, which can be used in conjunction with the customer.
Delivery method: CBT.
Minimum hardware requirement: 486PC; CD-ROM; 4Mb RAM; 30Mb hard disk.
Price: Available on application.
Source: CBL Technology Ltd, St Katherine's House, Mansfield Road, Derby DE1 3TQ. Tel: 01332 205800

Motivation

CBT
Title: **Motivate!**
Purpose: To explain how to motivate effectively.
Suitable for: Team leaders and managers.
Prerequisites: None.
Description: This course explains: how to recognise key motivational factors; how to identify and exploit opportunities to motivate; how to identify and eliminate demotivational threats; how to create conditions for self-motivation; and how harmony of personal needs and organisational goals is achieved.
Delivery method: CBT.
Minimum hardware requirement: PC.
Price: £413.00.
Source: Electrovision UK Ltd, Hamble Point Marina, School Lane, Hamble, Southampton SO31 4JD. Tel: 01703 452221

Title: **Motivating With Praise**
Purpose: To introduce the benefits of providing feedback.
Suitable for: Team leaders and managers.
Prerequisites: None.
Description: Introduces the benefits of providing feedback and how this can enhance employee performance. Discusses individual reaction to praise and how you can effectively include praise in your management style.
Delivery method: CBT.
Minimum hardware requirement: PC.
Price: £175.00.
Source: Electrovision UK Ltd, Hamble Point Marina, School Lane, Hamble, Southampton SO31 4JD. Tel: 01703 452221

CD-i

Title: **Motivating The Team**
Purpose: To encourage and teach basics of successful motivation.
Suitable for: First line managers.
Prerequisites: None.
Description: The film lays down an easily remembered and applied structure for motivation, following the mnemonic SPUR: specific; purposeful; useful; rewarding.
Delivery method: CD-i.
Minimum hardware requirement: TV and CD-i player.
Price: Purchase: £995.00 + carriage + VAT; 2-day hire: £165.00 + carriage + VAT.
Source: Melrose, 16 Bromells Road, London SW4 0BL. Tel: 0171 627 8404

CD-ROM

Title: **Motivation at Work**
Purpose: To provide a strategy for improving motivation.
Suitable for: Team leaders and managers.
Prerequisites: None.
Description: The course covers the basic motivational drivers, and the fact that performance is a factor of ability, back-up and motivation. It then develops a strategy which helps to increase motivation.
Delivery method: CD-ROM.
Minimum hardware requirement: 386 PC; 8Mb RAM; 6Mb hard-disk space; CD-ROM drive; sound card.
Price: £295.00.
Source: Comput-Ed Ltd, Long Lane, Dawlish EX7 0QR. Tel: 01626 889955

Title: **Motivation at Work**
Purpose: To take you through a motivational strategy which identifies needs,

establishes rewards, defines performance, and ensures a successful result for both individuals and teams.
Suitable for: Team leaders.
Prerequisites: None.
Description: This is an introductory course which will enable you to: recognise the needs of surviving, socialising and developing; plan actions and motivations; take four steps through the motivational model; concentrate on the possible; set out clear tasks, goals and deadlines; and see the importance of generating enthusiasm in a team.
Delivery method: CD-ROM.
Minimum hardware requirement: 486 PC; 8Mb RAM; 256 Colour VGA; sound card; and 8Mb hard-disk space.
Price: £295.00.
Source: Ivy Business Training Software plc, Ivy House, 233–235 Roehampton Lane, London SW15 4LB. Tel: 0181 780 1494

Multimedia

CD-ROM

Title: **Professor Multimedia**
Purpose: To provide a wonderful introduction to the world of multimedia.
Suitable for: Anyone.
Prerequisites: None.
Description: This course, with 50 video and animation clips, will help you learn about multimedia and experience at first hand hundreds of multimedia capabilities. The three main sections cover: multimedia around you; what is multimedia; and multimedia presentations.
Delivery method: CD-ROM.
Minimum hardware requirement: PC; 8Mb RAM; CD-ROM drive and sound card.
Price: £49.95 (multiple copy price on request).
Source: Electrovision UK Ltd, Hamble Point Marina, School Lane, Hamble, Southampton SO31 4JD. Tel: 01703 452221

Negotiation

CBT

Title: **Negotiating Skills**
Purpose: To introduce the importance of planning and preparing for a negotiation.
Suitable for: Anyone.
Prerequisites: None.

Description: Comprehensively covers actual negotiation techniques such as opening, exploring, testing, bargaining and closing.
Delivery method: CBT.
Minimum hardware requirement: PC.
Price: £348.00.
Source: Electrovision UK Ltd, Hamble Point Marina, School Lane, Hamble, Southampton SO31 4JD. Tel: 01703 452221

CD-i
Title: **Agreed**
Purpose: To show how to influence others in negotiation and reach 'win-win' outcomes.
Suitable for: Everyone working within teams and cross-departmental teams.
Prerequisites: None.
Description: A drama illustrating the negotiation process and how to reach 'win-win'.
Delivery method: CD-i.
Minimum hardware requirement: TV and CD-i player.
Price: Purchase: £995.00 + carriage + VAT; 2-day hire: £165.00 + carriage + VAT.
Source: Melrose, 16 Bromells Road, London SW4 0BL. Tel: 0171 627 8404

CD-ROM
Title: **Negotiating for a Positive Outcome**
Purpose: To provide an understanding of the negotiating process and the negotiation skills which are required to achieve the best possible outcome for everyone concerned.
Suitable for: Managers.
Prerequisites: None.
Description: This course develops positive attitudes towards negotiation and will help you acquire practical negotiating skills. The key messages are: the importance of gathering information; developing the right attitude; and how to reach agreement and commitment.
Delivery method: CD-ROM.
Minimum hardware requirement: 486 PC; 8Mb RAM; 420Mb hard disk; CD-ROM drive; audio card.
Price: £1195.00.
Source: Intelligent Training Solutions, 29 Narrow Street, London E14 8DP. Tel: 0171 791 3000

Title: **The Art of Negotiating**
Purpose: To help you to learn and apply the techniques you need to achieve 'win-win' every time.
Suitable for: Managers, staff and union personnel who conduct negotiations.

Prerequisites: None.
Description: This course, which uses a series of dramatic sequences, will help you to understand: the importance of planning ahead and setting targets; the four stages of a successful negotiation; how to use 'if' and 'then' successfully; how to recognise concessions by reading signals; how to minimise your own concessions.
Delivery method: CD-ROM.
Minimum hardware requirement: 486 PC; 8Mb RAM; 420Mb hard disk; CD-ROM drive; audio card.
Price: £895.00.
Source: Training Direct, North Court, Edinburgh Gate, Harlow, Essex CM20 2JE. Tel: 01279 623927

Title: **The Negotiator**
Purpose: To help users improve and hone their negotiation skills.
Suitable for: Sales representatives, sales managers, business managers, marketers, and anyone who has to negotiate a deal.
Prerequisites: None.
Description: Users are encouraged, first, to research thoroughly the basics of negotiation, learn about their particular situation/position in the case-study negotiation, and conduct an actual negotiation with the computer using real-life English sentences. The CD then assesses the performance and suggests areas for improvement or further reading.
Delivery method: CD-ROM or CBT.
Minimum hardware requirement: 386 PC; CD-ROM drive; 4Mb RAM; 12Mb hard disk.
Price: CD: £35.95 + VAT; CBT: £68.00 + VAT.
Source: Bookstores/CD-ROM Distributors or McGraw-Hill Publishing Co., Shoppenhangers Rd, Maidenhead, Berkshire SL6 2QL. Tel: 01628 23432

Networking

General

CBT
Title: **Network or Hierarchy? Linking With Others to be Effective**
Purpose: To teach you how to establish and maintain the complex network of interdependent relationships that is so necessary to 'get the job done!'
Suitable for: Anyone.
Prerequisites: None.
Description: This is an introductory course which will enable you to understand: the changes that have occurred in organisational structures; the properties of

network links and the characteristics of the key participants in a network; and how to manage, maintain and use your own network. The course includes a model that you can use and reuse.
Delivery method: CBT and supporting text.
Minimum hardware requirement: IBM PC or compatible; 512k RAM.
Price: £165.00.
Source: Ivy Business Training Software plc, Ivy House, 233–235 Roehampton Lane, London SW15 4LB. Tel: 0181 780 1494

Title: **Networking Technologies**
Purpose: To provide the concepts of data communications, networking and connectivity.
Suitable for: Technical staff.
Prerequisites: None.
Description: This course covers the concepts of data communications, networking and connectivity, including: the OSI reference model; communication protocols and standards; data translations; data transmission; network structures; lower-layer communications protocols, IEEE.x 802 communications protocols, TCP/IP, OSI, Netware, SNA, DNA, ISDN and Appletalk, to name but a few.
Delivery method: CBT.
Minimum hardware requirement: PC.
Price: £795.00.
Source: Electrovision UK Ltd, Hamble Point Marina, School Lane, Hamble, Southampton SO31 4JD. Tel: 01703 452221

LANS

CBT
Title: **Introducing LANS**
Purpose: To provide a comprehensive introduction to LANS.
Suitable for: Technical staff.
Prerequisites: None.
Description: This course includes topics on an overview of: LANS; PC LANS; communications architectures and protocols; network components and technologies; MA/CD LANS and standards; token passing LANS; and LANS management.
Delivery method: CBT.
Minimum hardware requirement: PC.
Price: £520.00.
Source: Mindware Training Technologies Ltd, Block 2, International Business Centre, Plassey, Limerick, Ireland. Tel: (353) 6133 1430

Title: **Training for LANS and Datacomms**
Purpose: To provide a general overview of LANS.
Suitable for: LAN users and potential users.
Prerequisites: None.
Description: An extremely useful tutorial for LAN users or anyone who needs a general overview of LANS. It provide an introduction to networks: what they are and how they work; LAN components; network software; LAN management; telecomms basics; and PC to mainframe communications.
Delivery method: CBT.
Minimum hardware requirement: PC.
Price: £69.95 (multiple copy price on application).
Source: Electrovision UK Ltd, Hamble Point Marina, School Lane, Hamble, Southampton SO31 4JD. Tel: 01703 452221

Netware

CBT

Title: **Netware 4.1 Advanced Administration**
Purpose: To teach the skills necessary to perform advanced Netware systems management tasks effectively.
Suitable for: Experienced administrators.
Prerequisites: Some knowledge of Netware 4.1.
Description: This course covers: network and server optimisation; NDS design administration and security; NDS partitioning and replicas; and managing the environment.
Delivery method: CBT.
Minimum hardware requirement: PC.
Price: £695.00.
Source: Electrovision UK Ltd, Hamble Point Marina, School Lane, Hamble, Southampton SO31 4JD. Tel: 01703 452221

Title: **Netware 4.1 Installation/Configuration**
Purpose: To teach Netware installation/configuration.
Suitable for: Intermediate to advanced Netware personnel.
Prerequisites: Knowledge of Netware to intermediate level.
Description: This course covers: planning; setting timelines; directory tree structures; migration schedules; installation and customising installation; managing users; modifying; parameters; and troubleshooting.
Delivery method: CBT.
Minimum hardware requirement: PC.
Price: £395.00.
Source: Electrovision UK Ltd, Hamble Point Marina, School Lane, Hamble, Southampton SO31 4JD. Tel: 01703 452221

Title: **Netware 4.1 Service and Support**
Purpose: To provide training for Netware service and support staff.
Suitable for: Netware service and support staff.
Prerequisites: None.
Description: This course covers: troubleshooting and researching problem areas; adapter cards and cabling; network storage devices; diagnostic tools; and techniques.
Delivery method: CBT.
Minimum hardware requirement: PC.
Price: £1195.00.
Source: Electrovision UK Ltd, Hamble Point Marina, School Lane, Hamble, Southampton SO31 4JD. Tel: 01703 452221

Title: **Netware 4.1 Systems Administration**
Purpose: To teach the skills necessary to perform Netware systems management tasks effectively.
Suitable for: Administrators.
Prerequisites: None.
Description: Topics include: Netware basics; resources; security; printing; workstation automation; server security; and data protection. Also covers: basic configuration; automating the user environment; managing directory services; and performing administrative tasks.
Delivery method: CBT.
Minimum hardware requirement: PC.
Price: £795.00.
Source: Electrovision UK Ltd, Hamble Point Marina, School Lane, Hamble, Southampton SO31 4JD. Tel: 01703 452221

Title: **Netware 4.1 TCP/IP**
Purpose: To provide training for configuration, management and troubleshooting the TCP/IP protocol stack on Netware servers.
Suitable for: Netware systems managers.
Prerequisites: None.
Description: This course provides instruction on: the TCP/IP protocol suite; Novell's TCP/IP product line; Telnet; FTP; and IP protocol configurations. It also covers: IP addressing; SNMP; and TCPCON.NLM, IPTUNNEL and internet working problems.
Delivery method: CBT.
Minimum hardware requirement: PC.
Price: £495.00.
Source: Electrovision UK Ltd, Hamble Point Marina, School Lane, Hamble, Southampton SO31 4JD. Tel: 01703 452221

Noise

CD-ROM
Title: **Noise at Work**
Purpose: To understand and comply with the Noise at Work Regulations.
Suitable for: Managers, supervisors and staff.
Prerequisites: None.
Description: The course examines noise, the damage it can do, and the steps which should be taken to prevent damage. It explains both employers' and employees' obligations under the regulations. The modules are: what is noise; noise and deafness; quantifying noise; the regulations; ear protection; and a self-test.
Delivery method: CD-ROM.
Minimum hardware requirement: 486 PC; 4Mb RAM; dual speed CD-ROM drive; sound card.
Price: On application.
Source: Instinct Training, Strawberry How Business Centre, Lorton Road, Cockermouth, Cumbria CA13 9XQ. Tel: 01900 827600

Non-verbal communication

Interactive video
Title: **Non-verbal Communication**
Purpose: To show how body language qualifies our verbal messages, and how to use it to your advantage.
Suitable for: Anyone.
Prerequisites: None.
Description: This course is set in an advertising agency and comprises three modules: the basics explained; recognising the signs; and applying the lessons.
Delivery method: Interactive video.
Minimum hardware requirement: Interactive video workstation.
Price: £1135.00.
Source: Training Direct, North Court, Edinburgh Gate, Harlow, Essex CM20 2JE. Tel: 01279 623927

NVQ

CBT
Title: **Everything about NVQs**
Purpose: To help you to understand NVQs, SVQs and their value.
Suitable for: Anyone.

Prerequisites: None.
Description: This course will assist you in matching NVQs to previous work experience and in identifying the NVQs essential for your career development.
Delivery method: CBT.
Minimum hardware requirement: PC.
Price: £267.00.
Source: Electrovision UK Ltd, Hamble Point Marina, School Lane, Hamble, Southampton SO31 4JD. Tel: 01703 452221

Objective setting

CD-i
Title: **Targeting For Performance**
Purpose: To encourage effective target setting.
Suitable for: All managers.
Prerequisites: None.
Description: To work targets need to be SMART: specific; measurable; agreed; realistic; and timed.
Delivery method: CD-i.
Minimum hardware requirement: TV and CD-i player.
Price: Purchase: £995.00 + carriage + VAT; 2-day hire: £165.00 + carriage + VAT.
Source: Melrose, 16 Bromells Road, London SW4 0BL. Tel: 0171 627 8404

Operating environments

Client

CBT
Title: **Client/Server Configuration Management**
Purpose: To provide the management principles required to configure client/server systems.
Suitable for: Professional and technical staff.
Prerequisites: 'Intro to Client/Server Architecture'.
Description: The course topics include: user interface; transaction processing; multiserver databases; and server management functions.
Delivery method: CBT.
Minimum hardware requirement: PC.
Price: £1995.00.
Source: Electrovision UK Ltd, Hamble Point Marina, School Lane, Hamble, Southampton SO31 4JD. Tel: 01703 452221

Title: **Intro to Client/Server Architecture**
Purpose: To describe the principles and knowledge required to design and configure client/server systems.
Suitable for: Professional and management.
Prerequisites: None.
Description: The course topics include: systems; middleware; distributed data management issues; administration and technological subjects related to building client/server applications; hardware platforms; and operating systems.
Delivery method: CBT.
Minimum hardware requirement: PC.
Price: £1995.00.
Source: Electrovision UK Ltd, Hamble Point Marina, School Lane, Hamble, Southampton SO31 4JD. Tel: 01703 452221

Title: **Introduction to Client/Server Computing**
Purpose: To provide an introduction to the potential of client/server computing.
Suitable for: Decision makers.
Prerequisites: None.
Description: The emphasis of the course is on teaching the concepts of client/server technology and providing the information needed to evaluate this technology and decide on its implementation.
Delivery method: CBT.
Minimum hardware requirement: PC.
Price: £795.00.
Source: Electrovision UK Ltd, Hamble Point Marina, School Lane, Hamble, Southampton SO31 4JD. Tel: 01703 452221

JCL

CBT
Title: **JCL Coding Level 1 (XA) or (ESA)**
Purpose: To provide students with a working knowledge of how to write JCL statements.
Suitable for: Persons with some experience in job processing in a S/370 environment.
Prerequisites: None.
Description: This course provides students with a working knowledge of writing JCL statements. Student manual provided.
Delivery method: CBT.
Minimum hardware requirement: PC.
Price: £1995.00 (multiple copy price on application).

Source: Electrovision UK Ltd, Hamble Point Marina, School Lane, Hamble, Southampton SO31 4JD. Tel: 01703 452221

Title: **JCL Coding Level 2 (XA) or (ESA)**
Purpose: To provide students with an understanding of the more advanced JCL processing concepts.
Suitable for: Persons with some working knowledge of JCL.
Prerequisites: Working knowledge of JCL commands and structures.
Description: This course provides students with an understanding of the more advanced JCL commands and structures. Student manual provided.
Delivery method: CBT.
Minimum hardware requirement: PC.
Price: £1995.00 (multiple copy price on application).
Source: Electrovision UK Ltd, Hamble Point Marina, School Lane, Hamble, Southampton SO31 4JD. Tel: 01703 452221

UNIX

CBT

Title: **Advanced UNIX User**
Purpose: To expand on the topics of UNIX User.
Suitable for: UNIX users.
Prerequisites: 'UNIX User'.
Description: This course is designed to expand on the topics covered in UNIX User, including: commands to manage files and directories; monitor processes; create and use script files; and use UNIX utilities.
Delivery method: CBT; also available via the Internet.
Minimum hardware requirement: Any PC capable of running Microsoft Windows.
Price: On application.
Source: Oracle Corporation UK Ltd, The Oracle Centre, The Ring, Bracknell, Berks. RG12 1BW. Tel: 01344 860066

Title: **AIX Systems Administrator**
Purpose: To provide the tools to perform basic tasks.
Suitable for: New systems administrators.
Prerequisites: None.
Description: This course provides the new system administrator with the tools to perform basic tasks in an established AIX network environment and to troubleshoot problems unique to AIX. Topics include: managing files; managing users; resources; processing; start-up; and shutdown.
Delivery method: CBT.
Minimum hardware requirement: PC.
Price: £1495.00.

Source: Electrovision UK Ltd, Hamble Point Marina, School Lane, Hamble, Southampton SO31 4JD. Tel: 01703 452221

Title: **Complete AIX Course/DOS**
Purpose: To provide a complete AIX course.
Suitable for: Anyone.
Prerequisites: None.
Description: This course is in six modules: getting started; AIX system user; C programming; advanced system user; systems administrator; and advanced systems administrator. RS6000 network version also available.
Delivery method: CBT.
Minimum hardware requirement: PC.
Price: £1750.00.
Source: Electrovision UK Ltd, Hamble Point Marina, School Lane, Hamble, Southampton SO31 4JD. Tel: 01703 452221

Title: **Complete AIX Course/Windows**
Purpose: To provide a complete AIX course.
Suitable for: Anyone.
Prerequisites: None.
Description: This course is in six modules: getting started; AIX system user; C programming; advanced system user; systems administrator; and advanced systems administrator. RS6000 network version also available.
Delivery method: CBT.
Minimum hardware requirement: PC.
Price: £1750.00.
Source: Electrovision UK Ltd, Hamble Point Marina, School Lane, Hamble, Southampton SO31 4JD. Tel: 01703 452221

Title: **Complete UNIX and C Course/DOS**
Purpose: To provide complete UNIX training.
Suitable for: Anyone.
Prerequisites: None.
Description: This course is in six modules: getting started; UNIX system user; C programming; advanced system user; systems administrator; and advanced systems administrator. Available for all sorts of systems platforms.
Delivery method: CBT.
Minimum hardware requirement: PC.
Price: £1750.00.
Source: Electrovision UK Ltd, Hamble Point Marina, School Lane, Hamble, Southampton SO31 4JD. Tel: 01703 452221

DIRECTORY OF COURSES

Title: **Complete UNIX and C Course/Windows**
Purpose: To provide complete UNIX training.
Suitable for: Anyone.
Prerequisites: None.
Description: This course is in six modules: getting started; UNIX system user; C programming; advanced system user; systems administrator; and advanced systems administrator.
Delivery method: CBT.
Minimum hardware requirement: PC.
Price: £1750.00.
Source: Electrovision UK Ltd, Hamble Point Marina, School Lane, Hamble, Southampton SO31 4JD. Tel: 01703 452221

Title: **UNIX Advanced Programming**
Purpose: To give training at an advanced level.
Suitable for: Programmers.
Prerequisites: None.
Description: This course covers: the UNIX operating system; file structures; working with ordinary, directory and device files; working with terminals; working with processes; interprocess communication; and a case study.
Delivery method: CBT.
Minimum hardware requirement: PC.
Price: £795.00.
Source: Electrovision UK Ltd, Hamble Point Marina, School Lane, Hamble, Southampton SO31 4JD. Tel: 01703 452221

Title: **UNIX C Shell**
Purpose: To provide training for UNIX C Shell.
Suitable for: Power users, programmers and system administrators.
Prerequisites: None.
Description: The topics include: Shell basics – commands, redirection, piping, scripts; Shell environment – variables, term, path, prompt, exporting variables; Shell programming – parameters, test, if/then/else, echo/read, subscripts and loops. The course is accompanied by a comprehensive manual.
Delivery method: CBT.
Minimum hardware requirement: PC.
Price: £995.00 (multiple copy price on application).
Source: Electrovision UK Ltd, Hamble Point Marina, School Lane, Hamble, Southampton SO31 4JD. Tel: 01703 452221

Title: **UNIX Device Drivers**
Purpose: To enable you to develop UNIX device drivers.
Suitable for: Programmers.

Prerequisites: None.

Description: This course covers: introduction to device drivers; device driver design – interface, entry points, structures for communication; and device driver installation.

Delivery method: CBT.

Minimum hardware requirement: PC.

Price: £795.00.

Source: Electrovision UK Ltd, Hamble Point Marina, School Lane, Hamble, Southampton SO31 4JD. Tel: 01703 452221

Title: **UNIX Editors**

Purpose: To provide an overview of four editors and teaches vi and emacs editor in detail.

Suitable for: Programmers.

Prerequisites: None.

Description: The course covers: Ed; Sed; vi and emacs; show; save; retrieve files; navigate; erase; cut and paste; print files; and macros. A comprehensive student manual accompanies the course.

Delivery method: CBT.

Minimum hardware requirement: PC.

Price: £1295.00 (multiple copy price on application).

Source: Electrovision UK Ltd, Hamble Point Marina, School Lane, Hamble, Southampton SO31 4JD. Tel: 01703 452221

Title: **UNIX Electronic Mail**

Purpose: To provide instruction on electronic mail.

Suitable for: Anyone.

Prerequisites: None.

Description: This course presents two UNIX mail programs and details how to manage mail with a UNIX system. The topics include: the UNIX Mail Program; the Elm Mail PSystem; and more communications. A comprehensive student manual accompanies the course.

Delivery method: CBT.

Minimum hardware requirement: PC.

Price: £995.00 (multiple copy price on application).

Source: Electrovision UK Ltd, Hamble Point Marina, School Lane, Hamble, Southampton SO31 4JD. Tel: 01703 452221

Title: **UNIX Essentials**

Purpose: To provide a basic understanding of the features and capabilities of UNIX.

Suitable for: Anyone.

Prerequisites: None.

Description: This course gives a basic understanding of the features and capabilities of UNIX and how to use this operating system. Topics include: getting started; overview of the UNIX shell; applications and hardware; basic UNIX commands, files, directories, syntax explanations, background processing, etc. Supplied with a student manual.
Delivery method: CBT.
Minimum hardware requirement: PC.
Price: £1495.00 (multiple copy price on application).
Source: Electrovision UK Ltd, Hamble Point Marina, School Lane, Hamble, Southampton SO31 4JD. Tel: 01703 452221

Title: **UNIX Fundamentals**
Purpose: To provide an introduction to UNIX.
Suitable for: Programmers and trainee programmers.
Prerequisites: None.
Description: This course covers: an introduction to UNIX; the structure of UNIX; starting a UNIX session; UNIX file system, directory and ordinary file commands; text processing; using the editors; printing text files; online communications; piping and redirection; and data security.
Delivery method: CBT.
Minimum hardware requirement: PC.
Price: £795.00.
Source: Electrovision UK Ltd, Hamble Point Marina, School Lane, Hamble, Southampton SO31 4JD. Tel: 01703 452221

Title: **UNIX Internet**
Purpose: To introduce Internet.
Suitable for: Anyone.
Prerequisites: None.
Description: This course introduces Internet and teaches how to use it to communicate with other UNIX users, and how to transfer files to and from other sites. Topics include: how to access the Internet; how to use the Internet; and how to transfer files. Student manual supplied.
Delivery method: CBT.
Minimum hardware requirement: PC.
Price: £750.00 (multiple copy price on application).
Source: Electrovision UK Ltd, Hamble Point Marina, School Lane, Hamble, Southampton SO31 4JD. Tel: 01703 452221

Title: **UNIX Korn Shell**
Purpose: To provide training for UNIX Korn Shell.
Suitable for: Power users, programmers and system administrators.
Prerequisites: None.

Description: The topics include: Shell basics – commands, redirection, piping, scripts; Shell environment – profiles, variables, term, path, PS1, exporting variables; Shell programming – parameters, test, if/then/else, echo/read, case statements, subscripts and loops. The course is accompanied by a comprehensive manual.
Delivery method: CBT.
Minimum hardware requirement: PC.
Price: £995.00 (multiple copy price on application).
Source: Electrovision UK Ltd, Hamble Point Marina, School Lane, Hamble, Southampton SO31 4JD. Tel: 01703 452221

Title: **UNIX Network Administration**
Purpose: To provide training in installing and managing a UNIX network.
Suitable for: Network administrators
Prerequisites: None.
Description: This course covers: introduction to UNIX networking; setting up a UNIX network; interconnection of networks; file sharing; and troubleshooting.
Delivery method: CBT.
Minimum hardware requirement: PC.
Price: £795.00.
Source: Electrovision UK Ltd, Hamble Point Marina, School Lane, Hamble, Southampton SO31 4JD. Tel: 01703 452221

Title: **UNIX Network Programming**
Purpose: To enable students to develop network applications using TCP/IP.
Suitable for: Programmers.
Prerequisites: None.
Description: The course covers: networking fundamentals; working with sockets; socket support routines; working with TLI – modes of service; client server; and ends with a case study.
Delivery method: CBT.
Minimum hardware requirement: PC.
Price: £795.00.
Source: Electrovision UK Ltd, Hamble Point Marina, School Lane, Hamble, Southampton SO31 4JD. Tel: 01703 452221

Title: **UNIX Productivity Tools**
Purpose: To provide training in the use of the productivity tools.
Suitable for: Programmers and trainee programmers.
Prerequisites: 'UNIX Fundamentals' and C programming.
Description: This course covers: text processing tools – Using Vi, AWK, SED; program development tools – cc, lex, yacc, lex with yacc; debugging tools – sdb, ctrace, lint; and maintenance tools – make, SCCS.

Delivery method: CBT.
Minimum hardware requirement: PC.
Price: £795.00.
Source: Electrovision UK Ltd, Hamble Point Marina, School Lane, Hamble, Southampton SO31 4JD. Tel: 01703 452221

Title: **UNIX Shell Programming**
Purpose: To teach UNIX shell programming.
Suitable for: Programmers and trainee programmers.
Prerequisites: 'UNIX Fundamentals'.
Description: This course covers: introduction to the shell; shell variables; shell metacharacters; programming in the shell; writing shell scripts; organising commands; writing shell functions; advanced shell programming.
Delivery method: CBT.
Minimum hardware requirement: PC.
Price: £795.00.
Source: Electrovision UK Ltd, Hamble Point Marina, School Lane, Hamble, Southampton SO31 4JD. Tel: 01703 452221

Title: **UNIX System Administration**
Purpose: To give training in systems administration.
Suitable for: Administrators.
Prerequisites: None.
Description: This comprehensive course covers: introduction to system administration; managing user accounts; managing the file system; printing and communication; starting up and shutting down; handling system problems; activity; security and set-up; and configuring the system.
Delivery method: CBT.
Minimum hardware requirement: PC.
Price: £795.00.
Source: Electrovision UK Ltd, Hamble Point Marina, School Lane, Hamble, Southampton SO31 4JD. Tel: 01703 452221

Title: **UNIX System Administration Files**
Purpose: To teach how to effectively set up, maintain and manage disk partitions and file systems.
Suitable for: System Administrators.
Prerequisites: None.
Description: This course is designed to teach UNIX 5.4 system administrators how to effectively set up, maintain and manage disk partitions and file systems.
Delivery method: CBT; also available via the Internet.
Minimum hardware requirement: Any PC capable of running Microsoft Windows.
Price: On application.

Source: Oracle Corporation UK Ltd, The Oracle Centre, The Ring, Bracknell, Berks. RG12 1BW. Tel: 01344 860066

Title: **UNIX User**
Purpose: To introduce the major features and components of the UNIX operating system.
Suitable for: UNIX users.
Prerequisites: None.
Description: The key topics covered by this course include: logging on and off; basic shell commands; managing directories and files; navigating the directory; and file management.
Delivery method: CBT; also available via the Internet.
Minimum hardware requirement: Any PC capable of running Microsoft Windows.
Price: On application.
Source: Oracle Corporation UK Ltd, The Oracle Centre, The Ring, Bracknell, Berks. RG12 1BW. Tel: 01344 860066

Title: **Using vi Editor**
Purpose: To provide an understanding of the standard UNIX display editor.
Suitable for: UNIX users.
Prerequisites: None.
Description: This course is for the user who wishes to use the standard UNIX display editor to create and edit text files. Topics include: moving the cursor; editing text; and using the last line mode commands.
Delivery method: CBT; also available via the Internet.
Minimum hardware requirement: Any PC capable of running Microsoft Windows.
Price: On application.
Source: Oracle Corporation UK Ltd, The Oracle Centre, The Ring, Bracknell, Berks. RG12 1BW. Tel: 01344 860066

Pensions

CBT
Title: **Occupational Pensions**
Purpose: To provide a complete introduction to the subject of occupational pensions.
Suitable for: Anyone.
Prerequisites: None.
Description: The course covers: setting the scene; eligibility; contributions; retirement age; the members' pensions; options for members' pensions; tax free cash; and death benefits.
Delivery method: CBT.

Minimum hardware requirement: PC.
Price: £250.00.
Source: Marketing Department, The Chartered Insurance Institute, 20 Aldermanbury, London EC2V 7HY. Tel: 0171 417 4427

Personal

CBT

Title: **Managing Your Boss**
Purpose: To examine how beneficial it can be to work effectively with your boss.
Suitable for: Anyone.
Prerequisites: None.
Description: This course looks at the benefits that can be achieved by working effectively with your boss. It discusses the line between managing and manipulating, and the techniques that you can employ to effectively manage your boss.
Delivery method: CBT.
Minimum hardware requirement: PC.
Price: £175.00.
Source: Electrovision UK Ltd, Hamble Point Marina, School Lane, Hamble, Southampton SO31 4JD. Tel: 01703 452221

Title: **Managing Yourself**
Purpose: To introduce the concept of managing yourself by getting a perspective on your own working environment.
Suitable for: Anyone.
Prerequisites: None.
Description: Looks at time management techniques and the management of your own resources.
Delivery method: CBT.
Minimum hardware requirement: PC.
Price: £175.00.
Source: Electrovision UK Ltd, Hamble Point Marina, School Lane, Hamble, Southampton SO31 4JD. Tel: 01703 452221

Title: **Thinking Positively**
Purpose: To introduce the concept of positive thinking.
Suitable for: Anyone.
Prerequisites: None.
Description: Introduces the concept of positive thinking and how to apply it to yourself. Also looks at how to be positive with others and how positive thinking can be integrated into creating your future.

Delivery method: CBT.
Minimum hardware requirement: PC.
Price: £175.00.
Source: Electrovision UK Ltd, Hamble Point Marina, School Lane, Hamble, Southampton SO31 4JD. Tel: 01703 452221

Title: **Your Confidence Profile**
Purpose: To assess your confidence profile.
Suitable for: Everyone.
Prerequisites: 'Your Personality Profile'.
Description: This is a diagnostic programme that can help you observe a range of personality traits within the heading of confidence.
Delivery method: CBT and supporting text.
Minimum hardware requirement: IBM PC or compatible; 1Mb RAM.
Price: £165.00.
Source: Ivy Business Training Software plc, Ivy House, 233–235 Roehampton Lane, London SW15 4LB. Tel: 0181 780 1494

Title: **Your Personality Profile**
Purpose: To assess your personality profile.
Suitable for: Everyone.
Prerequisites: None.
Description: This is a diagnostic programme that can help you look at your personality traits. The results you receive are not to be taken as a medical or psychiatric assessment, but merely as a guideline.
Delivery method: CBT and supporting text.
Minimum hardware requirement: IBM PC or compatible, 1Mb RAM.
Price: £165.00.
Source: Ivy Business Training Software plc, Ivy House, 233–235 Roehampton Lane, London SW15 4LB. Tel: 0181 780 1494

Title: **Your Self-Esteem: Measure it, Improve it**
Purpose: To help you to focus on the traits of low and high self-esteem, so that you can use the exercises to measure your self-esteem and gain an insight into how you perceive yourself.
Suitable for: Anyone.
Prerequisites: None.
Description: This is an introductory course which will enable you to know: what self-esteem is and how it affects self confidence; how to recognise high and low self-esteem in yourself and others; how you can, after the exercises, get a better insight into your own self-concept; ways to increase your self-esteem.
Delivery method: CBT and supporting text.
Minimum hardware requirement: IBM PC or compatible; 1Mb RAM.

Price: £165.00.

Source: Ivy Business Training Software plc, Ivy House, 233–235 Roehampton Lane, London SW15 4LB. Tel: 0181 780 1494

CD-ROM
Title: **PLATO Curriculum**

Purpose: To provide a totally integrated learning system addressing all levels skills in: numeracy; literacy; communication; science; physics; chemistry; life and job skills; and workplace skills.

Suitable for: Young adult and adult learners.

Prerequisites: None.

Description: PLATO courseware incorporates effective instructional strategies for skill development with real-life applications to help learners establish a solid foundation of skills. From this base, learners develop the critical thinking skills necessary to function effectively in today's increasingly complex world.

Delivery method: CD-ROM; also currently installed on Microsoft (IIS).

Minimum hardware requirement: 486 PC; 4Mb RAM; CD-ROM drive and sound card.

Price: On application.

Source: TRO Learning (UK) Ltd, Brook House, Riverside Park, Poyle Road, Colnbrook, Berks. SL3 0AA. Tel: 01753 799111

Title: **Self-Development**

Purpose: To make you aware to a large measure of what you can achieve and how to set about achieving it.

Suitable for: Anyone.

Prerequisites: None.

Description: This course is about *you* and *your future*. If you are determined enough, this course of self-development will reflect in your domestic, social and working environments to the benefit of all.

Delivery method: CD-ROM.

Minimum hardware requirement: 386 PC; 8Mb RAM; 6Mb hard-disk space; CD-ROM drive; sound card.

Price: £295.00.

Source: Comput-Ed Ltd, Long Lane, Dawlish EX7 0QR. Tel: 01626 889955

Title: **Strategy**

Purpose: To teach and support a complete introductory course on strategy.

Suitable for: All business (or modular) students from HND level upwards.

Prerequisites: None.

Description: A detailed introduction to strategy.

Delivery method: CD-ROM.

Minimum hardware requirement: PC; 8Mb RAM; CD-ROM drive and sound card.

Price: £29.95 (inc. VAT) single-user licence; multi-user licences from £650.
Source: Pitman Publishing, 128 Long Acre, London WC2E 9AN. Tel: 0171 4472290

Personal finance

CBT

Title: **Introducing Pensions: What are They and Do You Need One?**
Purpose: To give you an overview of the subject of pensions and the recent changes in legislation.
Suitable for: Anyone.
Prerequisites: None.
Description: This is an introductory course which will enable you to gain the knowledge that is important to an understanding of the purposes, complexities and dynamics of pensions.
Delivery method: CBT and supporting text.
Minimum hardware requirement: IBM PC or compatible, 512k RAM.
Price: £165.00.
Source: Ivy Business Training Software plc, Ivy House, 233–235 Roehampton Lane, London SW15 4LB. Tel: 0181 780 1494

Title: **Money and You: Your Income, Your Taxes, Your Bank Account**
Purpose: To explain how to manage your own personal finances.
Suitable for: Anyone.
Prerequisites: None.
Description: This is an introductory course which will enable you to: calculate taxes and explain how they are collected through the PAYE system; calculate deductions to gross pay with consideration given to National Insurance Contributions, allowances and tax; understand the items on a bank statement and how to reconcile timing differences.
Delivery method: CBT and supporting text.
Minimum hardware requirement: IBM PC or compatible; 512k RAM.
Price: £165.00.
Source: Ivy Business Training Software plc, Ivy House, 233–235 Roehampton Lane, London SW15 4LB. Tel: 0181 780 1494

Personal skills

CBT
Title: **The Strategy Game**
Purpose: To help users gain high-level management experience in a non-real life situation.
Suitable for: Anyone who wants to move up the career ladder, whether they be new graduates or new managers.
Prerequisites: None.
Description: Users are put into a high-level position with a struggling subsidiary of a multinational company and given the task of turning the company's fortunes around to make it profitable.
Delivery method: CBT.
Minimum hardware requirement: 386 PC; 4Mb RAM; 5Mb hard disk.
Price: £32.00 + VAT.
Source: McGraw-Hill Publishing Co., Shoppenhangers Rd, Maidenhead, Berks. SL6 2QL. Tel: 01628 23432

CD-ROM
Title: **Job Fundamentals**
Purpose: To provide a wealth of information to anyone starting a new job.
Suitable for: Anyone starting their first job, returning to work or starting out with a new employer.
Prerequisites: None.
Description: This course is in five sections: introduction; clarifying your role; managing your work; being a professional; providing quality.
Delivery method: CD-ROM.
Minimum hardware requirement: 486PC; 8Mb; RAM; 10Mb hard-disk space.
Price: Single course £75.00; multiple course discount on request.
Source: Video Arts Ltd, Dumbarton House, 68 Oxford Street, London W1N OLH. Tel: 0171 637 7288

Plastics and polymers

CBT
Title: **Injection Moulding Training Course**
Purpose: To develop injection moulding machine operating skills from a very basic level up to setter level, using a systematic approach.
Suitable for: Anyone who wants or needs to improve their injection moulding process performance.
Prerequisites: None.
Description: Provides training and information in six key areas: introduction to

plastic; the injection moulding cycle; the injection moulding machine; mould design and principles; problem solving; and simulated machine operation.
Delivery method: CBT.
Minimum hardware requirement: PC; 640Kb RAM; 2Mb hard-disk space.
Price: £550.00 + VAT.
Source: British Polymer Training Association, Coppice House, Halesfield 7, Telford, Shropshire TF7 4NA. Tel: 01952 587020

Title: **PICAT (Polymer Industry Competence Assessment Tool)**
Purpose: To train and assess polymer processing production staff in fault finding and troubleshooting.
Suitable for: Anyone in plastics processing, who wants to reduce downtime and waste, and improve output, quality and profitability.
Prerequisites: Minimum 6 months' process experience.
Description: PICAT is a complete training support and assessment system that is available in: injection moulding; blow moulding; blown film; extrusion-pipe; extrusion-profile. PICAT allows the user to experience a 'real' processing environment.
Delivery method: CBT.
Minimum hardware requirement: 386 PC; 640Kb RAM: 4Mb hard-disk space.
Price: £825.00 + VAT.
Source: British Polymer Training Association, Coppice House, Halesfield 7, Telford, Shropshire TF7 4NA. Tel: 01952 587020

Title: **PICOS (Polymer Industry Core Operative Skills)**
Purpose: To help anyone working towards the achievement of N/SVQ levels 1 and 2 in polymer processing disciplines.
Suitable for: Anyone new to the polymer processing industry who needs to get an understanding of the basic key issues.
Prerequisites: None.
Description: Provides training and information in three key areas: quality; health and safety; and communication skills. An optional module 'Injection Moulding' is included. It provides a basic understanding on how it works, including basic operation of the machine, along with start-up and shutdown procedures.
Delivery method: CBT.
Minimum hardware requirement: 486 PC; 4Mb RAM; 20 Mb hard-disk space.
Price: On application.
Source: British Polymer Training Association, Coppice House, Halesfield 7, Telford, Shropshire TF7 4NA. Tel: 01952 587020

Pneumatics

CBT

Title: **PNEUSIM**
Purpose: Pneumatic circuit design and simulation software.
Suitable for: Engineering students and trainers.
Prerequisites: None.
Description: A six-lesson tutorial designed to progress the student through various aspects of the package. This starts with circuit examples and proceeds through simple file handling and display controls to the creation of an interactive electro-pneumatic circuit. The student can then experiment with circuit ideas and quickly simulate operation to test the design.
Delivery method: CBT.
Minimum hardware requirement: PC 640Kb RAM.
Price: On application.
Source: The Training Department, IMI Norgren Ltd, Brookside Business Park, Greengate, Middleton, Manchester M24 1GR. Tel: 0161 654 6540

Power generation

CD-ROM

Title: **A New Generation – Combined Cycle Gas Turbines (CCGT)**
Purpose: To study the main components of the power station and how the various elements interact to affect the overall process.
Suitable for: Persons involved in or interested in CCGT technology.
Prerequisites: None.
Description: This course covers: introduction; plant overview; gas turbine; heat recovery steam generator (HRSG); water steam cycle; steam turbine; cooling water system; water treatment; control systems; and an assessment.
Delivery method: CD-ROM.
Minimum hardware requirement: 486 PC; 4Mb RAM; dual speed CD-ROM drive; sound card.
Price: On application.
Source: Instinct Training, Strawberry How Business Centre, Lorton Road, Cockermouth, Cumbria CA13 9XQ. Tel: 01900 827600

Title: **Alternators and Electrical Systems**
Purpose: To provide training in alternators and electrical systems.
Suitable for: Persons in the power industry.
Prerequisites: None.
Description: The modules of this course are: alternators; electrical systems; and an assessment.

Delivery method: CD-ROM.
Minimum hardware requirement: 486 PC; 4Mb RAM; dual speed CD-ROM drive; sound card.
Price: On application.
Source: Instinct Training, Strawberry How Business Centre, Lorton Road, Cockermouth, Cumbria CA13 9XQ. Tel: 01900 827600

Title: **Atomic Structure**
Purpose: To provide training in atomic structure.
Suitable for: Those in the power industry.
Prerequisites: None.
Description: The modules of this course are: elements and compounds; the atom; mass number and atomic number; isotopes; Avogadro's number; chemical reactions; historical appendix; and a self-test.
Delivery method: CD-ROM.
Minimum hardware requirement: 486 PC; 4Mb RAM; dual speed CD-ROM drive; sound card.
Price: On application.
Source: Instinct Training, Strawberry How Business Centre, Lorton Road, Cockermouth, Cumbria CA13 9XQ. Tel: 01900 827600

Title: **Auxiliary Systems**
Purpose: To provide training for auxiliary systems.
Suitable for: Persons in the power industry.
Prerequisites: None.
Description: The modules of this course are: circulating water; compressed air systems; water treatment; fire prevention; and an assessment.
Delivery method: CD-ROM.
Minimum hardware requirement: 486 PC; 4Mb RAM; dual speed CD-ROM drive; sound card.
Price: On application.
Source: Instinct Training, Strawberry How Business Centre, Lorton Road, Cockermouth, Cumbria CA13 9XQ. Tel: 01900 827600

Title: **Biological Effects of Ionising Radiation**
Purpose: To provide training in biological ionising radiation.
Suitable for: Those in the power industry.
Prerequisites: None.
Description: The modules of this course are: introduction; early effects; late effects; stochastic and non-stochastic effects; risks factors; quantities and units; and an assessment.
Delivery method: CD-ROM.

Minimum hardware requirement: 486 PC; 4Mb RAM; dual speed CD-ROM drive; sound card.
Price: On application.
Source: Instinct Training, Strawberry How Business Centre, Lorton Road, Cockermouth, Cumbria CA13 9XQ. Tel: 01900 827600

Title: **Chain Reaction**
Purpose: To provide training in chain reaction.
Suitable for: Those in the power industry.
Prerequisites: None.
Description: The modules of this course are: neutron balance; multiplication constant k; cross-section values for natural uranium; sustaining the chain reaction; and an assessment.
Delivery method: CD-ROM.
Minimum hardware requirement: 486 PC; 4Mb RAM; dual speed CD-ROM drive; sound card.
Price: On application.
Source: Instinct Training, Strawberry How Business Centre, Lorton Road, Cockermouth, Cumbria CA13 9XQ. Tel: 01900 827600.

Title: **Contamination Detectors**
Purpose: To provide training in contamination detectors.
Suitable for: Those in the power industry.
Prerequisites: None.
Description: The modules of this course are: requirements of health physics instruments; principles of contamination detectors; contamination instruments; monitoring procedures; and an assessment.
Delivery method: CD-ROM.
Minimum hardware requirement: 486 PC; 4Mb RAM; dual speed CD-ROM drive; sound card.
Price: On application.
Source: Instinct Training, Strawberry How Business Centre, Lorton Road, Cockermouth, Cumbria CA13 9XQ. Tel: 01900 827600

Title: **Control of Ionising Radiation**
Purpose: To provide training in control of ionising radiation.
Suitable for: Those in the power industry.
Prerequisites: None.
Description: The modules of this course are: activity; annual limits on intake; control by design; working with radioactive substances; safety rules radiological; and an assessment.
Delivery method: CD-ROM.

Minimum hardware requirement: 486 PC; 4Mb RAM; dual speed CD-ROM drive; sound card.
Price: On application.
Source: Instinct Training, Strawberry How Business Centre, Lorton Road, Cockermouth, Cumbria CA13 9XQ. Tel: 01900 827600

Title: **Detection of Ionising Radiation**
Purpose: To provide training in detection of ionising radiation.
Suitable for: Those in the power industry.
Prerequisites: None.
Description: The modules of this course are: personal dosimetry; detection systems; and an assessment.
Delivery method: CD-ROM.
Minimum hardware requirement: 486 PC; 4Mb RAM; dual speed CD-ROM drive; sound card.
Price: On application.
Source: Instinct Training, Strawberry How Business Centre, Lorton Road, Cockermouth, Cumbria CA13 9XQ. Tel: 01900 827600

Title: **Dosimetry and Air Sampling**
Purpose: To provide training dosimetry and air sampling.
Suitable for: Those in the power industry.
Prerequisites: None.
Description: The modules of this course are: dosimetry responsibilities of SAP (NR); dosimeters; NRSI; airborne activity responsibilities of SAP (NR); airborne contamination; measurement of airborne activity; and an assessment.
Delivery method: CD-ROM.
Minimum hardware requirement: 486 PC; 4Mb RAM; dual speed CD-ROM drive; sound card.
Price: On application.
Source: Instinct Training, Strawberry How Business Centre, Lorton Road, Cockermouth, Cumbria CA13 9XQ. Tel: 01900 827600

Title: **Fission**
Purpose: To provide training in fission
Suitable for: Those in the power industry.
Prerequisites: None.
Description: The modules of this course are: fission; fission products; the emission of neutrons; energy and power; and an assessment.
Delivery method: CD-ROM.
Minimum hardware requirement: 486 PC; 4Mb RAM; dual speed CD-ROM drive; sound card.
Price: On application.

Source: Instinct Training, Strawberry How Business Centre, Lorton Road, Cockermouth, Cumbria CA13 9XQ. Tel: 01900 827600

Title: **Health Physics Measurements 1**
Purpose: To provide training health physics measurements.
Suitable for: Those in the power industry.
Prerequisites: None.
Description: The modules of this course are: introduction; types of monitoring; monitoring for external hazards; contamination monitoring; non-radioactive gases; legislation; and an assessment.
Delivery method: CD-ROM.
Minimum hardware requirement: 486 PC; 4Mb RAM; dual speed CD-ROM drive; sound card.
Price: On application.
Source: Instinct Training, Strawberry How Business Centre, Lorton Road, Cockermouth, Cumbria CA13 9XQ. Tel: 01900 827600

Title: **Health Physics Measurements 2**
Purpose: To provide training in health physics measurements.
Suitable for: Those in the power industry.
Prerequisites: None.
Description: The modules of this course are: legislation; surface contamination; airborne activity; radiation monitoring; factors affecting instruments; and an assessment.
Delivery method: CD-ROM.
Minimum hardware requirement: 486 PC; 4Mb RAM; dual speed CD-ROM drive; sound card.
Price: On application.
Source: Instinct Training, Strawberry How Business Centre, Lorton Road, Cockermouth, Cumbria CA13 9XQ. Tel: 01900 827600

Title: **Interactions of Radiation with Matter**
Purpose: To provide training in interactions of radiation with matter.
Suitable for: Those in the power industry.
Prerequisites: None.
Description: The modules of this course are: ionisation and electronic excitation; origin and nature of ionising radiation; interaction of ionising radiation; range and shielding; interactions with the human body; quantities and units; and an assessment.
Delivery method: CD-ROM.
Minimum hardware requirement: 486 PC; 4Mb RAM; dual speed CD-ROM drive; sound card.
Price: On application.

Source: Instinct Training, Strawberry How Business Centre, Lorton Road, Cockermouth, Cumbria CA13 9XQ. Tel: 01900 827600

Title: **Moderation**
Purpose: To provide training in moderation.
Suitable for: Those in the power industry.
Prerequisites: None.
Description: The modules of this course are: introduction; properties of an ideal moderator; moderator materials; properties of moderators; neutron behaviour; and an assessment.
Delivery method: CD-ROM.
Minimum hardware requirement: 486 PC; 4Mb RAM; Dual speed CD-ROM drive; sound card.
Price: On application.
Source: Instinct Training, Strawberry How Business Centre, Lorton Road, Cockermouth, Cumbria CA13 9XQ. Tel: 01900 827600

Title: **Nuclear Reactions**
Purpose: To provide training in nuclear reactions.
Suitable for: Those in the power industry.
Prerequisites: None.
Description: The modules of this course are: properties of the nuclei; nuclear reactions; the rate of reaction; appendices; and an assessment.
Delivery method: CD-ROM.
Minimum hardware requirement: 486 PC; 4Mb RAM; dual speed CD-ROM drive; sound card.
Price: On application.
Source: Instinct Training, Strawberry How Business Centre, Lorton Road, Cockermouth, Cumbria CA13 9XQ. Tel: 01900 827600

Title: **Our Generation**
Purpose: To describe how the parts of a coal-fired power station operate and how those components interact and affect the overall process.
Suitable for: New entrants to the power industry.
Prerequisites: None.
Description: This course covers: coal handling; turbines; cooling water systems; exhaust gases; feed heaters; generators; boilers; milling; and combustion.
Delivery method: CD-ROM.
Minimum hardware requirement: 486 PC; 4Mb RAM; dual speed CD-ROM drive; sound card.
Price: On application.
Source: Instinct Training, Strawberry How Business Centre, Lorton Road, Cockermouth, Cumbria CA13 9XQ. Tel: 01900 827600

DIRECTORY OF COURSES

Title: **Overview ICRP 60 and NRPB Advices**
Purpose: To provide training in Overview ICRP 60 and NRPB Advices.
Suitable for: Those in the power industry.
Prerequisites: None.
Description: The modules of this course are: introduction; biological effects of ionising radiation; quantities; system of radiological protection; dose limits and constraints; legislation; and an assessment.
Delivery method: CD-ROM.
Minimum hardware requirement: 486 PC; 4Mb RAM; dual speed CD-ROM drive; sound card.
Price: On application.
Source: Instinct Training, Strawberry How Business Centre, Lorton Road, Cockermouth, Cumbria CA13 9XQ. Tel: 01900 827600

Title: **Personal Dosimetry**
Purpose: To provide training in personal dosimetry.
Suitable for: Those in the power industry.
Prerequisites: None.
Description: The modules of this course are: overview of personal dosimetry; dosemeters; requirements for dosemeter issue; (CDRS) and an assessment.
Delivery method: CD-ROM.
Minimum hardware requirement: 486 PC; 4Mb RAM; dual speed CD-ROM drive; sound card.
Price: On application.
Source: Instinct Training, Strawberry How Business Centre, Lorton Road, Cockermouth, Cumbria CA13 9XQ. Tel: 01900 827600

Title: **Pulverised Fuel Codes of Practice**
Purpose: To provide an appreciation of the requirements for, and underlying philosophy of the pulverised fuel codes of practice.
Suitable for: Those who come into contact with pulverised fuel.
Prerequisites: None.
Description: The course also addresses the specific variations of the codes of practice relating to particular mill types. Modules covered are: why PF codes of practice; plant layout; general precautions; normal operations; abnormal conditions; operating a mill group; and an assessment.
Delivery method: CD-ROM.
Minimum hardware requirement: 486 PC; 4Mb RAM; dual speed CD-ROM drive; sound card.
Price: On application.
Source: Instinct Training, Strawberry How Business Centre, Lorton Road, Cockermouth, Cumbria CA13 9XQ. Tel: 01900 827600

Title: **Radiation Detectors**
Purpose: To provide training in radiation detectors.
Suitable for: Those in the power industry.
Prerequisites: None.
Description: The modules of this course are: principles of gas-filled detectors; detection instruments; how to use detectors; and an assessment.
Delivery method: CD-ROM.
Minimum hardware requirement: 486 PC; 4Mb RAM; dual speed CD-ROM drive; sound card.
Price: On application.
Source: Instinct Training, Strawberry How Business Centre, Lorton Road, Cockermouth, Cumbria CA13 9XQ. Tel: 01900 827600

Title: **Radioactive Quantities and Units**
Purpose: To provide training in radioactive quantities and units.
Suitable for: Those in the power industry.
Prerequisites: None.
Description: The modules of this course are: activity; absorbed dose and dose equivalent; committed dose equivalent; effective dose equivalent and committed effective dose equivalent; ionising radiations regulations; and an assessment.
Delivery method: CD-ROM.
Minimum hardware requirement: 486 PC; 4Mb RAM; dual speed CD-ROM drive; sound card.
Price: On application.
Source: Instinct Training, Strawberry How Business Centre, Lorton Road, Cockermouth, Cumbria CA13 9XQ. Tel: 01900 827600

Title: **Radioactivity**
Purpose: To provide training in radioactivity.
Suitable for: Those in the power industry.
Prerequisites: None.
Description: The modules of this course are: the nature of forces within the nucleus; chart of the nuclides; how nuclei become more stable; half-life; radioactive decay chains; and an assessment.
Delivery method: CD-ROM.
Minimum hardware requirement: 486 PC; 4Mb RAM; dual speed CD-ROM drive; sound card.
Price: On application.
Source: Instinct Training, Strawberry How Business Centre, Lorton Road, Cockermouth, Cumbria CA13 9XQ. Tel: 01900 827600

Title: **Radiological Calculators**
Purpose: To provide training in radiological calculators.
Suitable for: Those in the power industry.
Prerequisites: None.
Description: The modules of this course are: radioactive decay; radioactive equilibrium; external health hazard calculations; external radiation shielding calculations; neutron activation; and an assessment.
Delivery method: CD-ROM.
Minimum hardware requirement: 486 PC; 4Mb RAM; dual speed CD-ROM drive; sound card.
Price: On application.
Source: Instinct Training, Strawberry How Business Centre, Lorton Road, Cockermouth, Cumbria CA13 9XQ. Tel: 01900 827600

Title: **Radiological Quantities and Units**
Purpose: To provide training in radiological quantities and units.
Suitable for: Those in the power industry.
Prerequisites: None.
Description: The modules of this course are: activity; quantities concerned with individuals; quantities concerned with populations; and an assessment.
Delivery method: CD-ROM.
Minimum hardware requirement: 486 PC; 4Mb RAM; dual speed CD-ROM drive; sound card.
Price: On application.
Source: Instinct Training, Strawberry How Business Centre, Lorton Road, Cockermouth, Cumbria CA13 9XQ. Tel: 01900 827600

Title: **Steam Water Cycle**
Purpose: To provide training in steam water cycle.
Suitable for: Persons in the power industry.
Prerequisites: None.
Description: The modules of this course are: introduction; steam production; turbines; condensate system; feedwater system; and an assessment.
Delivery method: CD-ROM.
Minimum hardware requirement: 486 PC; 4Mb RAM; dual speed CD-ROM drive; sound card.
Price: On application.
Source: Instinct Training, Strawberry How Business Centre, Lorton Road, Cockermouth, Cumbria CA13 9XQ. Tel: 01900 827600

Presentation skills

CBT

Title: **Preparing a Presentation**
Purpose: To train you to analyse your audience and the administration requirements.
Suitable for: Anyone.
Prerequisites: None.
Description: This course starts by training you to analyse your audience and the administration requirements of your presentation. It then moves on to preparing a presentation, using visual aids, rehearsing, and room preparation.
Delivery method: CBT.
Minimum hardware requirement: PC.
Price: £175.00.
Source: Electrovision UK Ltd, Hamble Point Marina, School Lane, Hamble, Southampton SO31 4JD. Tel: 01703 452221

Title: **Succeeding With Your Presentation: Prepare it, Deliver it**
Purpose: To help you overcome 'presentation panic' by leading you through the steps of a successful presentation.
Suitable for: Anyone.
Prerequisites: None.
Description: This is an introductory course which includes a model which you can reuse to build the outline of a presentation, and rely on it as a speaking aid – just fill in the model, print it out and use it. Training staff will find this course invaluable in laying a solid foundation before role-playing exercises.
Delivery method: CBT and supporting text.
Minimum hardware requirement: IBM PC or compatible; 512k RAM.
Price: £165.00.
Source: Ivy Business Training Software plc, Ivy House, 233–235 Roehampton Lane, London SW15 4LB. Tel: 0181 780 1494

Title: **The Effective Presentation: Getting Started**
Purpose: To teach the fundamental concepts of effective presentations and offer practical suggestions that can overcome stage fright and produce a successful presentation.
Suitable for: Anyone.
Prerequisites: None.
Description: This is an introductory course which will enable you to understand: the listener's thinking sequence; the preparation points for each step in the thinking sequence; the structure of a presentation and how to conduct each phase; and the different types of visual aids, their advantages and disadvantages.

Delivery method: CBT and supporting text.
Minimum hardware requirement: IBM PC or compatible; 512k RAM.
Price: £165.00.
Source: Ivy Business Training Software plc, Ivy House, 233–235 Roehampton Lane, London SW15 4LB. Tel: 0181 780 1494

Production management

Simulation
Title: **Operations**
Purpose: To introduce production concepts.
Suitable for: Trainees, functional specialists, supervisors, junior through middle management.
Prerequisites: None.
Description: A simulation/game replicating the production operation of a manufacturing company. Involving purchasing, scheduling and shift planning decisions by teams of 4–5.
Delivery method: Teams use computerised simulator.
Minimum hardware requirement: PC; 640Kb RAM and printer.
Price: Rental: £125.00; purchase: £295.00; tutored from £500.00.
Source: Hall Marketing, Studio 11, Colman's Wharf, 45 Morris Road, London E14 6PA. Tel: 0171 537 2982

Project management

CBT
Title: **An Introduction to Project Management**
Purpose: To give an understanding of the principles, tools and techniques used to manage a project effectively.
Suitable for: Project managers.
Prerequisites: None.
Description: This is an introductory course which will enable you to: develop the skills for handling projects; structure a project and implement each of the four phases; prepare a project definition document, and a project planning document; monitor a project and prepare and use a project change document and a project finish document.
Delivery method: CBT and supporting text.
Minimum hardware requirement: IBM PC or compatible, 512k RAM.
Price: £165.00.
Source: Ivy Business Training Software plc, Ivy House, 233–235 Roehampton Lane, London SW15 4LB. Tel: 0181 780 1494

Title: **Project Management**
Purpose: To teach the concepts of project management.
Suitable for: Team leaders and managers.
Prerequisites: None.
Description: Looks at how to define a project and set objectives, and then identify issues and critical factors. Includes detailed planning and scheduling instruction. Also covers monitoring projects and common reasons for project failure.
Delivery method: CBT.
Minimum hardware requirement: PC.
Price: £348.00.
Source: Electrovision UK Ltd, Hamble Point Marina, School Lane, Hamble, Southampton SO31 4JD. Tel: 01703 452221

Title: **Project Management Fundamentals**
Purpose: To provide an overview of the basic principles of project management, the characteristics of a project and what is involved in project planning.
Suitable for: Anyone.
Prerequisites: None.
Description: The course has three lessons covering: overview of project management, organising a project; and the project life cycle.
Delivery method: CBT.
Minimum hardware requirement: 386 PC; 4Mb RAM; 7Mb hard-disk space.
Price: £300.00.
Source: Mindware Training Technologies Ltd, Block 2, International Business Centre, Plassey, Limerick, Ireland. Tel: (353) 6133 1430

Title: **Project Management Methods**
Purpose: To outline the use of methods and tools to help manage a project.
Suitable for: Anyone.
Prerequisites: None.
Description: This course has three lessons covering: project methods and tools; the PRINCE methods; and the PERT method.
Delivery method: CBT.
Minimum hardware requirement: 386 PC; 8Mb RAM; 7Mb hard-disk space.
Price: £300.00.
Source: Mindware Training Technologies Ltd, Block 2, International Business Centre, Plassey, Limerick, Ireland. Tel: (353) 6133 1430

Title: **Project Planning and Control**
Purpose: To provide an overview of the basic principles of project management and control; to identify the main areas of a project plan; to outline some techniques that can be used.

Suitable for: Anyone.
Prerequisites: None.
Description: The course has three lessons covering: project planning; project monitoring and control; and budget and cost control.
Delivery method: CBT.
Minimum hardware requirement: 386 PC; 4Mb RAM; 7Mb hard-disk space.
Price: £450.00.
Source: Mindware Training Technologies Ltd, Block 2, International Business Centre, Plassey, Limerick, Ireland. Tel: (353) 6133 1430

Title: **Purchasing for Projects**
Purpose: To outline the purchasing and supply requirements for running a project, and to explain what is involved in producing a purchasing plan.
Suitable for: Project managers.
Prerequisites: None.
Description: The course has three lessons covering: purchasing; the requirements specification; and evaluation of suppliers.
Delivery method: CBT.
Minimum hardware requirement: 386 PC; 4Mb RAM; 7Mb hard-disk space.
Price: £500.00.
Source: Mindware Training Technologies Ltd, Block 2, International Business Centre, Plassey, Limerick, Ireland. Tel: (353) 6133 1430

Title: **Software Development Project Management**
Purpose: To teach collaborative ways of using technical management systems and tools for effective projects.
Suitable for: Anyone.
Prerequisites: None.
Description: This course provides instruction for the development of a well-motivated team environment. The topics covered include: critical path; flowcharts; resource demands; meetings; project management; and duration and float of activities.
Delivery method: CBT.
Minimum hardware requirement: PC.
Price: £1995.00.
Source: Electrovision UK Ltd, Hamble Point Marina, School Lane, Hamble, Southampton SO31 4JD. Tel: 01703 452221

CD-ROM

Title: **Participating in Project Teams**
Purpose: To provide you with a good understanding of how a project team operates and a grasp of the skills demanded of team members.
Suitable for: Anyone.

Prerequisites: None.
Description: This course will help to give you a better knowledge of the structure of projects and the success factors that will make the individual a more valuable project team member.
Delivery method: CD-ROM.
Minimum hardware requirement: 486 PC, 8Mb RAM; 420Mb hard disk; CD-ROM drive; audio card.
Price: £1195.00.
Source: Intelligent Training Solutions, 29 Narrow Street, London E14 8DP. Tel: 0171 791 3000

Title: **Project Management**
Purpose: To provide a comprehensive grounding in the monitoring, control and general management of projects.
Suitable for: Team leaders and managers.
Prerequisites: None.
Description: The course has eight lessons covering: project management; the project life cycle; project estimating and planning; project monitoring and control; environmental change; procurement management; requirements and suppliers; formal management methods.
Delivery method: CD-ROM.
Minimum hardware requirement: 486 PC; 8Mb RAM; CD-ROM drive; sound card.
Price: £2250.00.
Source: Mindware Training Technologies Ltd, Block 2, International Business Centre, Plassey, Limerick, Ireland. Tel: (353) 6133 1430

Interactive video
Title: **Principles of Project Management**
Purpose: To explain the stages, techniques and situations unique to projects, and the importance of the interpersonal skills critical to successful project management.
Suitable for: Managers and supervisors.
Prerequisites: None.
Description: This course will enable you to: reduce costs and improve resource scheduling; avoid spending time on problems and less resolving them; bring projects in on time, on or under budget, and within quality specifications.
Delivery method: Interactive video.
Minimum hardware requirement: Interactive video workstation.
Price: £2880.00.
Source: Training Direct, North Court, Edinburgh Gate, Harlow, Essex CM20 2JE. Tel: 01279 623927

Simulation

Title: **PROTEST – Project Management**
Purpose: To teach project management.
Suitable for: Trainees, functional specialists, supervisors, junior through middle management.
Prerequisites: Basic project management knowledge.
Description: A customisable project management simulator involving project planning and implementation.
Delivery method: Teams use computerised simulator.
Minimum hardware requirement: PC; 640Kb RAM and printer.
Price: On application.
Source: Hall Marketing, Studio 11, Colman's Wharf, 45 Morris Road, London E14 6PA. Tel: 0171 537 2982

Protective equipment

CD-ROM

Title: **Personal Protective Equipment**
Purpose: To ensure that all users of PPE are aware of their responsibilities under the Personal Protective Equipment at Work Regulations 1992.
Suitable for: All users of PPE.
Prerequisites: None.
Description: This course explains why certain requirements have been introduced and stresses the importance of the use and storage of PPE. The modules of this course are: introduction; a little of the legislation; what your employer will do; your obligations; why you will need training; general points; and a self-test.
Delivery method: CD-ROM.
Minimum hardware requirement: 486 PC; 4Mb RAM; dual speed CD-ROM drive; sound card.
Price: On application.
Source: Instinct Training, Strawberry How Business Centre, Lorton Road, Cockermouth, Cumbria CA13 9XQ. Tel: 01900 827600

Questioning skills

Interactive video

Title: **Effective Questioning**
Purpose: To teach the effective use of questioning techniques to ensure that the correct information is elicited in an interview situation.
Suitable for: Anyone.

Prerequisites: None.
Description: This course comprises three modules, each set in a different location within a newspaper office. You will see the effectiveness of different techniques and have an opportunity to test your knowledge of question types.
Delivery method: Interactive video.
Minimum hardware requirement: Interactive video workstation.
Price: £1135.00.
Source: Training Direct, North Court, Edinburgh Gate, Harlow, Essex CM20 2JE. Tel: 01279 623927

Reading skills

CD-ROM
Title: **Speed Reading**
Purpose: To analyse how different people approach reading and outline the techniques to follow in order to speed up your reading and improve your comprehension.
Suitable for: Anyone.
Prerequisites: None.
Description: This is an introductory course that will help you: to learn about how people read; to become a faster reader; to improve levels of comprehension; to improve levels of concentration. The main body of this course is taken up with timed practice texts which are followed by questions to check your understanding.
Delivery method: CD-ROM.
Minimum hardware requirement: 486 PC; 8Mb RAM; 256 Colour VGA; sound card; and 8Mb hard-disk space.
Price: £295.00.
Source: Ivy Business Training Software plc, Ivy House, 233–235 Roehampton Lane, London SW15 4LB. Tel: 0181 780 1494

Recruitment and selection

CD-i
Title: **It's Your Choice**
Purpose: To teach selection interview skills.
Suitable for: Managers.
Prerequisites: None.
Description: Shows how a selection interview is like detective work. Key points are: prepare – think about the job and applicant; forestall interruptions; listen

– put applicants at ease and encourage them to talk; probe – control the interview; don't avoid awkward questions.
Delivery method: CD-i.
Minimum hardware requirement: CD-i player and television.
Price: £995.00; rental prices on request.
Source: Video Arts Ltd, Dumbarton House, 68 Oxford Street, London W1N OLH. Tel: 0171 637 7288

CD-ROM
Title: **Recruitment Interviewing**
Purpose: To teach you the specialist skills you need, and give you a chance to practise, so that when you actually do it, you get it right every time!
Suitable for: Managers.
Prerequisites: 'Essential Interviewing Skills'.
Description: This course will help you: to understand the need for writing a job description; in reviewing applications; in explaining what will happen during the interview; in controlling the interview; in assessing the candidate; in selling the job; in explaining what will happen after the interview; in writing up your interview notes; in checking references; and in choosing the appropriate candidate.
Delivery method: CD-ROM.
Minimum hardware requirement: 486 PC; 8Mb RAM; 420Mb hard disk; CD-ROM drive; audio card.
Price: £895.00.
Source: Training Direct, North Court, Edinburgh Gate, Harlow, Essex CM20 2JE. Tel: 01279 623927

Title: **Right the First Time**
Purpose: To teach the skills and techniques for successful recruitment interviewing.
Suitable for: Managers.
Prerequisites: None.
Description: This course provides the opportunity to interview three candidates for a vacancy. Complete with past employment information, you ask the questions, but can you get it right first time. Covers topics from advertising to job offer.
Delivery method: CD-ROM (2 discs).
Minimum hardware requirement: PC; 8Mb RAM; CD-ROM drive; sound card.
Price: £975.00.
Source: Electrovision UK Ltd, Hamble Point Marina, School Lane, Hamble, Southampton SO31 4JD. Tel: 01703 452221

Title: **The Selection Interview**
Purpose: To outline ways: of providing appropriate interview settings; of putting the interviewee at ease; of using questioning styles to extract information and match a candidate against specification.
Suitable for: Managers.
Prerequisites: None.
Description: This is an introductory course that will enable you to plan and prepare for an interview and conduct a successful selection interview.
Delivery method: CD-ROM.
Minimum hardware requirement: 486 PC; 8Mb RAM; 256 Colour VGA; sound card; and 8Mb hard-disk space.
Price: £295.00.
Source: Ivy Business Training Software plc, Ivy House, 233–235 Roehampton Lane, London SW15 4LB. Tel: 0181 780 1494

Title: **The Selection Interview**
Purpose: To provide practical and comprehensive advice on selecting the right person.
Suitable for: Business students, supervisors and managers at all levels.
Prerequisites: None.
Description: This course covers: overview; preparation; planning; structuring the interview; conducting the interview; and reviewing. Practice scenarios allow you to check your performance.
Delivery method: CD-ROM.
Minimum hardware requirement: 386 PC; 6Mb hard disk; sound card; CD-ROM drive.
Price: £295.00.
Source: Comput-Ed Ltd, Long Lane, Dawlish EX7 0QR. Tel: 01626 889955

Report writing

CBT
Title: **Report Writing**
Purpose: To teach how to write reports that will achieve their objectives.
Suitable for: Anyone.
Prerequisites: None.
Description: The topics include: action-oriented objectives; identifying essential and desirable content; structuring reports; how to write clearly and economically with flair. The step-by-step training starts with planning and ends with final editing.
Delivery method: CBT.
Minimum hardware requirement: PC.

Price: £413.00.
Source: Electrovision UK Ltd, Hamble Point Marina, School Lane, Hamble, Southampton SO31 4JD. Tel: 01703 452221

CD-i
Title: **Report Writing**
Purpose: To teach the art of writing a good report.
Suitable for: Everyone.
Prerequisites: None.
Description: This course looks at the six key steps to the production of a good report: list objectives; organise key points; structure the argument; use plain English; make it look readable; package it attractively.
Delivery method: CD-i.
Minimum hardware requirement: CD-i player and television.
Price: £995.00; rental prices on request.
Source: Video Arts Ltd, Dumbarton House, 68 Oxford Street, London. W1N 0LH. Tel: 0171 637 7288

Research and development

Simulation
Title: **RESERVE – Research and Development**
Purpose: To teach how research and development influences commercial success, with: business objectives and measures; basic finance and marketing; operational control and forecasting; and decision making and team working.
Suitable for: Engineers, scientists, trainees, functional specialists, supervisors, junior through middle management.
Prerequisites: Some basic business appreciation.
Description: A total enterprise business simulation/game replicating a manufacturing company. Involving marketing, operational and financial R & D decisions by teams of 4–5 in competition, with up to 8 teams.
Delivery method: Trainer uses computerised simulator.
Minimum hardware requirement: PC; 640Kb RAM and printer.
Price: Rental: £295.00; purchase: POA; fully tutored from £1200.00.
Source: Hall Marketing, Studio 11, Colman's Wharf, 45 Morris Road, London E14 6PA. Tel: 0171 537 2982

Risk management

CBT

Title: **Risk Manager Trading Simulation for Windows**
Purpose: To provide a real-time market trading simulation where users can learn about markets and products or perfect dealing skills.
Suitable for: Use as a self-contained study package or on training workshops.
Prerequisites: None.
Description: A realistic dealing environment with integrated markets covering major foreign exchanges, fixed income and derivative product areas. Markets are driven by mathematical models that generate trends, news items and price moves indefinitely.
Delivery method: CBT and workbooks.
Minimum hardware requirement: 486 PC; 8Mb RAM; 20 Mb hard-disk space.
Price: Available on request.
Source: Chisholm Roth & Company Ltd, 54 Warwick Square, London SW1V 2AJ. Tel: 0171 630 0161

Sales management

CBT

Title: **Staying Ahead of Your Competitors: From Analysis to Advantage**
Purpose: To show you how to build and sustain a competitive advantage.
Suitable for: Managers.
Prerequisites: None.
Description: This is an introductory course which will enable you to: undertake a thorough industry analysis; analyse your competitors with a thorough competitor profile analysis; gather industry and specific competitor data and use it to identify weaknesses and opportunities within the industry, your competitors and your own company.
Delivery method: CBT and supporting text.
Minimum hardware requirement: IBM PC or compatible; 512k RAM.
Price: £165.00.
Source: Ivy Business Training Software plc, Ivy House, 233–235 Roehampton Lane, London SW15 4LB. Tel: 0181 780 1494

Title: **The Sales Executive: Designing the Sales Management System**
Purpose: To consider selling strategy, and the building of sales policies and procedures which will try to make that strategy effective and economical.
Suitable for: Senior sales managers.
Prerequisites: The other two courses in this series.
Description: This is an introductory course which will enable you to: define the

skills and attributes needed by a salesman; know the techniques for selection and the criteria on which to decide the proper form of sales training; question and analyse a given sales management system.
Delivery method: CBT and supporting text.
Minimum hardware requirement: IBM PC or compatible; 512k RAM.
Price: £165.00.
Source: Ivy Business Training Software plc, Ivy House, 233–235 Roehampton Lane, London SW15 4LB. Tel: 0181 780 1494

Title: **The Sales Manager: Motivating, Directing and Evaluating the Sales Force**
Purpose: To give you insights into the effects of policies and procedures (or lack thereof) on the job of the field sales manager.
Suitable for: Sales managers.
Prerequisites: 'The Salesperson: Identifying Tasks and Attributes for Effective Selling'.
Description: This is an introductory course which will enable you to apply techniques in motivation and in exercising effective field supervision.
Delivery method: CBT and supporting text.
Minimum hardware requirement: IBM PC or compatible; 512k RAM.
Price: £165.00.
Source: Ivy Business Training Software plc, Ivy House, 233–235 Roehampton Lane, London SW15 4LB. Tel: 0181 780 1494

Title: **The Salesperson: Identifying Tasks and Attributes for Effective Selling**
Purpose: To help you understand and acquire the decision skills needed to build and maintain an effective sales organisation.
Suitable for: Anyone.
Prerequisites: None.
Description: This is an introductory course which will enable you to: look at the sales management operation within an organisation and analyse whether it is properly structured and used effectively within the overall corporate strategy; decide whether the selling task required is that of trade, missionary, technical or entrepreneurial.
Delivery method: CBT and supporting text.
Minimum hardware requirement: IBM PC or compatible; 512k RAM.
Price: £165.00.
Source: Ivy Business Training Software plc, Ivy House, 233–235 Roehampton Lane, London SW15 4LB. Tel: 0181 780 1494

Simulation

Title: **Sales Calls**
Purpose: To introduce sales management concepts.
Suitable for: Trainees, functional specialists, supervisors, junior through middle management.
Prerequisites: None.
Description: A simulation/game replicating call planning, and involving deciding call rates for customers depending on their potential. Teams of 4–5.
Delivery method: Teams use computerised simulator.
Minimum hardware requirement: PC; 640Kb RAM and printer.
Price: Rental: £125.00; purchase: £295.00; tutored from £500.00.
Source: Hall Marketing, Studio 11, Colman's Wharf, 45 Morris Road, London E14 6PA. Tel: 0171 537 2982

Title: **SMITE – Sales Management**
Purpose: To teach: sales management; staff selection and development; territory planning and control; performance assessment; and team working.
Suitable for: Senior sales staff and sales management.
Prerequisites: Basic sales management experience.
Description: A simulation/game replicating the sales function of a manufacturing company, and involving sales management decisions by teams of 4–5 in competition, with up to 4 teams.
Delivery method: Trainer uses computerised simulator.
Minimum hardware requirement: PC; 640Kb RAM and printer.
Price: Rental: £295.00; purchase: £1595.00; fully tutored from £1600.00.
Source: Hall Marketing, Studio 11, Colman's Wharf, 45 Morris Road, London E14 6PA. Tel: 0171 537 2982

Selling skills

CBT

Title: **Selling Products and Services**
Purpose: To train sales staff in the all-important skill of selling to corporate customers.
Suitable for: Those new to selling, and as a refresher to more experienced sales staff.
Prerequisites: None.
Description: The course mixes interaction tutorial sessions with a variety of other methods: simulations, role play, case studies. The course is supported by extensive documentation, including a course companion by Philip Lund which is a major work on selling techniques in itself.
Delivery method: CBT.

Minimum hardware requirement: IBM PC, 512Kb RAM.
Price: £395.00 + VAT. Copies are available on 30 days' approval.
Source: Bourne Training Systems Ltd, Bourne House, Sandy Lane, Romsey, Hampshire SO51 0PD. Tel: 01794 523301

Title: **Selling Skills: Techniques for Successful Sales**
Purpose: To introduce selling and buying behaviour; how to plan a sales call; and how to handle objections and post-sales call critiques.
Suitale for: Salespersons.
Prerequisites: None.
Description: This is an introductory course which will enable you to: secure an interview to make a sales presentation; know how to plan a sales call and construct the product needs analysis; conduct effective sales presentations; handle objections and close a sale; be able to analyse a sales call after it is made.
Delivery method: CBT and supporting text.
Minimum hardware requirement: IBM PC or compatible; 512k RAM.
Price: £165.00.
Source: Ivy Business Training Software plc, Ivy House, 233–235 Roehampton Lane, London SW15 4LB. Tel: 0181 780 1494

CD-i
Title: **A Good Person To Do Business With**
Purpose: To teach salespeople the value of relationship selling and how to build trust.
Suitable for: Salespeople, account management teams and agency personnel.
Prerequisites: Basic knowledge of sales principles.
Description: The course examines how attitudes and behaviour can affect sales skills adversely. It shows how to counter this by gaining and keeping a client's trust.
Delivery method: CD-i.
Minimum hardware requirement: TV and CD-i player.
Price: Purchase: £995.00 + carriage + VAT; 2-day hire: £165.00 + carriage + VAT.
Source: Melrose, 16 Bromells Road, London SW4 0BL. Tel: 0171 627 8404

CD-i
Title: **Sell It To Me!**
Purpose: To teach the essential skills for all salespeople.
Suitable for: Salespersons.
Prerequisites: None.
Description: The course is in two parts – 'Preparing the Way,' and 'Doing the Deal'. The key points are: ask open questions, keep control of meetings, listen to customers, explain benefits not features, make objections specific, put them

into perspective, set realistic objectives, prepare alternative closes and look for buying signals.
Delivery method: CD-i.
Minimum hardware requirement: CD-i player and television.
Price: £995.00; rental prices on request.
Source: Video Arts Ltd, Dumbarton House, 68 Oxford Street, London. W1N 0LH. Tel: 0171 637 7288

CD-ROM
Title: **Everyone Sells**
Purpose: To provide an all-round sales course.
Suitable for: Anyone.
Prerequisites: None.
Description: An all-round sales course. Topics include: adding value; establishing trust; questioning; presenting the product; handling objections; closing and follow up. Includes a case study and a workbook.
Delivery method: CD-ROM.
Minimum hardware requirement: PC; 8Mb RAM; CD-ROM drive; sound card.
Price: £1195.00.
Source: Intelligent Training Solutions, 29 Narrow Street, London E14 8DP. Tel: 0171 791 3000

Interactive video
Title: **Professional Selling: A Product**
Purpose: To teach all the basic skills your sales team needs to sell a product, from preparing for the first cold call to after-sales support.
Suitable for: Salesmen.
Prerequisites: None.
Description: This four-module course will help you to present a more professional image in the marketplace, and unlock new opportunities with existing customers. It will increase sales productivity and reduce sales costs by shortening the selling cycle.
Delivery method: Interactive video.
Minimum hardware requirement: Interactive video workstation.
Price: £4015.00.
Source: Training Direct, North Court, Edinburgh Gate, Harlow, Essex CM20 2JE. Tel: 01279 623927

Title: **Professional Selling: A Service**
Purpose: To teach all the basic skills your sales team needs to sell a service, from preparing for the first cold call to after-sales support.
Suitable for: Salesmen.
Prerequisites: None.

Description: This four-module course will help you to present a more professional image in the marketplace, and unlock new opportunities with existing customers. It will increase sales productivity and reduce sales costs by shortening the selling cycle.
Delivery method: Interactive video.
Minimum hardware requirement: Interactive video workstation.
Price: £4015.00.
Source: Training Direct, North Court, Edinburgh Gate, Harlow, Essex CM20 2JE. Tel: 01279 623927

Title: **Progressive Selling**
Purpose: To develop and try out new skills in the five key areas: customer qualification; cold calling; identifying customer personality types; appointment making; and face-to-face selling.
Suitable for: Experienced salesmen.
Prerequisites: None.
Description: In this course the user joins the sales team of Astech Systems and has inherited a prospect list from the previous salesperson. The user must identify those most likely to buy and turn them into customers. There are coaching sessions run by the sales manager and further tests of skill in the form of quizzes based on these coaching sessions.
Delivery method: Interactive video.
Minimum hardware requirement: Interactive video workstation.
Price: £2020.00.
Source: Training Direct, North Court, Edinburgh Gate, Harlow, Essex CM20 2JE. Tel: 01279 623927

Social care

CBT
Title: **CareMatch**
Purpose: To explain how to use NVQs to achieve quality assurance in caring.
Suitable for: Anyone concerned with NVQs in caring.
Prerequisites: None.
Description: Three modules, which may be purchased separately or together: NVQ database listing all NVQ Care awards and enabling you to link a care activity with its equivalent NVQ unit; manager, identifying organisations in geographical areas and matching NVQ units with particular care activities; and provider, enabling you to establish a staff database and match work with NVQ units.
Delivery method: CBT.
Minimum hardware requirement: PC with Windows.

Price: On application.
Source: Concord Video & Film Council, 201 Felixstowe Road, Ipswich IP3 9BJ. Tel: 01473 715754

Interactive Video
Title: **Assessment in Social Care series**
Purpose: To explain how to use NVQs to achieve quality assurance in caring.
Suitable for: Anyone concerned with NVQs in caring.
Prerequisites: None.
Description: A series of interactive video-based training programmes produced by the Central Council for Education and Training in Social Work (CCETSW) for use in the training of assessors and internal verifiers working with National Vocational Qualifications (NVQs) and Scottish Vocational Qualifications (SVQs).
Delivery method: Interactive video.
Minimum hardware requirement: IV workstation.
Price: On application.
Source: Concord Video & Film Council, 201 Felixstowe Road, Ipswich IP3 9BJ. Tel: 01473 715754

Software maintenance

CBT
Title: **Software Maintenance**
Purpose: To give an overview of the logistics of software maintenance as well as the steps that can reduce both the difficulty and cost of the function.
Suitable for: Managers of software development projects.
Prerequisites: None.
Description: This course, designed for managers with responsibility for software development projects and the relevant staff, covers topics including: support facilities; development tools; change requests; configuration management; and quality assurance.
Delivery method: CBT.
Minimum hardware requirement: PC.
Price: £1995.00.
Source: Electrovision UK Ltd, Hamble Point Marina, School Lane, Hamble, Southampton SO31 4JD. Tel: 01703 452221

Spanish

CBT
Title: **Spanish Tutor**
Purpose: To provide a highly successful aid to learning Spanish.
Suitable for: Anyone.
Prerequisites: None.
Description: This course provides a highly successful aid to modern language learning in vocabulary and grammar, with a variety of learning modes and test modes. All words and phrases are displayed complete with accents and special characters. In addition to the vast vocabulary supplied, the program also allows you to add your own lessons.
Delivery method: CBT.
Minimum hardware requirement: PC.
Price: £45.00.
Source: Electrovision UK Ltd, Hamble Point Marina, School Lane, Hamble, Southampton SO31 4JD. Tel: 01703 452221

CD-ROM
Title: **Expressions – Spanish**
Purpose: To provide practical language training.
Suitable for: Anyone.
Prerequisites: None.
Description: This course provides practical language training by concentrating on various scenarios – airport, train, eating out, etc. The CD also has practice, speaking test, playback and various exercises.
Delivery method: CD-ROM.
Minimum hardware requirement: PC; 8Mb RAM; CD-ROM; sound card.
Price: £69.00.
Source: Electrovision UK Ltd, Hamble Point Marina, School Lane, Hamble, Southampton SO31 4JD. Tel: 01703 452221

Title: **Think and Talk Spanish**
Purpose: To teach you to think and talk Spanish.
Suitable for: Anyone.
Prerequisites: None.
Description: Lively dialogue and engrossing scenes, using sound effects, music and other audio cues, make this an interesting training course. Eight CDs are contained in this pack, which has a 10,000-word dictionary and enough training to aim at a vocabulary in excess of 1,000 words.
Delivery method: CD-ROM.
Minimum hardware requirement: PC; 8Mb RAM; CD-ROM; sound card.
Price: £159.00.

Source: Electrovision UK Ltd, Hamble Point Marina, School Lane, Hamble, Southampton SO31 4JD. Tel: 01703 452221

Standards

CBT
Title: **The Standards Toolkit**
Purpose: To demystify the adoption of standards.
Suitable for: Managers and candidates involved with G/S/NVQs.
Prerequisites: None.
Description: The Standards Toolkit has been designed to provide all of the information and sample documentation you need to introduce Occupational Standards and G/S/NVQs for both the tutor and the student. It covers the five stages in organising or obtaining G/S/NVQs from planning to assessment.
Delivery method: CBT.
Minimum hardware requirement: 386 PC Windows 3.1; 4Mb RAM, 5Mb hard disk.
Price: Licences – single: £95.00; network: £250.00.
Source: MLS Ltd, 26 Warwick Road, London SW5 9UD. Tel: 0171 373 9489

Stock control

CBT
Title: **How to Control Stock: Holding and Ordering Stock**
Purpose: The first in a three-part series which aims to show you how to understand the principles of stock control and how to set up and maintain an effective stock control system.
Suitable for: Anyone controlling stock.
Prerequisites: Basic mathematical skills.
Description: This is an intermediate/advanced course which will enable you to: calculate the economic order interval; calculate the EOI for multiple items of stock; establish a reorder point; master the technique of calculating the economic order quantity.
Delivery Method: CBT and supporting text.
Minimum hardware requirement: IBM PC or compatible, 512k RAM.
Price: £165.00.
Source: Ivy Business Training Software plc, Ivy House, 233–235 Roehampton Lane, London SW15 4LB. Tel: 0181 780 1494

Title: **How to Control Stock: Material Requirements Planning**
Purpose: The third in a three-part series which aims to show you how to under-

stand the principles of stock control and how to set up and maintain an effective stock control system.
Suitable for: Anyone controlling stock.
Prerequisites: The first two in the series of how to control stock.
Description: This is an intermediate/advanced course which will enable you to construct, revise and use a master production schedule.
Delivery method: CBT and supporting text.
Minimum hardware requirement: IBM PC or compatible, 512k RAM.
Price: £165.00.
Source: Ivy Business Training Software plc, Ivy House, 233–235 Roehampton Lane, London SW15 4LB. Tel: 0181 780 1494

Title: **How to Control Stock: Safety Stock**
Purpose: The second in a three-part series which aims to show you how to understand the principles of stock control and how to set up and maintain an effective stock control system.
Suitable for: Anyone controlling stock.
Prerequisites: The first in the series of how to control stock.
Description: This is an intermediate/advanced course which will enable you to: conduct sensitivity analysis on EOQ; explain how the stock system will work if the lead time is longer than the order interval and when the EOQ is smaller than the demand during the lead time.
Delivery method: CBT and supporting text.
Minimum hardware requirement: IBM PC or compatible, 512k RAM.
Price: £165.00.
Source: Ivy Business Training Software plc, Ivy House, 233–235 Roehampton Lane, London SW15 4LB. Tel: 0181 780 1494

Street works

CBT
Title: **Street Works Code of Practice**
Purpose: Training and certification in the signing, lighting and guarding requirements of the new Roads and Street Works Act.
Suitable for: Road works operatives supervisors, inspectors and planners (approved by CABWI).
Prerequisites: Some practical experience of road works.
Description: Comprises seven modules: an introduction; five traffic control situations; and a site monitoring/inspection module.
Delivery method: CBT.
Minimum hardware requirement: 386PC; 4Mb RAM; 12Mb disk space.
Price: Site licence £1,050.00; discounts for multiple sites.

THE DIRECTORY

Source: Interac, PO Box 4, Winterslow, Salisbury SP5 1BR. Tel: 01980 862611

Stress management

CBT
Title: **Coping With Stress**
Purpose: To look at the causes and symptoms of stress.
Suitable for: Anyone.
Prerequisites: None.
Description: This course looks at the causes and symptoms of stress. It discusses mental attitudes and how lifestyle changes can affect stress. Proposes techniques such as exercise and breathing techniques to combat stress.
Delivery method: CBT.
Minimum hardware requirement: PC.
Price: £175.00.
Source: Electrovision UK Ltd, Hamble Point Marina, School Lane, Hamble, Southampton SO31 4JD. Tel: 01703 452221

Title: **Pressure Gauge**
Purpose: To help staff to learn how to reduce stress and recognise pressure.
Suitable for: Anyone.
Prerequisites: None.
Description: Comprising four modules and self-analysis tests, the course introduces and explains the concepts of pressure and stress. Presenting practical and common-sense suggestions to improve attitude and behaviour in our lives, the course analyses your stress profile and puts the suggestions to work in daily routines.
Delivery method: CBT.
Minimum hardware requirement: 386 PC; 3Mb hard disk; 640Kb RAM.
Price: £595.00: unlimited workstation licence; £1950.00: unlimited network licence.
Source: Easy i Ltd, 42 The Square, Kenilworth, Warwickshire CV8 1EB. Tel: 01926 854111

Title: **Turn Stress to Your Advantage**
Purpose: To understand stress, what it is, what causes it and what are its symptoms.
Suitable for: Anyone.
Prerequisites: 'Your Confidence Profile' and 'Your Personality Profile'.
Description: An introductory course which will enable you to: identify others who may be prone to stress; know when you are suffering from stress; know

the steps to control stress both on and off the job; give some guidance to others on how to recognise and manage stress within tolerable levels.
Delivery method: CBT and supporting text.
Minimum hardware requirement: IBM PC or compatible, 512k RAM.
Price: £165.00.
Source: Ivy Business Training Software plc, Ivy House, 233–235 Roehampton Lane, London SW15 4LB. Tel: 0181 780 1494

CD-ROM
Title: **Wellbeing: Managing Pressure and Stress at Work**
Purpose: To help the user to actively manage work and domestic pressures, making them more able to cope, less likely to suffer from stress and thus more effective.
Suitable for: Anyone.
Prerequisites: None.
Description: The programme has three elements: diagnosis – identifying key sources of pressure; coping strategy development – through better understanding and positive action; training and development – short-term training survival kit to help through peak pressure periods.
Delivery method: CD-ROM.
Minimum hardware requirement: 486PC; 24Mb hard disk space; 8Mb RAM; SVGA Monitor and 16-bit sound card.
Price: £750.00.
Source: TDA Consulting Ltd, 4 Thameside Centre, Kew Bridge Road, Brentford, Middlesex TW8 0HF. Tel: 0181 568 3040

Interactive video
Title: **Stress at Work**
Purpose: To make the user aware of the early signs of stress and explain how to tackle them.
Suitable for: Anyone.
Prerequisites: None.
Description: Through a series of dramatic sequences which follow the takeover of a publishing company, the course demonstrates how to recognise the telltale symptoms, in oneself and in others.
Delivery method: Interactive video.
Minimum hardware requirement: Interactive video workstation.
Price: £2020.00.
Source: Training Direct, North Court, Edinburgh Gate, Harlow, Essex CM20 2JE. Tel: 01279 623927

Study skills

CBT

Title: **The Secrets of Study**
Purpose: Introduces all the key study skills and provides users with an opportunity to practice these skills.
Suitable for: Those studying for exams or are enrolled in a distance-learning programme.
Prerequisites: None.
Description: An introduction to the key study skills, using seven study modules: survey of preferred learning styles; getting down to it; writing; note taking; memory; revision; and exams.
Delivery method: CBT.
Minimum hardware requirement: 386 PC; 128Kb RAM; 2.5Mb hard disk.
Price: Licences – single: £150.00; network: £500.00.
Source: MLS Ltd, 26 Warwick Road, London SW5 9UD. Tel: 0171 373 9489

CD-ROM

Title: **Winning the Brain Game**
Purpose: To help you improve your study skills and examination preparation.
Suitable for: Anyone.
Prerequisites: None.
Description: This course has been developed from the 'Right system' training programs written by Neil Taylor. It covers: getting organised for study; learning how the right-brain works and how to use it; revision techniques; and sitting exams.
Delivery method: CD-ROM.
Minimum hardware requirement: Pentium PC; 8Mb RAM; quad speed CD-ROM drive; sound card.
Price: £35.00.
Source: Marketing Department, The Chartered Insurance Institute, 20 Aldermanbury, London EC2V 7HY. Tel: 0171 417 4427

Team leadership and development

CBT

Title: **Ace Teams**
Purpose: To identify team performance and the dynamics of the team.
Suitable for: Team leaders, line managers, training and HR professionals.
Prerequisites: None.
Description: This is a 50-question assessment package which looks at the performance of any team or can be used as an integral preliminary or dynamic

element in: team building and teamwork; change; quality and TQM; and performance management.
Delivery method: CBT.
Minimum hardware requirement: IBM compatible.
Price: £695.00.
Source: Pba Training Services Ltd, 1 Waterloo Street, Birmingham B2 5PG. Tel: 0121 643 4060

Title: **Team Building**
Purpose: To provide guidelines to achieve a clear understanding of the factors that make a team effective.
Suitable for: Anyone.
Prerequisites: None.
Description: Teaches the skills required to build, strengthen and maintain any team. The student learns the features a team requires to work effectively and a range of simple but effective team-building techniques.
Delivery method: CBT.
Minimum hardware requirement: PC.
Price: £413.00.
Source: Electrovision UK Ltd, Hamble Point Marina, School Lane, Hamble, Southampton SO31 4JD. Tel: 01703 452221

Title: **Working in Teams**
Purpose: To define what it is to work in a team, and the role that you and others play.
Suitable for: Anyone.
Prerequisites: None.
Description: The stages of teamwork and team building; how to address the task at hand; and how to maintain and improve your team.
Delivery method: CBT.
Minimum hardware requirement: PC.
Price: £175.00.
Source: Electrovision UK Ltd, Hamble Point Marina, School Lane, Hamble, Southampton SO31 4JD. Tel: 01 703 452221

CD-i
Title: **Teams And Leaders**
Purpose: To get groups of people to work together as a team.
Suitable for: Team leaders and team members.
Prerequisites: None.
Description: The film looks at both sides of the team: the leaders and the led – and how they learn to work together as a productive, well-motivated team.
Delivery method: CD-i.

Minimum hardware requirement: TV and CD-i player.
Price: Purchase: £995.00 + carriage + VAT; 2-day hire: £165.00 + carriage + VAT.
Source: Melrose, 16 Bromells Road, London SW4 0BL. Tel: 0171 627 8404

Title: **The Best of Motives**
Purpose: To explain how, by informing and involving their teams, team leaders can improve motivation and productivity.
Suitable for: Team leaders and managers.
Prerequisites: None.
Description: This course deals with the two most common complaints: 'Nobody ever tells us' and 'Nobody ever asks us.' The key points are inform, feed back, recognise, listen, involve and empower.
Delivery method: CD-i.
Minimum hardware requirement: CD-i player and television.
Price: £995.00; rental prices on request.
Source: Video Arts Ltd, Dumbarton House, 68 Oxford Street, London W1N 0LH. Tel: 0171 637 7288

CD-ROM

Title: **Building a Team**
Purpose: To look at the reasons why individuals lack the effectiveness of teams and consider different attributes needed to make up the essential key roles in a team.
Suitable for: Team leaders.
Prerequisites: None.
Description: This is an introductory course which will enable you to set up an effective team and identify the problems created in certain teams.
Delivery method: CD-ROM.
Minimum hardware requirement: 486 PC; 8Mb RAM; 256 Colour VGA; sound card; and 8Mb hard-disk space.
Price: £295.00.
Source: Ivy Business Training Software plc, Ivy House, 233–235 Roehampton Lane, London SW15 4LB. Tel: 0181 780 1494

Title: **Building a Team**
Purpose: To provide an understanding of the concepts needed for transforming ordinary groups of people into powerful teams, with greater motivation and productivity.
Suitable for: Team leaders and managers.
Prerequisites: None.
Description: The course looks at the reasons why individuals lack the effectiveness of teams and considers their different attributes. These attributes are looked at in detail, starting with the essential key roles in a team. Attention

is given to the characteristics which can cause conflicts in a team, and the elements of a successful team are highlighted.
Delivery method: CD-ROM.
Minimum hardware requirement: 386 PC; 8Mb RAM; 6Mb hard-disk space; CD-ROM drive; sound card.
Price: £295.00.
Source: Comput-Ed Ltd, Long Lane, Dawlish EX7 0QR. Tel: 01626 889955

Telephone skills

CD-ROM

Title: **Business Calls**
Purpose: To make people at all levels in your organisation much more effective on the telephone.
Suitable for: Everyone.
Prerequisites: None.
Description: This course explains and demonstrates telephone skills and techniques. It is a modular course which covers every aspect of using the telephone.
Delivery method: CD-ROM.
Minimum hardware requirement: 486 PC; 8Mb RAM; 420Mb hard disk; CD-ROM drive, audio card.
Price: £1199.00.
Source: Xebec Multi Media Solutions Ltd, The Critchley Building, Bath Road, Woodchester, Stroud, Glos. GL5 5EY. Tel: 01453 835482

Title: **Phone Fundamentals**
Purpose: To teach basic telephone skills, from answering a call correctly to reassuring the caller that their message has been understood.
Suitable for: All staff who use the telephone in business.
Prerequisites: None.
Description: The course has four key modules: basics – establishing facts and summarising details; behaviour – introducing yourself, showing you're listening and closing the call; confidence – dealing with unfamiliar situations, difficult accents and bad connections; quality – handling complaints.
Delivery method: CD-ROM.
Minimum hardware requirement: 486 PC; 8Mb RAM; 10Mb hard disk; CD-ROM drive; sound card.
Price: On application.
Source: Video Arts Interactive Learning, Dumbarton House, 68 Oxford Street, London W1N 0LH. Tel: 0171 637 7288

Interactive video
Title: **Make the Telephone Sell for You**
Purpose: To provide detailed and effective training at every stage of the sales call, allowing you and your staff to optimise every selling opportunity.
Suitable for: Telemarketers.
Prerequisites: None.
Description: This five-module course covers: communicating over the telephone; planning your telephone sales tactics; making a telephone sales presentation; dealing with objections and difficult customers; closing a telephone sale; and following up.
Delivery method: Interactive video.
Minimum hardware requirement: Interactive video workstation.
Price: £4380.00.
Source: Training Direct, North Court, Edinburgh Gate, Harlow, Essex CM20 2JE. Tel: 01279 623927

Title: **Make the Telephone Work for You**
Purpose: To ensure that everyone uses the telephone efficiently and effectively.
Suitable for: Everyone.
Prerequisites: None.
Description: This course helps users learn the importance of making the right impression and the effect their attitude and actions can have. They will acquire the fundamental skills for using the telephone and receive extensive tuition in every aspect of making and taking calls.
Delivery method: Interactive video.
Minimum hardware requirement: Interactive video workstation.
Price: £2880.00.
Source: Training Direct, North Court, Edinburgh Gate, Harlow, Essex CM20 2JE. Tel: 01279 623927

Title: **Making the Most of the Telephone**
Purpose: To demonstrate the techniques which give the right impression over the telephone. Users are given the opportunity to put their skills to the test throughout.
Suitable for: Everyone.
Prerequisites: None.
Description: This two-part course deals with general telephone skills and techniques and shows the consequences of both correct and incorrect techniques. These principles are expanded and applied to the specific business areas of enquiry, customer service, after-sales, and sales.
Delivery method: Interactive video.
Minimum hardware requirement: Interactive video workstation.
Price: £2020.00.

Source: Training Direct, North Court, Edinburgh Gate, Harlow, Essex, CM20 2JE. Tel: 01279 623927

Time management

CBT

Title: **How Well Do You Manage Your Time?**
Purpose: To act as a learning needs assessment which will be an aid to both learning and revision.
Suitable for: Anyone.
Prerequisites: None.
Description: A self-assessment tool consisting of about 100 questions that will help you to develop your knowledge through repeated practice on questions covering all areas of the subject.
Delivery method: CBT and supporting text.
Minimum hardware requirement: IBM PC or compatible, 512k RAM.
Price: £165.00.
Source: Ivy Business Training Software plc, Ivy House, 233–235 Roehampton Lane, London SW15 4LB. Tel: 0181 780 1494

Title: **Manage Your Time Effectively**
Purpose: To show how, by setting goals and reassessing priorities, you can make better use of time.
Suitable for: Anyone.
Prerequisites: None.
Description: This is an introductory course which will enable you to: set objectives; use a flow chart to plan; categorise actions as vital or urgent; set and follow priorities; plan your time; distinguish between proactive and reactive time; and know how to expand proactive time.
Delivery method: CBT and supporting text.
Minimum hardware requirement: IBM PC or compatible, 1Mb RAM.
Price: £165.00.
Source: Ivy Business Training Software plc, Ivy House, 233–235 Roehampton Lane, London SW15 4LB. Tel: 0181 780 1494

Title: **Managing Interruptions**
Purpose: To teach you how to manage interruptions.
Suitable for: Anyone.
Prerequisites: None.
Description: Discusses how interruptions can affect you and the techniques for reducing these by prevention and filtering. Also looks at managing interruptions by delaying, rejecting and accepting certain interruptions.

Delivery method: CBT.
Minimum hardware requirement: PC.
Price: £175.00.
Source: Electrovision UK Ltd, Hamble Point Marina, School Lane, Hamble, Southampton SO31 4JD. Tel: 01703 452221

Title: **Planning Your Work**
Purpose: To introduce the concept of work planning.
Suitable for: Anyone.
Prerequisites: None.
Description: Introduces the concept of work planning, why it should be used and the benefits that can be derived from it, including job satisfaction and greater productivity. Proposes useful work-planning techniques and explains how to integrate them on a day-to-day basis.
Delivery method: CBT.
Minimum hardware requirement: PC.
Price: £175.00.
Source: Electrovision UK Ltd, Hamble Point Marina, School Lane, Hamble, Southampton SO31 4JD. Tel: 01703 452221

Title: **Setting Priorities**
Purpose: To establish why priorities need to be set.
Suitable for: Anyone.
Prerequisites: None.
Description: Asks why priorities need to be set and shows common methods for doing so. Identifies the issues and key factors, and explains how to rank importance, urgency and trend. Also lays out guidelines for action.
Delivery method: CBT.
Minimum hardware requirement: PC.
Price: £175.00.
Source: Electrovision UK Ltd, Hamble Point Marina, School Lane, Hamble, Southampton SO31 4JD. Tel: 01703 452221

Title: **The Time Challenge**
Purpose: To help all employees who may need to improve their personal organisation or time management.
Suitable for: Everyone.
Prerequisites: None.
Description: The package allows the user to select which areas of their time management skills they wish to develop and builds upon some of the basic techniques that are vital in working effectively. It contains nine modules and self-tests, in which the trainee will cover: setting goals and priorities; prime

time planning; handling paperwork; handling interruptions; and preparing for meetings.
Delivery method: CBT.
Minimum hardware requirement: 386 PC; 3Mb hard disk; 640Kb RAM.
Price: £595.00: unlimited workstation licence; £1950.00: unlimited network licence.
Source: Easy i Ltd, 42 The Square, Kenilworth, Warwickshire CV8 1EB. Tel: 01926 854111

Title: **Time Management (DOS Version)**
Purpose: To learn how to construct your own time management action plan.
Suitable for: Anyone.
Prerequisites: None.
Description: With a variety of stimulating exercises, you can learn how to construct your own time management action plan. Covers such topics as: direction setting, objectives at work; self-management; time planning; and time bandits.
Delivery method: CBT.
Minimum hardware requirement: PC.
Price: £359.00.
Source: Electrovision UK Ltd, Hamble Point Marina, School Lane, Hamble, Southampton SO31 4JD. Tel: 01703 452221

Title: **Time Management (Windows Version)**
Purpose: To learn how to construct your own time management action plan.
Suitable for: Anyone.
Prerequisites: None.
Description: With a variety of stimulating exercises, you can learn how to construct your own time management action plan. Covers such topics as: direction setting; objectives at work; self-management; time planning; and time bandits.
Delivery method: CBT.
Minimum hardware requirement: PC.
Price: £476.00.
Source: Electrovision UK Ltd, Hamble Point Marina, School Lane, Hamble, Southampton SO31 4JD. Tel: 01703 452221

CD-i

Title: **The Paper Chase**
Purpose: To show how paperwork can hinder efficiency and how to deal with this.
Suitable for: Managers and team leaders.
Prerequisites: None.
Description: This course explains the rules to follow to make sure that you control the paper around you, rather than let yourself be dominated by it. The

four simple key points in dealing with paperwork are action it, pass it on, file it or bin it.
Delivery method: CD-i.
Minimum hardware requirement: CD-i player and television.
Price: £995.00; rental prices on request.
Source: Video Arts Ltd, Dumbarton House, 68 Oxford Street, London W1N 0LH. Tel: 0171 637 7288

Title: **The Unorganised Manager**
Purpose: To improve management effectiveness.
Suitable for: Managers.
Prerequisites: None.
Description: This four-part series is designed to improve the performance in three critical areas: time management, delegation and motivation. Key points are: organise time; establish priorities; delegate; brief and train people properly; allow time for people to learn; define responsibilities; set measurable standards and, agree targets.
Delivery Method: CD-i.
Minimum hardware requirement: CD-i player and television.
Price: £995.00; rental prices on request.
Source: Video Arts Ltd, Dumbarton House, 68 Oxford Street, London W1N 0LH. Tel: 0171 637 7288

CD-ROM

Title: **Getting the Work Done**
Purpose: To show how to organise yourself and your teams so that work gets done more efficiently.
Suitable for: Manager and supervisors.
Prerequisites: 'Building a Partnership'.
Description: This course will enable you to: plan for time management; deal with interruptions and confront problems; understand the benefits of delegation and what to delegate and to whom; know what your staff can handle; use delegation for motivation; get to the root of poor performance.
Delivery method: CD-ROM.
Minimum hardware requirement: 486 PC; 8Mb RAM; 420Mb hard disk; CD-ROM drive; audio card.
Price: £895.00.
Source: Training Direct, North Court, Edinburgh Gate, Harlow, Essex CM20 2JE. Tel: 01279 623927

Title: **Making Your Time Count**
Purpose: To provide the skills needed to plan well in order to achieve the day's

objectives. It explains the effect one person's efficiency (or lack of it) has on others.
Suitable for: Everyone.
Prerequisites: None.
Description: This course will change your attitude to time management and self-management, and will provide practical plans for taking those strategies on board.
Delivery method: CD-ROM.
Minimum hardware requirement: 486 PC; 8Mb RAM; 420Mb hard disk; CD-ROM drive; audio card.
Price: £1195.00.
Source: Intelligent Training Solutions, 29 Narrow Street, London E14 8DP. Tel: 0171 791 3000

Title: **Managing Tasks and Activities**
Purpose: To offer practical and realistic advice on a whole range of topics including: scheduling and budgeting; organising yourself and your time, delegating effectively; and setting and monitoring standards.
Suitable for: Managers.
Prerequisites: None.
Description: This course will help to improve productivity from managers and their teams. It is a four-module course dealing with: management; planning; organisation; monitoring and control.
Delivery method: CD-ROM.
Minimum hardware requirement: 486 PC; 8Mb RAM; 420Mb hard disk; CD-ROM drive; audio card.
Price: £1199.00.
Source: Xebec Multi Media Solutions Ltd, The Critchley Building, Bath Road, Woodchester, Stroud, Glos. GL5 5EY. Tel: 01453 835482

Title: **Practising Time Management**
Purpose: To show you how to deal with disruption, and to develop the skills which will enable you to make the very best use of your working day.
Suitable for: Anyone.
Prerequisites: 'Principles of Time Management'.
Description: This course will teach you: how to deal with interruptions; telephone tactics; how to analyse your paper work; how to deal with the post and memos; how to develop people for delegation; and how to make meetings work.
Delivery method: CD-ROM.
Minimum hardware requirement: 486 PC; 8Mb RAM; 420Mb hard disk; CD-ROM drive; audio card.
Price: £895.00.

Source: Training Direct, North Court, Edinburgh Gate, Harlow, Essex, CM20 2JE. Tel: 01279 623927

Title: **Principles of Time Management**
Purpose: To look at the general concepts of time management and analyse how efficiently time is used. To teach principles that will help you to make more productive use of your time.
Suitable for: Anyone.
Prerequisites: None.
Description: This course will help you to: accept responsibility for your own time management; determine goals and personal skills; set goals and establish priorities; avoid procrastination and over-management; keep time logs; analyse and plan information.
Delivery method: CD-ROM.
Minimum hardware requirement: 486 PC; 8Mb RAM; 420Mb hard disk; CD-ROM drive; audio card.
Price: £895.00.
Source: Training Direct, North Court, Edinburgh Gate, Harlow, Essex CM20 2JE. Tel: 01279 623927

Title: **The Office Professional**
Purpose: To teach the techniques of streamlining performance at work.
Suitable for: All administrators.
Prerequisites: None.
Description: This course will help to develop all the key administrative skills. The key training messages are: the importance of planning and quantifying tasks; setting priorities and deadlines; the importance of team building and rapport; how to plan projects and set objectives; and why delegation should be encouraged.
Delivery method: CD-ROM.
Minimum hardware requirement: 486 PC; 8Mb RAM; 420Mb hard disk; CD-ROM drive; audio card.
Price: £995.00.
Source: Training Direct, North Court, Edinburgh Gate, Harlow, Essex CM20 2JE. Tel: 01279 623927

Total quality

CBT
Title: **Quality in Practice**
Purpose: To provide an introduction into what quality is and what it is not.
Suitable for: Anyone.

Prerequisites: None.

Description: Provides a thorough introduction into what quality is and is not. The student learns how to produce: a quality action plan which provides a precise statement of their customer's requirements; a step-by-step plan to satisfy those requirements; and a method for measuring performance and conformance to the plan.

Delivery method: CBT.

Minimum hardware requirement: PC.

Price: £413.00.

Source: Electrovision UK Ltd, Hamble Point Marina, School Lane, Hamble, Southampton SO31 4JD. Tel: 01703 452221

Title: **Total Quality Improvement: Why It Involves You**

Purpose: To test how good you and your team are at Total Quality Improvement.

Suitable for: Anyone.

Prerequisites: None.

Description: A self assessment tool consisting of about 60 questions that will enable you to assess your strengths and weaknessess and those of your team.

Delivery method: CBT and supporting text.

Minimum hardware requirement: IBM PC or compatible, 512k RAM.

Price: £165.00.

Source: Ivy Business Training Software plc, Ivy House, 233–235 Roehampton Lane, London SW15 4LB. Tel: 0181 780 1494

CD-i

Title: **Quality – The Only Way**

Purpose: To get everyone thinking about quality and find out what it means.

Suitable for: Everyone.

Prerequisites: None.

Description: It is the story of a man, prepared to settle for second-best at work, who finds out what that means when on holiday – on the receiving end.

Delivery method: CD-i.

Minimum hardware requirement: TV and CD-i player.

Price: Purchase: £995.00 + carriage + VAT; 2-day hire: £165.00 + carriage + VAT.

Source: Melrose, 16 Bromells Road, London SW4 0BL. Tel: 0171 627 8404

CD-ROM

Title: **An Introduction to Statistical Process Control**

Purpose: To introduce the basic concepts of statistical process control, and its role in controlling quality through improved process performance.

Suitable for: All production personnel.

Prerequisites: None.

Description: This course will give you a better understanding of the need for quality and the techniques for achieving it.
Delivery method: CD-ROM.
Minimum hardware requirement: 486 PC; 8Mb RAM; 420Mb hard disk; CD-ROM drive; audio card.
Price: £395.00.
Source: Training Direct, North Court, Edinburgh Gate, Harlow, Essex CM20 2JE. Tel: 01279 623927

Title: **An Introduction to Total Quality Management**
Purpose: To show you how embracing Total Quality Management throughout your organisation can help you to be as efficient as possible and improve your business profitability.
Suitable for: All staff.
Prerequisites: None.
Description: This course will help you to understand: that total quality management demands 100 per cent commitment from everyone; who your customer is and how to meet their needs; how to manage change effectively and project the right image.
Delivery method: CD-ROM.
Minimum hardware requirement: 486 PC; 8Mb RAM; 420Mb hard disk; CD-ROM drive; audio card.
Price: £395.00.
Source: Training Direct, North Court, Edinburgh Gate, Harlow, Essex CM20 2JE. Tel: 01279 623927

Title: **FASTRAQ 9000 – Learn all about ISO 9000**
Purpose: To assist organisations in implementing and maintaining a quality management system as well as assisting with their programme of awareness and staff development training.
Suitable for: Everyone.
Prerequisites: None.
Description: This training programme, through ten modules, provides training on ISO 9000, from awareness to understanding, through to implementing and maintaining an effective quality management system to the internationally recognised ISO 9000 standard. Fastraq allows you to select particular sections to create a personal training programme for an individual or group.
Delivery method: CD-ROM.
Minimum hardware requirement: 486 PC; 8Mb RAM; CD-ROM drive; sound card.
Price: BSI registered: £995.00 + VAT + delivery; non-registered: £1250.00 + VAT + delivery.
Source: BSI Training Services, 389 Chiswick High Road, London W4 4AL. Tel: 0181 996 7337

Title: **Improving Quality**

Purpose: To support team working by introducing tools for problem solving which can be used by the whole team.

Suitable for: People needing to solve problems.

Prerequisites: None.

Description: This course recognises that the people who work in any given environment are often the best placed to tackle a problem which arises, and it shows the potential of an empowered team to achieve real quality and cost improvements for the business.

Delivery method: CD-ROM; also available on interactive video.

Minimum hardware requirement: 486 PC; 8Mb RAM; 420Mb hard disk; CD-ROM drive; audio card.

Price: CD-ROM: £1135.00; IV £2020.00.

Source: Training Direct, North Court, Edinburgh Gate, Harlow, Essex CM20 2JE. Tel: 01279 623927

Title: **Training for Quality**

Purpose: To help all employees understand the concepts and practices of the implementation of a quality programme and how they take part in that implementation.

Suitable for: Anyone.

Prerequisites: None.

Description: Covers concepts and is divided into eight sections: commitment to quality; persistence; tools and techniques; calculating the cost; meeting requirements; performance standard; preventing errors; taking action. Six languages available on CD plus local language workbooks on application: French, German, English, Dutch, Portuguese and Italian.

Delivery method: CD-ROM.

Minimum hardware requirement: 386 PC; CD-ROM drive; sound card.

Price: On application.

Source: McGraw-Hill Publishing Co., Shoppenhangers Rd, Maidenhead, Berks. SL6 2QL. Tel: 01628 23432

Simulation

Title: **QUAD – Quality Advantage**

Purpose: To teach: business objectives and measures; basic finance and marketing; operational control and forecasting; decision-making; and team working, with a bias towards equality.

Suitable for: Trainees, functional specialists, supervisors, junior through middle management.

Prerequisites: Some basic business appreciation.

Description: A total enterprise business simulation/game replicating a manufacturing company, and involving marketing, operational and financial decisions by teams of 4–5 in competition, with up to eight teams.
Delivery method: Trainer uses computerised simulator.
Minimum hardware requirement: PC; 640Kb RAM and printer.
Price: Rental: £295.00; purchase: £995.00; fully tutored from £800.00.
Source: Hall Marketing, Studio 11, Colman's Wharf, 45 Morris Road, London E14 6PA. Tel: 0171 537 2982

Training and development

CBT
Title: **One-to-One Training**
Purpose: To teach the concept of one-to-one training.
Suitable for: Team leaders and managers.
Prerequisites: None.
Description: Explains the concept of one-to-one training, using the PETS method: prepare; explain; show; try out. Each section is discussed in detail to ultimately achieve the goal of successful one-to-one training skills.
Delivery method: CBT.
Minimum hardware requirement: PC.
Price: £413.00.
Source: Electrovision UK Ltd, Hamble Point Marina, School Lane, Hamble, Southampton SO31 4JD. Tel: 01703 452221

Title: **Questioning Techniques for Open Learning**
Purpose: To enable the development of relevant and attractive questions and exercises in open-learning materials.
Suitable for: Designers of open-learning materials.
Prerequisites: None.
Description: Interactive CBT modules that illustrate and explain ten questioning techniques.
Delivery method: CBT.
Minimum hardware requirement: 386 PC; 386Kb RAM.
Price: £49.00 plus VAT (£58.58) including postage.
Source: Dean Associates, 9 The South West Centre, Troutbeck Road, Sheffield S7 2QA. Tel: 0114 258 1171

Title: **Training for Non Trainers**
Purpose: To help to remove the fear many have about training groups of people.
Suitable for: Anyone.
Prerequisites: None.

Description: This course is aimed at inexperienced trainers and helps to remove the fear many have about training groups of people. It provides a broad range of practical advice including: identifying training needs; preparing a training session; writing a lesson plan; and selecting appropriate training methods.
Delivery method: CBT.
Minimum hardware requirement: PC.
Price: £413.00.
Source: Electrovision UK Ltd, Hamble Point Marina, School Lane, Hamble, Southampton SO31 4JD. Tel: 01703 452221

Transport

CBT

Title: **Goods Vehicle Drivers' Hours: EC and UK Rules**
Purpose: To provide advice and instruction to drivers and operators of goods vehicles, whether used privately or commercially.
Suitable for: Drivers and operators of goods vehicles.
Prerequisites: None.
Description: This is an introductory course which will enable you to: know the driving limits with respect to time, and when you can and must take a break; the exemptions from the rules; the rules for domestic drivers' hours, as well as for mixed EC and domestic driving.
Delivery method: CBT and supporting text.
Minimum hardware requirement: IBM PC or compatible, 512k RAM.
Price: £165.00.
Source: Ivy Business Training Software plc, Ivy House, 233–235 Roehampton Lane, London SW15 4LB. Tel: 0181 780 1494

Title: **Goods Vehicle Operator Licensing**
Purpose: To provide an understanding of how to apply for a licence, the requirements, and most of the issues that you need to know about the subject.
Suitable for: Goods vehicle operators and potential operators.
Prerequisites: None.
Description: This is an introductory course which will enable you to: know how to apply for a licence; be able to state the requirements for a licence; clearly explain who can object to an application and what you would do; be aware of the convictions, sentences and rehabilitation rules; list the main check points needed for vehicle roadworthiness.
Delivery method: CBT and supporting text.
Minimum hardware requirement: IBM PC or compatible, 512k RAM.
Price: £165.00.

Source: Ivy Business Training Software plc, Ivy House, 233–235 Roehampton Lane, London SW15 4LB. Tel: 0181 780 1494

Title: **Tachograph Rules for Goods Vehicle Operators**
Purpose: To teach you when and how to use a tachograph, and when and how to keep written records.
Suitable for: Goods vehicle operators.
Prerequisites: None.
Description: This is an introductory course which will enable you to: know how tachographs work; fill in written records; be familiar with driver's responsibilities relating to tachographs; know the penalties and enforcement for infractions.
Delivery method: CBT and supporting text.
Minimum hardware requirement: IBM PC or compatible, 1Mb RAM.
Price: £165.00.
Source: Ivy Business Training Software plc, Ivy House, 233–235 Roehampton Lane, London SW15 4LB. Tel: 0181 780 1494

Title: **Teach Yourself the Highway Code**
Purpose: To allow you to learn more effectively and also to assess what you know by self-testing on every topic that is covered in the Highway Code.
Suitable for: Anyone.
Prerequisites: None.
Description: This is an introductory course which will enable you to: know the rules and advice for pedestrians, drivers and cyclists; know the various speed limits; recognise traffic signs, road markings and vehicle markings; and be familiar with rules on motorways, railway level crossings, tramways.
Delivery method: CBT and supporting text.
Minimum hardware requirement: IBM PC or compatible, 512k RAM.
Price: £165.00.
Source: Ivy Business Training Software plc, Ivy House, 233–235 Roehampton Lane, London SW15 4LB. Tel: 0181 780 1494

VDU Safety

CD-ROM
Title: **Display Screen Equipment**
Purpose: To explain the implications of the regulations for both employers and users and to provide a means of analysing workstations and recording each analysis.
Suitable for: Employers, managers and users of display screen equipment.
Prerequisites: None.

Description: The modules cover: background; inside the VDU; health effects; radiation; workstation requirements; breaks; eye tests; information and training; assessment and self-test.
Delivery method: CD-ROM.
Minimum hardware requirement: 486 PC; 4Mb RAM; dual speed CD-ROM drive; sound card.
Price: On application.
Source: Instinct Training, Strawberry How Business Centre, Lorton Road, Cockermouth, Cumbria CA13 9XQ. Tel: 01900 827600

Title: **What You Must Know ... About Working With VDUs**
Purpose: To teach the legal requirements of working with VDUs and how to work comfortably and correctly.
Suitable for: Everyone working with VDUs or supervisors managing user teams.
Prerequisites: None.
Description: 20-minute programme plus test.
Delivery method: CD-ROM.
Minimum hardware requirement: PC or MAC with CD-ROM drive and sound card.
Price: £195.00 + VAT.
Source: Melrose, 16 Bromells Road, London SW4 0BL. Tel: 0171 627 8404

Title: **Working with Display Screen Equipment**
Purpose: To set out the information and training requirements of Article 6 of the EU Directive covering display screen equipment.
Suitable for: Anyone who uses a VDU at work.
Prerequisites: None.
Description: This course covers all the key points regarding office environment, workstations and the operator in a tutorial style.
Delivery method: CD-ROM.
Minimum hardware requirement: 486 PC; 8Mb RAM; 420Mb hard disk; CD-ROM drive; audio card.
Price: £195.00.
Source: Training Direct, North Court, Edinburgh Gate, Harlow, Essex CM20 2JE. Tel: 01279 623927

Web sites

CD-ROM
Title: **Webwise**
Purpose: To help users develop, design and maintain their own web site.
Suitable for: Webmasters, marketers, small business owners, entrepreneurs.

Prerequisites: None.
Description: This CD offers a complete tutorial to setting up a World Wide Web site. Coverage includes HTML, hyperlinking, using sound and video discussion of future developments including Java, JavaScript and Shockwave.
Delivery method: CD-ROM (PC or Apple versions).
Minimum hardware requirement: 486 PC; CD-ROM drive; 4Mb RAM.
Price: £44.95 + VAT.
Source: McGraw-Hill Publishing Co., Shoppenhangers Road, Maidenhead, Berks. SL6 2QL. Tel: 01628 23432

Word processing

AmiPro

CBT

Title: **Perception Lite for AmiPro v3**
Purpose: To present a concise view of AmiPro v3.
Suitable for: Anyone.
Prerequisites: None.
Description: This course is suitable for novice to intermediate-level user. Topics include: creating and formatting documents; document tools; presentation tools; text controls; cut; paste; copy; page layout; graphics; tables; and outlines.
Delivery method: CBT.
Minimum hardware requirement: PC with Windows.
Price: £75.00 (multiple copy price on application).
Source: Electrovision UK Ltd, Hamble Point Marina, School Lane, Hamble, Southampton SO31 4JD. Tel: 01703 452221

Title: **Teach Yourself AmiPro v3/Win**
Purpose: To teach you how to use AmiPro v3.
Suitable for: Anyone.
Prerequisites: None.
Description: This course uses a simulation tutorial with summaries and quizzes to reinforce learning points. It covers an introduction to: the screen; smart icons; the status bar; creating and editing documents; formatting; cut; copy; paste; fonts; multiple documents; different views and more.
Delivery method: CBT.
Minimum hardware requirement: PC with Windows.
Price: £79.95 (multiple copy price on application).
Source: Electrovision UK Ltd, Hamble Point Marina, School Lane, Hamble, Southampton SO31 4JD. Tel: 01703 452221

Title: **Understanding AmiPro v3/Windows**
Purpose: To give an introduction to AmiPro which will take the user through all the basics right up to intermediate level.
Suitable for: Anyone.
Prerequisites: None.
Description: This course, which is available in DOS and Windows versions, covers topics including: AmiPro introduction; a tour of the screen bars and buttons; creating a document; paragraphs; text formatting. The course includes glossary, quizzes and summaries.
Delivery method: CBT.
Minimum hardware requirement: PC.
Price: £75.00 (multiple copy price on application).
Source: Electrovision UK Ltd, Hamble Point Marina, School Lane, Hamble, Southampton SO31 4JD. Tel: 01703 452221

CD-ROM
Title: **AmiPro for Windows**
Purpose: To teach the fundamentals of AmiPro.
Suitable for: Everyone.
Prerequisites: None.
Description: The basic course teaches how to: start AmiPro; become familiar with screen layout; and practise basic document editing and printing techniques. It is followed by the intermediate course covering: templates; built-in writing aids; macros; tables; and graphics.
Delivery method: CD-ROM.
Minimum hardware requirement: Pentium 90; 16Mb RAM; quad speed CD-ROM drive; sound card; MPEG card.
Price: £2599.00.
Source: Intelligent Training Solutions, 29 Narrow Street, London E14 8DP. Tel: 0171 791 3000

Interactive video
Title: **Using AmiPro for Windows**
Purpose: To teach users basic word-processing skills, and then progressing to more advanced skills.
Suitable for: Anyone.
Prerequisites: None.
Description: This course is in two parts: basics and intermediate. The basics course covers: screen layout; and basic document editing and printing techniques. The intermediate course covers: templates; built-in writing aids; macros; tables; and graphics.
Delivery method: Interactive video.
Minimum hardware requirement: Interactive video workstation.

Price: £2300.00 each course.
Source: Training Direct, North Court, Edinburgh Gate, Harlow, Essex CM20 2JE. Tel: 01279 623927

DisplayWrite

Interactive video
Title: **Using DisplayWrite IV**
Purpose: To teach word-processing using all the techniques offered by DisplayWrite IV.
Suitable for: Anyone.
Prerequisites: None.
Description: This course covers: editing and formatting; moving and copying blocks of text; and using search functions. There is a comprehensive introduction to spelling verification, printing and using document utilities.
Delivery method: Interactive video.
Minimum hardware requirement: Interactive video workstation.
Price: £2300.00.
Source: Training Direct, North Court, Edinburgh Gate, Harlow, Essex CM20 2JE. Tel: 01279 623927

Word

CBT
Title: **Perception Lite for Word v2 (Win)**
Purpose: To provide concise training on how to use Word v2 (Win).
Suitable for: Anyone.
Prerequisites: None.
Description: This course is suitable for novice through to intermediate-level user. It includes glossaries, quizzes and quick search. The topics include: working with text; cut; paste; delete; copy; move; use fonts; automate repetitive tasks; spell check; search and replace; and creating and running macros.
Delivery method: CBT.
Minimum hardware requirement: PC with Windows.
Price: £75.00 (multiple copy price on application).
Source: Electrovision UK Ltd, Hamble Point Marina, School Lane, Hamble, Southampton SO31 4JD. Tel: 01703 452221

Title: **Perception Lite for Word v6 (Win)**
Purpose: To provide concise training on how to use Word v6 (Win).
Suitable for: Anyone.
Prerequisites: None.

Description: This course is suitable for novice through to intermediate-level user. It includes glossaries, quizzes and quick search. The topics include: menus and toolbar; working with text; cut; paste; delete; copy; move; applying styles; formatting text; grammar checker; automate repetitive tasks; and using wizards.
Delivery method: CBT.
Minimum hardware requirement: PC with Windows.
Price: £75.00 (multiple copy price on application).
Source: Electrovision UK Ltd, Hamble Point Marina, School Lane, Hamble, Southampton SO31 4JD. Tel: 01703 452221

Title: **Perception of Word v6 (Windows)**
Purpose: To provide in-depth instruction on how to use Word v6 (Windows).
Suitable for: Anyone.
Prerequisites: None.
Description: This course uses attractive and realistic simulation techniques to simulate the Word environment. The topics include: editing text; formatting; styles; templates; page views; macros and more. There is a comprehensive student manual.
Delivery method: CBT.
Minimum hardware requirement: PC with Windows.
Price: £119.00 (multiple copy price on application).
Source: Electrovision UK Ltd, Hamble Point Marina, School Lane, Hamble, Southampton SO31 4JD. Tel: 01703 452221

Title: **Perception of Word7 (Office95)**
Purpose: To provide in-depth instruction on how to use Word7 (Office95).
Suitable for: Anyone.
Prerequisites: None.
Description: This course uses attractive and realistic simulation techniques to simulate the Word environment. The topics include: editing text; formatting; styles; templates; page views; macros and more. There is a comprehensive student manual.
Delivery method: CBT.
Minimum hardware requirement: PC with Windows.
Price: £119.00 (multiple copy price on application).
Source: Electrovision UK Ltd, Hamble Point Marina, School Lane, Hamble, Southampton SO31 4JD. Tel: 01703 452221

Title: **Teach Yourself Word v2/Windows**
Purpose: To teach you how to use Word v2 for Windows.
Suitable for: Anyone.
Prerequisites: None.

Description: This course is an excellent introductory/intermediate package that simulates the Word environment. Easy to use, but thorough, each section has instruction, summary and quiz.
Delivery method: CBT.
Minimum hardware requirement: PC with Windows.
Price: £69.95 (multiple copy price on application).
Source: Electrovision UK Ltd, Hamble Point Marina, School Lane, Hamble, Southampton SO31 4JD. Tel: 01703 452221

Title: **Teach Yourself Word v6/Windows**
Purpose: To teach you how to use Word v6 for Windows.
Suitable for: Anyone.
Prerequisites: None.
Description: This course is an excellent introductory/intermediate package that simulates the Word environment. Easy to use, but thorough, each section has instruction, summary and quiz.
Delivery method: CBT.
Minimum hardware requirement: PC with Windows.
Price: £75.00 (multiple copy price on application).
Source: Electrovision UK Ltd, Hamble Point Marina, School Lane, Hamble, Southampton SO31 4JD. Tel: 01703 452221

Title: **Training for Word v6**
Purpose: To teach you how to use Word v6.
Suitable for: Anyone.
Prerequisites: None.
Description: This course teaches: Word basics; formatting; creating and handling multiple documents; layout; search tools; printing; inserting pictures; objects; and tables.
Delivery method: CBT.
Minimum hardware requirement: PC with Windows.
Price: £79.95 (multiple copy price on application).
Source: Electrovision UK Ltd, Hamble Point Marina, School Lane, Hamble, Southampton SO31 4JD. Tel: 01703 452221

Title: **Understanding Word v6 (Windows)**
Purpose: To teach you how to use Word v6 (Windows).
Suitable for: Anyone.
Prerequisites: None.
Description: This course uses summaries and quizzes, and covers topics including: a tour of the Word screen; text formatting and editing; paragraphs; fonts; headers and footers; spelling; layout; thesaurus and glossary; outlining; sorting; and printing.

Delivery method: CBT.
Minimum hardware requirement: PC with Windows.
Price: £75.00 (multiple copy price on application).
Source: Electrovision UK Ltd, Hamble Point Marina, School Lane, Hamble, Southampton SO31 4JD. Tel: 01703 452221

CD-ROM
Title: **Discoverware Word v6**
Purpose: To teach you how to use Word v6.
Suitable for: Anyone.
Prerequisites: None.
Description: This full multimedia course, which includes video introductions, shows and tells you how to do something, and then lets you try, using simulation exercises. Suitable up to intermediate level. Topics include: character formatting; document formatting and proofing columns; graphics; outlining; and macros.
Delivery method: CD-ROM.
Minimum hardware requirement: PC; 8Mb RAM; CD-ROM drive; sound card.
Price: £99.00.
Source: Comput-Ed Ltd, Long Lane, Dawlish EX7 0QR. Tel: 01626 889955

Title: **Using Word for Windows**
Purpose: To teach the fundamentals of Word.
Suitable for: Everyone.
Prerequisites: None.
Description: The basic course teaches you: how to start Word; become familiar with screen layout and practise basic document editing; and printing techniques. The intermediate course covers: Word templates; built-in writing aids; macros; tables; and graphics.
Delivery method: CD-ROM.
Minimum hardware requirement: Pentium 90; 16Mb RAM; quad speed CD-ROM drive; sound card; MPEG card.
Price: £2599.00.
Source: Intelligent Training Solutions, 29 Narrow Street, London E14 8DP. Tel: 0171 791 3000

Interactive video
Title: **Using Word 6 for Windows**
Purpose: To teach basic and more advanced word-processing skills with Word for Windows.
Suitable for: Anyone.
Prerequisites: None.
Description: There are two courses: basics and intermediate. The basics course

covers: the basic concepts of word processing; and how to create documents in Word. The intermediate course covers: using templates; built-in writing aids; macros; tables; and graphics.
Delivery method: Interactive video.
Minimum hardware requirement: Interactive video workstation.
Price: £2300.00 each course.
Source: Training Direct, North Court, Edinburgh Gate, Harlow, Essex CM20 2JE. Tel: 01279 623927

WordPerfect

CBT

Title: **Perception Lite for WordPerfect 5.2/Win**
Purpose: To give concise training for novice through to intermediate level in how to use WordPerfect.
Suitable for: Anyone.
Prerequisites: None.
Description: This course uses glossaries, quizzes and quick search. It covers topics including: file management; basic editing functions; formatting; layout; tables; graphics; creating styles; object linking and embedding files; and using macros.
Delivery method: CBT.
Minimum hardware requirement: PC with Windows.
Price: £75.00 (multiple copy price on application).
Source: Electrovision UK Ltd, Hamble Point Marina, School Lane, Hamble, Southampton SO31 4JD. Tel: 01703 452221

Title: **Perception Lite for WordPerfect v6/DOS**
Purpose: To give concise training for novice through to intermediate level in how to use WordPerfect.
Suitable for: Anyone.
Prerequisites: None.
Description: This course uses glossaries, quizzes and quick search. It covers topics including: file management; basic editing functions; formatting; layout; tables; graphics; creating styles; object linking and embedding files; and using macros.
Delivery method: CBT.
Minimum hardware requirement: PC.
Price: £75.00 (multiple copy price on application).
Source: Electrovision UK Ltd, Hamble Point Marina, School Lane, Hamble, Southampton SO31 4JD. Tel: 01703 452221

DIRECTORY OF COURSES

Title: **Perception Lite for WordPerfect v6/Win**
Purpose: To give concise training for novice through to intermediate level in how to use WordPerfect.
Suitable for: Anyone.
Prerequisites: None.
Description: This course uses glossaries, quizzes and quick search and covers topics including: file management; basic editing functions; formatting; layout; tables; graphics; creating styles; object linking and embedding files; and using macros.
Delivery method: CBT.
Minimum hardware requirement: PC with Windows.
Price: £75.00 (multiple copy price on application).
Source: Electrovision UK Ltd, Hamble Point Marina, School Lane, Hamble, Southampton SO31 4JD. Tel: 01703 452221

Title: **Perception of WordPerfect 6 (DOS)**
Purpose: To give in-depth training for novice through to intermediate level in how to use WordPerfect.
Suitable for: Anyone.
Prerequisites: None.
Description: This course uses on-line glossary, quick search index, easy-to-use pull-down menus and student testing. It covers: text; paragraphs and document handling; merge; graphics; tables; macros and more.
Delivery method: CBT.
Minimum hardware requirement: PC.
Price: £119.00 (multiple copy price on application).
Source: Electrovision UK Ltd, Hamble Point Marina, School Lane, Hamble, Southampton SO31 4JD. Tel: 01703 452221

Title: **Perception of WordPerfect 6 (Windows)**
Purpose: To give in-depth training for novice through to intermediate level in how to use WordPerfect.
Suitable for: Anyone.
Prerequisites: None.
Description: This course uses on-line glossary, search facilities and student testing. The instruction includes: use of screen tools; button bar; power bar; file management; formatting techniques; editing; printing; graphics; and tables. It includes a comprehensive manual containing more exercises.
Delivery method: CBT.
Minimum hardware requirement: PC with Windows.
Price: £119.00 (multiple copy price on application).
Source: Electrovision UK Ltd, Hamble Point Marina, School Lane, Hamble, Southampton SO31 4JD. Tel: 01703 452221

Title: **Teach Yourself WordPerfect v6.2/Win**
Purpose: To teach you how to use WordPerfect.
Suitable for: Anyone.
Prerequisites: None.
Description: A visually attractive training package that simulates the real environment. Easy to use menus and extensive user controls allow you to access a wealth of interactive instruction including: use of screen tools; button bar; power bar; file management; formatting techniques; editing; printing; graphics; and tables.
Delivery method: CBT.
Minimum hardware requirement: PC with Windows.
Price: £75.00 (multiple copy price on application).
Source: Electrovision UK Ltd, Hamble Point Marina, School Lane, Hamble, Southampton SO31 4JD. Tel: 01703 452221

Title: **Teach Yourself WordPerfect v6/DOS**
Purpose: To teach you how to use WordPerfect.
Suitable for: Anyone.
Prerequisites: None.
Description: A comprehensive introductory/intermediate-level training programme that uses attractive and realistic simulation techniques to address features and functions of WordPerfect. It covers: text; paragraph and document handling to merge; graphics; tables; and macros.
Delivery method: CBT.
Minimum hardware requirement: PC.
Price: £75.00 (multiple copy price on application).
Source: Electrovision UK Ltd, Hamble Point Marina, School Lane, Hamble, Southampton SO31 4JD. Tel: 01703 452221

Title: **Teach Yourself WordPerfect v6/Win**
Purpose: To teach you how to use WordPerfect.
Suitable for: Anyone.
Prerequisites: None.
Description: A visually attractive training package that simulates the real environment. Easy-to-use menus and extensive user controls allow you to access a wealth of interactive instruction including: use of screen tools; button bar; power bar; file management; formatting techniques; editing; printing; graphics; and tables.
Delivery method: CBT.
Minimum hardware requirement: PC with Windows.
Price: £75.00 (multiple copy price on application).
Source: Electrovision UK Ltd, Hamble Point Marina, School Lane, Hamble, Southampton SO31 4JD. Tel: 01703 452221

DIRECTORY OF COURSES

Title: **Training for WordPerfect 6/DOS**
Purpose: To teach you how to use WordPerfect.
Suitable for: Anyone.
Prerequisites: None.
Description: This course gives an introduction to WordPerfect and the basic concepts. It teaches how to use commands such as file, edit, and layout, and tools including spelling and grammar checkers, thesaurus, creating outlines and indices. Also covers intermediate-level concepts and contains a comprehensive test disk.
Delivery method: CBT.
Minimum hardware requirement: PC.
Price: £79.95 (multiple copy price on application).
Source: Electrovision UK Ltd, Hamble Point Marina, School Lane, Hamble, Southampton SO31 4JD. Tel: 01703 452221

Title: **Training for WordPerfect 6/Windows**
Purpose: To teach you how to use WordPerfect.
Suitable for: Anyone.
Prerequisites: None.
Description: This course gives an introduction to WordPerfect and the basic concepts. It teaches how to use commands such as file, edit, and layout, and tools including spelling and grammar checkers, thesaurus, creating outlines and indices. Also covers intermediate-level concepts and contains a comprehensive test disk.
Delivery method: CBT.
Minimum hardware requirement: PC with Windows.
Price: £79.95 (multiple copy price on application).
Source: Electrovision UK Ltd, Hamble Point Marina, School Lane, Hamble, Southampton SO31 4JD. Tel: 01703 452221

Title: **Understanding WordPerfect v6 (DOS)**
Purpose: To teach you how to use WordPerfect.
Suitable for: Anyone.
Prerequisites: None.
Description: This course uses on line glossary, index, summaries and quizzes. Instruction includes: understanding the WordPerfect screen; creating and working with documents; text editing; formatting; layout commands and features; speller; thesaurus; graphics; columns; tables; and more.
Delivery method: CBT.
Minimum hardware requirement: PC.
Price: £75.00 (multiple copy price on application).
Source: Electrovision UK Ltd, Hamble Point Marina, School Lane, Hamble, Southampton SO31 4JD. Tel: 01703 452221

Title: **Understanding WordPerfect v6 (Windows)**
Purpose: To teach you how to use WordPerfect.
Suitable for: Anyone.
Prerequisites: None.
Description: A sophisticated package containing comprehensive interactive instruction at introductory to intermediate level. Topics include: Windows introduction; mouse tutorial; button bar; ruler; status bar; entering formatting and editing text; working with paragraphs and documents; clipboard; styles; tabs; columns; speller; thesaurus; file manager; viewer; and printing.
Delivery method: CBT.
Minimum hardware requirement: PC with Windows.
Price: £75.00 (multiple copy price on application).
Source: Electrovision UK Ltd, Hamble Point Marina, School Lane, Hamble, Southampton SO31 4JD. Tel: 01703 452221

CD-ROM

Title: **Discoverware WordPerfect 6.1/Win**
Purpose: To teach you how to use WordPerfect.
Suitable for: Anyone.
Prerequisites: None.
Description: This course instructs and then lets you practise using simulation exercises. Topics covered include: word processing tips; Windows techniques; creating and editing documents; formatting; tables; indices; macros; proofing; graphics; templates, etc.
Delivery method: CD-ROM.
Minimum hardware requirement: PC; 8Mb RAM; CD-ROM drive; sound card.
Price: £99.00.
Source: Comput-Ed Ltd, Long Lane, Dawlish EX7 0QR. Tel: 01626 889955

Interactive video

Title: **Using WordPerfect 6 for Windows**
Purpose: To teach the basics and more advanced techniques of using this word processor.
Suitable for: Anyone.
Prerequisites: None.
Description: There are two courses: basics and intermediate. The basics course covers: the basic concepts of word processing; and how to create documents in WordPerfect. The intermediate course covers: using styles; tables; and mail merge.
Delivery method: Interactive video.
Minimum hardware requirement: Interactive video workstation.
Price: £2300.00 each course.

Source: Training Direct, North Court, Edinburgh Gate, Harlow, Essex CM20 2JE. Tel: 01279 623927

Working capital

CBT

Title: **Working Capital: How to Manage Cash**
Purpose: To provide competence to manage working capital by balancing liquidity and profitability.
Suitable for: Managers needing to manage the day-to-day operations of a business.
Prerequisites: Knowledge of financial statements and basic maths.
Description: An advanced course which covers: the use of ratio analysis to analyse liquidity; how to calculate working capital needs; how to prepare a cash forecast and cash budget.
Delivery method: CBT with supporting text.
Minimum hardware requirement: IBM PC or compatible, 512k RAM.
Price: £165.00 single copy. Price for multiple copies on request.
Source: Ivy Business Training Software plc, Ivy House, 233–235 Roehampton Lane, London SW15 4LB. Tel: 0181 780 1494

Title: **Working Capital: Managing Debtors**
Purpose: This course addresses credit policy, bad debts, and collection procedures.
Suitable for: Persons needing to control credit.
Prerequisites: 'Working Capital: How to Manage Cash'.
Description: An intermediate course that instructs you: how to calculate the three primary ratios for assessing creditworthiness; how to calculate the cost of granting credit, rejecting credit and delaying the decision; how to calculate the average expected allowance for bad debts as a percentage of credit sales.
Delivery method: CBT with supporting text.
Minimum hardware requirement: IBM PC or compatible, 512k RAM.
Price: £165.00 single copy. Price for multiple copies on request.
Source: Ivy Business Training Software plc, Ivy House, 233–235 Roehampton Lane, London SW15 4LB. Tel: 0181 780 1494

Title: **Working Capital: Managing Stocks and Creditors**
Purpose: Concentrates on managing the stock inventory as it represents such a large investment on the balance sheet.
Suitable for: People dealing with managing stock.
Prerequisites: An understanding of the basics of working capital.
Description: An intermediate course which will enable you to: calculate re-order

levels and economic order quantities; use and understand stock turnover ratios and age-of-stock calculation.
Delivery method: CBT and supporting text.
Minimum hardware requirement: IBM PC or compatible, 512k RAM.
Price: £165.00.
Source: Ivy Business Training Software plc, Ivy House, 233–235 Roehampton Lane, London SW15 4LB. Tel: 0181 780 1494

CD-ROM
Title: **Controlling Working Capital**
Purpose: To explain the elements of working capital and why it must be controlled.
Suitable for: Managers involved in managing resources.
Prerequisites: 'How Money Works in Business'.
Description: This course, including its case study, will help you use a variety of control methods and give you practical experience.
Delivery method: CD-ROM.
Minimum hardware requirement: 486 PC; 8Mb RAM; 420Mb hard disk; CD-ROM drive; audio card.
Price: £895.00.
Source: Training Direct, North Court, Edinburgh Gate, Harlow, Essex CM20 2JE. Tel: 01279 623927

Index 1   Alphabetical List of all Courses

A Good Person To Do Business With	333
A New Generation – Combined Cycle Gas Turbines (CCGT)	311
Accounting	100
Accounting and Finance for Managers in Insurance	247
Ace Teams	342
Active Listening	266
Active Listening	266
Administer the Oracle 7.1 Database I	204
Administer the Oracle 7.1 Database II	204
Advanced C	137
Advanced C++ Programming and Workshop	137
Advanced C Programming in Windows	137
Advanced Financial Planning Certificate	233
Advanced Oracle Forms 4.5	204
Advanced SQL	210
Advanced UNIX User	297
Advanced X.25	134
Agreed	289
AIX Systems Administrator	297
Alternators and Electrical Systems	311
AmiPro for Windows	361
An Inside Job	186
An Introduction to Assertiveness	105
An Introduction to Financial Futures	224
An Introduction to Marketing	282
An Introduction to Project Management	321
An Introduction to Safety In The Office	243
An Introduction to Statistical Process Control	353
An Introduction to Total Quality Management	354
An Introduction to Traded Options	224

Analysing Financial Statements: How Successful Are We?	224
Appraisal and Counselling	103
Appraisal for Performance	101
Appraisal Interviewing	102
Assessment in Social Care series	336
Atomic Absorption Spectrometry Softbook	121
Atomic Structure	312
Auxiliary Systems	312
Backup and Recovery with Server Manager	205
Banking and Money: How They Work and What it Means to You	225
Banking Law: The Banking–Customer Relationship	107
Basic Communications	129
Basic Skills – English	220
Basic Skills – French and German and Spanish	239
Biological Effects of Ionising Radiation	312
Budgeting	114
Budgeting Basics	113
Building a Partnership	271
Building a Team	344
Business Accounting	97
Business Acumen Marketing	279
Business Awareness	273
Business Calls	345
Business Communications	127
Business English Activities	220
Business Functions	115
Business Insurance	264
Business Interruption Insurance	248
Business Management	271
Business Meetings	285
Business of Balance	105
Business Words	264
C Fundamentals	138
C Programming Level 1	138
C Programming Level 2	138
CAPITA	255
CareMatch	335
Caring for Your Customer	191
Cash Flow Statements: The Naked Truth About Financial Performance	225
CDM – Getting It Right	183
Certificate of Insurance Practice – Testing	248
Chain Reaction	313
Checking Understanding	129

ALPHABETICAL LIST OF ALL COURSES

Chemical Safety	120
CISCO – Contract Business	274
Client/Server Configuration Management	295
Coaching for Results	124
Coaching for Success	124
Coaching in the Workplace	125
Coaching Skills	123
Coatings for Life	125
Communication at Work	127
Complete AIX Course/DOS	298
Complete AIX Course/Windows	298
Complete UNIX and C Course/DOS	298
Complete UNIX and C Course/Windows	299
Computing for the Terrified	153
Configure the Multi-Threaded Server	205
Connections	240
Contamination Detectors	313
Contract Law and Insurance	248
Contract Law: What Contracts Are and How They Affect You	183
Control of Ionising Radiation	313
Controlling Working Capital	372
Coping With Stress	340
Corporate Finance: Projecting Profits and Cash Flow	225
Corporate Finance: The Cost of Capital	226
Corporate Finance: The Creation of Value	226
Creative Thinking Techniques	185
Creative Writing Version 2.0	118
Customer Fundamentals	188
Customise Applications with Oracle Terminal	145
Data Networks	129
Data Warehousing	192
DB2 Application Programming (COBOL/PL1)	195
DB2 Design and Administration	195
DB2 Essentials	196
Dealing with Conflict	183
Deciding on a Business Strategy: Your Capabilities Determine Your Choices	117
Delegation	215
Design MultiTasking Win32 Applications	143
Designer/2000 Forms Design and Generation	145
Designer/2000 Model Business Systems	146
Designer/2000 Server Design and Generation	146
Detection of Ionising Radiation	314

375

THE DIRECTORY

Develop Applications with PL/SQL (V2.0)	211
Develop Basic Data Models	142
Develop Basic Function Models	143
Develop Reports with SQL*Report Writer (V1.1)	211
Developer/2000: Enhancing Applications with Graphics	146
Developer/2000: Introduction to Oracle Forms 4.5	147
Developer/2000: MS Windows Extensions with Forms	147
Developer/2000: Oracle Advanced Forms 4.5	147
Developer/2000: Using Oracle Procedure Builder	148
Developer/2000: Using Oracle Reports 2.5	148
Developing Applications with Oracle Power Objects	148
Developing Leadership Styles	262
Developing People	272
Discover Office 95	168
Discoverware Access v2	194
Discoverware Excel v5	198
Discoverware Freelance v2/Win	165
Discoverware Learn Windows 3.11	178
Discoverware Lotus v5	202
Discoverware Powerpoint v4	172
Discoverware Win 3.11 and Mail/Schedule+	163
Discoverware Windows 95	178
Discoverware Word v6	365
Discoverware WordPerfect 6.1/Win	370
Display Screen Equipment	358
Distributed Computing Environment	181
Do or Delegate?	214
Do You Know Basic Accounting?	97
Do You Know Business Law?	116
Do You Know Costing?	184
Do You Know Economics?	216
Do You Know Financial Accounting?	98
Do You Know Financial Management?	232
Do You Know Foundation Business Mathematics?	109
Do You Know How to Interpret Accounts?	98
Do You Know Information Technology?	154
Do You Know Management Accounting?	226
Documentary Collections	227
Doing Business in Europe	222
Dosimetry and Air Sampling	314
Economics	216
Effective Communication	128
Effective English for Business Letters	263

Effective Meetings	285
Effective Questioning	325
Electrical Safety	217
Electricity at Work	217
Empowerment	219
Encouraging Upward Communication	126
Equal Opportunities	221
Equal Opportunities at Work	221
Essential Interviewing Skills	255
Euroquest	223
Everybody Has a Customer	191
Everyone Sells	334
Everything about NVQs	294
Exceeding Your Customers' Expectations	189
Excel for Windows	199
Expressions – English	221
Expressions – French	241
Expressions – German	242
Expressions – Spanish	337
Facilitation Skills	223
FASTRAQ 9000 – Learn all about ISO 9000	354
Financial Analysis	232
Financial Planning Certificate – Paper 1	233
Financial Planning Certificate – Paper 2	233
Financial Planning Certificate – Paper 3	234
Fire Instructions and Fire Precautions	238
Fission	314
Focus on Management	273
FPA (Financial Performance Assessment)	227
FPC3	234
French Mistress	240
Front Line Customer Care – Challenges	189
Front Line Customer Care – Handle with Care	189
Front Line Customer Care – Prepare to Care	190
Fundamentals of Oracle Forms 4.5	205
Gas Chromatography Method Development Softbook	121
Gas Chromatography Softbook	121
General Investment and Financial Services Knowledge	234
Generic Mortgages	286
German Master	241
Getting Started with PowerBuilder	151
Getting the most out of the Internet	253
Getting the Work Done	350

Giving Clear Instructions	126
Global Custody: A Practical Overview	227
Global Operations	117
Goods Vehicle Drivers' Hours: EC and UK Rules	357
Goods Vehicle Operator Licensing	357
Grammar Quiz	260
Grievance and Disciplinary Interviewing	215
GUI Design	140
GUI Design Essentials	140
GUI Standards for Windows 3.x	141
GUI Testing Essentials	141
Handle with Care	191
Health and Safety at Work	244
Health Physics Measurements 1	315
Health Physics Measurements 2	315
High Performance Liquid Chromatography Softbook	122
Hope and Glory	268
How Money Works in Business	107
How to Communicate With Other People	126
How to Control Stock: Holding and Ordering Stock	338
How to Control Stock: Material Requirements Planning	338
How to Control Stock: Safety Stock	339
How to Lose Customers Without Really Trying	187
How to Make Computers Work for You	155
How to Make Computers Work for You	156
How to Master Book-Keeping (Part 1)	111
How to Master Book-Keeping (Part 2)	111
How to Master Book-Keeping (Part 3)	112
How Well Do You Manage Your Time?	347
IDMS	200
Ideas Into Action	185
If Looks Could Kill	187
Improving Profitability	231
Improving Quality	355
IMS/DB Programming	142
IMS/DC Programming	142
INTEX – Industrialising Nation	274
Induction	247
Inductively Coupled Plasma Softbook	122
InfoCheck	154
Information Technology	156
Injection Moulding Training Course	309
Insurance Practice	249

ALPHABETICAL LIST OF ALL COURSES

Integrate Applications with SQL*Menu	152
Interactions of Radiation with Matter	315
Interactive Accounting Tutor	98
Interactive Book-Keeping Tutor	112
Interactive Taxation Tutor	98
International Banking	107
Interviewing Skills	254
Intro to Client/Server Architecture	296
Introducing ISDN	131
Introducing LANS	291
Introducing Numbers: Numbers and Fractions Made Easy	109
Introducing Pensions: What are They and Do You Need One?	308
Introduction to C++ Programming and Workshop	138
Introduction to Client/Server Computing	296
Introduction to Commercial General Insurances	249
Introduction to Logistics	266
Introduction to Management	268
Introduction to Object Oriented Technology	143
Introduction to Oracle Networking	206
Introduction to OSI	132
Introduction to Personal General Insurances	249
Introduction to Personal Oracle	149
Introduction to SQL	211
Italian Tutor	255
It's Your Choice	326
Japanese – Kana Kun	256
Japanese – Kantaro	257
JCL Coding Level 1 (XA) or (ESA)	296
JCL Coding Level 2 (XA) or (ESA)	297
Job Fundamentals	309
Keeping Customers Cool	187
Keeping Staff Informed	127
Large Systems Overview	182
Law	116
Leadership: Do You Have What it Takes?	261
Leadership Skills	261
Leading Teams	262
Learn Windows 95	178
Legal Aspects of Insurance	249
Life and Disability Underwriting	265
Lotus Notes – Advanced Application Development	165
Lotus Notes – Application Development	166
Lotus Notes for End Users	159

379

THE DIRECTORY

Lotus Smartsuite	166
Lotus 1-2-3 for Windows	203
Make the Telephone Sell for You	346
Make the Telephone Work for You	346
Making The Money Go Round	228
Making the Most of the Telephone	346
Making Your Time Count	350
Manage Your Time Effectively	347
Management Experience	274
Management of Change	120
Management of Health and Safety at Work	245
Management Techniques	272
Management 2000	268
Managing Assertiveness	104
Managing Change	120
Managing Information Overload: Getting the Message Across	128
Managing Information Overload: Taking in Information Effectively	272
Managing Interruptions	347
Managing Meetings	284
Managing Tasks and Activities	351
Managing the Reprimand	100
Managing Your Boss	305
Managing Your Budget	113
Managing Yourself	305
Marketing	282
Marketing Essentials	278
Marketing Essentials for Everyone in Business	279
Marketing for Profit	280
Marketing Planning	280
Marsgame	267
Mass Spectrometry Softbook	123
Mavis Beacon Teaches Typing/CD-ROM	260
Mavis Beacon Teaches Typing/Windows	257
Meetings, Bloody Meetings	284
MENTA	269
Mentoring Skills	123
Microsoft Office	167
Moderation	316
Modern Business Practice	250
Money and You: Your Income, Your Taxes, Your Bank Account	308
Money Business 1: Managing Cash	231
Money Business 2: Effective Budgeting	115
More Bloody Meetings	285

ALPHABETICAL LIST OF ALL COURSES

More Numbers: Ratios, Percentages and Charts Made Easy	109
Motivate!	286
Motivating The Team	287
Motivating With Praise	287
Motivation at Work	287
Motor Insurance	250
Multimedia Typing Instructor	260
Navigate Oracle Applications (GUI)	168
Negotiating for a Positive Outcome	289
Negotiating Skills	288
Netware 4.1 Advanced Administration	292
Netware 4.1 Installation/Configuration	292
Netware 4.1 Service and Support	293
Netware 4.1 Systems Administration	293
Netware 4.1 TCP/IP	293
Network Design	130
Network Management	131
Network or Hierarchy? Linking With Others to be Effective	290
Network Security	132
Networking Technologies	291
No Complaints?	188
Noise at Work	294
Non-verbal Communication	294
Nuclear Reactions	316
Numbusters	110
Object Oriented Analysis	144
Object Oriented Analysis	144
Object Oriented Design	144
Object Oriented Design	145
Object Oriented Programming in C++	139
Occupational Pensions	304
One-to-One Training	356
Operations	321
Oracle Online Mentor: Building Forms with Developer/2000	149
Oracle Online Mentor: Building Reports with Developer/2000	150
Oracle 7 – Advanced Administration	206
Oracle 7 – An Overview	206
Oracle 7 – Basic Administration	206
Oracle 7 – New Features for DBAs	207
Oracle 7 – Server Programming	149
Oracle 7 – SQL Programming	207
Oracle 7.1 Architecture	207
Organisational Behaviour	273

OSI Model and Related Standards 132
Our Generation 316
Overview ICRP 60 and NRPB Advices 317
Overview of Networks 130
Overview of Sybase System 10 213
Participating in Project Teams 323
PC Skills 154
PCs to Supercomputers 182
Perception for Windows 95 174
Perception Lite for Access v2 192
Perception Lite for AmiPro v3 360
Perception Lite for cc:Mail (Network) 160
Perception Lite for Excel v5 196
Perception Lite for Exchange (Office95) 160
Perception Lite for Freelance (Win) 164
Perception Lite for Lotus Notes v3 160
Perception Lite for Lotus v5 (Win) 200
Perception Lite for Mail/Schedule+ 161
Perception Lite for MS DOS v6.2 158
Perception Lite for Powerpoint v4 170
Perception Lite for Project v4 173
Perception Lite for Schedule (Office95) 174
Perception Lite for Windows 3.1 174
Perception Lite for Windows 95 175
Perception Lite for Word v2 (Win) 362
Perception Lite for Word v6 (Win) 362
Perception Lite for WordPerfect v6/DOS 366
Perception Lite for WordPerfect v6/Win 367
Perception Lite for WordPerfect 5.2/Win 366
Perception Lite for Works v3 180
Perception of Access v2 193
Perception of Access 7 (Office 95) 193
Perception of Corel Draw v4 157
Perception of DOS v6.2 158
Perception of Excel v5 197
Perception of Excel 7 (Office95) 197
Perception of Lotus v5 (Windows) 200
Perception of Powerpoint v4 170
Perception of Powerpoint7 (Office95) 171
Perception of the Internet 254
Perception of Windows 3.1 175
Perception of Word v6 (Windows) 363
Perception of WordPerfect 6 (DOS) 367

ALPHABETICAL LIST OF ALL COURSES

Perception of WordPerfect 6 (Windows)	367
Perception of Word7 (Office95)	363
Perception of Works v3	181
Performance Review	103
Performance Troubleshooting	100
Perform! Managing to Win	269
Personal Dosimetry	317
Personal Protective Equipment	325
Phone Fundamentals	345
PICAT (Polymer Industry Competence Assessment Tool)	310
PICOS (Polymer Industry Core Operative Skills)	310
Planning Your Work	348
PLATO Curriculum	307
PNEUSIM	311
Power to the Customer	190
PowerBuilder: Creating Business Reports	151
PowerBuilder: Creating MDI Applications	151
PowerPoint 4 Basics	172
Practical Finance	230
Practical Marketing	283
Practice of Reinsurance	250
Practising Time Management	351
Preparing a Presentation	320
Preparing Your Budget	113
Presenting Numbers (DOS Version)	110
Presenting Numbers (Windows Version)	110
Pressure Gauge	340
Principles of Project Management	324
Principles of Reinsurance	251
Principles of Time Management	352
Problem Solving	185
Problem Solving at Work	186
Product Launch	283
Product Modules – Life, Investments and Pensions	265
Products Related to Life Assurance	235
Products Related to Mortgage Arrangements	235
Products Related to Pensions: Occupational Pensions	235
Products Related to Pensions: Personal Pensions	236
Products Related to Pensions: The State Pension	236
Professional Selling: A Product	334
Professional Selling: A Service	334
Professor DOS v6.2	158
Professor Multimedia	288

383

Professor PC	155
Professor Windows 3.1	175
Professor Windows 95	179
Progressive Selling	335
Project Management	322
Project Management	324
Project Management Fundamentals	322
Project Management Methods	322
Project Planning and Control	322
Project/Investment Appraisal and Capital Spending: Compounding and Discounting	118
Project/Investment Appraisal and Capital Spending: Making the Decision	119
Project/Investment Appraisal and Capital Spending: Projecting Cash Flows	119
Property Insurance Risk Assessment and Control	251
PROTEST – Project Management	325
Pulverised Fuel Codes of Practice	317
Purchasing for Projects	323
Pushing for Profit	228
QUAD – Quality Advantage	355
Quality in Practice	352
Quality – The Only Way	353
Quantitative Method	231
Questioning Techniques for Open Learning	356
Radiation Detectors	318
Radioactive Quantities and Units	318
Radioactivity	318
Radiological Calculators	319
Radiological Quantities and Units	319
RDBMS Fundamentals	210
Recruitment Interviewing	327
Regulatory and Compliance Knowledge	236
Relational Database Concepts	182
Report Writing	328
Report Writing	329
RESERVE – Research and Development	329
Resource Accounting and Budgeting	114
Right the First Time	327
Risk and Insurance	251
Risk Management	252
Risk Manager Trading Simulation for Windows	330
Safe Manual Handling	278
Safe Working at Heights	246

ALPHABETICAL LIST OF ALL COURSES

Safety for Women: Confronting Danger	244
Safety in Excavations	244
Safety Rules – Acceptors	218
Safety Rules – Contractors	246
Safety Rules – Issuers	218
Safety Rules – Safety Controllers	219
Sales Calls	332
Sales Mix	283
Say The Right Thing	105
Say What You Want	104
Scaffold Inspection	245
Self-Assessment for FPC 1	237
Self-Assessment for FPC 2	237
Self-Development	307
Sell It To Me!	333
Selling Products and Services	332
Selling Skills: Techniques for Successful Sales	333
Seminar-On-A-Disk	155
Seminar-On-A-Disk: Multimedia Edition	157
Setting Objectives	269
Setting Priorities	348
Sexual Harassment: Define it, Deal With it	243
SMART – Service Marketing	284
SMITE – Sales Management	332
Software Development Project Management	323
Software Maintenance	336
Spanish Tutor	337
Speed Reading	326
SQL Data Management	212
SQL Queries	212
SQL/DS Essentials	212
Staying Ahead of Your Competitors: From Analysis to Advantage	330
Steam Water Cycle	319
Straight Talking	104
Strategic Management	275
Strategy	307
Street Works Code of Practice	339
Stress at Work	341
Styles of Leadership	263
Succeeding With Your Presentation: Prepare it, Deliver it	320
Successful Marketing – Deciding on Product, Price, Promotion and Distribution	280
Superskills	270

385

Supervisory and Managerial Leadership: From Analysis to Action	261
Surf the Internet	254
SWOT	270
Sybase System 10 – Advanced Admin	213
Sybase System 10 – Server Programming	153
Sybase System 10 – System Administration	214
Sybase System 10 – T-SQL Programming	214
SYCOPS – Systems Company Operations	275
Tachograph Rules for Goods Vehicle Operators	358
Targeting For Performance	295
Taxation and Social Security Knowledge	237
TCP/IP Explained	133
Teach Yourself Access v2/Win	193
Teach Yourself AmiPro v3/Win	360
Teach Yourself Basic	136
Teach Yourself Basic	136
Teach Yourself C++ and OOP	139
Teach Yourself C Language	139
Teach Yourself COBOL	140
Teach Yourself cc:Mail v2/Windows	161
Teach Yourself Dataease v4	195
Teach Yourself DOS v6.2	159
Teach Yourself Excel v5/Windows	197
Teach Yourself Freelance v2/Win	164
Teach Yourself Lotus Notes v3/Win	161
Teach Yourself Lotus v3.1/DOS	201
Teach Yourself Lotus v5/Win	201
Teach Yourself Mail/Schedule+	162
Teach Yourself OS/2 v2.1	169
Teach Yourself Pascal	150
Teach Yourself Powerpoint v4/Win	171
Teach Yourself Project v4	173
Teach Yourself Supercalc 5	213
Teach Yourself the Highway Code	358
Teach Yourself Windows 3.1	176
Teach Yourself Windows 95	176
Teach Yourself Word v2/Windows	363
Teach Yourself Word v6/Windows	364
Teach Yourself WordPerfect v6/DOS	368
Teach Yourself WordPerfect v6/Win	368
Teach Yourself WordPerfect v6.2/Win	368
Team Building	343
Teams And Leaders	343

ALPHABETICAL LIST OF ALL COURSES

TEAMSKILL – Production Management	275
TECHNIQUE – High Technology	246
Telephone Behaviour	188
The Appraisal Interview	101
The Appraisal Interview	102
The Appraisal Interview	102
The Art of Negotiating	289
The Balance Sheet and Profit and Loss Account: Where Finance Begins	106
The Balancing Act	228
The Best of Motives	344
The Business Environment	252
The Casino Challenge	276
The Cheese Market	267
The Counselling Interview	184
The Discipline Interview	215
The Dreaded Appraisal	101
The Effective Leader	262
The Effective Presentation: Getting Started	320
The Empowering Manager	220
The European Community: Its History and Institutions	223
The Executive Challenge	276
The Helping Hand	124
The Hotel Europa Series, France/Deutschland/España	239
The Letters Game	264
The Management Challenge	276
The Marketing Executive: Do We Need a Sales Force?	281
The Mathematics of Profit: Pricing and Discounts	281
The Mathematics of Survival: Costs and Breakeven	282
The McGraw-Hill Interactive Guide to World Business and Economics	217
The Negotiator	290
The Newcomers	245
The Office Professional	115
The Office Professional	352
The Paper Chase	349
The Power of Positive Criticism	242
The Principles of Lending: How Banks Lend Money to Businesses	108
The Reinsurance Market	252
The Retail Challenge	277
The Sales Executive: Designing the Sales Management System	330
The Sales Manager: Motivating, Directing and Evaluating the Sales Force	331
The Salesperson: Identifying Tasks and Attributes for Effective Selling	331
The Secrets of Study	342
The Selection Interview	328

The Selection Interview	328
The Service Challenge	277
The SFA Rules: A Management and Staff Training Programme	229
The Single Insurance Market and You	253
The Standards Toolkit	338
The Strategy Game	309
The Time Challenge	348
The Unorganised Manager	350
Think and Talk French	241
Think and Talk German	242
Think and Talk Italian	256
Think and Talk Spanish	337
Thinking Positively	305
Time Management (DOS Version)	349
Time Management (Windows Version)	349
Total Quality Improvement: Why It Involves You	353
Trade Tutor	229
Training for cc:Mail v2	162
Training for dBase IV (v1.1 to 1.5)	196
Training for Excel v5	198
Training for Freelance v2	164
Training for LANS and Datacomms	292
Training for Lotus v2.4 to 3.4/DOS	201
Training for Lotus v5	202
Training for Mail/Schedule+	162
Training for Non Trainers	356
Training for Powerpoint v4	171
Training for Project Management	173
Training for Quality	355
Training for Smartsuite	166
Training for Windows 3.1	176
Training for Windows 95	177
Training for Word v6	364
Training for WordPerfect 6/DOS	369
Training for WordPerfect 6/Windows	369
Tune the Oracle 7.1 Database	208
Turn Stress to Your Advantage	340
Turning Problems Into Opportunities	186
TutorPro for Microsoft Office	167
TutorPro for Word, Excel, PowerPoint, Mail/Schedule and Exchange	167
Tycoon	270
Typequick for DOS	257
Typequick for Windows	258

Typequick Skill Evaluator	258
Typing Instructor/DOS	258
Typing Tutor/DOS	259
Typing Tutor for DOS	259
Typing Tutor for Windows	259
UK Domestic Banking	108
UMIX – Functional Interaction	278
UNIX Advanced Programming	299
UNIX C Shell	299
UNIX Device Drivers	299
UNIX Editors	300
UNIX Electronic Mail	300
UNIX Essentials	300
UNIX Fundamentals	301
UNIX Internet	301
UNIX Korn Shell	301
UNIX Network Administration	302
UNIX Network Programming	302
UNIX Productivity Tools	302
UNIX Shell Programming	303
UNIX System Administration	303
UNIX System Administration Basics	135
UNIX System Administration Files	303
UNIX User	304
Understand Accounts	99
Understand Management Accounting	99
Understanding AmiPro v3/Windows	361
Understanding Approach v3	194
Understanding Book-Keeping	112
Understanding Business Finance	229
Understanding Business Planning	116
Understanding cc:Mail	162
Understanding DOS v6.2	159
Understanding Equal Opportunities	222
Understanding Excel v5	198
Understanding Freelance v2	165
Understanding Lotus v5	202
Understanding Mail/Schedule+	163
Understanding Management Accounting	230
Understanding of Access v2	193
Understanding Organiser	169
Understanding OS/2 v2	170
Understanding Powerpoint v4	171

Understanding Quattro Pro v5	209
Understanding Windows for Workgroups 3.1	177
Understanding Windows 3.1	177
Understanding Windows 95	177
Understanding Word v6 (Windows)	364
Understanding WordPerfect v6 (DOS)	369
Understanding WordPerfect v6 (Windows)	370
Unit Trusts, Investment Trusts, Bonds, PEPs, Annuities, Single Premium Endowments	238
Up to Standard Series: French/German	239
Using AmiPro for Windows	361
Using DisplayWrite IV	362
Using Excel 4 for Windows	199
Using Excel 5 for Windows	199
Using Lotus 1-2-3 for Windows Release 4	203
Using Oracle Enterprise Manager	208
Using Oracle Forms (V4.0)	150
Using Oracle Office 2.1	168
Using Oracle Reports 2.5	208
Using Oracle7 Workgroup Server I	209
Using Oracle7 Workgroup Server II	209
Using PCs for Windows	157
Using Personal Computers for Windows	179
Using SQL*Forms (V3.0) I	152
Using SQL*Forms (V3.0) II	152
Using TCP/IP	133
Using vi Editor	304
Using Windows	179
Using Word for Windows	365
Using Word 6 for Windows	365
Using WordPerfect 6 for Windows	370
Voice Networks	130
Webwise	359
Wellbeing: Managing Pressure and Stress at Work	341
What You Must Know ... About Working With VDUs	359
Where do Balance Sheets and Profit and Loss Accounts Come From?	106
Windows Basics 4×	180
Windows Intermediate	180
Winning the Brain Game	342
Working Capital: How to Manage Cash	371
Working Capital: Managing Debtors	371
Working Capital: Managing Stocks and Creditors	371
Working in Teams	343

Working with Display Screen Equipment	359
Working with Numbers	110
Writing Bourne Shell Scripts	135
Writing C Shell Scripts	135
Writing for Results	118
Writing Korn Shell Scripts	136
X.25 and Related Protocols	134
X.400 Getting the Message	134
Your Confidence Profile	306
Your Personality Profile	306
Your Self-Esteem: Measure it, Improve it	306

Index 2 List of Courses by Delivery Method

CBT

Accounting and Finance for Managers in Insurance	247
Ace Teams	342
Active Listening	266
Administer the Oracle 7.1 Database I	204
Administer the Oracle 7.1 Database II	204
Advanced C	137
Advanced C Programming in Windows	137
Advanced C++ Programming and Workshop	137
Advanced Financial Planning Certificate	233
Advanced Oracle Forms 4.5	204
Advanced SQL	210
Advanced UNIX User	297
Advanced X.25	134
AIX Systems Administrator	297
An Introduction to Financial Futures	224
An Introduction to Project Management	321
An Introduction to Safety In The Office	243
An Introduction to Traded Options	224
Analysing Financial Statements: How Successful Are We?	224
Atomic Absorption Spectrometry Softbook	121
Backup and Recovery with Server Manager	205
Banking and Money: How They Work and What it Means to You	225
Banking Law: The Banking–Customer Relationship	107
Budgeting Basics	113
Business Accounting	97
Business Acumen Marketing	279
Business Insurance	264

THE DIRECTORY

Business Interruption Insurance	248
Business of Balance	105
C Fundamentals	138
C Programming Level 1	138
C Programming Level 2	138
CareMatch	335
Cash Flow Statements: The Naked Truth About Financial Performance	225
CDM – Getting It Right	183
Certificate of Insurance Practice – Testing	248
Client/Server Configuration Management	295
Coaching Skills	123
Complete AIX Course/DOS	298
Complete AIX Course/Windows	298
Complete UNIX and C Course/DOS	298
Complete UNIX and C Course/Windows	299
Computing for the Terrified	153
Configure the Multi-threaded Server	205
Contract Law and Insurance	248
Contract Law: What Contracts Are and How They Affect You	183
Coping With Stress	340
Corporate Finance: Projecting Profits and Cash Flow	225
Corporate Finance: The Cost of Capital	226
Corporate Finance: The Creation of Value	226
Creative Thinking Techniques	185
Creative Writing Version 2.0	118
Customise Applications with Oracle Terminal	145
Data Warehousing	192
DB2 Application Programming (COBOL/PL1)	195
DB2 Design and Administration	195
DB2 Essentials	196
Deciding on a Business Strategy: Your Capabilities Determine Your Choices	117
Design MultiTasking Win32 Applications	143
Designer/2000 Forms Design and Generation	145
Designer/2000 Model Business Systems	146
Designer/2000 Server Design and Generation	146
Develop Applications with PL/SQL (V2.0)	211
Develop Basic Data Models	142
Develop Basic Function Models	143
Develop Reports with SQL*Report Writer (V1.1)	211

LIST OF COURSES BY DELIVERY METHOD

Developer/2000: Enhancing Applications with Graphics	146
Developer/2000: Introduction to Oracle Forms 4.5	147
Developer/2000: MS Windows Extensions with Forms	147
Developer/2000: Oracle Advanced Forms 4.5	147
Developer/2000: Using Oracle Procedure Builder	148
Developer/2000: Using Oracle Reports 2.5	148
Developing Applications with Oracle Power Objects	148
Distributed Computing Environment	181
Do or Delegate?	214
Do You Know Basic Accounting?	97
Do You Know Business Law?	116
Do You Know Costing?	184
Do You Know Economics?	216
Do You Know Financial Accounting?	98
Do You Know Financial Management?	232
Do You Know Foundation Business Mathematics?	109
Do You Know How to Interpret Accounts?	98
Do You Know Information Technology?	154
Do You Know Management Accounting?	226
Documentary Collections	227
Doing Business in Europe	222
Effective English for Business Letters	263
Empowerment	219
Encouraging Upward Communication	126
Equal Opportunities	221
Equal Opportunities at Work	221
Euroquest	223
Everything about NVQs	294
Facilitation Skills	223
Financial Planning Certificate – Paper 1	233
Financial Planning Certificate – Paper 2	233
Financial Planning Certificate – Paper 3	234
Fire Instructions and Fire Precautions	238
FPA (Financial Performance Assessment)	227
FPC3	234
French Mistress	240
Fundamentals of Oracle Forms 4.5	205
Gas Chromatography Method Development Softbook	121
Gas Chromatography Softbook	121
General Investment and Financial Services Knowledge	234

Generic Mortgages	286
German Master	241
Getting Started with PowerBuilder	151
Getting the most out of the Internet	253
Giving Clear Instructions	126
Global Custody: A Practical Overview	227
Goods Vehicle Drivers' Hours: EC and UK Rules	357
Goods Vehicle Operator Licensing	357
Grammar Quiz	260
GUI Design	140
GUI Design Essentials	140
GUI Standards for Windows 3.x	141
GUI Testing Essentials	141
Handle with Care	191
Health and Safety at Work	244
High Performance Liquid Chromatography Softbook	122
Hope and Glory	268
How to Communicate With Other People	126
How to Control Stock: Holding and Ordering Stock	338
How to Control Stock: Material Requirements Planning	338
How to Control Stock: Safety Stock	339
How to Master Book-Keeping (Part 1)	111
How to Master Book-Keeping (Part 2)	111
How to Master Book-Keeping (Part 3)	112
How Well Do You Manage Your Time?	347
IDMS	200
IMS/DB Programming	142
IMS/DC Programming	142
Inductively Coupled Plasma Softbook	122
InfoCheck	154
Injection Moulding Training Course	309
Insurance Practice	249
Integrate Applications with SQL*Menu	152
Interactive Accounting Tutor	98
Interactive Book-Keeping Tutor	112
Interactive Taxation Tutor	98
International Banking	107
Interviewing Skills	254
Intro to Client/Server Architecture	296
Introducing ISDN	131
Introducing LANS	291

Introducing Numbers: Numbers and Fractions Made Easy	109
Introducing Pensions: What are They and do You Need One?	308
Introduction to C++ Programming and Workshop	138
Introduction to Client/Server Computing	296
Introduction to Commercial General Insurances	249
Introduction to Management	268
Introduction to Object Oriented Technology	143
Introduction to Oracle Networking	206
Introduction to OSI	132
Introduction to Personal General Insurances	249
Introduction to Personal Oracle	149
Introduction to SQL	211
Italian Tutor	255
JCL Coding Level 1 (XA) or (ESA)	296
JCL Coding Level 2 (XA) or (ESA)	297
Keeping Staff Informed	127
Large Systems Overview	182
Leadership: Do You Have What it Takes?	261
Leadership Skills	261
Legal Aspects of Insurance	249
Life and Disability Underwriting	265
Lotus Notes – Advanced Application Development	165
Lotus Notes – Application Development	166
Lotus Notes for End Users	159
Lotus Smartsuite	166
Making The Money Go Round	228
Manage Your Time Effectively	347
Management 2000	268
Management of Change	120
Managing Assertiveness	104
Managing Interruptions	347
Managing Meetings	284
Managing the Reprimand	100
Managing Your Boss	305
Managing Your Budget	113
Managing Yourself	305
Marketing Essentials for Everyone in Business	279
Marketing for Profit	280
Marketing Planning	280

Mass Spectrometry Softbook	123
Mavis Beacon Teaches Typing/Windows	257
MENTA	269
Mentoring Skills	123
Microsoft Office	167
Modern Business Practice	250
Money and You: Your Income, Your Taxes, Your Bank Account	308
More Numbers: Ratios, Percentages and Charts Made Easy	109
Motivate!	286
Motivating With Praise	287
Motor Insurance	250
Navigate Oracle Applications (GUI)	168
Negotiating Skills	288
Netware 4.1 Advanced Administration	292
Netware 4.1 Installation/Configuration	292
Netware 4.1 Service and Support	293
Netware 4.1 Systems Administration	293
Netware 4.1 TCP/IP	293
Network or Hierarchy? Linking With Others to be Effective	290
Networking Technologies	291
Numbusters	110
Object Oriented Analysis	144
Object Oriented Analysis	144
Object Oriented Design	144
Object Oriented Design	145
Object Oriented Programming in C++	139
Occupational Pensions	304
One-to-One Training	356
Oracle 7 – Advanced Administration	206
Oracle 7 – An Overview	206
Oracle 7 – Basic Administration	206
Oracle 7 – Server Programming	149
Oracle 7 – SQL Programming	207
Oracle 7 New Features for DBAs	207
Oracle 7.1 Architecture	207
Oracle Online Mentor: Building Forms with Developer/2000	149
Oracle Online Mentor: Building Reports with Developer/2000	150
OSI Model and Related Standards	132
Overview of Sybase System 10	213
PC Skills	154

LIST OF COURSES BY DELIVERY METHOD

PC's to Supercomputers	182
Perception for Windows 95	174
Perception Lite for Access v2	192
Perception Lite for AmiPro v3	360
Perception Lite for cc:Mail (Network)	160
Perception Lite for Excel v5	196
Perception Lite for Exchange (Office95)	160
Perception Lite for Freelance (Win)	164
Perception Lite for Lotus Notes v3	160
Perception Lite for Lotus v5 (Win)	200
Perception Lite for Mail/Schedule+	161
Perception Lite for MS DOS v6.2	158
Perception Lite for Powerpoint v4	170
Perception Lite for Project v4	173
Perception Lite for Schedule (Office95)	174
Perception Lite for Windows 3.1	174
Perception Lite for Windows 95	175
Perception Lite for Word v2 (Win)	362
Perception Lite for Word v6 (Win)	362
Perception Lite for WordPerfect 5.2/Win	366
Perception Lite for WordPerfect v6/DOS	366
Perception Lite for WordPerfect v6/Win	367
Perception Lite for Works v3	180
Perception of Access 7 (Office 95)	193
Perception of Access v2	193
Perception of Corel Draw v4	157
Perception of DOS v6.2	158
Perception of Excel 7 (Office95)	197
Perception of Excel v5	197
Perception of Lotus v5 (Windows)	200
Perception of Powerpoint v4	170
Perception of Powerpoint7 (Office95)	171
Perception of Windows 3.1	175
Perception of Word v6 (Windows)	363
Perception of Word7 (Office95)	363
Perception of WordPerfect 6 (DOS)	367
Perception of WordPerfect 6 (Windows)	367
Perception of Works v3	181
Perform! Managing to Win	269
Performance Troubleshooting	100
PICAT (Polymer Industry Competence Assessment Tool)	310
PICOS (Polymer Industry Core Operative Skills)	310
Planning Your Work	348

399

PNEUSIM	311
PowerBuilder: Creating Business Reports	151
PowerBuilder: Creating MDI Applications	151
Practice of Reinsurance	250
Preparing a Presentation	320
Preparing Your Budget	113
Presenting Numbers (DOS Version)	110
Presenting Numbers (Windows Version)	110
Pressure Gauge	340
Principles of Reinsurance	251
Product Modules – Life, Investments and Pensions	265
Products Related to Life Assurance	235
Products Related to Mortgage Arrangements	235
Products Related to Pensions: Occupational Pensions	235
Products Related to Pensions: Personal Pensions	236
Products Related to Pensions: The State Pension	236
Professor DOS v6.2	158
Professor PC	155
Professor Windows 3.1	175
Project Management	322
Project Management Fundamentals	322
Project Management Methods	322
Project Planning and Control	322
Project/Investment Appraisal and Capital Spending: Compounding and Discounting	118
Project/Investment Appraisal and Capital Spending: Making the Decision	119
Project/Investment Appraisal and Capital Spending: Projecting Cash Flows	119
Property Insurance Risk Assessment and Control	251
Purchasing for Projects	323
Pushing for Profit	228
Quality in Practice	352
Questioning Techniques for Open Learning	356
RDBMS Fundamentals	210
Regulatory and Compliance Knowledge	236
Relational Database Concepts	182
Report Writing	328
Report Writing	329
Resource Accounting and Budgeting	114
Risk and Insurance	251
Risk Management	252
Risk Manager Trading Simulation for Windows	330

Safety for Women: Confronting Danger	244
Safety in Excavations	244
Scaffold Inspection	245
Self-Assessment for FPC 1	237
Self-Assessment for FPC 2	237
Selling Products and Services	332
Selling Skills: Techniques for Successful Sales	333
Seminar-On-A-Disk	155
Setting Objectives	269
Setting Priorities	348
Sexual Harassment: Define it, Deal With it	243
Software Development Project Management	323
Software Maintenance	336
Spanish Tutor	337
SQL Data Management	212
SQL/DS Essentials	212
SQL Queries	212
Staying Ahead of Your Competitors: From Analysis to Advantage	330
Street Works Code of Practice	339
Succeeding With Your Presentation: Prepare it, Deliver it	320
Successful Marketing – Deciding on Product, Price, Promotion and Distribution	280
Superskills	270
Supervisory and Managerial Leadership: From Analysis to Action	261
SWOT	270
Sybase System 10 – Advanced Admin	213
Sybase System 10 – Server Programming	153
Sybase System 10 – System Administration	214
Sybase System 10 – T-SQL Programming	214
Tachograph Rules for Goods Vehicle Operators	358
Taxation and Social Security Knowledge	237
TCP/IP Explained	133
Teach Yourself Access v2/Win	193
Teach Yourself AmiPro v3/Win	360
Teach Yourself Basic	136
Teach Yourself C++ and OOP	139
Teach Yourself C Language	139
Teach Yourself cc:Mail v2/Windows	161
Teach Yourself COBOL	140
Teach Yourself Dataease v4	195
Teach Yourself DOS v6.2	159
Teach Yourself Excel v5/Windows	197

401

Teach Yourself Freelance v2/Win	164
Teach Yourself Lotus Notes v3/Win	161
Teach Yourself Lotus v3.1/DOS	201
Teach Yourself Lotus v5/Win	201
Teach Yourself Mail/Schedule+	162
Teach Yourself OS/2 v2.1	169
Teach Yourself Pascal	150
Teach Yourself Powerpoint v4/Win	171
Teach Yourself Project v4	173
Teach Yourself Supercalc 5	213
Teach Yourself the Highway Code	358
Teach Yourself Windows 3.1	176
Teach Yourself Windows 95	176
Teach Yourself Word v2/Windows	363
Teach Yourself Word v6/Windows	364
Teach Yourself WordPerfect v6.2/Win	368
Teach Yourself WordPerfect v6/DOS	368
Teach Yourself WordPerfect v6/Win	368
Team Building	343
The Balance Sheet and Profit and Loss Account: Where Finance Begins	106
The Balancing Act	228
The Business Environment	252
The Effective Leader	262
The Effective Presentation: Getting Started	320
The European Community: Its History and Institutions	223
The Letters Game	264
The Marketing Executive: Do We Need a Sales Force?	281
The Mathematics of Profit: Pricing and Discounts	281
The Mathematics of Survival: Costs and Breakeven	282
The Negotiator	290
The Office Professional	115
The Power of Positive Criticism	242
The Principles of Lending: How Banks Lend Money to Businesses	108
The Reinsurance Market	252
The Sales Executive: Designing the Sales Management System	330
The Sales Manager: Motivating, Directing and Evaluating the Sales Force	331
The Salesperson: Identifying Tasks and Attributes for Effective Selling	331
The Secrets of Study	342
The SFA Rules: A Management and Staff Training Programme	229
The Single Insurance Market and You	253
The Standards Toolkit	338
The Strategy Game	309
The Time Challenge	348

LIST OF COURSES BY DELIVERY METHOD

Thinking Positively	305
Time Management (DOS Version)	349
Time Management (Windows Version)	349
Total Quality Improvement: Why It Involves You	353
Trade Tutor	229
Training for cc:Mail v2	162
Training for dBase IV (v1.1 to 1.5)	196
Training for Excel v5	198
Training for Freelance v2	164
Training for LANS and Datacomms	292
Training for Lotus v2.4 to 3.4/DOS	201
Training for Lotus v5	202
Training for Mail/Schedule+	162
Training for Non Trainers	356
Training for Powerpoint v4	171
Training for Project Management	173
Training for Smartsuite	166
Training for Windows 3.1	176
Training for Windows 95	177
Training for Word v6	364
Training for WordPerfect 6/DOS	369
Training for WordPerfect 6/Windows	369
Tune the Oracle 7.1 Database	208
Turn Stress to Your Advantage	340
TutorPro for Microsoft Office	167
TutorPro for Word, Excel, PowerPoint, Mail/Schedule and Exchange	167
Tycoon	270
Typing Instructor/DOS	258
Typing Tutor for DOS	259
Typing Tutor for Windows	259
Typing Tutor/DOS	259
Typequick for DOS	257
Typequick for Windows	258
Typequick Skill Evaluator	258
UK Domestic Banking	108
Understand Accounts	99
Understand Management Accounting	99
Understanding AmiPro v3/Windows	361
Understanding Approach v3	194
Understanding Book-Keeping	112
Understanding Business Finance	229
Understanding Business Planning	116

403

Understanding cc:Mail	162
Understanding DOS v6.2	159
Understanding Equal Opportunities	222
Understanding Excel v5	198
Understanding Freelance v2	165
Understanding of Access v2	193
Understanding Lotus v5	202
Understanding Mail/Schedule+	163
Understanding Management Accounting	230
Understanding Organiser	169
Understanding OS/2 v2	170
Understanding Powerpoint v4	171
Understanding Quattro Pro v5	209
Understanding Windows 3.1	177
Understanding Windows 95	177
Understanding Windows for Workgroups 3.1	177
Understanding Word v6 (Windows)	364
Understanding WordPerfect v6 (DOS)	369
Understanding WordPerfect v6 (Windows)	370
Unit Trusts, Investment Trusts, Bonds, PEPs, Annuities, Single Premium Endowments	238
UNIX Advanced Programming	299
UNIX C Shell	299
UNIX Device Drivers	299
UNIX Editors	300
UNIX Electronic Mail	300
UNIX Essentials	300
UNIX Fundamentals	301
UNIX Internet	301
UNIX Korn Shell	301
UNIX Network Administration	302
UNIX Network Programming	302
UNIX Productivity Tools	302
UNIX Shell Programming	303
UNIX System Administration	303
UNIX System Administration Basics	135
UNIX System Administration Files	303
UNIX User	304
Using Oracle Enterprise Manager	208
Using Oracle Forms (V4.0)	150
Using Oracle Office 2.1	168
Using Oracle Reports 2.5	208
Using Oracle7 Workgroup Server I	209

Using Oracle7 Workgroup Server II	209
Using SQL*Forms (V3.0) I	152
Using SQL*Forms (V3.0) II	152
Using TCP/IP	133
Using vi Editor	304
Where do Balance Sheets and Profit and Loss Accounts Come From?	106
Working Capital: How to Manage Cash	371
Working Capital: Managing Debtors	371
Working Capital: Managing Stocks and Creditors	371
Working in Teams	343
Working with Numbers	110
Writing Bourne Shell Scripts	135
Writing C Shell Scripts	135
Writing Korn Shell Scripts	136
X.25 and Related Protocols	134
X.400 Getting the Message	134
Your Confidence Profile	306
Your Personality Profile	306
Your Self-Esteem: Measure it, Improve it	306

CBT (tutor led)

Practical Finance	230

CD-i

A Good Person To Do Business With	333
Agreed	289
An Inside Job	186
How to Lose Customers Without Really Trying	187
Ideas Into action	185
If Looks Could Kill	187
It's Your Choice	326
Keeping Customers Cool	187

Managing Change	120
Meetings, Bloody Meetings	284
More Bloody Meetings	285
Motivating The Team	287
No Complaints?	188
Quality – The Only Way	353
Report Writing	328
Report Writing	329
Say What You Want	104
Sell It To Me!	333
Straight Talking	104
Targeting For Performance	295
Teams and Leaders	343
Telephone Behaviour	188
The Appraisal Interview	101
The Best of Motives	344
The Dreaded Appraisal	101
The Empowering Manager	220
The Helping Hand	124
The Newcomers	245
The Paper Chase	349
The Unorganised Manager	250

CD-ROM

A New Generation – Combined Cycle Gas Turbines (CCGT)	311
Accounting	100
Alternators and Electrical Systems	311
AmiPro for Windows	361
An Introduction to Assertiveness	105
An Introduction to Statistical Process Control	353
An Introduction to Total Quality Management	354
Appraisal for Performance	101
Appraisal Interviewing	102
Atomic Structure	312
Auxiliary Systems	312

LIST OF COURSES BY DELIVERY METHOD

Basic Communications	129
Basic Skills – English	220
Basic Skills – French and German and Spanish	239
Biological Effects of Ionising Radiation	312
Budgeting	114
Building a Partnership	271
Building a Team	344
Business Calls	345
Business Communications	127
Business English Activities	220
Business Functions	115
Business Management	271
Business Meetings	285
Business Words	264
CAPITA	255
Chain Reaction	313
Chemical Safety	120
Coaching for Results	124
Coaching for Success	124
Coaching in the Workplace	125
Coatings for Life	125
Communication at Work	127
Contamination Detectors	313
Control of Ionising Radiation	313
Controlling Working Capital	372
Data Networks	129
Dealing with Conflict	183
Delegation	215
Detection of Ionising Radiation	314
Developing Leadership Styles	262
Developing People	272
Discover Office 95	168
Discoverware Access v2	194
Discoverware Excel v5	198
Discoverware Freelance v2/Win	165
Discoverware Learn Windows 3.11	178
Discoverware Lotus v5	202
Discoverware Powerpoint v4	172
Discoverware Win 3.11 and Mail/Schedule+	163
Discoverware Windows 95	178
Discoverware Word v6	365

THE DIRECTORY

Discoverware WordPerfect 6.1/Win	370
Display Screen Equipment	358
Dosimetry and Air Sampling	314
Economics	216
Effective Communication	128
Electrical Safety	217
Electricity at Work	217
Essential Interviewing Skills	255
Everyone Sells	334
Exceeding Your Customers' Expectations	189
Excel for Windows	199
Expressions – English	221
Expressions – French	241
Expressions – German	242
Expressions – Spanish	337
FASTRAQ 9000 – Learn all about ISO 9000	354
Fission	314
Front Line Customer Care – Challenges	189
Front Line Customer Care – Handle with Care	189
Front Line Customer Care – Prepare to Care	190
Getting the Work Done	350
Grievance and Disciplinary Interviewing	215
Health Physics Measurements 1	315
Health Physics Measurements 2	315
How Money Works in Business	107
How to Make Computers Work for You	155
How to Make Computers Work for You	156
Improving Profitability	231
Improving Quality	355
Induction	247
Information Technology	156
Interactions of Radiation with Matter	315
Introduction to Logistics	266
Japanese – Kana Kun	256
Japanese – Kantaro	257
Law	116

408

LIST OF COURSES BY DELIVERY METHOD

Leading Teams	262
Learn Windows 95	178
Lotus 1-2-3 for Windows	203
Making Your Time Count	350
Management of Health and Safety at Work	245
Management Techniques	272
Managing Information Overload: Getting the Message Across	128
Managing Information Overload: Taking in Information Effectively	272
Managing Tasks and Activities	351
Marketing	282
Mavis Beacon Teaches Typing/CD-ROM	260
Moderation	316
Money Business 1: Managing Cash	231
Money Business 2: Effective Budgeting	115
Motivation at Work	287
Multimedia Typing Instructor	260
Negotiating for a Positive Outcome	289
Network Design	130
Network Management	131
Network Security	132
Noise at Work	294
Nuclear Reactions	316
Organisational Behaviour	273
Our Generation	316
Overview ICRP 60 and NRPB Advices	317
Overview of Networks	130
Participating in Project Teams	323
Perception of the Internet	254
Personal Dosimetry	317
Personal Protective Equipment	325
Phone Fundamentals	345
PLATO Curriculum	307
Power to the Customer	190
Practising Time Management	351
Principles of Time Management	352
Problem Solving	185
Problem Solving at Work	186
Professor Multimedia	288
Professor Windows 95	179

409

THE DIRECTORY

Project Management	324
Pulverised Fuel Codes of Practice	317
Quantitative Method	231
Radiation Detectors	318
Radioactive Quantities and Units	318
Radioactivity	318
Radiological Calculators	319
Radiological Quantities and Units	319
Recruitment Interviewing	327
Right the First Time	327
Safe Manual Handling	278
Safe Working at Heights	246
Safety Rules – Acceptors	218
Safety Rules – Contractors	246
Safety Rules – Issuers	218
Safety Rules – Safety Controllers	219
Say The Right Thing	105
Self-Development	307
Seminar-On-A-Disk: Multimedia Edition	157
Speed Reading	326
Steam Water Cycle	319
Strategy	307
Styles of Leadership	263
Surf the Internet	254
The Appraisal Interview	102
The Art of Negotiating	289
The Counselling Interview	184
The Discipline Interview	215
The Hotel Europa Series, France/Deutschland/España	239
The McGraw-Hill Interactive Guide to World Business and Economics	217
The Negotiator	290
The Office Professional	352
The Selection Interview	328
Think and Talk French	241
Think and Talk German	242
Think and Talk Italian	256
Think and Talk Spanish	337
Training for Quality	355
Turning Problems Into Opportunities	186

Up to Standard Series: French/German — 239
Using Personal Computers for Windows — 179
Using Windows — 179
Using Word for Windows — 365

Voice Networks — 130

Webwise — 359
Wellbeing: Managing Pressure and Stress at Work — 341
What You Must Know ... About Working With VDUs — 359
Winning the Brain Game — 342
Working with Display Screen Equipment — 359

Interactive video

Active Listening — 266
An Introduction to Marketing — 282
Appraisal and Counselling — 103
Assessment in Social Care series — 336

Caring for Your Customer — 191
Checking Understanding — 129
Connections — 240

Effective Meetings — 285
Effective Questioning — 325
Everybody Has a Customer — 191

Focus on Management — 273

Make the Telephone Sell for You — 346
Make the Telephone Work for You — 346
Making the Most of the Telephone — 346

Non-verbal Communication — 294

Performance Review — 103
PowerPoint 4 Basics — 172
Practical Marketing — 283
Principles of Project Management — 324
Professional Selling: A Product — 334
Professional Selling: A Service — 334

411

THE DIRECTORY

Progressive Selling 335

Stress at Work 341

Using AmiPro for Windows 361
Using DisplayWrite IV 362
Using Excel 4 for Windows 199
Using Excel 5 for Windows 199
Using Lotus 1-2-3 for Windows Release 4 203
Using PCs for Windows 157
Using Word 6 for Windows 365
Using WordPerfect 6 for Windows 370

Windows Basics 4x 180
Windows Intermediate 180
Writing for Results 118

Internet

Advanced UNIX User 297

Backup and Recovery with Server Manager 205

Configure the Multi-Threaded Server 205
Customise Applications with Oracle Terminal 145

Designer/2000 Forms Design and Generation 145
Designer/2000 Model Business Systems 146
Designer/2000 Server Design and Generation 146
Develop Applications with PL/SQL (V2.0) 211
Develop Basic Data Models 142
Develop Basic Function Models 143
Develop Reports with SQL*Report Writer (V1.1) 211
Developer/2000: Enhancing Applications with Graphics 146
Developer/2000: Introduction to Oracle Forms 4.5 147
Developer/2000: MS Windows Extensions with Forms 147
Developer/2000: Oracle Advanced Forms 4.5 147
Developer/2000: Using Oracle Procedure Builder 148
Developer/2000: Using Oracle Reports 2.5 148
Developing Applications with Oracle Power Objects 148

Integrate Applications with SQL*Menu 152

Introduction to C++ Programming and Workshop	138
Introduction to Object Oriented Technology	143
Introduction to Oracle Networking	206
Introduction to Personal Oracle	149
Introduction to SQL	211
Navigate Oracle Applications (GUI)	168
Object Oriented Analysis	144
Object Oriented Design	145
Oracle 7 New Features for DBAs	207
Oracle 7.1 Architecture	207
Oracle Online Mentor: Building Forms with Developer/2000	149
Oracle Online Mentor: Building Reports with Developer/2000	150
Tune the Oracle 7.1 Database	208
UNIX System Administration Basics	135
UNIX System Administration Files	303
UNIX User	304
Using Oracle Enterprise Manager	208
Using Oracle Forms (V4.0)	150
Using Oracle Office 2.1	168
Using Oracle7 Workgroup Server I	209
Using Oracle7 Workgroup Server II	209
Using SQL*Forms (V3.0) I	152
Using SQL*Forms (V3.0) II	152
Using TCP/IP	133
Using vi Editor	304
Writing Bourne Shell Scripts	135
Writing C Shell Scripts	135
Writing Korn Shell Scripts	136

Simulation

Business Awareness	273
CISCO – Contract Business	274
Financial Analysis	232

THE DIRECTORY

Global Operations 117

INTEX – Industrialising Nation 274

Management Experience 274
Marketing Essentials 278
Marsgame 267

Operations 321

Product Launch 283
PROTEST – Project Management 325

QUAD – Quality Advantage 355
RESERVE – Research and Development 329

Sales Calls 332
Sales Mix 283
SMART – Service Marketing 284
SMITE – Sales Management 332
Strategic Management 275
SYCOPS – Systems Company Operations 275

TEAMSKILL – Production Management 275
TECHNIQUE – High Technology 246
The Casino Challenge 276
The Cheese Market 267
The Executive Challenge 276
The Management Challenge 276
The Retail Challenge 277
The Service Challenge 277

UMIX – Functional Interaction 278

Index 3 List of Courses by Supplier

April Training Executive Ltd
Tarvin Road, Frodsham, Cheshire WA6 6XN. Tel: 01928 735868

Business Awareness	273
Marketing Essentials	278
Practical Finance	230
Strategic Management	275

Bourne Training Systems Ltd
Bourne House, Sandy Lane, Romsey, Hampshire SO51 0PD. Tel: 01794 523301

Marketing for Profit	280
Marketing Planning	280
Selling Products and Services	332

British Coatings Federation Ltd
James House, Bridge Street, Leatherhead, Surrey KT22 7EP. Tel: 01372 360660

Coatings for Life	125

British Polymer Training Association
Coppice House, Halesfield 7, Telford, Shropshire TF7 4NA. Tel: 01952 587020

Injection Moulding Training Course	309
PICAT (Polymer Industry Competence Assessment Tool)	310
PICOS (Polymer Industry Core Operative Skills)	310

BSI Training Services
389 Chiswick High Road, London W4 4AL. Tel: 0181 996 7337

FASTRAQ 9000 – Learn all about ISO 9000	354

CBL Technology Ltd
St Katherine's House, Mansfield Road, Derby DE1 3TQ. Tel: 01332 205800

Equal Opportunities	221
FPC3	234
Generic Mortgages	286

The Chartered Insurance Institute, Marketing Department
20 Aldermanbury, London EC2V 7HY. Tel: 0171 417 4427

Accounting and Finance for Managers in Insurance	247
Advanced Financial Planning Certificate	233
Business Insurance	264
Business Interruption Insurance	248
Certificate of Insurance Practice – Testing	248
Contract Law and Insurance	248
Euroquest	223
Financial Planning Certificate – Paper 1	233
Financial Planning Certificate – Paper 2	233
Financial Planning Certificate – Paper 3	234
Insurance Practice	249
Introduction to Commercial General Insurances	249
Introduction to Personal General Insurances	249
Legal Aspects of Insurance	249
Life and Disability Underwriting	265
Modern Business Practice	250
Motor Insurance	250
Occupational Pensions	304
Practice of Reinsurance	250
Principles of Reinsurance	251
Product Modules – Life, Investments and Pensions	265
Property Insurance Risk Assessment and Control	251
Risk and Insurance	251
Risk Management	252
The Business Environment	252
The Reinsurance Market	252
The Single Insurance Market and You	253
Winning the Brain Game	342

Chisholm Roth & Company Ltd
54 Warwick Square, London SW1V 2AJ. Tel: 0171 630 0161

Risk Manager Trading Simulation for Windows	330

CITB, Publications Department
Bircham Newton, Kings Lynn PE31 6RH. Tel: 01553 776677 or 01553 776651

CDM – Getting It Right	183
Safety in Excavations	244
Scaffold Inspection	245

Cognitive Solutions Ltd
13 Herries Road, Glasgow G41 4DE. Tel: 0141 423 1060

Atomic Absorption Spectrometry Softbook	121

Comput-Ed Ltd
Long Lane, Dawlish EX7 0QR. Tel: 01626 889955

Building a Team	344
Communication at Work	127
Developing Leadership Styles	262
Discover Office 95	168
Discoverware Access v2	194
Discoverware Excel v5	198
Discoverware Freelance v2/Win	165
Discoverware Learn Windows 3.11	178
Discoverware Lotus v5	202
Discoverware Powerpoint v4	172
Discoverware Win 3.11 and Mail/Schedule+	163
Discoverware Windows 95	178
Discoverware Word v6	365
Discoverware WordPerfect 6.1/Win	370
Motivation at Work	287
Problem Solving at Work	186
Self-Development	307
The Appraisal Interview	102
The Counselling Interview	184
The Discipline Interview	215
The Selection Interview	328

THE DIRECTORY

Concord Video & Film Council
201 Felixstowe Road, Ipswich IP3 9BJ. Tel: 01473 715754

Assessment in Social Care series	336
Care Match	335

Daedal Training Ltd
309 High Street, Orpington, Kent BR6 0NN. Tel: 01689 873637

Marsgame	267
The Cheese Market	267

Dean Associates
9 The South West Centre, Troutbeck Road, Sheffield S7 2QA. Tel: 0114 258 1171

CAPITA	255
Effective English for Business Letters	263
Questioning Techniques for Open Learning	356

Easy i Ltd
42 The Square, Kenilworth, Warwickshire CV8 1EB. Tel: 01926 854111

Handle with Care	191
Pressure Gauge	340
Superskills	270
The Letters Game	264
The Time Challenge	348
Understanding Equal Opportunities	222

Electrovision UK Ltd
Hamble Point Marina, School Lane, Hamble, Southampton SO31 4JD. Tel: 01703 452221

Active Listening	266
Advanced C	137
Advanced C Programming in Windows	137
Advanced Oracle Forms 4.5	204
AIX Systems Administrator	297
Basic Skills – English	220
Basic Skills – French and German and Spanish	239
Budgeting Basics	113
Business English Activities	220
Business of Balance	105
C Fundamentals	138

LIST OF COURSES BY SUPPLIER

C Programming Level 1	138
C Programming Level 2	138
Client/Server Configuration Management	295
Coaching Skills	123
Complete AIX Course/DOS	298
Complete AIX Course/Windows	298
Complete UNIX and C Course/DOS	298
Complete UNIX and C Course/Windows	299
Coping With Stress	340
Creative Thinking Techniques	185
Data Warehousing	192
DB2 Application Programming (COBOL/PL1)	195
DB2 Design and Administration	195
DB2 Essentials	196
Design MultiTasking Win32 Applications	143
Distributed Computing Environment	181
Do or Delegate?	214
Empowerment	219
Encouraging Upward Communication	126
Everything about NVQs	294
Expressions – English	221
Expressions – French	241
Expressions – German	242
Expressions – Spanish	337
Facilitation Skills	223
French Mistress	240
Fundamentals of Oracle Forms 4.5	205
German Master	241
Getting Started with PowerBuilder	151
Getting the most out of the Internet	253
Giving Clear Instructions	126
Grammar Quiz	260
GUI Design	140
GUI Design Essentials	140
GUI Standards for Windows 3.x	141
GUI Testing Essentials	141
How to Make Computers Work for You	155
IDMS	200
IDMS/DB Programming	142
IMS/DC Programming	142
Interviewing Skills	254
Intro to Client/Server Architecture	296
Introduction to Client/Server Computing	296

419

Introduction to Management	268
Italian Tutor	255
Japanese – Kana Kun	256
Japanese – Kantaro	257
JCL Coding Level 1 (XA) or (ESA)	296
JCL Coding Level 2 (XA) or (ESA)	297
Keeping Staff Informed	127
Large Systems Overview	182
Leadership Skills	261
Learn Windows 95	178
Lotus Notes – Advanced Application Development	165
Lotus Notes – Application Development	166
Lotus Notes for End Users	159
Making The Money Go Round	228
Management of Change	120
Managing Assertiveness	104
Managing Interruptions	347
Managing Meetings	284
Managing the Reprimand	100
Managing Your Boss	305
Managing Your Budget	113
Managing Yourself	305
Mavis Beacon Teaches Typing/CD-ROM	260
Mavis Beacon Teaches Typing/Windows	257
Mentoring Skills	123
Motivate!	286
Motivating With Praise	287
Mulitmedia Typing Instructor	260
Negotiating Skills	288
Netware 4.1 Advanced Administration	292
Netware 4.1 Installation/Configuration	292
Netware 4.1 Service and Support	293
Netware 4.1 Systems Administration	293
Netware 4.1 TCP/IP	293
Networking Technologies	291
Numbusters	110
Object Oriented Analysis	144
Object Oriented Design	144
Object Oriented Programming in C++	139
One-to-One Training	356
Oracle 7 – Advanced Administration	206
Oracle 7 – An Overview	206
Oracle 7 – Basic Administration	206

LIST OF COURSES BY SUPPLIER

Oracle 7 – Server Programming	149
Oracle 7 – SQL Programming	207
Overview of Sybase System 10	213
PCs to Supercomputers	182
Perception for Windows 95	174
Perception Lite for Access v2	192
Perception Lite for AmiPro v3	360
Perception Lite for cc:Mail (Network)	160
Perception Lite for Excel v5	196
Perception Lite for Exchange (Office95)	160
Perception Lite for Freelance (Win)	164
Perception Lite for Lotus Notes v3	160
Perception Lite for Lotus v5 (Win)	200
Perception Lite for Mail/Schedule+	161
Perception Lite for MS DOS v6.2	158
Perception Lite for Powerpoint v4	170
Perception Lite for Project v4	173
Perception Lite for Schedule (Office95)	174
Perception Lite for Windows 3.1	174
Perception Lite for Windows 95	175
Perception Lite for Word v2 (Win)	362
Perception Lite for Word v6 (Win)	362
Perception Lite for WordPerfect 5.2/Win	366
Perception Lite for WordPerfect v6/DOS	366
Perception Lite for WordPerfect v6/Win	367
Perception Lite for Works v3	180
Perception of Access 7 (Office 95)	193
Perception of Access v2	193
Perception of Corel Draw v4	157
Perception of DOS v6.2	158
Perception of Excel 7 (Office95)	197
Perception of Excel v5	197
Perception of Lotus v5 (Windows)	200
Perception of Powerpoint v4	170
Perception of Powerpoint7 (Office95)	171
Perception of the Internet	254
Perception of Windows 3.1	175
Perception of Word v6 (Windows)	363
Perception of Word7 (Office95)	363
Perception of WordPerfect 6 (DOS)	367
Perception of WordPerfect 6 (Windows)	367
Perception of Works v3	181
Performance Troubleshooting	100

Planning Your Work	348
PowerBuilder: Creating Business Reports	151
PowerBuilder: Creating MDI Applications	151
Preparing a Presentation	320
Preparing Your Budget	113
Presenting Numbers (DOS Version)	110
Presenting Numbers (Windows Version)	110
Professor DOS v6.2	158
Professor Multimedia	288
Professor PC	155
Professor Windows 3.1	175
Professor Windows 95	179
Project Management	322
Pushing for Profit	228
Quality in Practice	352
RDBMS Fundamentals	210
Relational Database concepts	182
Report Writing	328
Report Writing	329
Right the First Time	327
Say The Right Thing	105
Setting Objectives	269
Setting Priorities	348
Software Development Project Management	323
Software Maintenance	336
Spanish Tutor	337
SQL Data Management	212
SQL Queries	212
SQL/DS Essentials	212
Surf the Internet	254
SWOT	270
Sybase System 10 – Advanced Admin	213
Sybase System 10 – Server Programming	153
Sybase System 10 – System Administration	214
Sybase System 10 – T-SQL Programming	214
Teach Yourself Access v2/Win	193
Teach Yourself AmiPro v3/Win	360
Teach Yourself Basic	136
Teach Yourself C++ and OOP	139
Teach Yourself C Language	139
Teach Yourself cc:Mail v2/Windows	161
Teach Yourself COBOL	140
Teach Yourself Dataease v4	195

LIST OF COURSES BY SUPPLIER

Teach Yourself DOS v6.2	159
Teach Yourself Excel v5/Windows	197
Teach Yourself Freelance v2/Win	164
Teach Yourself Lotus Notes v3/Win	161
Teach Yourself Lotus v3.1/DOS	201
Teach Yourself Lotus v5/Win	201
Teach Yourself Mail/Schedule+	162
Teach Yourself OS/2 v2.1	169
Teach Yourself Pascal	150
Teach Yourself Powerpoint v4/Win	171
Teach Yourself Project v4	173
Teach Yourself Supercalc 5	213
Teach Yourself Windows 3.1	176
Teach Yourself Windows 95	176
Teach Yourself Word v2/Windows	363
Teach Yourself Word v6/Windows	364
Teach Yourself WordPerfect v6/DOS	368
Teach Yourself WordPerfect v6/Win	368
Teach Yourself WordPerfect v6.2/Win	368
Team Building	343
The Effective Leader	262
The Office Professional	115
The Power of Positive Criticism	242
Think and Talk French	241
Think and Talk German	242
Think and Talk Italian	256
Think and Talk Spanish	337
Thinking Positively	305
Time Management (DOS Version)	349
Time Management (Windows Version)	349
Training for cc:Mail v2	162
Training for dBase IV (v1.1 to 1.5)	196
Training for Excel v5	198
Training for Freelance v2	164
Training for LANS and Datacomms	292
Training for Lotus v2.4 to 3.4/DOS	201
Training for Lotus v5	202
Training for Mail/Schedule+	162
Training for Non Trainers	356
Training for Powerpoint v4	171
Training for Project Management	173
Training for Smartsuite	166
Training for Windows 3.1	176

THE DIRECTORY

Training for Windows 95	177
Training for Word v6	364
Training for WordPerfect 6/DOS	369
Training for WordPerfect 6/Windows	369
Typequick for DOS	257
Typequick for Windows	258
Typequick Skill Evaluator	258
Typing Instructor/DOS	258
Typing Tutor for DOS	259
Typing Tutor for Windows	259
Typing Tutor/DOS	259
Understanding AmiPro v3/Windows	361
Understanding Approach v3	194
Understanding cc:Mail	162
Understanding DOS v6.2	159
Understanding Excel v5	198
Understanding Freelance v2	165
Understanding Lotus v5	202
Understanding Mail/Schedule+	163
Understanding of Access v2	193
Understanding Organiser	169
Understanding OS/2 v2	170
Understanding Powerpoint v4	171
Understanding Quattro Pro v5	209
Understanding Windows 3.1	177
Understanding Windows 95	177
Understanding Windows for Workgroups 3.1	177
Understanding Word v6 (Windows)	364
Understanding WordPerfect v6 (DOS)	369
Understanding WordPerfect v6 (Windows)	370
UNIX Advanced Programming	299
UNIX C Shell	299
UNIX Device Drivers	299
UNIX Editors	300
UNIX Electronic Mail	300
UNIX Essentials	300
UNIX Fundamentals	301
UNIX Internet	301
UNIX Korn Shell	301
UNIX Network Administration	302
UNIX Network Programming	302
UNIX Productivity Tools	302
UNIX Shell Programming	303

UNIX System Administration	303
Using Oracle Reports 2.5	208
Working in Teams	343
Working with Numbers	110

EQL International Ltd
Scottish Software Partner Centre, South Queensferry, West Lothian EH30 9TG. Tel: 0131 331 7371

Interactive Accounting Tutor	98
Interactive Book-Keeping Tutor	112
Interactive Taxation Tutor	98
Understand Accounts	99
Understand Management Accounting	99

Hall Marketing
Studio 11, Colman's Wharf, 45 Morris Road, London E14 6PA. Tel: 0171 537 2982

CISCO – Contract Business	274
Financial Analysis	232
Global Operations	117
INTEX – Industrialising Nation	274
Management Experience	274
Operations	321
Product Launch	283
PROTEST – Project Management	325
QUAD – Quality Advantage	355
RESERVE – Research and Development	329
Sales Calls	332
Sales Mix	283
SMART – Service Marketing	284
SMITE – Sales Management	332
SYCOPS – Systems Company Operations	275
TEAMSKILL – Production Management	275
TECHNIQUE – High Technology	246
The Casino Challenge	276
The Executive Challenge	276
The Management Challenge	276
The Retail Challenge	277
The Service Challenge	277
UMIX – Functional Interaction	278

IMI Norgren Ltd, Training Department
Brookside Business Park, Greengate, Middleton, Manchester M24 1GR. Tel: 0161 654 6540

PNEUSIM	311

InfoSource International
InfoSource House, 54 Marston Street, Oxford OX4 1JU. Tel: 0800 318923

InfoCheck	154
Seminar-On-A-Disk	155
Seminar-On-A-Disk: Multimedia Edition	157

Instinct Training
Strawberry How Business Centre, Lorton Road, Cockermouth, Cumbria CA13 9XQ. Tel: 01900 827600

A New Generation – Combined Cycle Gas Turbines (CCGT)	311
Alternators and Electrical Systems	311
Atomic Structure	312
Auxiliary Systems	312
Biological Effects of Ionising Radiation	312
Chain Reaction	313
Chemical Safety	120
Contamination Detectors	313
Control of Ionising Radiation	313
Detection of Ionising Radiation	314
Display Screen Equipment	358
Dosimetry and Air Sampling	314
Electrical Safety	217
Electricity at Work	217
Fission	314
Health Physics Measurements 1	314
Health Physics Measurements 2	315
Interactions of Radiation with Matter	315
Management of Health and Safety at Work	245
Moderation	316
Noise at Work	294
Nuclear Reactions	316
Our Generation	316
Overview ICRP 60 and NRPB Advices	317
Personal Dosimetry	317
Personal Protective Equipment	325
Pulverised Fuel Codes of Practice	317

LIST OF COURSES BY SUPPLIER

Radiation Detectors	318
Radioactive Quantities and Units	318
Radioactivity	318
Radiological Calculators	319
Radiological Quantities and Units	319
Safe Manual Handling	278
Safe Working at Heights	246
Safety Rules – Acceptors	218
Safety Rules – Contractors	246
Safety Rules – Issuers	218
Safety Rules – Safety Controllers	219
Steam Water Cycle	319

Intellexis International Ltd
Lyric House, 149 Hammersmith Road, London W14 0QL. Tel: 0171 371 4444

FPA (Financial Performance Assessment)	227

Intelligent Training Solutions
29 Narrow Street, London E14 8DP. Tel: 0171 791 3000

AmiPro for Windows	361
Coaching in the Workplace	125
Dealing with Conflict	183
Everyone Sells	334
Exceeding Your Customers' Expectations	189
Excel for Windows	199
Front Line Customer Care – Challenges	189
Front Line Customer Care – Handle with Care	189
Front Line Customer Care – Prepare to Care	190
Lotus 1-2-3 for Windows	203
Lotus Smartsuite	166
Making Your Time Count	350
Microsoft Office	167
Negotiating for a Positive Outcome	289
Participating in Project Teams	323
Turning Problems Into Opportunities	186
Using Personal Computers for Windows	179
Using Windows	179
Using Word for Windows	365

427

Interac
PO Box 4, Winterslow, Salisbury SP5 1BR. Tel: 01980 862611

Street Works Code of Practice	339

Investment Education plc
20 Dickinson Street, Manchester M1 4LF. Tel: 0161 228 2400

Documentary Collections	227
Global Custody: A Practical Overview	227
The SFA Rules: A Management and Staff Training Programme	229

Ivy Business Training Software plc
Ivy House, 233–235 Roehampton Lane, London SW15 4LB. Tel: 0181 780 1494

An Introduction To Financial Futures	224
An Introduction to Project Management	321
An Introduction to Safety In The Office	243
An Introduction To Traded Options	224
Analysing Financial Statements: How Successful Are We?	224
Banking and Money: How They Work and What it Means to You	225
Banking Law: The Banking–Customer Relationship	107
Building A Team	344
Cash Flow Statements: The Naked Truth About Financial Performance	225
Computing for the Terrified	153
Contract Law: What Contracts Are and How They Affect You	183
Corporate Finance: Projecting Profits and Cash Flow	225
Corporate Finance: The Cost of Capital	226
Corporate Finance: The Creation of Value	226
Deciding on a Business Strategy: Your Capabilities Determine Your Choices	117
Do You Know Basic Accounting?	97
Do You Know Business Law?	116
Do You Know Costing?	184
Do You Know Economics?	216
Do You Know Financial Accounting?	98
Do You Know Financial Management?	232
Do You Know Foundation Business Mathematics?	109
Do You Know How to Interpret Accounts?	98
Do You Know Information Technology?	154
Do You Know Management Accounting?	226
Doing Business in Europe	222

Fire Instructions and Fire Precautions	238
General Investment and Financial Services Knowledge	234
Goods Vehicle Drivers' Hours: EC and UK Rules	357
Goods Vehicle Operator Licensing	357
Health and Safety at Work	244
How to Communicate With Other People	126
How to Control Stock: Holding and Ordering Stock	338
How to Control Stock: Material Requirements Planning	338
How to Control Stock: Safety Stock	339
How to Master Book Keeping (Part 1)	111
How to Master Book Keeping (Part 2)	111
How to Master Book Keeping (Part 3)	112
How Well Do You Manage Your Time?	347
International Banking	107
Introducing Numbers: Numbers and Fractions Made Easy	109
Introducing Pensions: What are They and Do You Need One?	308
Leadership: Do You Have What it Takes?	261
Manage Your Time Effectively	347
Marketing Essentials for Everyone in Business	279
Money and You: Your Income, Your Taxes, Your Bank Account	308
More Numbers: Ratios, Percentages and Charts Made Easy	109
Motivation At Work	287
Network or Hierarchy? Linking With Others to be Effective	290
Problem Solving	185
Products Related to Life Assurance	235
Products Related to Mortgage Arrangements	235
Products Related to Pensions: Occupational Pensions	235
Products Related to Pensions: Personal Pensions	236
Products Related to Pensions: The State Pension	236
Project/Investment Appraisal and Capital Spending: Compounding and Discounting	118
Project/Investment Appraisal and Capital Spending: Making the Decision	119
Project/Investment Appraisal and Capital Spending: Projecting Cash Flows	119
Regulatory and Compliance Knowledge	236
Safety for Women: Confronting Danger	244
Self-Assessment for FPC 1	237
Self-Assessment for FPC 2	237
Selling Skills: Techniques for Successful Sales	333
Sexual Harassment: Define it, Deal With it	243
Speed Reading	326
Staying Ahead of Your Competitors: From Analysis to Advantage	330

Styles of Leadership	263
Succeeding With Your Presentation: Prepare it, Deliver it	320
Successful Marketing – Deciding on Product, Price, Promotion and Distribution	280
Supervisory and Managerial Leadership: From Analysis to Action	261
Tachograph Rules for Goods Vehicle Operators	358
Taxation and Social Security Knowledge	237
Teach Yourself the Highway Code	358
The Appraisal Interview	102
The Balance Sheet and Profit and Loss Account: Where Finance Begins	106
The Effective Presentation: Getting Started	320
The European Community: Its History and Institutions	223
The Marketing Executive: Do We Need a Sales Force?	281
The Mathematics of Profit: Pricing and Discounts	281
The Mathematics of Survival: Costs and Breakeven	282
The Principles of Lending: How Banks Lend Money to Businesses	108
The Sales Executive: Designing the Sales Management System	330
The Sales Manager: Motivating, Directing and Evaluating the Sales Force	331
The Salesperson: Identifying Tasks and Attributes for Effective Selling	331
The Selection Interview	328
Total Quality Improvement: Why It Involves You	353
Turn Stress to Your Advantage	340
UK Domestic Banking	108
Unit Trusts, Investment Trusts, Bonds, PEPs, Annuities, Single Premium Endowments	238
Where do Balance Sheets and Profit and Loss Accounts Come From?	106
Working Capital: How to Manage Cash	371
Working Capital: Managing Debtors	371
Working Capital: Managing Stocks and Creditors	371
Your Confidence Profile	306
Your Personality Profile	306
Your Self-Esteem: Measure it, Improve it	306

Logistics Training International Ltd
Development House, Newton Road, Heather, Coalville, Leicestershire LE67 2RD. Tel: 01530 262666

Introduction to Logistics	266

McGraw-Hill Publishing Co
Shoppenhangers Road, Maidenhead, Berks. SL6 2QL. Tel: 01628 23432

The McGraw-Hill Interactive Guide to World Business and Economics	217
The Negotiator	290
The Strategy Game	309
Training for Quality	355
Webwise	359

Mantissa Ltd
1 Cresswell Park, London SE3 9RD. Tel: 0181 297 0441

Trade Tutor	229

Melrose
16 Bromells Road, London, SW4 0BL. Tel: 0171 627 8404

A Good Person To Do Business With	333
Agreed	289
Ideas Into Action	185
Keeping Customers Cool	187
Managing Change	120
Motivating The Team	287
Quality – The Only Way	353
Say What You Want	104
Targeting For Performance	295
Teams And Leaders	343
The Appraisal Interview	101
The Empowering Manager	220
The Newcomers	245
What You Must Know ... About Working With VDUs	359

Mindware Training Technologies Ltd
Block 2, International Business Centre, Plassey, Limerick, Ireland. Tel: (353) 6133 1430

Advanced X.25	134
Basic Communications	129
Business Management	271
Data Networks	129
Introducing ISDN	131
Introducing LANS	291
Introduction to OSI	132
Management Techniques	272
Network Design	130

Network Management	131
Network Security	132
OSI Model and Related Standards	132
Overview of Networks	130
Project Management	324
Project Management Fundamentals	322
Project Management Methods	322
Project Planning and Control	322
Purchasing for Projects	323
TCP/IP Explained	133
Voice Networks	130
X.25 and Related Protocols	134
X.400 Getting the Message	134

MLS Ltd
26 Warwick Road, London SW5 9UD. Tel: 0171 373 9489

Equal Opportunities at Work	221
The Hotel Europa Series, France/Deutschland/España	239
The Secrets of Study	342
The Standards Toolkit	338
Up to Standard Series: French/German	239

Mobile Training Ltd
Green Acres, Sibford Gower, Banbury OX15 5RW. Tel: 01295 788115

Understanding Book-Keeping	112

Oracle Corporation UK Ltd
The Oracle Centre, The Ring, Bracknell, Berks. RG12 1BW. Tel: 01344 860066

Advanced UNIX User	297
Backup and Recovery with Server Manager	205
Configure the Multi-Threaded Server	205
Customise Applications with Oracle Terminal	145
Designer/2000 Forms Design and Generation	145
Designer/2000 Model Business Systems	146
Designer/2000 Server Design and Generation	146
Develop Applications with PL/SQL (V2.0)	211
Develop Basic Data Models	142
Develop Basic Function Models	143
Develop Reports with SQL*Report Writer (V1.1)	211
Developer/2000: Enhancing Applications with Graphics	146

Developer/2000: Introduction to Oracle Forms 4.5	147
Developer/2000: MS Windows Extensions with Forms	147
Developer/2000: Oracle Advanced Forms 4.5	147
Developer/2000: Using Oracle Procedure Builder	148
Developer/2000: Using Oracle Reports 2.5	148
Developing Applications with Oracle Power Objects	148
Integrate Applications with SQL*Menu	152
Introduction to C++ Programming and Workshop	138
Introduction to Object Oriented Technology	143
Introduction to Oracle Networking	206
Introduction to Personal Oracle	149
Introduction to SQL	211
Navigate Oracle Applications (GUI)	168
Object Oriented Analysis	144
Object Oriented Design	144
Oracle 7 New Features for DBAs	207
Oracle 7.1 Architecture	207
Oracle Online Mentor: Building Forms with Developer/2000	149
Oracle Online Mentor: Building Reports with Developer/2000	150
Tune the Oracle 7.1 Database	208
UNIX System Administration Basics	135
UNIX System Administration Files	303
UNIX User	304
Using Oracle Enterprise Manager	208
Using Oracle Forms (V4.0)	150
Using Oracle Office 2.1	168
Using Oracle7 Workgroup Server I	209
Using Oracle7 Workgroup Server II	209
Using SQL*Forms (V3.0) I	152
Using SQL*Forms (V3.0) II	152
Using TCP/IP	133
Using vi Editor	304
Writing Bourne Shell Scripts	135
Writing C Shell Scripts	135
Writing Korn Shell Scripts	136

Pan European Courseware Ltd
The Old Vicarage, Bishopswood, Chard, Somerset TA20 3RS. Tel: 01460 234232/234644

TutorPro for Microsoft Office	167
TutorPro for Word, Excel, PowerPoint, Mail/Schedule and Exchange	167

Pba Training Services Ltd
1 Waterloo Street, Birmingham, B2 5PG. Tel: 0121 643 4060

Ace Teams	342

Pitman Publishing
128 Long Acre, London, WC2E 9AN. Tel: 0171 4472290

Accounting	100
Business Functions	115
Economics	216
Information Technology	156
Law	116
Marketing	282
Organisational Behaviour	273
Quantitative Method	231
Strategy	307

QWIZ (UK) Ltd
QWIZ House, 219a Hatfield Road, St Albans, Hertfordshire AL1 4SY. Tel: 01727 868600

PC Skills	154

Simulation Training Ltd
The New Hall, Methwold, Thetford, Norfolk IP26 4NR. Tel: 01366 728215

Hope and Glory	268
Management 2000	268
MENTA	269
Tycoon	270

Stanley Thornes (Publishers) Ltd
Ellenborough House, Wellington Street, Cheltenham, Gloucestershire GL50 1YW. Tel: 01242 228888

Business Accounting	97

TDA Consulting Ltd
4 Thameside Centre, Kew Bridge Road, Brentford, Middlesex TW8 0HF. Tel: 0181 568 3040

Wellbeing: Managing Pressure and Stress at Work	341

LIST OF COURSES BY SUPPLIER

Training Direct
North Court, Edinburgh Gate, Harlow, Essex CM20 2JE. Tel: 01279 623927

Active Listening	266
An Introduction to Assertiveness	105
An Introduction to Marketing	282
An Introduction to Statistical Process Control	353
An Introduction to Total Quality Management	354
Appraisal and Counselling	103
Appraisal Interviewing	102
Budgeting	114
Building a Partnership	271
Caring for Your Customer	191
Checking Understanding	129
Coaching for Success	124
Connections	240
Controlling Working Capital	372
Delegation	215
Developing People	272
Effective Communication	128
Effective Meetings	285
Effective Questioning	325
Essential Interviewing Skills	255
Everybody Has a Customer	191
Focus on Management	273
Getting the Work Done	350
Grievance and Disciplinary Interviewing	215
How Money Works in Business	107
How to Make Computers Work for You	155
Improving Profitability	231
Improving Quality	355
Make the Telephone Sell for You	346
Make the Telephone Work for You	346
Making the Most of the Telephone	346
Managing Information Overload: Getting the Message Across	128
Managing Information Overload: Taking in Information Effectively	272
Non-verbal Communication	294
Performance Review	103
Power to the Customer	190
PowerPoint 4 Basics	172
Practical Marketing	283
Practising Time Management	351

435

THE DIRECTORY

Principles of Project Management	324
Principles of Time Management	352
Professional Selling: A Product	334
Professional Selling: A Service	334
Progressive Selling	335
Recruitment Interviewing	327
Stress at Work	341
The Art of Negotiating	289
The Office Professional	352
Using AmiPro for Windows	361
Using DisplayWrite IV	362
Using Excel 4 for Windows	199
Using Excel 5 for Windows	199
Using Lotus 1-2-3 for Windows Release 4	203
Using PCs for Windows	157
Using Word 6 for Windows	365
Using WordPerfect 6 for Windows	370
Windows Basics 4x	180
Windows Intermediate	180
Working with Display Screen Equipment	359
Writing for Results	118

TRO Learning (UK) Ltd
Brook House, Riverside Park, Poyle Road, Colnbrook, Berks. SL3 0AA. Tel: 01753 799111

PLATO Curriculum	307

Unicorn Training
Copsham House, Broad Street, Chesham HP5 3EA. Tel: 01494 791064

Resource Accounting and Budgeting	114

Video Arts Ltd
Dumbarton House, 68 Oxford Street, London W1N 0LH. Tel: 0171 637 7288

An Inside Job	186
Customer Fundamentals	188
How To Lose Customers Without Really Trying	187
If Looks Could Kill	187
It's Your Choice	326
Job Fundamentals	309
Meetings, Bloody Meetings	284

LIST OF COURSES BY SUPPLIER

More Bloody Meetings	285
No Complaints?	188
Phone Fundamentals	345
Report Writing	329
Sell It To Me!	333
Straight Talking	104
Telephone Behaviour	188
The Best of Motives	344
The Dreaded Appraisal	101
The Helping Hand	124
The Paper Chase	349
The Unorganised Manager	350
Phone Fundamentals	345

Way Ahead Electronic Publishing
27 Woodford Green, Bratton, Telford, Shropshire TF5 0NS. Tel: 01952 243153

Business Acumen Marketing	279
Creative Writing Version 2.0	118
Perform! Managing to Win	269

Xebec Multi Media Solutions Ltd
The Critchley Building, Bath Road, Woodchester, Stroud, Glos. GL5 5EY. Tel: 01453 835482

Appraisal for Performance	101
Business Calls	345
Business Communications	127
Business Meetings	285
Business Words	264
Coaching for Results	124
Induction	247
Leading Teams	262
Managing Tasks and Activities	351
Money Business 1: Managing Cash	231
Money Business 2: Effective Budgeting	115